AF519601

Education in Third World and India

A Development Perspective

EDUCATION IN THIRD WORLD AND INDIA

A Development Perspective

Edited by

Dr. Meenu Agrawal

KANISHKA PUBLISHERS, DISTRIBUTORS
NEW DELHI-110 002

KANISHKA PUBLISHERS, DISTRIBUTORS
4697/5-21A, Ansari Road, Daryaganj
New Delhi-110 002
Phones : 2327 0497, 2328 8285
Fax : 011-2328 8285
e-mail: kanishka_publishing@yahoo.co.in

First Published 2008

ISBN 978-81-8457-023-6

PRINTED IN INDIA

Published by Madan Sachdeva for Kanishka Publishers, Distributors, 4697/5-21A, Ansari Road, Daryaganj, New Delhi-110 002; Typeset by Sunshine Graphics, Delhi, and Printed at Nice Printing Press, Delhi.

Preface

"If you ask what is the good of education in general, the answer is easy: that education makes good men, and that good men act nobly."

— Plato, Greek Philosopher (c. 428-c. 348)

When Tony Blair was sworn in as the Prime Minister of Britain, he was asked what would be three major areas on which his government would focus. He replied, "Education, education and education."

There are significant social and economic differences between developed and developing countries. Many of the underlying causes of these differences are rooted in the long history of development of such nations and include social, cultural and economic variables, historical and political elements, international relations and geographical factors. These, however, do not tell the whole story. The differences in the scientific and technological infrastructure and in the popularization of science and technology in the two groups of countries are the most important causes of differential social and economical levels. An essential prerequisite to a country's technological progress is early recognition of necessity of a good educational system. This was one of the key factors that contributed to Japan's economic success.

In developing countries economic growth can mainly be enhanced by a science and technology policy. However, science and technology can play their role in development only when the integrity of the whole enterprise-research institutions, universities, publications research priorities and emphasis and the education of creative scientists, as well as those active in science is preserved. Thus, the simplest strategy in developing countries is first of all, to increase the percentage of GNP that is to be devoted to universities and research institutions.

Developing countries should understand the fact that perceiving investment in sciences as a time-consuming, wasteful and costly activity will bring further limitations on their economic growth. Human development is partly a matter of people and communities improving their own lives and taking greater control of their destinies. Education is broadly used as an instrument for social change. The critical point of such belief can be traced far back to the 1960s when Theodre Schultz systematically articulated the human capital theory of development. In his voluminously printed works, Schultz argued that population quality and knowledge constitute the principal determinants of the future welfare of mankind (Schultz, 1961). Adding to this argument, Harbison and Hanushek (1992) contended that a country which is unable to develop the skills and knowledge of its people and to utilize them effectively in the national economy will be unable to develop anything else. And according to Psacharopoulos (1985, p. 5), education is widely regarded as the route to economic prosperity, the key to scientific and technological advancement, the means to combat unemployment, the foundation of social equity, and the spread of political socialization and cultural vitality.

One can also make up an intricate argument in that educating all the children provides stratificational costs to oneself and one's children since only in this way will one protect one's own rights. Equalizing the welfare of the individual in society is therefore an important modern desideratum.

For more than 40 years, different stakeholders have partnered to support the development of basic education throughout the developing countries. Education is one of the most powerful instruments for reducing poverty and inequality and for laying the basis for sustained economic growth. Education also has powerful synergistic effects on the other development objectives: empowerment, better health and good governance. The literature has shown that the continued under-enrolment of some children may be caused as much as by lack of demand for schooling as its supply. All the evidence is pointing to the fact that education should be inclusive, responding to the diverse needs and circumstances of learners and giving appropriate weight to the abilities, skills, and knowledge they bring to the teaching learning process.

However, the high level of education (as we can see in the developed countries of the world) in fact stimulates economic progress of the country and plays a great role in building civil society and in establishing dynamic and competitive economic systems in global scale. That is why it is important to reveal the problems in the sphere of education (making impact on the developing countries). They must be discussed by the members of global community.

In the developing countries especially in South America and South Africa over the last 10 years the percentage of children involved in the system of education has increased greatly, but *the problem of limited access to education* is still on the agenda. More than 1 million of children, especially girls in developing countries do not attend school and many leave it because of misery. Despite the colossus efforts devoted to wiping out illiteracy about 860 million of *adults remain illiterate*. Of the estimated 862 million illiterate people in 2000, over one-third lives in India.

To achieve universal education another problem should be solved - *gender inequality*. This means that in many developing countries men and women have different access to education. Worldwide, girls' enrolment in primary school improved in the 1990s. Girls' indices increased by 3 per cent, from 93.1 per cent in 1990 to 96.5 per cent in 1999 while over the same period, indices for boys fell from 105.5 per cent to 104 per cent. The Gender Parity Index (GPI) improved in all regions and in nearly two-thirds of the 92 countries for which data are available. But overall the GPI remained below 0.9 and in favour of boys in South and West Asia, the Arab States and sub-Saharan Africa.

The problems of education are always connected with other social, political, economic and cultural problems:

Health protection: The major part of today's population in developing countries suffers from different illnesses, including AIDS. Epidemics and diseases make access to educational process more difficult. Good primary education has a positive impact on lower fertility rates, better diets and the earlier and more effective diagnosis of illness. The link between literacy and life expectancy is strong. Parents – particularly women – with greater amounts of schooling have healthier, longer-living children.

In general, the world community introduces a "formula" of achieving success in the developing countries: enlightenment—the spread of education—must be connected with tolerance, peace and must deal with real peculiarities of the regions. These principles must and in fact make the basis of the emerging programmes devoted to the problems of education.

In spite of the vital role of basic education, it is also important to ensure balanced development of education, in other words improved education systems at all levels.

"Education is a progressive discovery of our ignorance."

Meenu Agrawal

Contents

List of Contributors

Harender Kumar, Lecturer, T.P.S.T.K.P.T.M. Degree College, Muradnagar (U.P.).

Dr. Meenu Agrawal, Reader and Head, Economics, Major Research Project Director, UGL and IIPA, GDMG (PG) College, Modinagar (U.P.).

Miss Meenakshi Sharma, Research Scholar, GDMG (PG) College, Modinagar (U.P.).

Dr. Rajeev Tyagi, Economics Department, GDMG College, Modinagar (U.P.).

Dr. Rupesh Tyagi, Economics Department, GDMG College, Modinagar (U.P.).

Mrs. Rakhi Mittal, Lecturer in Home Science, GDMG Girls (PG) College, Modinagar (U.P.).

Dr. K.D. Gaur, Deputy Director, Indian Council of Social Science Research, N. Delhi.

Dr. Pooja Gaur, R.S. Ginni Devi Modi Girls (PG) College, Modinagar (U.P.).

Sarita Jain, Lecturer (Economics Deptt.), Ginni Devi Modi Girls (PG) College, Modinagar (U.P.).

Dr. R.C. Agrawal, Retd. Principal, A.G.P.G. College, Sikandrabad (U.P.).

Miss Roona, Project-Fellow, Department of Economic, Ginni Devi Modi Girls (P.G.) College, Modinagar (U.P.).

Dr. Upasna Sharma, Lecturer in Economics, Dr. Sushila Tiwari Degree College, Sitarganj, Dist. Udham Singh Nagar, Uttaranchal.

Dr. H.M. Mittal, Assistant Prof. of Law, University of Rajasthan, Jaipur (Raj.).

Dr. Babita Agrawal, Reader and Head, Department of Economics, A.K.P. College, Hapur (U.P.).

Ms. Sarika, R.S. Ginni Devi Modi Girls (PG) College, Modinagar (U.P.).

Ms. Dipti Singh, Research Scholar, GDMG. P.G. College, Modinagar (U.P.).

Dr. Pratima Kumari, Lecturer in Department of Economics, DERPP, NCERT, New Delhi.

Ms. Prabha Singh, Research Scholar, Department of Economics, G.D.M.G. (PG) College, Modinagar (U.P.).

Mr. Arun Kumar Singh, Research Scholar, Department of Economics, G.D.M.G. (PG) College, Modinagar (U.P.).

Dr. Suman Lata, Lecturer in Department of Economics, Ginni Devi Modi Girls (PG) College, Modinagar (U.P.).

Dr. Pravesh, Lecturer, Department of Political Science, Ginni Devi Modi Girls (PG) College, Modinagar (U.P.).

Dr. (Mrs.) Anupam Sharma, Lecturer, Department of Political Science, I.N.M. (PG) College, Meerut (U.P.).

Dr. J.C. Pant, Reader and Head, Department of Economics, D.N. College, Meerut (U.P.).

Dr. (Mrs.) Deepa Rawat, Reader, Department of Economics, Agra College, Agra (U.P.).

Shelendra Kumar, Research Scholar, Agra College, Agra (U.P.).

Dr. Vikram Singh, Lecturer, Department of Economics, Government Degree College, Tuppal, Aligarh (U.P.).

Gunjan Agarwal, Research Scholar, Agra College, Agra (U.P.).

Meenakshi Madan, Research Scholar, GDMG (PG) College, Modinagar (U.P.).

Dr. Birendra Kumar Jha, Reader and Head Department of Economics, D.B.K.N. College, Narhan, Shamastipur (Bihar).

Dr. Shyam Sunder Singh Chauhan, Reader and Head, Department of Economics, Government Girls (PG) College, Badalpur (U.P.).

Dr. (Mrs.) Sangita Gupta, Sr. Lecturer, Department of Home Science, Government Girls (PG) College, Badalpur (U.P.).

Dr. Sanjeev Bharadwaj, Sr. Lecturer, Department of Economics, Government Girls (PG) College, Sirsaganj, Firozabad (U.P.).

Manish Dev, P.G. Scholar, Department of Economics, R.B.S. College, Agra (U.P.).

Dr. A.K. Tomar, Reader, Department of Economics, D.S. College, Aligarh (U.P.).

Ms. Neerja Sharma, Department of Economics, Government P.G. College, Noida (U.P.).

Dr. Bhavna Agrawal, Lecturer, Jaipuria Institute, Ghaziabad (U.P.).

Ms. Bhawana, Project-Fellow, Research Scholar, GDMG (PG) College, Modinagar (U.P.).

G.M. Bhat, Prof. and Head, Post-Graduate Department of Economics, University of Kashmir, Srinagar (J & K).

Shabir Ahmad Paddar, Research Scholar, Post-Graduate Department of Economics, University of Kashmir, Srinagar (J & K).

Prof. Ram Naresh Thakur, Head of Department, Department of Economics, Samastipur College, Samastipur (Bihar).

Ranju Narang, Senior Lecturer, Department of Economics, S.S.S.S. (PG) College, Rasna, Meerut (U.P.).

Dr. Jyotsna Chauhan, Lecturer, Department of Economics, D.S. College, Aligarh (U.P.).

Anuj Agrawal, Lecturer in Department of Economics, Jaipuria Institute of Management, Ghaziabad (U.P.).

Vipin Agrawal, Assistant Professor, Jaipuria Institute of Management, Ghaziabad (U.P.).

Dr. Sandeep Shandilya, Lecturer, Department of Economics, Government Degree College, Fatehabad, Agra (U.P.).

1

Role of Education in Developing Countries

HARENDER KUMAR

Education has always been associated with providing a better quality of life for human beings. It has been regarded as a major means of imparting knowledge and skills to individuals and helping the process of social transformation. It is believed to have the capacity to facilitate a flow of vital ideas and information to the masses increasing their awareness of the situation in which they live and of the possibilities and choices before them.

Even as education is supposed to enhance the quality of life and provide more opportunities for individuals in society, conceptualisations of what constitutes a better life have changed over the ages. The spiritual, thinking mind of a millennium ago has perhaps yielded place to a more production-oriented human being in recent times. And therefore, besides seeing education as a creative experience, several scholars have expressed faith in its merit as a major dimension of whatever 'development' takes place in society.[1]

The various components of human capital, education and heath have been found to be most important. Accordingly, several developing and developed countries have invested huge resources in education—Education had a 'Golden period' during the 1960s with substantial public investment in education have been the highest during the 1960s.[2] In the recent past, the role of education and its contribution to economic growth has been the major area of investigation among the researchers in the economies of education.[3]

Developing countries and also international agencies began

paying serious attention to investment in human capital. The contribution of education to economic growth is found to be positive and significant, when measured not only in monetary terms, but also in physical terms such as farm efficiency, labour productivity, etc. This contribution has been found to be significant in not only economic growth, but also in the reduction of poverty, improvement in income distribution and in various dimensions of social, demographic and political development. The relative significance of human capital has also found to be higher in developing countries, and in poor people, then in developed countries and rich people.[4]

Harbison and Myer in their famous study have examined the nature of relationship between educational development and the patterns of economic growth of various countries. However, one thing is very clear both from Denison's and Schultz's studies that a substantial part of the growth in output in both the developed and the developing countries could be explained in terms of their educational advancement. During the last three decades, the faith in the critical role of education in inducing development impulses has become so strong that most of the developing countries have accorded a very high priority to investment in education. Consequently, the proportion of GNP spent on education witnessed a rapid rise till about a decade ago.

There are many analytical difficulties in the precise measurement of social benefits and costs, especially in the developing countries, the approach has helped the planners to rationalise the processes of resource allocations for various educational programmes. Education has also direct and indirect links with other components of human resource development like child health, fertility and family welfare.[5] Over a billion young people—nearly one fifth of the world's population—are enrolled in formal education today, compared to around 300 million or one-tenth of the world's population in 1953, the earliest year for which UNESCO has global estimates of enrolment.[6]

As regards the developed countries, it may be noted firstly that there are very few differences between the school life and school survival expectancies, which is to be expected since virtually all children enter formal education. In the handful of cases (Belgium, Bulgaria, Croatia, Estonia, Germany, Netherlands, Romania and Switzerland) where the estimated school life expectancies are lower than the corresponding school survival expectancies, this is probably due either to a small proportion of children not being recorded as entering formal education, or to an overestimate of the size of the population in the reference age group.[7]

Education is a major social institution, which can contribute to democracy and equality. Through education, a culture is transmitted and transformed, social functions and status reproduced and created. Culture acts upon and is acted upon by education, and the problem of inequality of educational opportunity, be it geographical, sexual, and/or socio-economic, is closely linked to inequality of distribution of income, cultural goods, and political power. It is widely agreed that in the developed countries a student's performance correlates with the socio-economic position of his or her parents, but this does not necessarily apply in the developing countries.[8]

Priorities in education are dependent on complex and volatile factors, some of which are usually recognised and taken into consideration in planning and decision making at least in the rhetoric such as certain societal goals (political, cultural etc.), on the needs of economic development, and particularly on national capacities for financing manpower training. The impacts of environment of family and home backgrounds, and in a more extended way, social and cultural factors are sometimes not adequately taken into consideration by donors.[9]

Developing countries made impressive efforts and progress in education in the 1960s and 1970s. Quantitative indicators, including both the number of educated people—the stock of human capital and enrolment rates—the additions to that stock-show that considerable progress was made between 1960 and 1980. Both governments and individuals gave high priority to education and development of human resources during this period. The expansion in the stock of human capital took place against a backdrop of considerable political change, as many countries achieved political independence, and took responsibility for determining their own educational policies and choices.

Governments gave high priority to education in allocating their resources, reflecting both a strong political will to generalise access to education, in the conviction that it would help foster national unity and satisfy social justice and respect for on essential human right, and at the same time an urgent need to develop their human resources in order to contribute to the economic and social growth of their societies.[10]

Perhaps the most striking educational achievement is the overall expansion of literacy in the developing countries since the 1950s. The number of people who have at least passed through primary school, and the number who have actually become literate, has vastly increased as the opportunity to attend school has widened.

As these young people grew into adulthood they often became fervent supporters of education for their children, which helped to foster a strong social demand for schooling. For the late 1960s, UNESCO statistics showed rates of illiteracy falling below 50 per cent, which implied that the number of literates actually outstripped the number of illiterates, perhaps for the first time in the history of mankind. By the mid-1980s, the proportion of the adult populations of developing countries classified as illiterate had fallen to 38 per cent, and overall and numerically the total literate adult population of the world grew from about 900 million in 1950 to 2,300 million in 1985. The figures are all the more impressive when seen in the context of rapid population growth, resulting from progress in health and life expectancy.[11]

However, population growth also meant that the absolute number of illiterates was growing; from 700 million in 1950, they reached 880 million in 1985. In absolute numbers, the largest pockets of illiteracy are concentrated in a few countries in southern and Western Asia, a few in Latin America, and more in Africa.

Nevertheless, in relative terms, the percentage of illiterates in most developing countries diminished between 1950 and 1985, and from a historical perspective, the performance of the developing countries is extraordinary, when compared with the much longer time taken by industrialised countries to eliminate illiteracy in the nineteenth century.[12]

Over the last three decades, the developing countries have made tremendous efforts in education aiming to concretise a basic human right and to promote, at the same time economic and social development. In view of the present signs of stagnation or even deterioration of educational coverage and quality and by no means direct linkage between HRD and economic progress in practice, them is an urgent need for setting priorities in education and implementing programme for improvement.[13]

A developing country's capability of participating in the benefits of technological innovation, depends on a number of educational prerequisites. High-level researchers, engineers, and technicians must be trained and used effectively. It is not because developing countries must look to others to provide technology that they need not produce their own professionals, managers, technicians and skilled workers. Without them, they cannot assess the possible choices, select appropriately, or apply what they choose to their own contexts. Without them, there is no choice but to fall behind forever.[14]

The authorities of most countries, particularly the developing countries, are seriously preoccupied with the problem of urbanisation, which is worldwide and irreversible; by the end of the century it will affect more than half the planet, and in many cases be quite possibly out of control. Research on urban systems is generally limited to the structures and functions of and forms of adaptation to, urban life, and to the most disadvantaged sectors of communities; it has not yet adequately addressed the cultures of marginalised and excluded populations, nor those, which have developed original forms of organisation and management. Education must contribute to train urban migrants and respond to their particular needs, whether in the modern or the informal sector.[15]

The increased contribution of education to economic growth and the principle of equality of opportunity appear at first glance to lie peacefully side by side, the twin objectives of any system of education. Each would appear to reinforce the other, to be in its most cherished interests. Yet the moment one seeks of make policy choices in favour of one or the other, conflicts arise. Most developing countries have pledged and are striving to achieve rapid economic growth and social justice, and the two seem complementary in the long run; but the short-term demands of countries suffering from chronic paucity of resources, and acute pressures of cyclic recessions and austerity measures, tend to minimise the weight assigned to equality of opportunity and social justice in the formulation of policy.[16]

For many developing countries, vocational schools represent the sole possibility for training workers. The production sector is generally poorly organised and small. When an employer lacks the technical expertise to direct training or finds it uneconomical to employ a training specialist, the only recourse is to a training school; but the effectiveness of the training found there will also depend on the quality of the relationships between schools and employers, and between them and the government authorities. The stronger these links, and the greater the degree of involvement of employers, the better the chances of the school being effective, and of their producing graduates who are employable. The lack of employer organisations reduces the real possibilities for developing such links in many developing countries, and even in many industrialised countries, and weakens the arguments in favour of rapid development of the technical/vocational sector.[17]

Changes and trends in education are long-term phenomena, which must be considered in their historical context. Educational progress cannot be completely separated from that of other social and political institutions, and both the progress and the problem of education in developing countries need to be viewed in a long-term perspective.

It is difficult of course, to generalise about experience which occur in different social context at different times in history, but the histories of educational development in Europe and North America in the nineteenth century are interesting and of some relevance in interpreting and assessing trends of enrolment in developing countries over the past three decades.[18]

The effects of reforms were found to be varying significantly across the three major developing continents: Africa, Latin America and Asia. Latin America fell into a debt trap and Africa suffered very severely in the levels of living and educational development in particular. But the experience of Asian countries is generally believed to be different, and of East Asian countries, indeed relatively favourable, due to which many seen to be keen on emulating them.[19]

Generally, the relationship between investment in education and economic conditions is not simple and straight. Under normal condition of economic well-being, including situations characterised by economic progress, allocation of resources to education is generally found to be least significantly influenced by economic factors. Economic ability factors such as gross national product (GNP) per capita and public spending on education, are not significantly related. That the benefits of education are not tangible, and do not flow immediately, adds to the tightening of the flow of resources to education. As a result, education becomes a highly vulnerable sector under deteriorating economic conditions.[20]

If education is considered to be a human right, it is because it leads to individual creativity, improved participation in the economic, social and cultural roles in society, and hence a more effective contribution to human development.[21]

REFERENCES

1. Kaul, Rekha and Shukla, Sumesh Chandra, *"Education Development and Underdevelopment"*, (1998), p. 11.
2. *Ibid.*, p. 99.
3. Aggarwal, Y.P., *"Education and Human Resource Development"*, (1998), p. 273.
4. Kaul, Rekha and Shukla, Sumesh Chandra, *"Education Development and Underdevelopment"*, (1998), p. 100.
5. Aggarwal, Y.P., *"Education and Human Resource Development"*, (1998), p. 274.
6. *World Education Report*, 1995, p. 19.
7. *Ibid.*, p. 39.
8. Carron, G. & Ngoc, C. Ta, *"Reducing Regional Disparities: The Role of Educational Planning*, Paris, UNESCO: IIEP, 1981.
9. Hallak, Jacques, *"Investing in the Future: Setting Educational Priorities in the Developing World"*, (1990), p. 2.
10. Hill-Roy, Carr and Lintott, John, *"Comparative Analysis of Statistical Data on Adult Education for 84 Countries"*, Paris, UNESCO Office of Statistics, 1985.
11. Hallak, Jacques, *"Investing in the Future: Setting Educational Priorities in the Developing World"*, (1990), p. 20.
12. *Ibid.*, p. 21.
13. Coombs, P.H.; Prosser, R.C. and Ahmed, M., In: *New Paths to Learning for Rural Children and Youth*, New York, International Council for Educational Development, 1973.
14. Gottelmann, G., "Strategies d' innovation technologique et politiques educatives en France, en Republique Federale d' Allemaghe et an Royaume—Uni", Paris, UNESCO: IIEP, 1989.
15. Hallak, Jacques, *"Investing in the Future: Setting Educational Priorities in the Developing World"*, (1990), p. 59.
16. *Ibid.*, p. 89.

17. *Ibid.*, p. 127.
18. Hill-Roy, Carr and Lintott, John, "*Comparative Analysis of Statistical Data on Adult Education for 84 Countries*", Paris, UNESCO Office of Statistics, 1985.
19. Kaul, Rekha and Shukla, Sumesh Chandra, "*Education Development and Underdevelopment*", (1998), p. 101.
20. *Ibid.*, p. 102.
21. Hallak, Jacques, "*Investing in the Future: Setting Educational Priorities in the Developing World*", (1990), p. 45.

2

Education is the Key for Development in Developing Countries

DR. MEENU AGRAWAL

GATE's Chairman and CEO, Mr. Glenn Jones, has said "*Education is the great hope for the survival of humankind and for the forward progress of civilization." The French revolutionary Danton said more than two centuries ago, "After bread, education."* Education is the most basic necessity after those that are vital to life itself—food, clothing, and shelter. It is education that lifts people out of the state of chronic poverty in which they are constantly struggling to fulfill basic needs such as these. The truth is that all people have a right to have these basic needs fulfilled, and they also have a right to education. In this regard, the world is not doing very well.

According to UNESCO Survey, more than 836 million adults in the developing countries are illiterate. Around the world, one of every eight children is not enrolled in primary school, and more than one third of adolescents are not in high school. It is no coincidence that the vast majority of these unschooled youngsters and illiterate adults can be found in the poorest countries on earth. The direct link between poverty and lack of educational opportunities has been demonstrated many times over. As Lyndon Johnson said during the War on Poverty in the 1960s, "*Poverty has many roots, but the tap root is ignorance.*"

While everyone has a contribution to make in furthering our educational progress, basic education is a fundamental right, and it is the responsibility of governments to provide it. The huge gaps in opportunity that we witness in our world are just one form of injustice, and states are bound by duty and by law to strive for justice. Quite simply, developing countries are not investing enough in education. Instead of preparing children for the twenty-first century, we are sending them back to the nineteenth century. One can do better than this.

Around the world, 121 million children—including 65 million girls—have no opportunity to attend primary school. Many children—especially girls—break off their education early; in developing countries, only one child in three completes five years of schooling. For socially disadvantaged groups such as rural or indigenous communities, poor urban dwellers, AIDS orphans or the disabled, access to education is especially problematical. The United Nations Educational, Scientific and Cultural Organization (UNESCO) estimates that around 90 per cent of disabled children in developing countries do not attend school.

"If you have knowledge, let others light their candles by it." This is the philosophical underpinning of the freedom of information movement. Freedom of information and in particular, the right of access to information held by public bodies, has attracted a substantial amount of attention recently. In recent years many countries have taken steps to enact legislation giving effect to this right. By doing so, these countries join others around the world which have a long tradition to right to information, such as Sweden, the United States, Finland, the Netherlands, Australia and Canada. However, the right to access to information has not been realized by the majority of India's people. Rather than protecting citizens right to information, India and other developing countries have created a "poverty of information" through sanctioning an official culture of secrecy. And the media in these countries has not done enough to counter this culture by procuring information and putting it in the public domain.

Education is likely the single most important factor in improving a woman's life; the more schooling she has, the brighter her future (Neft and Levine, 1997). Educating women is also advantageous to society. There is a positive correlation between education enrolment rates of girls and GNP per capita (Karl, 1995). In the past, education was the path to professions and careers open only to men. Earlier there was an illusion about woman, she was mentally and morally inferior that's why she would learn only domestic skills. The roots of these beliefs can be found in the writings of the educator Jean-Jacques Rousseau who believed that women were created for the purpose of entertaining and caring for men, and that their education should equip them for the task (Spender, 1992).

According to a survey one-sixth of the world's population is illiterate in which two-thirds are women. In primary and higher education girls continue to lag behind boys, perpetuating a cycle of inequality and poverty that impedes developing countries from moving forward. In much of the developing world, girls represent an untapped resource and a hope for the future. Educating girls is a crucial component of building a foundation for democracy, and a prerequisite for creating and sustaining free, open, prosperous societies. Nations that marginalize half of their population cannot function and thrive as full democracies. Nor can countries that ignore this vital source of human capital be competitive in today's globalized economy.

Education for women in Europe and North America has never been as accessible as it is today. For almost two centuries American education, following European traditions, barred girls from academic higher learning. Women were not allowed to learn Latin or Greek, the sign of an educated person, on the scientific grounds that their brains would burst or that they would become unfit for child-bearing (Spender, 1992). While developed countries have seen an increase in the number of women receiving education, some developing countries are still notably biased towards educating males over females. Some countries maintain policies that limit or forbid girls and women from education. The most notable example is Afghanistan where the education of girls and women has been banned (Marsden, 1998). Inherent in women's struggle for educational opportunities are issues of power and institutionalized perceptions of women's role in society.

September 25, 2006 a conference was organized in New York on *"The Education of Girls in the Developing World"*. In that conference Laura Bush said, *"Education as a means of empowering children and building bridges of tolerance and understanding. Ending illiteracy is a challenge for every country. And every country must do its part." In that context, Mrs. Bush further said, "Investing in education, governments build their economies. When people read, they're more likely to participate in business and trade, which leads to greater economic development."*

By investing in literacy instruction for women and girls now, governments ensure that future generations will enjoy the benefits of reading. Women who can read are much more likely to be advocates for their children's education. In order to fulfill their responsibilities as architects of a better future, leaders around the globe must pursue the education of girls as a high priority. The education of girls holds the promise of improving lives, spurring economic growth, and creating opportunities in under-developed and developing countries. Following points are creating the problem in the development of developing countries:

Lack of Funds

In many developing countries, delivering on the commitment to compulsory education fails due to lack of funds. In most developing countries, public funding for primary education is inadequate to meet demand. High levels of public debt also restrict these countries' opportunities. According to UNESCO, developing countries' average spending on education amounts to just 3.4-5.7 per cent of gross national income. Developed countries are investing more money for this project of the National Income. Unwieldy administrative structures and corruption also impede the provision of a nationwide education system.

Lack of Primary Schools

Rural regions in particular but also poor urban districts often lack a comprehensive primary school network. Children in rural regions often have to walk unacceptably long distances to school. Many girls are not allowed to attend schools some distance away as parents are concerned about their daughters' safety. The classrooms in the available schools are overcrowded. In some sub-Saharan African countries, one teacher may have more than 70 pupils in their class.

Lack of Equipments in Schools

In developing countries schools are not properly equipped. Teaching staff and textbooks are also less and when these are available, they are often as outdated as the furnishings. Many schools have no funding to cover overheads such as water, electricity or transport for pupils. However, the absence of infrastructure in many developing countries makes communication and distribution of information a difficult task. It can take days of rough travel to reach schools in rural areas. Education in these places is poor and often not available at all. Consequently, illiteracy rates are extremely high in West Africa. Colleges and universities also lack proper funding and amenities. Very few are able to fulfill their research and teaching responsibilities satisfactorily. Yet colleges and universities play an important role in the education system as a whole, in the provision of training for specialists and managers, and in resolving development-relevant challenges in the economy, state and society.

Lack of Good Teaching Staff

Most developing countries lack well-qualified teachers. Sub-Saharan Africa in particular also faces a burgeoning health problem: In some regions, so many teachers have fallen victim to AIDS that schools have had to close. In developing countries teachers struggle to make the right to education a reality. Motivation can be low in desperate conditions and dire poverty. According to UNESCO, there are still 15 million teachers needed worldwide to educate all those children who are not yet included in schools.

Poor Working Conditions for Teachers

Teachers' working conditions are unacceptable in many developing countries. Many teachers have to teach two or three shifts a day— in classes with very high student numbers. A teaching career is often an unattractive prospect due to the poor pay as well. Many teachers have to take an extra job in order to support themselves and their families. Teachers are also poorly trained and inadequately prepared for their professional role.

Teachers working in isolated schools have no access to additional training or means of communicating with colleagues. Providing new communication and information services will help them to perform their educational task and improve the distribution of up-to-date information into rural communities.

Low-Quality Teaching

Quality of teachers plays a pivotal role in education reforms and systems. Teachers are increasingly in the spotlight; recent reports such as the World Bank World Development Report and the UNESCO EFA Global Monitoring Report give high profile to teacher issues. Receiving quality education is highly dependent on sufficient numbers of teachers. Well-trained teachers are the critical factor in providing access and quality in education, yet rarely are their voices listened to by education policy makers.

This year Handicap International has joined the numerous international and national non-governmental organisations, teachers unions, schools, and general public in support of the Global Campaign for Education (GCE). Since the GCE began in 1999 it has gradually been gaining momentum and now in 2007 hopes to be the biggest ever. With this year's campaign entitled 'Every Child Needs a Teacher' the focus is on the quality of education and the teachers themselves.

Many developing countries face the problem of low-quality teaching. No clear targets are defined within the curricula, which are overloaded with subjects and do not meet the learning needs of primary school children. Too little account is taken of cultural and regional factors. For example, the use of a teaching language that is unfamiliar to students reduces learning outcomes in many cases. An innovative approach is also lacking in teaching methods. Group work and independent learning are not encouraged, while the capacity for independent critical thought and problem solving, the use of new technologies and the promotion of life skills are not given adequate priority in many curricula. In the field of vocational training as well, the courses are often far too theoretical and lack market relevance.

Unable to Afford Fee Structure of Schools

Many people in developing countries cannot afford to pay for books and other learning materials, school uniforms and transport to school. Despite the human rights conventions, which oblige states to provide free and compulsory primary schooling for all children, school fees are still levied in at least 101 countries. There are many indications that these costs are the main reason why many children stay away from school or break off their schooling early.

Gender Disparities

In many countries, the traditional role of women and girls militates against their enrolment in school—especially in societies where women's sphere of activity is centred on the home. Gender disparities—also in education—are most marked in the countries and regions with a strong cultural preference for sons: North Africa, the Middle East, and Pakistan, much of Bangladesh and India, and some East Asian countries. Early marriage or pregnancy may prevent girls from attending school. Many countries have resorted to hiring ill-trained and badly paid teachers as a cost saving strategy. However, this has resulted in declining levels of quality, especially in rural or disadvantaged areas, where such schemes tend to be trilled, further exacerbating and reproducing educational inequalities. Including girls, and children belonging to ethnic and other minorities requires education that is relevant and free of discrimination. Good teachers, especially female teachers, are particularly important for helping girls stay in school.

Education for Disabled Children

Quality of education is a subject of particular interest to Handicap International and its education projects which promote education opportunities for disabled children and children with intellectual impairments in developing countries around the world. For the 150 million disabled children in developing countries, of whom only 2 per cent attend a school, the GCE is crucial in making a difference. The majority of disabled children in these countries do not receive any opportunity of an education at all.

For Handicap International it is imperative that the issue of inclusive education is at the forefront of the campaign. We promote an education that is accessible and appropriate for the needs of all children whatever their ability. Currently Handicap International is working with teachers in Burkina Faso, Cambodia, Nicaragua and Madagascar to provide training on curriculum adaptation, child-centred teaching methodologies and accessibility of teaching and learning materials.

Child Labour

According to the International Labour Organization (ILO), around

186 million children between five and 15 years of age have to work—often up to 16 hours a day. In sub-Saharan Africa, almost one child in three works; in Asia, the figure is one child in five and in Latin America one child in six. Many families depend on their children's contribution to their income. In Africa, there are a great many AIDS orphans who have to provide for their families. These children have no time or money to attend school, and the teaching hours and curriculum also take no account of these children's life situation.

Worldwide Progress of Literacy

A number of governments have made important strides in improving the status of girls' education. Successful government programmes in Bangladesh, Brazil, Colombia, Kenya, and Mexico, for example, have helped more girls gain access to education through scholarships and stipends that help poor families send their daughters to school. Guinea, Guatemala, Peru, and Morocco likewise have successfully increased girls' school enrolment rates. Despite these gains, however, much more needs to be done to remove gender barriers to learning and literacy for girls.

No country can thrive in which women's voices are silenced, their rights are violated, and their potential is left unrealized. That fact will grow ever more prominent as the world's markets and opportunities continue to interconnect. Guaranteeing the human rights of women and children, including the education of girls, is fundamental to building stable, democratic, economically prosperous societies. The education gap for girls in developing countries and post-conflict societies remains a collective global task. We must continue to work together to lay the foundation for a more sustainable, secure world.

Suggestions

- Women's Teacher Training Institute should start as Kabul has trained 384 village literacy teachers.
- This programme has provided learning materials to approximately 10,000 youths and adults through its Literacy and Community Empowerment Programme.
- Under the Alternative Livelihoods programme, women

in poppy-producing provinces of developing countries are taught skills such as tailoring, poultry and dairy production, value-added farming, business development, and literacy.

- In micro-financing programme women should start home-based businesses, which provide a viable alternative to income from poppy production.
- Government should start new technology programme so that women can earn more.
- Private sectors, universities, NGOs, and active members of civil society should create synergies and mobilize resources.
- Issues of Education For All are about the poor and the disadvantaged and the aim of educational policy should therefore be to give every person a chance of developing his/her inherent potential. However, there remains considerable social selection in education and disparities in particular have persisted and it is the low socio-economic groups, which manifest.
- To achieve universal education another problem should be solved—gender inequality. This means that in many developing countries men and women have different access to education. Worldwide, girls' enrolment in primary school improved in the 1990s.
- Extension agents, researchers, teachers and students should be educated and informed about rural women's problems, potentials and aspirations.
- Education system should establish which provide an opportunity to learn more technical skills through vocational training. Specialist centres and apprenticeships are some examples of services that could be created for this purpose.
- Supporting educational strategies, systems and processes that promote the demand for education and the acquisition of qualifications needed to pave the way for the country's economic growth.
- Introducing innovative approaches that go beyond the formal education sector, focusing on women in particular. These could include promoting self-employment and access to other forms of capital (land, loans, for example)

introducing active policies to ensure a closer link between training and employment.

- Increase investment should increase on S&T education and higher education for the benefit of young people and especially women. To this end, the universities need to be more involved as they can support the creation of new companies, introduce entrepreneurial training, and participate in projects, which will serve local societies.

These policies could integrate job-seeking aid and direct assistance for job creation.

Conclusion

In the past, women have been excluded from the domains of both development and technology. The material presented here attempts to uncover the vital role that women can play in the developmental process through the use of new technology and science.

The quality of education is also poor in many developing countries. According to current estimates, by the end of four to six years of primary education, 30-50 per cent of school-leavers cannot read or write confidently and lack basic numeracy skills. In the Sub-Saharan African countries in particular, the poor quality of teaching results in 18 per cent of children, on average, repeating a year of schooling. Lack of access and the often-poor quality of the education systems mean that in developing countries, around 16 per cent of young people in the 15-24 age group are illiterate. There are 862 million adults and young people worldwide who cannot read and write, and 64 per cent of them are women. The illiteracy rate dropped from 37 per cent to 20 per cent worldwide between 1970 and 2000—but due to demographic growth, the number of illiterate persons increased in absolute terms by 15 million. 98 per cent of people who cannot read and write live in developing countries.

Of the 121 million children worldwide who do not attend school more than 80 per cent live in crisis and post-conflict regions. In the 17 Sub-Saharan African countries where school attendance fell during the 1990s, six are affected by or have just come out of a major armed conflict. In Rwanda, more than two -thirds of teachers fled or were killed in the genocide in 1994.

In Mozambique, the civil war destroyed 45 per cent of schools. The number of refugees has also risen as a result of armed conflict. Most refugees are women and children. Today, there are around millions uneducated people in the world—the equivalent of the populations of Europe, the USA and Australia put together. Amongst the millions of illiterate children, most have no hope of receiving an education and many of those who do attend a school dropout before achieving a basic level of education.

The campaign is based on the Education For All goals (EFA), which set out benchmarks to be achieved so that children and adults worldwide can realise their potential and their rights. At the 2000 World Education Forum in Dakar, 180 governments committed themselves to achieving these goals and providing Education For All by 2015. Many governments have already begun to take up this challenge through changes to their education strategies. The EFA goals were further endorsed by the 2000 Millennium Development Goals. The Global Action Week takes place every year from April 24-28th. The campaign is aimed at both poor and rich countries to urge them to take responsibility to provide quality education for all. This week also provides a collective forum for the public to exert pressure on governments and funding agencies around the world to provide free and quality education to all.

Education is not only essential to the creation of democracies, it is essential to development, and in particular to what we today call "sustainable development". Sustainable development implies a balance between meeting immediate needs and looking to the future with a long-term vision. Everyone knows by now that the hierarchy of human needs dictates that someone who is hungry and has a family to feed is not going to think of protecting the environment first. Because of this, much environmental destruction has been caused by the subsistence farming of poor families throughout the developing world. To reverse this phenomenon, concerted efforts to meet the basic needs of poor families, as well as strong programmes of education that are capable of instilling a long-term vision and teaching the responsible use of resources, will be indispensable.

REFERENCES

Ahmed, A. and Carron, G. (1989), The Challenges of Basic Education For All, *Prospects*, 14, 4.

Anderson, M.B. (1988), *Improving Access to Schooling in Third World: A Review*, Bridge Research Report Series 1.

Apple, M.W. (1990), *Ideology and Curriculum*, New York: Routledge.

Ashby, J.A. (1985), Equity and Discrimination Among Children: Schooling Decisions in Rural Nepal, *Comparative Education Review*, 29(1), pp. 68-79.

Bawden, R. (1996), A Learning Approach to Sustainable Agriculture and Rural Development: Reflections from Hawkesbury, University of Western Sydney, Hawkesbury, Richmond, *NSW*, 2753, Australia.

Bhalla, A.S., Introduction, Globalization, Growth and Marginalization, Ed., A.S. Bhalla, Ottawa, *IDRC*, 1998, pp. 1-7.

Boehrer, J. and Linsky, M. (1990), Teaching with Cases: Learning to Question (In): M.D. Svinicki (Ed.), *The Changing Face of College Teaching*, Jossey-Bass Inc., San Francisco, California.

Brock-Utne, B. (2000), *Whose Education for All? The Recolonization of the African Mind*, NewYork: Falmer Press.

Bryant, C. (1990), *Investigating in People*, World Bank Lending for Human Resource Development in Malawi, Washington, DC.

Burney, N.A. and Irfan, M. (1991), Parental Characteristics, Supply of Schools and Child-School Enrolment in Pakistan, *The Pakistan Development Review*, 30(1), pp. 21-62.

Chimombo, J.P.G. (1986), *Secondary School Curricula Diversification: The Case for Practical Subjects in Malawi Evaluated*, A Dissertation submitted as a Partial Requirement for the Degree of Masters of Education—M.Ed. in the University of Bristol, School of Education, England.

Chimombo, J.P.G. (1999), *Implementing Educational Innovations: A Study of Free Primary Education in Malawi*, Unpublished D. Phil. thesis, University of Sussex.

Chimombo, J.P.G. and Kadzamira E. (2001), *Community Participation in Education*, Zomba: CERT.

Crowder, L.V. (1998), Women in Higher Agricultural Education and Employment Opportunities, (In), A.H. Ronning and M. Kearney (Eds.), *Graduate Prospects in a Changing Society*, UNESCO Publishing, Lillois-Witterzee, Belgium.

FAO (1996), *Improving Extension Work With Rural Women*, The Food and Agriculture Organization of the United Nations (FAO), Rome, Italy.

Heitzman, J., "Information Systems and Development in the Third World," *Information Processing and Management*, 26.4 (1990), pp. 489-502.

Long, Sarah Ann., *Sister Libraries*, Internet publication date unknown, 13 April, 2000 (http://www.ala.org/sisterlibraries/).

McChesney, Robert W., "The Political Economy of Global Communication," In *Capitalism and the Information Age: The Political Economy of the Global Communication Revolution*, Eds. Robert, W. McChesney, Ellen Meiksins Wood and John Bellamy Foster, New York: Monthly Review Press, 1998, p. 1.

Swift, Jamie and the Ecumenical Coalition for Economic Justice, "The Debt Crisis: A Case of Global Usury." In Conflicts of Interest: Canada and the Third World, Eds, Jamie Swift and Brian Tomlinson, Toronto, *Between the Lines*, 1991, p. 97.

Unesco, *Draft Medium-term Plan* (1984-89), Second part, VII. Information Systems and Access to Knowledge, General Conference Fourth Extraordinary Session, Paris, 1982, p. 157.

3

Role of Education in Agriculture and Developing Countries

DR. MEENU AGRAWAL AND MISS MEENAKSHI SHARMA

"The roots of education are bitter but the fruit is sweet."

The bureau for Economics Growth Agriculture and Trade (EGAT) was established in FY 2002 as one of three pillars of technical, bureaus within the U.S. Agency for International Development (USAID). In its initial year, EGAT articulated its overall goal—to reduce poverty and promote prosperity in development and transition countries; shaped a new organization capable of providing or accessing expertise and information in the fields of economics growth, trade and investment, micro enterprise development, urban development, development credit, education, agriculture, natural resources management, science policy, energy, information and communication technology and technology transfer; began to restructure its portfolio with the intention of providing high-quality support to USAID missions worldwide; and both led and supported U.S. Government (USG) participation in key international forums—the Doha Ministerial of the World Trade Organization (WTO), the Monterrey Conference on Financing for Development, the World Food Summit: Five years later, and the World Summit on Sustainable Development (WSSD).

Strategic Objective

In FY 2003, EGAT further refined its strategies, approaches, and portfolio to carry out its mandate of technical leadership and field support. The Bureau embarked upon an ambitious effort to expand the scope and quality of interactions with professional and operational networks, e.g., with U.S. universities, the women in development community, those U.S. Government and private sector leaders in trade and investment, and the growing network of scientists and policy-makers dealing with agricultural development, and education and training benefited from this external input. EGAT strategic planning and programme design, best-practices implementation, and assessments. Significant progress was made in launching projects addressing the President's Water for the Poor Initiative, the Digital Freedom Initiative, and other WSSD commitments. Alliances with the private sector for potable water expansion in West Africa and for increasing the sustainability of forest management moved from concept to action on the ground.

EGAT's agenda in FY 2004 includes a commitment to: developing a more focused and efficient approach to field support, while maintaining or improving the quality of our responsive to field needs; nurturing new partnerships and alliances for the achievement of mutually set goals; sustaining a highly successful programme in trade capacity building; and finalizing and launching strategies for USAID support of agricultural development, education and training, and women in development. The Bureau expects to develop guidelines for the design of programmes and training, and women in development. The Bureau expects to develop guidelines for the design of programmes and activities targeted at the poor both bilaterally and in the context of participation in the Organization for Economic Cooperation and development's Development Assistance Committee's (OECD/DAC) Poverty Network. EGAT will also direct increased cross-sectoral attention to infrastructure development, drawing on the lessons of experience with energy and telecommunications development and privatization as well as our understanding of the potential for public-private partnerships in this sector. With other bureaus in USAID, EGAT will contribute to the development of greater collaboration with the State Department of key issues in economic growth and the environment.

FY 2005 will see continued progress in these programmes as well as a greater integration of effort across all of the sectors covered by the EGAT Bureau. EGAT will work with the Democracy, Conflict, and Humanitarian Assistance (DCHA) Bureau on conflict recovery strategies, anti-corruption, human rights, and the prevention of famine. EGAT will also work with the Global Health Bureau on HIV/AIDS and human nutrition issues. There is already increased collaboration on developing more comprehensive approaches to dealing with the HIV/AIDS crisis, multicultural approaches to achievement of the Millennium Development Goals, and strengthening of the financial sector to ensure that trade, agriculture, business development, and overall economic growth can develop effectively.

The Development Challenge

The past 50 years have witnessed progress in reducing poverty and improving human well-being. Incomes have more than doubled and life expectancy has increased by as much as twenty years for much of the developing world. Food production has increased and world prices for staple grains continue to fall. New developments in science, especially agricultural biotechnology, offer the promise of meeting future food needs even as populations in developing countries continue to grow. Globalization has resulted in remarkable increases in world trade and investment as well as a quantum leap in the transmission of information from one part of the world to another. Economies oriented to market forces have been shown to be more efficient and more sustainable that state-led systems. Good governance has emerged as a critical factor in determining national prospects for growth and for the expansion of markets are essential to poverty reduction and increased prosperity.

In spite of such progress, over 1.2 billion people still live on less than one dollar a day, measure of extreme poverty. Close to half the world's population (2.5-3 billion people) live on less than two dollars a day, well below the poverty line in most countries. Seventy per cent of the world's poor are women and girls. Hunger has decreased in Asia and Latin America, but continues to increase in sub-Saharan Africa. Pressure on natural resources continues to increase, with both fertile land and water in increasingly scarce supply.

More than 125 million children, mostly girls, are out of school; only 25 per cent children complete five years of education. Most of the world's 900 million illiterate adults (mostly women) live in developing countries. Despite the importance of modern infrastructure to development and economic growth, two billion people worldwide still live without access to modern energy services and one billion lack access to safe drinking water; three billion people have never used a telephone; and only slightly more than 500 million use the Internet.

The expansion of trade has largely bypassed the least developed countries, which have seen their share of world trade drop over the last decade. Primary commodities (coffee, cocoa) have faced falling prices, with consequent impacts on rural incomes and employment in many countries. Overall competition in global markets has increased and developing incomes and employment in many countries. Overall competition in global markets has increased and developing country firms seeking to participate in these markets face a steep learning curve.

While national governments and leaders are responsible for their own development—as the Monterrey Convention of the Conference on Financing for International Development makes clear—donors such as USAID can play a role in bringing to bear the technical knowledge and expertise needed to solve problems. USAID can build local capacity to harness science and technology to increase productivity as well as to preserve the environment; train future generations as well as those youth unemployed today; and devise and shape the policies that will align individuals' incentives with national development goals.

The USAID Programme

EGAT's portfolio of technical leadership, research and field support activities is designed to address the multi-faceted challenge of reducing poverty and promotion prosperity. Each of the Bureau's Programmes focuses on a specific aspect of this challenge. As already noted, however, the programmes collaborate frequently on issues that cross sectors to ensure more effective impact of their activities.

The Economic Growth Programme (EGAT/EG)

The Economic Growth programme provides economic growth-related technical leadership and field support to strengthen the policy, legal, and institutional foundations that developing or transition countries need to achieve open and competitive economies. EGAT/EG provides leadership to the U.S. Government's commitment to provide trade capacity building assistance to developing and transition countries. In FY 2003, the programme developed and began to implement USAID's Trade Capacity Building Strategy by focusing its efforts and focusing its efforts and resources on innovative an cutting edge programmes in developing and transition countries that: (1) enhance their capacity to participate in, and benefit form, global trade and investment; (2) improve macroeconomic stability and economic governance in order to foster favourable business environments; and (3) enhance private sector and financial sector capacity to respond to opportunities in the global market place. In FY 2004, EGAT/EG will complete a Financial Sector Strategy that will be used to guide USAID missions in efforts to strengthen financial sector development programmes. It will also begin a new competitiveness initiative that will provide USAID missions with expertise, best practices and tools to design and initiate activities to enhance the competitiveness of the private sector in developing/transition countries.

The Agriculture Programme (EGAT/AG)

The Agriculture programme leads the Agency's efforts to help developing countries increase their agricultural productivity and stimulate economies growth in rural areas. It exercises its leadership role through support of agricultural research in development of country problems and through the provision of technical advice and training to USAID field missions that are implementing agriculture development programmes. Both the research and the technical services supported by EGAT/AG are organized around three themes: (1) agribusiness development; (2) agriculture and rural policy and governance; and (3) agriculture technology generation and outreach.

The Natural Resources Management Programme (EGAT/NRM)

The Natural Resources Management programme provides technical leadership and field support for the design and implementation of activities that assure the sustainable use of natural resources in four key areas: biodiversity, forestry, land resources management and use carried out by U.S. universities and a number of international research centers. It coordinates and supports three Presidential initiatives: The Initiative Against Illegal Logging; the President's Signature Initiative on water for the poor; and the White Water to Blue Water Initiative. In addition, the Programme works closely with several Global Alliance, which promotes sustainable forest management; the West Africa; and the Coffee Corps, which Provides U.S. private sector expertise to coffee producer groups in support of sustainable small farmer coffee systems.

The Environment and Science Policy Programme (EGAT/ESP)

The Environment and Science Policy programme manages activities in three specific areas that involve scientific and technological innovation-biotechnology and agricultural research, climate change, and multilateral police. Specifically, EGAT/ESP oversees USAID's agriculture, natural resource management and environment research portfolios and seeks to improve food security, protect the environment and reduce poverty through the use of biotechnology. The programme oversees and reports in USAID's efforts to international agenda on agriculture development, natural resources management and environment issues.

The Education Programme (EGAT/ED)

The Education programme provides technical leadership, field support and donor coordination in the education sector, focusing on:

(*a*) Improved basic education; (*b*) strengthened higher education institutions to address local and national needs; and (*c*) improved performance through training of public and private sector organizations. EGAT/ED places particular emphasis on access to education and quality issue support for Presidential Initiatives in Africa and Latin America, expansion of the role of higher education partnerships, and improvement of the development impact of training programmes. The programme manages a Global Development Alliance in teacher training, community partnership, and youth and workforce development.

EGAT/ED also serves as the U.S. Government lead in multilateral efforts to provide education for all with the United Nations Educational, Scientific and Cultural Organization (UNESCO), Word Bank, United Nations Children's Education Fund (UNICEF) and other donors.

The Energy and Information Technology Programme (EGAT/EIT)

The Energy and Information Technology programme provides technical leadership and field support to developing countries aimed at providing: (1) expanded access to, and sustainable use of, modern, efficient, and affordable energy services; (2) expanded access to and application of information and telecommunications services; (3) expanded access to enabling technologies for sustainable production and trade; and (4) expanded effective use of transportation and distribution infrastructure. EIT plays a major role in the implementation of the U.S. Government Clean Energy Initiative announced at the World Summit on Sustainable Development and in the Global Village Energy Partnership aimed at increasing the poor's access to modern and affordable energy services. EIT also provides leadership to the U.S. Government Digital Freedom Initiative, which promotes e-commerce in the developing world through policy reform and small business training. In addition, it promotes the effective use of transportation and distribution infrastructure in addressing transportation barriers and trade facilitation. Finally, the programme supports the Global Trade and Technology Network (GTN) which provides developing country private enterprises with enabling technologies for sustainable production and trade.

The Poverty Reduction Programme (EGAT/PR)

The Poverty Reduction programme works with USAID field missions to translate economic growth into poverty reduction by advancing market-led policies and other activities that specifically benefit the poor. The focus of these efforts is on initiatives that can help poor households protect, develop, leverage, or acquire enduring assets, exert control over their lives and participate in their communities in meaningful ways. EGAT/PR supports interventions that build up and protect the assets of the poor, increase the return on these assets, and help the poor cope with external adverse shocks. Equally important, it supports USAID efforts to increase the responsiveness of public institutions to poor people and to strengthen the poor's participation in local decision that affect their lives. Key activities include micro enterprise development, property systems reform, municipal service improvements and urban slum upgrading programmes.

The Women in Development Programme (EGAT/WID)

The Women in Development programme is the focal point within USAID for technical expertise and leadership on gender issues. Specifically, it assists USAID missions and offices in understanding the differential impacts of programmes on men and women and the unique contributions made by both men and women; addresses constraints that limit demand for girls' education; works with host country governments and non-governmental organizations to advance the status of women's legal rights and to increase opportunities for women; and takes a leadership role on emerging issues with critical gender dimensions. EGAT/WID seeks to increase the capacities of USAID and its partners to address these issues and coordinates with the donor community on critical gender issues such as trafficking in persons.

The Policy Analysis, Information, Communication and Outreach Programme (EGAT/PAICO)

The Policy Analysis, Information, Communication and Outreach Programme focuses on improving EGAT's ability to finance programme development costs, conduct programme assessments, implement special programmes/initiatives, conduct programme evaluations, and develop better information management tools.

The Development Credit Programme (DC)

The Development Credit programme manages the Development Credit Authority (DCA), a broad, general funding authority enacted by Congress that allows USAID to issue partial loan guarantees of upto 50 per cent for development purposes. DCA augments grant assistance by mobilizing private capital in developing countries for sustainable development projects, thereby supporting the capacity of host countries to finance their own development. In FY 2004, USAID plans to commit $ 15 million in transfer authority to an innovative programme to support the financing of water and sanitation facilities in developing countries under the Presidential Water Initiatives.

The Middle East Cooperation Programme

The Middle East Cooperation programme funds the U.S.-Israeli Cooperative Development Research programme, which provides grants to support cooperative research efforts by U.S., Israeli and developing country scientists. The programme also supports the Middle East Regional Cooperation programme, which promotes cooperative research efforts by Arab and Israeli researchers on topics relevant to the Middle East.

Other Programme Elements

USAID field missions buy into EGAT mechanisms and services. Over the past year, EGAT has taken the lead in developing a number of USAID sectoral strategies in the areas of trade capacity building, agriculture, education and women in development. The Trade Capacity Building Strategy was launched in February 2003 and has provided a framework for USAID efforts to meet commitments made at the Doha World Trade Organization (WTO) Trade Ministerial meetings in November 2001. The remaining strategies will be approved in early 2004. In line with these new strategies and the new strategic directions and its new organizational structure. EGAT is developing a new Bureau Strategic Plan that will reflect new strategic directions and its new organizational structure. EGAT's new Strategic Objectives, which have received interim Agency approval, are presented in this document. EGAT expects the Plan to be completed and submitted for Agency review in 2004. In FY 2004, EGAT will begin and innovative new field support programme—the Volunteers in Economic Growth Assistance programme (VEGA)—that will mobilize American volunteers, primarily private sector executives, farmers and business associations, to provide services to developing countries in private market development, agribusiness development and improvements to municipal services. EGAT has also developed more effective ways of informing missions of its field support services and developed and improved system for prioritising and responding to field requests for assistance. The responsiveness of these field support mechanisms was recently comfirmed by USAID missions responding to a USAID management survey.

4

Can Education Promote Rural Development?

DR. RAJEEV TYAGI AND DR. RUPESH TYAGI

For many years the proposition that education expansion promoted and in some cases even determined the rate of overall GNP growth remained the unquestioned. The logic seemed fairly straightforward. Developing countries are very deficient in their supply of semiskilled and skilled manpower. Without such manpower, which it was assumed could be created only through the formal education system, development leadership in both the public and private sectors would be woefully lacking.

Impressive statistics and numerous quantitative studies of the sources of economic development in the west were paraded out to demonstrate that it was not the growth of physical capital but rather of human capital that was the principal source of economic progress in the developed countries, clearly, in the newly independent nations of Africa and Asia, there was an immediate need to build up the human as well as physical capital infrastructure in order to provide indigenous leadership for the major task of development. It is extremely difficult to document statistically, it seems clear that the expansion of education opportunities at all levels has probably contributed to aggregate development by:

(*a*) Creating a more productive labour force and endowing it with increased knowledge and skills.

(*b*) Providing widespread employment and income earning opportunities for teachers, school and construction workers, textbook and paper printers, school uniform manufacturers, etc.

(*c*) Creating a class of educated leaders to fill vacancies left by departing expatriates or otherwise vacant positions in governmental services, public corporations, private businesses and professions.

(*d*) Providing the kind of training and education that would promote literacy and basic skill while encouraging "modern" attitudes on the part of diverse segments of the population. Even if alternative investment in the economy could have generated greater growth, this would not detract from the important contributions, education can make and has made to promoting aggregate economic development. That an educated and skilled labour force is a necessary condition cannot be denied.

Basic Problems of Education in Developing Countries

The school in many developing countries is a reflection and a fruit of the surrounding underdevelopment, from which arise its deficiency, its quantitative and qualitative poverty. But little by little, and there lies the really serious risk the school in these developing countries risks becoming in turn a factor of underdevelopment. Said Joseph Kizerbo, former minister of education Upper Volta.

Basic Problems of Primary and Secondary Education

There are two major problems related to primary and secondary education; firstly, poor management and distorted incentives, secondary maladjustment to social needs at the primary level. These problems of education arise in part becomes socially perceived needs within the educational system vastly exceed available funds and other resources. Given the tremendous importance of primary education for national development and the distinctive economic, social, and cultural conditions of developing countries. One must seriously question the advisability and utility of a system that for all practical purposes is no deterrent in structure and content from its counterpart in the advanced countries.

The basic problems of primary education, especially in the rural areas, and the reasons why it is often out of tune with the real needs of poor societies can best be summarized as follows:

1. Over 70 per cent of the children in developing countries live and attend school in rural areas.
2. Over 80 per cent of these children are likely to send their lives earning a living either directly the land from unskilled paid employments in rural areas. Yet primary schools spend little time giving these students the knowledge, skills, and ideas necessary to function efficiently in their rural environment (e.g., ferrying practices and management, hygiene, nutrition, community development).
3. Primary schools typically attempt to prepare students for secondary school, with training in literacy, basic arithmetic, and foreign languages receiving highest priority. The training, moreover, usually consists of recitation training, moreover, usually consists of recitation, repetition, and frill learning rather than thinking and problem solving.
4. In those developed nations in which the vast majority of primary school entrants precede to secondary school, which in turn tends to concentrate on college, prepares less questionable. But it has been estimated that it takes approximately 5 years (depending on age of entry) for a child to achieve literacy and even longer to master arithmetic and this foreign languages (even if languages were really relevant).
5. The problem with this approach to primary school curriculum solely as a preparation for secondary school in the developing countries is that:
   (*a*) For a variety of economic and social will dropout after year, with an additional 10 per cent dropping out the following year.
   (*b*) Approximately 50 per cent of those who enter the first class of primary school are unlikely to complete four years.
   (*c*) Less than 10 per cent of those who enter primary school are likely to succeed in reaching secondary

school, even though 25-30 per cent of the original entrants might complete the school.

(*d*) Of those who do get to secondary school, less than 60 per cent are likely to complete the course (the ratio is much lower in Africa) and only about 20 per cent will proceed to a university.

(*e*) For those who do make it through secondary school but do not continue on, the probability of finding a job in the modern sector (toward which their secondary education has been oriented) gets lower with each passing year.

Clearly something is seriously wrong with a primary and secondary education system modelled on its counterpart in economically advanced societies and transferred to an environment to which it has little if relevance (we deal with the problems is not the same thing as offering solutions. What is urgently needs are detailed studies and well-conceived experiments to answer such critical questions as the following:

1. At what age should a child who is going to have only a few years of primary education enter school?
2. Should primary education in a rural community in a developing country be full-time or part-time?
3. Assuming that some type of formal education is desirable do literacy and basic arithmetic skills constitute the highest-priority areas of instruction for children destined to spend lives in rural areas?
4. If the medium of instruction in higher and secondary education is language other than the mother tongue, it is therefore necessary to teach this language in primary school?
5. Given that for financial reasons it is not possible to language the training of teachers (salaries are usually directly related to length of training). Can the training give to teacher be changes and the curriculum and inspection system altered so that the teacher becomes more affective?
6. If children are given certain ideas that they forget because they have no possibility of practising them, are they more or less likely to accept and practice these ideas again when they are reintroduced later in adult life?

7. Have the children who drop of primary school after one, two, or there years gained much, if anything? If not, can a curriculum be designed so that they would benefit more?
8. Are the highest priority areas of instruction the same for (*a*) those children proceeding to secondary education, (*b*) those children getting paid employment in the modern sector, and (*c*) those children remaining in the rural areas/ if not is it possible to structure the system in such a way as to both provide some equality of opportunity and fulfill their differing requirements?
9. Related to (8), is it possible to design a reasonably just and incorruptible the procedure (for entrance into the next level) that does not over influence what is taught in the school?
10. Should the school and community be integrated? Should adult and child education be integrated? Should mass education (or community development) is designed to solve particular development problems? If so, how?

These and other questions of great significance to the nation-building aspirations of developing countries need to be answered if their primary (and secondary) education systems are to make maximum contributions to development.

Problems of Higher Education

Higher education in the developing countries is a very much smaller world than that of primary and secondary educations. Students in higher education make up less than 5 per cent of the total, and teachers less than 8 per cent. Although there are a considerable way of institutions in higher education the university is generally identified as the most important apex institution.

But these universities face some problems such as:

(1) Shortage of university.

(2) Malfunctioning of these institutions.

(3) Autonomy of universities; the Kithara Commission strongly recommended that university be given adequate authority and freedom of action

(4) Financial Arrangement is the one of major problem facing the university. The Radhakrishnan Commission concluded that

grants should be given for the fulfillment of the following objectives: (*a*) Grants for constructing buildings in university and college, (*b*) Means grants, (*c*) Library grants, (*d*) Hostel grants, (*e*) Salaries provident fund, pension, etc., (*f*) Scholarships and fellowships, (*g*) Study leaves travel grants, (*h*) Postgraduate work and research grants, industrial and vocational education.

(5) In general, there has been a dearth of academic research in developing countries; the standard education depends upon research. The need for higher education and research in developing counties is as follow:

(*a*) Many university and college try to introduce postgraduate course, but they have neither adequate resources teachers. Only those students take admission in such institutions who cannot fired a place elsewhere, but this leads to a decline in students.

(*b*) Before setting up a postgraduate department, a university should reflect upon the possibilities many times. According to S.N. base, it will be found in every university that younger teachers want to work, and they often express their resentment at the lack of space, lack of research material and even more at the absence of the people whom they can voice their problems and their grievances.

(*c*) The standard of post-graduate instruction and research should be equivalent consternation standards.

(*d*) Research centers should be set-up for facilitating research.

(6) According to James Rowland Angles, universities are biological organisms, which are governed by the principals of evolution. They cannot remain stagnant, and if forces to do so, they perish. Two programmers should be taken up for the spread of education.

(*a*) Adult education—for this programmers, education should be given the prevailing in classes specialist should introduce programmers for training and leadership in their own areas.

(*b*) Community service-order to arouse the desire for education in the community, university should set-up community centers.

In addition to this student welfare services are part of the university function. The reality is that the functions which are universities we conclude this issue with a quotation from a lecture by cardinal new man delivered a hundred years age, "A university training aims at raising mind at purifying the national taste, at supplying true principals to popular enthusiasm and fixed aim to popular aspiration, at giving enlargement and sobriety to the idea of the age, at vacillating the exercise of political power and refining the intercourse of private life."

Education and Rural Development

If economic development is to become a reality in developing countries there needs to be a better balance between rural and urban development. Since most of the priority projects of the past few decades focused on the modernization and development of the urban sector, much more emphasis needs to be placed in future years on expanding economic and social opportunities in rural areas. While agricultural development represents the main component of any successful rural development programme simply because 70 per cent of Third World rural population are engaged directly or indirectly in agricultural activities rural development nevertheless must be viewed in a broader perspective.

First and foremost, it needs to be viewed in the context of far reaching transformations of economic and social structures, institutions, relationships, and processes in rural areas. The goals of rural development cannot simply be restricted to agricultural and economic growth. Rather, they must be viewed in terms of a balanced economic and social development with emphasis on the equitable distortion, as well as the rapid generation, of the benefits on higher levels of living. Among these broader goals, therefore, are the creation of more productive employment opportunities both on and off the farm; more equitable access to arable land; more equitable distribution of the rural income; more widely distributes improvements in health, nutrition, and, finally, a broadened axes to both formal (in-school) and conformal (out-of-school) education, for adults as well as children, of a sort that will have direct relevance to the needs and aspirations of rural dwellers.

How do present developing countries systems of education fit into this holistic view of the meaning of rural development?

Basically, not very well. As we saw earlier in the formal primary school systems in most developing countries is with minor modifications a direct transplant of the system in developed countries. The overriding goal is to prepare all children to pass standard qualifying examinations for secondary schools; hence the curricula have strong urban bias. The priority needs of the greatest proportion of students those who will live and work in rural areas—are given minimal attention. Organized educational programmes, both formal and nonformal, largely neglect major groups with important rural training needs such as out-of-school children and youth, woman, and small subsistence farmers. As a result, much of the education in the rural communities of developing nations contributes little toward improving levels of agricultural productivity or toward assisting the student to function more effectively in the rural environment.

What, then might be the real and lasting educational needs for rural development? Philip H. Combs a noted educational economist, has provided one appealing typology. He groups these educational needs for both young people and adults, males and females, into four main categories:

1. General for basic education (literacy, an elementary understanding of science and one's environment, etc.)—What most primary and secondary schools now seek to achieve.
2. Family improvement education—designed primarily to impart knowledge, skills, and attitudes useful for improving the quality of family life and nutrition, home-making and childcare, home repairs and improvement, and family planning.
3. Community improvement education—designed to strengthen local and national institutions and processes through instruction in such matters as local and national government, cooperatives and community projects.
4. Occupational education—designed to develop particular knowledge and skills associated with various economic activities that are useful in making a living.

For the most part only Category 1—general education—has been emphasized in developing countries. But the learning needs of the three principal occupational subgroups of rural areas—farmers and farm workers. Persons engaged in non-farm rural enterprises, and rural general personnel—are likely in each case to fit quite poorly with most formal educational curricula. Table 4.1 shows how these learning needs vary among the three groups. Effective and well-designed educational programmes catering to each of these three diverse occupational groups are needed if education is to make its essential contribution to rural development.

Table 4.1: Illustrative Rural Occupational Groups and Their Learning Needs

Groups	*Types of Learning Needs (At Varying Levels of Sophistication and Specialization)*
A. Persons Directly Engaged in Agriculture	
1. Commercial farmers	Farm planning and management rational decision-making, recordkeeping, cost and revenue computations and use of credit.
2. Small subsistence and semi-subsistence farm families	
3. Landless farm workers practices	Application of new inpute, varieties, improved farm
	Storage, processing, food preservation
	Supplementary skills for farm maintenance and improvement, and sideline jobs for extra income.
	Knowledge of government services, policies, programmes, targets
	Knowledge and skills for family improvement (e.g., health, nutrition, home economics, child-care, family planning)
	Civic skills (e.g., knowledge of how cooperatives, local government, national government function).
B. Persons Engaged in Off-farm Commercial Activities	
1. Retailers and wholesalers of farm supplies and equipment, goods and other items	New and improved technical skills applicable to particular goods and services
2. Suppliers of repair and maintenance services	Quality control
	Technical knowledge of goods handled

(Contd.)

Groups	Types of Learning Needs (At Varying Levels of Sophistication and Specialization)
3. Processors, storers, and shippers of agricultural commodities	Sufficient to advise customers on their use, maintenance, etc.
4. Suppliers of banking and credit services	Management skills (business planning; record-keeping and cost accounting; and inventory control; market analysis and sales methods; customer and employee relations; knowledge of government services, regulations, taxes; use of credit).
5. Construction and other artisans	
6. Suppliers of general transport services	
C. General Services Personnel: Rural Administrators, Planners, Technical Experts	
1. General public administrators, broad-gauged analysts, and planners at sub-national promotional levels.	General skills for administration, planning, implementation, information flows, activities.
2. Managers, planners, technicians and trainers for specific public services (e.g., agriculture, transport, irrigation, health, small industry, education, family services, local government).	Technical and management skills applying to particular specialities.
	Leadership skills for generating community enthusiasm and collective action, staff team work, and support from higher echelons.
3. Managers of co-operatives and other farmer associations.	
4. Managers and other personnel of credit services.	

Now we concluded, that the education and rural as well as overall economic development of an economic are directly interrelated. So education plays an important role in the process of economic development of the developing countries. Since education in developing countries is underdeveloped, it would be desirable to expand it rapidly at every level. A strong case could be made for a crash programmer to extend and improve primary education. Secondary education is, of course, the most critical bottleneck in providing new additions to the desperately short supply of high-level manpower of all kinds. Expansion of higher education is indispensable if foreigners are to be replaced by local nationals.

REFERENCES

F.H. Harbison and C.A. Meyers, *Manpower and Economic Growth*, 1964.

Jagdish Bhagwati, "Education, Class Structure and Income Equality", *World Development*, no. 5 (1973).

John, Simmons, "Education for Development, Reconsidered", Reading 24 in *The Struggle for Economic Development*.

John, Simmons, "Education, Povertyment and Development", World Bank Staff Working Papers No. 188 (1974); p. 32.

Johns, Brubacker, *Bases for Policy in Higher Education*, pp. 76-77.

Marc, Blaug *et al.*, *Causes of Graduate Unemployment in India*, Harmmondworth, England: Penguin, 1967.

M.P. Aiyar, *Politics of University Higher Education in India*, Bombay, 1967, p. 76.

P.R. Panchmukhi, Education, Capital in India, *IJE*, January-March, 1965.

R. Islam, "Graduate Unemployment in Bangladesh: A Preliminary Analysis", *Bangladesh Development Studies*, Autumn 1980, pp. 47-74.

Shridharnath Mukerjee, *Education in India, Today and Tomorrow*, p. 210.

T.W. Schultz, *Education and Economic Growth in Social Forces Influencing*, American Education, N.B. Hentryced, 1951.

W.A. Lewis, "Education Economic Development", *TSCJ*, Vol. XIV, No. 4, 1952.

World Bank, "Human Development Issues and Policies: Education", Reading 13 in *The Struggle for Economic Development*.

5

Role of Extension Education in Rural Development

MRS. RAKHI MITTAL

"Poor Education if allowed to be continued for a longer period it will as such the rap of nation and will kill it."

Relevant, locally controlled educational programmes play key roles in rural development in developing nations. Education has a desirable controlling influence over development of the rural individual, family, community, and society, leading to reduced poverty, income equity, and controlled unemployment. The failure of trickle-down development and recognition of the importance of rural areas and rural people to the economic emancipation of developing countries has given education a key role in rural systems of supply, production, marketing, personnel maintenance, education, health-care and governance. Functions of education include imparting social change, improving individual social position and standard of living, activating participation in rural and cultural development, increasing critical abilities of rural people to diagnose their needs, assert their rights, and take greater control of decisions affecting their lives, providing trained manpower in rural areas, linking rural and urban sectors, providing employment and income opportunities, increasing labour force productivity, and developing leadership. Education oriented to urban rather than rural needs may do more harm than good by accelerating rural to urban migration, generating youth unemployment, and leaving students ill-equipped to succeed in a rural environment. Education contributing to rural development must be locally controlled, practical, applied, problem posing and focused on functional specialization.

Food security and its relationship to sustainable agricultural and rural development have increasingly become matters of concern for developing countries and for the international community. While there are many complex factors that influence sustainable development and food security, it is clear that education in agriculture plays an important role in preparing farmers, researchers, educators, extension staff, members of agri-businesses and others to make productive contributions. A critical issue in the 21st century will be the changes and adaptations required in agricultural education in order for it to more effectively contribute to improved food security, sustainable agricultural production and rural development.

According to Rogers (1996, p. 86), "poor training of agricultural extension staff has been identified as part of the problem of the relative ineffectiveness of much of extension in the field." This applies not only to extension staff, but to agricultural professionals in general. Unfortunately, the training of human resources in agriculture is often not a high priority in the development plans of countries. As a result, curricula and teaching programmes are not particularly relevant to the production needs and employment demands of the agricultural sector.

The situation has become more serious in recent years due to the economic crises in the public sector in many developing countries. In the past, the public sector absorbed nearly all agriculture graduates. This is no longer the case, and agriculture graduates are finding it increasingly difficult to find employment. Governments can no longer afford to hire every graduate, and education in agriculture has not kept up with the increasingly sophisticated labour demands of the private sector. These and other factors, such as environmental degradation, rapid changes in technical knowledge and the increasing marginalisation of rural areas, all call for changes in the current systems of education in agriculture in many developing countries.

In response to the need to review and adjust curricula and teaching programmes in agriculture, FAO conducted a series of regional round tables that were completed in 1994. Participants at the round tables were staff of agricultural universities, colleges and technical schools and officials of Ministries of Agriculture and

Education. In addition, two expert consultations were held in Rome— one to discuss the results of a survey of 20 agricultural education institutions from throughout the world and the other to address obstacles and challenges to integrating environmental themes into agricultural education programmes based on 10 institutional case studies.

From the regional round tables, expert consultations, and recent staff analysis it is possible to identify a number of common issues, which affect the teaching of agriculture in developing countries currently, as well as into the next century. These issues can be categorized in the following groups:

Contextual Constraints

- Changing employment opportunities in agriculture;
- Budgetary and financial crises;
- Marginalisation of agriculture and rural life, and the increase of urban-based students; and
- The relationship between agricultural education and research and extension.

Changes to Curricular Content and Emphasis

- Rapid scientific progress and technical change;
- Increased awareness of environmental issues in agricultural education;
- Increased awareness of gender issues and the roles of women in agriculture; and
- The need to integrate population issues into agricultural education.

Changes to Educational Processes

- The need to revise the pre-service education of extension workers; and
- The need for an inter-disciplinary, systems approach to agricultural education.

An analysis of these issues clearly demonstrates that agricultural universities, colleges and schools face major challenges in the 21st century. Meeting these challenges will require new educational strategies, innovative leadership and institutional reforms that take into account the current trends and factors that influence agricultural and rural development.

Contextual Constraints

Changing Employment Opportunities in Agriculture

Reduced government spending as a result of structural adjustment has put pressure on agricultural education institutions to better relate curricula to employment opportunities. The dramatic reduction in employment by Ministries of Agriculture in recent years, in some cases over 50 per cent staff reductions, means that students increasingly need to learn knowledge and skills for private sector employment. It is also likely that employment opportunities outside the agricultural sector will grow at a faster rate than in agriculture. This requires a continuous analysis of job markets and employers' requirements in order to plan and develop appropriate curricula.

The message of sizable reductions in the public sector workforce is not lost on students who are demanding curricular changes that will prepare them for employment opportunities in the private sector. University and college administrators and teaching staff, however, have been slower to accept the need for changes. What is required is that they engage frequently in consultations with prospective private sector employers to obtain estimates of the numbers and types of jobs that are likely to be available for graduates and to plan curricula accordingly.

To adjust training to private sector employment requires that agricultural education institutions develop ways of keeping in touch with the labour market. Ideally, institutions should set up permanent mechanisms for observations of the job market and continuous adaptation of courses. However, a lack of financial and human resources often makes this difficult to accomplish. Some institutions are taking action, however, to establish better contact with potential employers of graduates. For example, the Institut Agricole de Bouaké in the Ivory Coast has set up a committee to study the agricultural employment market and identify related training needs. The Institut also makes use of visiting instructors from agri-business firms and has arrangements for attaching students to agricultural enterprises so that they gain practical experience and possible entry to jobs.

A similar approach is being used by a secondary agricultural school in Zaragoza, Colombia. With FAO assistance, the school established an educational advisory committee consisting of school staff, local government organizations, representatives of farmers' cooperatives and students and their families. The committee helps the school formulate educational policy and programmes and also serves as a resource for internships and job placement for graduates.

Recent changes in employment opportunities mean that the curricula and training programmes in agriculture need to be reoriented to meet the learning requirements of diverse groups—unemployed and under-employed people, dismissed public sector workers, agricultural professionals seeking career changes and advancement and young graduates seeking employment for the first time. Only by involving potential employers in the curriculum development process will it be possible to ensure that agricultural education will result in gainful employment for graduates.

Improving the employment opportunities for graduates requires that curricula focus less on specific technical knowledge that will quickly become obsolete and more on processes and abilities of students to think and solve problems that are relevant to societal needs. Students should learn skills and abilities that are transferable to a wide range of occupations. For example, excellent communication skills are as needed by agricultural graduates who plan to work in extension as business school graduates who hope for a career in the banking industry. Likewise, teaching methods should be changed to reflect the needs of society, and thus better respond to demands for trained human resources. Teaching with practical, reality-based cases is a good example of how teachers can change methods to meet student needs and those of the larger society (Boeher and Linsky, 1990).

Budgetary and Financial Crisis

In most developing countries, the major source of funding and financial support for agricultural education is the national government, or the provincial/municipal government level where decentralization has been implemented. Generally, agricultural education institutions operate on the basis of an annual budget which depends on the number of students enrolled, previous funding levels and government capacity to support the institutions. Tuition, fees and other possible sources of income, such as donations and institutional revenue from farms or the provision of various kinds of services (e.g., veterinary services), are often of limited significance.

The economic crises of recent years and recurrent structural adjustment measures have imposed severe budgetary restrictions in many countries which have negatively affected support to agricultural education. For example, the analysis of 20 case studies carried out for the 1991 FAO expert consultation showed that institutions use upto 85 per cent of the total budget for salaries. If the educational infrastructure were in place (teaching labs, instructional equipment and materials) spending 80-85 per cent for salaries is within an acceptable range. However, in most developing countries this is not the case.

Agricultural education is expensive. It requires teaching aids and materials, scientific and technical equipment as well as adequately equipped training and experimental farms. The initial funds for buildings, teaching equipment, textbooks, and agricultural machinery have usually been provided in the past by governments and donor assistance. The maintenance and replacement of these facilities is generally beyond the existing financial resources of many institutions. The result is that agricultural education institutions face great difficulties in ensuring properly equipped, maintained and functioning laboratories and practice farms. Not surprisingly, the objectives of experimentation, teaching, outreach or agricultural production are inadequately achieved.

Budget cutbacks have also made it difficult to maintain teaching standards due to reductions in recruitment and in staff development programmes, especially those involving training abroad. Limited budgetary resources often do not allow teachers to obtain the scientific and technical publications necessary to keep their knowledge current, or to conduct up-to-date research. This has resulted in a decline in the standards of teaching, research and extension in many countries.

New innovative ways of funding institutions need to be

explored. A small percentage of money received from the sale of cash crops could be used as "check-off money" for research and extension efforts. Agribusiness support of funding schemes for research could also contribute revenue. An example of funding diversification that addresses the "capitalization" needs of both the institution and individual faculty members, is the Faculty of Agriculture, Cairo University, Egypt. The university has established specialized centres (e.g., Reclamation and Development Centre for Desert Soils) which provide fee-based services to commercial agricultural enterprises. The income that is generated is shared by both the faculty members and the teaching and research programmes of the centres.

Marginalisation of Agriculture and Rural Life

As they develop, almost all countries of the world have decreasing proportions of their economically active populations dependent on agriculture. Despite increased demand for food production, the percentage of the population which makes a living directly from agriculture continues to fall in developing countries. Intensification of production through improved technology and increased inputs is responsible in most cases for increased production, rather than from increased numbers of producers.

High rural population growth rates and increased efficiency in agricultural production have led to increased levels of unemployment and underemployment, and a consequent migratory drift (some would say flood) to cities in search of work and better standards of living. National budgets tend to be directed to satisfying the needs of urban centres at the cost of funding and services for rural areas. This urban bias and rural neglect has led to decreasing levels of real income in the rural areas.

Funds and resources for agricultural education are reduced as national budgetary restrictions are applied to rural areas. Reduced funding for primary and secondary education in rural areas means poorer educational standards. In many developing countries, rural youth find difficulty in obtaining a basic education of the same quality as urban youth, and hence have difficulty in gaining entrance to higher education institutions. This in turn means fewer agricultural students with an in-depth understanding of rural life.

This situation is unlikely to change as long as admission to these institutions is based solely on academic qualifications which place rural young people in direct competition with better schooled urban youth. The result is a significant waste of human resources, since rural youth possess unique aptitudes and qualities for understanding and working in the rural sector and are well suited for technical work in agriculture.

In some cases, the urban origin of agricultural students is now so dominant that it is becoming difficult to teach them about agriculture without special, often expensive, educational efforts. The result is that urban-based graduates, with little practical knowledge of rural development and agricultural production, are working as extension agents and agricultural advisers.

The increasing number of students with urban backgrounds has led some institutions to look for ways to ensure that these students gain a practical understanding of the realities of rural and farm life. One way is early integration of students in rural life through practical training before final admission and a series of practical training periods throughout the programme of study. Agricultural universities and colleges need to take into consideration during admission the willingness of students to follow an agricultural career and their ability to adapt to work in rural areas.

Policies and strategies need to be developed that ensure representation of rural youth in higher agricultural education. Bright but economically disadvantaged students need access to education. Quotas or community representation schemes are one means to ensure opportunities for rural youth. Another option is community or regional scholarships for capable youth interested in studying agriculture. Intellectually capable rural youth lacking academic skills may require an adjustment period and a make-up year to meet standards. Similarly, urban youth may need to obtain agricultural competencies through mandatory internships and systematic exposure to rural life.

Relationship between Agricultural Education and Research and Extension

With few exceptions, the institutional relationships between agricultural teaching and research and extension services are inadequate. In many countries, this is the result of the deliberate separation of education, research and extension into different ministries and agencies and a lack of functional mechanisms to link them together to solve common problems.

Agricultural research is usually conducted at government research stations and laboratories, the majority of which are not linked with universities. Research activities are often carried out as part of postgraduate programmes of higher agricultural education, but they are seldom directly related to national research priorities and programmes.

There are some significant exceptions to this separation of education and research. In India, for example, agricultural universities carry out an important part of research activities and are integrated within the programmes of the Indian Council for Agricultural Research (ICAR). Some specialised centres of ICAR (called University Centres), in turn, offer postgraduate M.Sc. or Ph.D. training programmes. Another examples is the Colegio de Postgraduados in Mexico, which was created specifically to balance research, postgraduate teaching and extension activities.

The participation of higher education institutions in research activities needs to be planned as part of the regular activities of the teaching staff and their students. The credibility of these activities, and the possibility of obtaining the necessary research resources, depends on the activities being relevant to farmers and to national research priorities. For agricultural education institutions to participate more fully in research, the role of research should be clearly defined in the institutional policies and in the responsibilities of faculty members.

As with research, close working relationships between agricultural education institutions and extension systems are indispensable in order to ensure the relevance and contribution of agricultural education. As with research, however, the involvement of agricultural education institutions in extension and community outreach is often limited. Even in those countries where extension and agricultural education are not separated into different ministries, the lack of resources and linking mechanisms greatly limits joint activities.

Notable exceptions are those institutions, which have been organized with outreach or extension responsibilities and are provided with the necessary means to carry them out. Looking again at the example of India, the responsibility for extension falls to a large extent on universities. They provide training and technical support to extension subject-matter specialists and have direct contacts with significant number of farmers. The universities often maintain their own units of extension and communication for this purpose. In the case of Mexico, the Colegio de Postgraduados has established a Centre for Development Studies with four regional units, one in each ecological zone of the country. These units provide a link between academic programmes, extension activities and rural producers.

One way for universities and technical institutes to implement development outreach activities is by follow-up technical support to graduates working in agri-businesses or managing their own production enterprises. Also, short courses of continuing education can be designed to update extension officers' knowledge and to qualify extension staff for career advancement. Continuing education should, wherever possible, make use of farmers' associations, graduate associations, NGOs, commercial enterprises and research and extension centres.

Agricultural education institutions, working with appropriate government agencies and NGOs, need to develop research and demonstration plots that directly address farmers' needs. This requires that farmers be valued for their contribution to production through their innovations and sharing of local knowledge. For their part, farmers' organizations need to do a better job of communicating the needs of their members to agricultural education institutions. Farmer advisory boards are one way to improve communication between agricultural education institutions and local producers.

Changes to Curricular Content and Emphasis

Rapid Scientific Progress and Technical Change

Although agriculture generally kept up with scientific progress in the past, the pace of change is much faster today, requiring continual updating of curricula. Scientific knowledge is changing very quickly as modern communication technologies facilitate the global sharing of information among scientists and educators. Since "new" knowledge becomes "old" knowledge so quickly, it is essential that students develop the skills and attitudes that will allow them to continue to learn and develop their competencies throughout their professional lives.

Rapid advances in information technologies (e.g., electronic mail and the Internet) now make possible new modes of collaboration and cooperation between institutions of agricultural education. Reduced funding for education makes inter-institutional collaboration both increasingly necessary and difficult to achieve. Access or lack of access to the Internet will determine if the information gap is reduced, or if it will widen even further. If institutions are to keep pace with rapid changes in science and technology, continuing education for faculty members is necessary through scientific meetings and inter-institutional exchanges, including those that apply innovative uses of electronic information systems (e.g., electronic networks for collaborative curriculum development and distance education). A commitment must be made by institutions to improve the information infrastructure to ensure that students and faculty have access to the new information technologies (Richardson, 1997).

New global developments in science and technology have profound implications for agricultural education institutions. New advances in science and technology influence the subject-matter and types of courses students need to understand today's agriculture. Food processing and post-harvest technologies, biotechnology, agri-business management and farming systems development are some of the subject areas which need to be incorporated into curricula. These subjects will attract increasing number of students as new employment opportunities are created which demand expertise in these fields. Advances in biological sciences increase the complexity of agriculture and complicate access to technology by poor nations. Regional cooperation and centers are a possible solution. Partnerships with private companies should also be explored as a means to improve access to new technologies.

In addition to new scientific knowledge, the most important source of knowledge for agricultural development is rural people themselves and the time-tested systems of production that embody their knowledge. An understanding of rural people and their production systems should be an integral part of agricultural education. This requires that agricultural education institutions play not only an academic role, but also a community development or outreach role that allows them to understand local knowledge and combine it with modern agricultural science. Understanding the contributions that local people can make to solving their own problems is the key to sustainable rural development.

Environmental Issues in Agricultural Education

In many parts of the world, the increasing needs of growing populations for food, fuel and fibers have led to deforestation, severe soil erosion, loss of water resources, and eventually declining crop production. It is clear that the loss of natural resources and environmental degradation affects food security. It is also clear that institutions of education in agriculture need to incorporate environmental and sustainable agricultural development issues into their curricula.

Environmental and sustainable agricultural development problems require an inter-disciplinary approach to curricula since sustainable development relates not only to technological concerns, but also to economic, social, cultural, ecological, and public policy matters. Furthermore, curricula need to provide students with opportunities to observe first-hand the physical, technological and social aspects of natural resource uses for agriculture through learning activities that are experiential and problem-focused.

Experience shows that institutions of agricultural education can play a vital role in bringing about changes in peoples' attitudes and practices so that they are more environmentally responsible. Developed countries have for some time included environmental concerns in their teaching curricula, research activities and outreach programmes. Current practice in agricultural education in many developing countries, however, does not demonstrate widespread integration of environmental and sustainable agriculture topics into academic programmes. Rather, these topics are added piecemeal to existing curricula, if at all.

Three main issues can be identified which affect the challenge of integrating environmental and sustainable development themes or issues into agricultural education programmes. First, such issues are complex and diverse. They involve social, cultural, political and economic aspects as well as technical and scientific information. Thus, an interdisciplinary approach is essential (Bawden, 1996).

Second, agricultural education institutions are not always structured to deal with the complexity of these issues. Substantial institutional reorientation and attitude change among faculty members may be necessary. In order to achieve such changes, the training and redeployment of teachers may be needed along with greater involvement of students, younger, environmentally-aware staff and rural communities in the design of new curricula.

Third, new approaches to learning and knowing which incorporate the environmental knowledge of local people are needed. These new approaches should involve people (students, teachers, producers) learning together in collaborative, knowledge-sharing situations on campus and in the field. The ultimate aim should be to make environmental issues inseparable from the professionalism of graduates, the production practices of farmers, the commercial objectives of agri-businesses and the interests of society for a safe and secure environment.

Integrating Population Issues into Agricultural Education

Population projections suggest that the world population will continue to increase from the present figure of nearly six billion people to between 11 and 14 billion people by the end of the next century. There is a great need in the developing countries to teach agricultural students population issues in relation to development problems. Institutions of agricultural education need to incorporate population education concepts and principles into curricula since many agricultural graduates will become managers, planners, and policy-makers who need to understand the dynamic inter-relationships between food, population, the environment and socio-economic development. Furthermore, students trained to work as extension agents need to be able to engage farm families in dialogue about sensitive population issues and to effectively communicate population messages to rural people.

Population education should develop awareness and understanding of the nature, causes and implications of population growth and distribution as they relate to agricultural productivity and rural development, and how these issues affect, and are affected by farmers, their families and society as a whole.

Population education can be integrated into training institutes by creating a separate population education course required of all students; by introducing population education as modules into existing courses; and by integrating population education issues and content into relevant topics in courses of study within existing curricula.

An FAO project in Malawi has taken the route of integrating population issues into existing courses of study at the Natural Resources College and the National Forestry College. The country has one of the highest annual population growth rates in Africa and its population density is one of the highest on the continent (Sigman, 1998). The project was a response to escalating concerns about the relationships between rapid population growth, food security, land use, environmental stress and poverty in Malawi. The basic strategy of the project was to enable extension agents to include population education, as it relates to agriculture and forestry, in their work with farm families. To implement this strategy, the project had two training components—pre-service training for students and in-service training for agents in the field.

Population's issues are a good example of how to integrate the teaching of values and attitudes into an agricultural subject area. Educators need to develop teaching strategies that emphasize and help students develop their affective reasoning skills. Since the attitudes and values that people possess are difficult to change, educators need to place greater emphasis on the psychology of the change process, thus improving the likelihood that change in practice will come as a result of educational efforts.

Gender Issues in Agricultural Education

Women play a major role in the world's agricultural production systems. In the less developed countries, an estimated one-third of all rural households are managed by women. In Sub-Saharan Africa and the Caribbean, women produce 60-80 per cent of basic foodstuffs, while in Asia they perform over 50 per cent of the labor involved in intensive rice cultivation.

In recent years, there has been widespread recognition of the vital roles played by women in all areas of agriculture and the need for women to have access, through formal and non-formal training, to the knowledge and skills needed for improved agricultural production, processing and marketing. Extension agents, researchers, teachers and students all need to be educated and informed about rural women's problems, potentials and aspirations.

The 1991 FAO expert consultation urged that special efforts be made to recruit and support female students from rural areas who could become extension agents, agricultural researchers, teachers and policy-makers. One of the reasons why there are few women extension workers, researchers and other agricultural professionals is the small number of female graduates from intermediate and higher-level agricultural education institutions. Yet, there are various countries where the enrolments of women are proportionately high. On average in Africa, FAO data show that there has been a 10 per cent increase from 1983 to 1993 from about 15 to 25 per cent female enrolment in agricultural education institutions.

The question of how to attract more female students to agricultural disciplines is linked to the issue of encouraging students from rural areas to enter higher education. As noted above, the number of female students has increased over the past ten years and this trend should be supported and encouraged. Also, more role models for young women to emulate are needed, including teachers in agricultural education institutions. Raising the number of women in agricultural education, both as educators, administrators and students is important as a means of reinforcing a commitment to understanding and changing the status of women in agriculture.

Educators need to become more responsive to gender related issues by taking into account women's roles and contributions in the total agricultural industry. While there is a trend for increased enrolment of women students in agricultural sciences at the technical or higher levels, this has not resulted in the dissemination of improved technology to women farmers because few female graduates are employed in extension work. Agricultural education institutions may increasingly have gender-sensitive admittance policies, but due to traditional barriers female graduates continue to have problems finding employment in agriculture (Crowder, 1998). Strategies, curricula, and policy shifts need to emphasize and include women as role models and leaders in agriculture.

Gender-sensitive policies have, at best, resulted in training programmes in which women are treated equally with men. However, it is not only the equal treatment of women that is important, it is equal employment benefits that are important. Equal treatment does not necessarily lead to equal benefits for women; indeed, the treatment may have to be different in order to take into consideration the different needs, time constraints and productive activities of women.

Gender-sensitive educational policies should be developed with a wide-range of stakeholders, including community leaders, politicians, potential employers and especially women themselves. Measures should be put in place to encourage young women and better prepare them to take up agricultural studies. For example, special attention should be paid to revising admissions policies that discriminate against women and to the creation of special scholarships for women to study agriculture. There is also a need to provide gender sensitisation courses for teaching staff and to eliminate stereotyping of females in agricultural studies. In some cases, professional organizations of women agriculturalists can act as pressure groups for these changes.

Changes to Educational Processes

Extension Education

Extension, as a non-formal educational input, can make important contributions to sustainable agricultural production and rural development. There is a critical need for well-trained extension workers in many developing countries. However, the extension methodology portion of the curricula and programmes of study of many agricultural education institutions is inadequate and in need of review and revision.

There is a tendency among many institutions to place emphasis primarily on providing students with scientific and technical knowledge in the various agricultural disciplines. Often, too little attention is paid to providing the types of courses that are important for preparing students as agricultural extension workers who can effectively communicate with diverse rural groups as well as support these groups in a process of collaborative problem-solving. In revising curricula for extension training, it is important to recognize that there has been a shift in thinking and in practice from expert-driven, technology-transfer extension approaches to collaborative learning approaches with participant groups.

Students studying extension need to see and work with applied technology on farms. Curricula should place less emphasis on theoretical models and more on practical application of research. There is a need to provide an interdisciplinary perspective into which a wide range of different disciplinary components can be integrated and to provide experiential, field-based learning activities. Learning should emphasize inductive reasoning skills so that students can interpret problems and devise solutions. Furthermore, curricular revisions for training extension workers should take into account a number of the issues identified in this chapter—the decline in public sector employment, the deterioration of the natural environment, population education, and the changes in the roles and responsibilities of women farmers.

In many cases, the lack of relevance of extension education to the rural world is a problem for students graduating from agricultural institutions. The gap between the methods and content taught and the rural socio-cultural context causes difficulties for graduates in establishing good communication with rural people. As noted above, this is especially serious for those with an urban background who go into extension work.

In many developing countries, small-scale family farms constitute the majority of the total number of agricultural holdings. A major challenge for extension is helping them advance in sustainable ways from subsistence agriculture to commercial agriculture. Agricultural education institutions, especially those at the intermediate technical level, have a key role in training extension workers so that they are oriented towards addressing the improvement of small-farmer agriculture, and in particular improving their food crop production and marketing capabilities.

This situation calls for more interaction among academic staff and students with members of the farming community, including the NGOs and agri-business firms that provide production services to farmers. The development of mechanisms and channels of communication which facilitate the understanding and utilization of local agricultural knowledge is of vital importance for the training of extension workers. Periodic curriculum review and revision, with a focus on local development problems and solutions, are needed in order to keep the knowledge base relevant and to ensure that there is not a "cultural gap" between extension workers and the ultimate beneficiaries—farmers and rural dwellers.

The implications for extension education are clear: an improved effort needs to be made to better relate local knowledge systems to scientific farming methods. Teachers and students need to use applied, field-based practices when learning how to improve agricultural production. Participatory teaching and learning strategies need to be incorporated into all aspects of educational delivery.

Extension Education combines both adult and informal education. It is concerned with educating adults, i.e., farmers or homemakers, not in the letters and alphabet, grammar or language, but in the techniques of raising better crops, better animals, better fruit trees, managing the home in a more efficient way, rearing children scientifically, taking care of the nutrition of the family, etc.

The areas of our concern can be defined thus:

1. *Agricultural Extension*:-Extending knowledge to the agriculturists;
2. *Veterinary and Animal Husbandry Extension*: Extending knowledge about breeding, marriage, feeding and care of animals and birds, etc.;
3. *Agricultural Engineering Extension*: Extending knowledge about agricultural machinery such as tractors and pumps, the levelling of land, water use, soil conservation, etc.;
4. *Home Science Extension*: Extending technical knowledge to farm wives, or ladies in urban and rural areas on food, child care, home decoration, kitchen gardening; and
5. *Industry Extension*: Extending knowledge on the managing and running of industries.

Similarly it can be sanitation and health extension, or any area which seeks to extend technical and scientific knowledge to a client system or the audience or the people who are to be educated along the lines of the innovation developed in the respective technological disciplines.

Extension Education is not formal which means:

1. It is flexible.

2. It is life, environment and leaner oriented.
3. It is diversified in content and method.
4. It is non-authoritarian.
5. It is built as leaner-participation.
6. It mobilizes local resources.
7. It enriches human and environmental potential.

Principles of Extension Education

Understanding of Principles

Before taking up the discussion of the Principles of Extension it will be worthwhile to examine what is meant by the word "Principle". A Principle is a statement of policy to guide decision and action in a consistent manner" (Mathews).

Its meaning will be clear when we try to understand the sequence of generalization. When something is put forth as a point of view, or an assumption, and its proof is not known, it is called a hypothesis. When a hypothesis is put to a test and the point of view, or the assumption, turn out to be acceptable, it is called a theory. When different individuals put a theory to several rigorous tests, under different setting, and the findings are found to be a substantial agreement, then it is given the name of a principle. Thus, a principle is a universal truth that has been observed and found to be true under varying conditions and circumstances. A principal is a fundamental truth and a settled rule of action.

Importance of Principles in Extension Work

It is usually believed that the knowledge of the principles is of no value to an extension worker. These principles are considered to be academic interest for the students taking advance courses in extension. Lagans, however, holds out clearly on the need for a sound knowledge of the principles for the extension workers. He points out that without this knowledge extension workers either keeps on labouring under some handicaps, or make grave mistakes, particularly in the initial stages. Further, if an extension worker aspires to become an administrator or a supervisor, it will be all the more necessary for him to possess a sound knowledge of the principles of extension.

Relative Sequence of Extension Principles

The Principles of extension is relative and not necessarily fixed in importance or sequence. Generally, however, it is also true that all the principles are important. It may also be relevant to point out that it is never possible to prepare a complete and final list of the extension principles. The principles discussed below are those, which are either fundamental in nature or widely accepted in literature on the subject.

Principles of Interest and Needs

To be effective, extension work must begin with the interests and needs of the people. Many times the interests of the rural people are not the interests of the extension worker. Even though he sees the needs of the people better than they do themselves, he must begin with the interests and needs as they (the people) see them.

In this way only can the extension agency mould the needs and interests of the people into realistic needs? Needs that can be fulfilled with the available resources, and the needs that should be fulfilled first.

Grassroots Principle of Organization

For extension work to be effective and real, it has to be a synthesis of democracy obtained at the level of the family and more particularly at the village level. Things must spring from below and spread like grass.

At the same time, modern science calls for an advanced stage of organization and a wiser coordination of thinking and action than is feasible in a single family or a single village. A higher level of living means wider specialization in a village. This calls for the corresponding organization of different professions and evocations. These will have to be woven together at the level of the enlarged family at the village community level. The Panchayats, as social institutions, have also to be established at the Block and the District levels. Thus, the establishment of the three-tier system namely, Village-Panchayat, Block-Samiti and Zila-Parishad, followed by State Legislatures and Parliament satisfies the grass-roots principle of organization in the extension.

Principle of Cultural Differences

In order to make extension programmes effective, the approach and procedure must be suited to the culture of the people who are taught. Different culture requires different approaches. A blue-print of work designed for one part globe cannot be applied effectively to another part, mainly because of the cultural differences. These differences can be perceived in the way of the life of the people, their attitudes, values, loyalties, habits and customs.

Principle of Cultural Change

Because changed ways must be learnt and because all learning must be grafted on what is already known, it is obvious that the change agent who works personally with the villagers must know what the villagers know and what they think. With this in mind and with an attitude of mutual respect and receptiveness, the worker must seek to discover and understand the limitations, the taboos and the cultural values related to each phase of his programme, before it is introduced, in order that an acceptable approach may be selected.

This principle can be summed up in the words of Earl Moncur:

> " As each culture is unique and each particular situation within which a change is occurring, or is to made, is unique, it is not possible to lay down prescription for what to identify and to describe the process which occurs so that each particular individual or team charged with responsibility for planning execution or adjusting to some type of change, may be able to act in terms of the process."

Principle of Cooperation and Participation

In an attempt to involve a great number of persons in achieving desired common ends, there seems to be no acceptable alternative but to let them choose the ends, and then aiding them to organize their self-help efforts successfully to do the things they want to do. Most members of the village community will willingly cooperate in carrying out a project which they helped to decide to undertake. It has been the experience of many countries that people become dynamic if they are permitted to take decisions concerning their own affairs, exercise responsibility for, and are helped to carry out projects in their own villages.

The participation of the people is of fundamental importance for the success of any educational endeavour. People must share in the development of a programme and must feel that it is their own programme.

Principle of Applied Science and Democratic Approach

Applied agricultural science is not a one-way process. The problems of the people are taken to the scientists who do the experimentation necessary to find out the solutions. The extension worker translates the scientific findings of the laboratories in such a way that the farm families can voluntarily adopt them to satisfy their own needs.

However, extension work is democratic both in philosophy and procedure. It aims to operate through discussion and suggestion. Facts about a situation are shared with the people. All possible alternative solutions are placed before the participants, and their merits are highlighted through mutual discussions. Ultimately, the people are left free to decide their line of action, the methods to be adopted in the local situation with their own resources and available government assistance.

Principle of Learning by Doing

In extension work, farmers should be encouraged to learn new things by doing and by direct participation. As Dr. Newman (1889) said, "Farmers, like other people, hesitate to believe and set on theories, or even facts, until they see with their own eyes the proof of them in material form. We must, in some way, bring this work to their personal attention. We must carry it home to them."

The motive for improvement must come from the people, and they must practice the new ideas by actually doing them. It is learning by doing, which is most effective in changing people's behaviour and developing the confidence to use the new methods in future.

Principle of Trained Specialists

It is very difficult for a multi-purpose extension worker to keep himself abreast with all the latest findings of research in all the branches of science he has to deal with in his day-to-day activity. Trained specialists have to be provided, who keep themselves in touch with their respective research institutes on the one hand, and extend to the extension workers, meaningful terms, and the latest scientific developments, which have scope for adoption in particular areas.

Adoptability Principle in the Use of Extension Teaching Methods

No single extension teaching method is effective under all situations. Reading material is for those who can read, radio programmes for those who have radios, meetings for those who can attend, demonstrations of recommended practices are for those who can come to the farmers where the demonstrations of recommended practices are laid. Farm and home visits are, by far, the most valuable, but they take up considerable time. New situations also arise where a special combination of method is necessary.

Extension agents have found that they need a large number of teaching methods out of which they can select and revise the one effective for the purpose and best suited to the culture of the people. At times, new methods must be devised to meet new situations and changing conditions.

Further, the use of teaching methods must have flexibility to be adopted to the members of a community who differ in age, education, economic status, sex and proneness to change, etc.

Principle of Leadership

A good rule in extension work is "Never do anything yourself that you can get someone to do for you." This calls for the development of local voluntary leadership. The involvement of leaders in extension programmes is the one single factor that determines the success or failure of those programmes. Local leaders are the guardians of local thought and action and can be trained and developed to best serve as interpreters of new ideas to the villagers. There is no dearth of local leaders. All communities have leaders or potential leaders; it is a question of searching them out and creating an environment, which will permit and encourage their development and performance.

In the promotion of change, however, it is neither right nor wise to disregard old organized groups and leaders. Old leaders, if they are trusted can open—as well as close—the gates to new types of community action. If such leaders are converted to new functions, the multiplication of new things to be done will almost certainly lead or drive them to share the role of leadership with others.

Whole Family Principle

The family is the unit of any society. All the members of the family to be developed equally by involving all of them. This is because of the following reasons:

- The Extension programme effects all members of the family.
- The family members have great influence in decision-making.
- It creates mutual understanding.
- It aids in money management.
- It balances farm and family needs.
- It educates the younger members.
- It provides an activity outlet for all.
- It unifies related aspects, such as the social, economic and cultural, of the family.
- It assures family service to the community and society.

It is not difficult to adopt this type of approach in extension programmes. There is much work in the field for the men and at home for the women. The 4-H clubs play a remarkable role in this regard so far as young boys and girls are concerned. A comparative study has shown that the young 4-H club members have greater confidence in scientific information than the non-members.

Principle of Satisfaction

Satisfaction of the people is very essential in extension work. Unless the people are satisfied with the end product of any programme, it is not going to be able to run. In democratic societies people cannot be made to move like machines. They must continue to act of their own conviction and that is possible only when they drive full satisfaction through adoption of innovations well suited to their needs and resources.

Difference between Formal Education and Extension Education

S.No	*Formal Education*	*Extension Education*
1.	Formal education starts from a theoretical Or conceptual framework and leads to Practical or actual field work.	Extension education is practical, field and farmer's problem-oriented, thus it starts from a practical and develops into a theoretical or basic understanding.
2.	In this type of education there is a fixed Or pre-decided curriculum.	In extension education there is no fixed Curriculum. It has also possible flexibilities depending on the needs of the learners.
3.	The audience in this type of education is Homogeneous with common goals.	The audience is heterogeneous and have diversified goals.
4.	Teaching is vertical and curriculum-centred.	Teaching is horizontal and mostly need-based and problem-oriented.
5.	Strict adherence to institutional norms and no free choice for the learners.	Freedom and choice of subject-matter left to the learners.
6.	This education is of a specialized nature, i.e., V Class-oriented, subject-centred and degree-oriented.	Informal, with some elements of formal education in class teaching, but not degree-oriented.
7.	Learners are taught, directly by the teachers.	Local teachers are used for training and dissemination of knowledge.

An Inter-Disciplinary Systems Approach to Agricultural Education

At a relatively early stage of their education, students need an overview of the agricultural and rural systems of their countries. Throughout their training, they need not only specialized courses which deal in-depth with specific technical subject-matter, but courses that help them think holistically, or in terms of integrated agricultural systems, so that they can understand the multi-dimensional nature of sustainable agricultural production. This requires an inter-disciplinary systems approach to agricultural education.

Training in the systems approach is essential for agricultural education because of the increasing complexity of agriculture, food and rural systems, the problems of environmental protection and management, women farmers and household issues and the needs of small-scale farmers. Even conventional subject-matter teaching should take place within an inter-disciplinary framework of agricultural systems rather than as isolated subjects.

Increasingly, education in agriculture needs to take the form of courses in agro-forestry, agro-ecology, and the socio-economics of integrated production systems. Local food production systems need to be studied in terms of the complexities of the larger economic and social context. A systems approach to agricultural education makes it possible to understand, evaluate and integrate the many disparate elements of production systems into a unified study of how those systems work and how they affect the biological, economic and social environments.

Teaching an inter-disciplinary, systems approach to agricultural and rural development applies to training students at every level of agricultural education (secondary, intermediate and higher levels). A systems approach to agricultural education requires a team-teaching methodology using case studies, problem-solving approaches and practical, field-based exercises. The goals of education in agricultural systems can be achieved through approaches that:

- Focus on whole-farm systems rather than single disciplines;
- Incorporate methods (e.g., participatory rural appraisal) to assess socio-economic impacts on agricultural productivity;
- Use agro-ecological systems as the unit of study and analysis;
- Encourage multi-disciplinary teams in teaching and encourage students to work in problem-solving groups; and
- Emphasize the linkages between basic and applied science, between research, education and extension, and between people, the environment, sustainable agricultural production and rural development.

Students need to be provided with more active learning roles within a farming systems perspective. Curricula need to integrate course work so that students can apply a range of skills to solving agricultural problems. To be effective agricultural change agents, students need to learn how to effectively communicate with farmers. Finally, more of their education needs to be experientially based.

Conclusions and Recommendations

Agriculture will remain for many years a major contributor to the economies of most developing countries. In some countries, however, its share of GDP will progressively decline. The agricultural sector in developing countries is undergoing rapid changes as a consequence of both technological progress and economic forces, which call for an increased market focus, competitiveness and higher productivity. Employment opportunities in the off-farm sector are expected to increase at a faster rate than in agriculture. This will further emphasize the present employment shift of agricultural graduates to related sectors, requiring a revision of existing curricula to better address educational needs.

Agricultural education curricula need to be redirected to address the labour demands of the private sector. Curricular reorientation will need to incorporate both the new role of market-oriented agriculture as well as issues of direct relevance to food security and rural poverty. Curricula also will need to better reflect the importance of social and environmental issues for sustainable agricultural development. Meaningful curricular revisions will require a better understanding and incorporation of the underlying psychological processes that influence learning, with special attention to experiential learning and participatory learning strategies that focus on inductive reasoning skills.

Agricultural colleges and universities need to determine their unique functions and the special attributes that they can offer students and the agricultural community. They will need to do a better job of communicating these attributes if they expect to remain financially sustainable, given current economic constraints. Moreover, agricultural institutions need to do a better job of carrying through with their unique ability to solve the agricultural problems of the communities they serve. A holistic approach to teaching agricultural production through a multi-disciplinary systems perspective will increase the utility of both scientific and local knowledge.

Inter-university alliances offer a means to capitalize on individual university strengths and to reduce costs reflected in the duplication of efforts. Regional collaborative strategies should be explored as a means to keep pace with accelerated scientific advancement. A commitment to developing communication infrastructure, especially with regard to the new computer-based communication technologies, should be a priority because of the potential to reduce the information gap.

The curricula of agricultural colleges and universities in developing countries need to adjust to the current and future employment needs of graduates. The emphasis in curricular revisions should be on process skills of problem solving and on skill sets that are transferable to a diverse employment sector. New options for programmes of study should be based on enabling students to meet the expectations of agricultural employers, and increasingly the employment needs of the private sector.

Given the severe restrictions on financial resources, governments in developing countries need to determine levels of continued support to higher education in agriculture based on the ability of colleges and universities to carry out curricular modifications that reflect employment markets. In some countries, there has been excessive growth in the number of diploma and degree granting agricultural education institutions. The challenge is to achieve a "better fit" between the supply and the demand for trained human resources in agriculture.

In the next century, agricultural education institutions in developing countries will need to address not only immediate production needs, but also long-term food security, sustainable agriculture and rural development needs. This will require moving from a single-disciplinary approach to an inter-disciplinary, systems approach, which incorporates a wide range of new topics, including gender, environmental and population issues.

A major challenge will be the transformation of agricultural education institutions into dynamic promoters of change within their environments. This will require that they abandon long-established traditions of academic isolation and become active contributors to sustainable agricultural and rural development through innovative teaching, research and extension.

6

Education: Need of Nation

DR. K.D. GAUR AND DR. POOJA GUPTA

Introduction

"The Function of Nayee-Talim is not to teach an occupation, but through it to develop the whole man."

—*Mahatma Gandhi*

Basic education links the children, whether of cities or the villages, to all that is best and lasting. Riding on one of the highest growth rates in the world, at around eight per cent in the tenth plan, India has launched the most ambitious education project since independence, Sarva Shiksha Abhiyan, under which primary education will be provided to all children by 2007. The purpose of education is not only to make our children literate but to make this earth a better place to live in.

While India takes a quantum jump into the developed world in the Tenth Plan the youth in the rural areas need to be trained to get absorbed in our new found industries and economic sectors. Every individual must be in a position to keep learning throughout his life. The idea of lifelong education is the keynote of the learning society.

Education has been looked upon as the most vital and crucial investment in human development. In recent years, studies on developed and developing countries have clearly demonstrated that development of human capital through universal basic education has contributed significantly to economic progress. The returns on investments in basic education is one of the highest. The strong linkage that the basic education has with improvement in levels of human well-being specially with regard to life expectancy, in fact mortality, nutritional status of children adds to the case of universal basic education.

It was the Ninth Plan (1999-2000) which drew up a detailed strategy for achieving the above objectives. The thrust areas for educational development in the Ninth Plan include universalisation of elementary education, achievement of full adult literacy, raising the quality of education at all levels, improving learner achievement, enlistment of the educational status of disadvantages groups including SC/ST girls and disabled children, removing of regional disparities, vocationalisation of education, retrieval of curriculum to meet emerging challenges in information technology and support for development of centers of excellence at the tertiary levels.

Investment in Education Since 1950-51

There has been an increase in investment in education since the 1950s. The expenditure on Education Sector was lightly less than 1 per cent in GDP 1951-52, continuing to rise, it reached a level of 4.11 per cent of GDP in 2000-01. During 1950-51, an expenditure of Rs. 64.46 crore was incurred on education. This has increased to Rs. 77847.66 crore in the year 2000-01 (this includes expenditure by Centre and States and plan and non-plan expenditure).

The allocations made in the Ninth and the Tenth Plan for the various sub-sectors of education in the central sector are given in the Table 6.1.

Department of Elementary Education and Literacy

Table 6.1: Ninth Plan Outlay/Expenditure and Tenth Plan (2002-07) Approved Outlay

S. No.	*Name of the Scheme*	*Ninth Plan 1997-02 Allocation*	*Ninth Plan Expenditure*	*Tenth Plan 1997-02, 2002-07 Approved Outlay*
1.	Elementary Education	16369.59	14523.29	28750.00
2.	Adult Education	630.39	520.38	1250.00
	Total	16999.98	15043.67	30000.00

Scenario in 1947

The educational scene at dawn of our independence was dismal, of technical and vocational education depressing. The rate of literacy was 16.67 per cent only one child out of three has access to the school, one out of twenty reached a middle school and one out of a hundred ever went to a college. The number of primary schools the British bequeathed was 1,41,000, the number of colleges around 600 and the number of universalities just 17. The educational expenditure was only 57 crores. In technical education system there were only 38 technical institutes and 53 polytechnic schools. The number of students receiving technical education at degree level was 2940 and at diploma level was 3650. There was no such thing as vocational schools or vocational education at any stage in general education system. That was the legacy the British left after about 200 of rule. That was a big challenge which the country accepted.

Current Scene

Today the rate of literacy as per census 2001 is 65.38 per cent (75.85% male and 64.10% female). The educational expenditure in 2000-01 was Rs. 77847 crore. There are about seven lakh primary schools, 12000 degree colleges, 234 universities out of which 12 are exclusively science and technology universities and 28 are agricultural universities. We have more than 200 technical institutes and degree level and more than 1000 polytechnics (1011 to be exact) at diploma level. We have 2721 Industrial Training Institutes. There are several other vocational institutes at diploma level. All told the intake capacity of these institutes is more than six lakhs. There are 17 Regional Engineering Colleges run by the Government and more than 200 run privately. There are eight Indian Institutes of Technology (IIT) including two Institutes of Information Technology. These are located at Kharagpur, Mumbai, Chennai, Kanpur, Delhi, Guwahati, Allahabad and Varanasi.

Four Pillars of Education

The first pillar is Learning to know in other words developing the capacity to absorb new knowledge. What is taught is not as important as whether the young persons' minds are being trained so that throughout their lives they can continue to absorb the exploding knowledge that now doubles every five years.

Indeed learning begins when the child is still in the womb and continues upto the very moment of death. What is needed, therefore, is that young people should have sharp and well trained minds which can cover a broad background and yet study in depth a small number of subjects. The curricula in Asia Pacific countries are not always designed with this in view. There is still too much learning by rote, rather than development of the intellectual faculty. The first object of our education, therefore particularly at the secondary level must be to impress young minds with a love for knowledge, spirit of inquiry and openness to new ideas, and a capacity to discriminate between what is really significant and what is simply an information overload.

The second pillar is Learning to do and this implies that the knowledge imparted to young people should also make them capable of gainful employment so that they become productive members of society in many of our countries the problem of the educated unemployed is getting increasingly serious, mainly because the secondary education system does not give adequate education in technical skills, and the aimless drift from school to college ultimately produce graduates who are not only unemployed but also, to an extent, unemployable. Third is pillar is Learning to live together. Here we deal with the all important social elements of education. Education does not involve merely developing individual skills, it also needs to encompass the necessary for young people to become positive and integrated elements of their respective societies. Thus such values as punctuality, cleanliness, respect for elders, helping the less fortunate, teamwork and discipline, although they may be looked down as being "old fashioned" do provide the foundations for socially integrated citizens. It is also necessary to point out that the process of social integration begins with the family and goes all way upto the global society itself. Each one of us has finally we come to the fourth pillar which is some ways in the most important, and that is Learning to be. At our very first meeting, the commission, and I quote education must contribute to the all round development of each individual mind and body, intelligence, sensitivity, aesthetic sense, personal responsibility and spiritual values.

Review of Literature

Most of the economists have given their views. Some of them are given below:

K.K. Khullar (2003), suggested that Technical education and Vocational education are the two major components of the human resource development, together they raise the quality of life as also its outlook. Although they are functioning separately at present it is essential to look at them together because of their close relationship and complementary concerns keeping in view the unprecedented expansion of knowledge in science, technology and vocational thinking, in the last five decades, making India one of the greatest technical education system in the world.

Vimal Ramachandaran (2003) had depicted that it is widely acknowledged that a significant proportion of children especially those from underprivileged backgrounds and girls, either dropout of primary school or even if they attend school, learn very little. Moreover there is a wide gap in learning achievement between government schools and private schools. The active participation of children is primary education hinges on a plethora of factors. Besides access, a range of demand and supply issues influence, why children choose to attend school regularly. Thus far, policy makers and education administrators have focused mainly on the formal school system and on improving access to education. The creating of backward and forward linkages is essential to creating an environment where every child not only goes to school but benefits from it.

C. Jayanti (2003) has concluded that education renewed commitment and faith in basic human rights upholding the dignity of man and woman. The Indian Government is taking small steps towards the bigger goal of education for all. Fifty years down the line once have a stronger nation, however the benefits of economic and social advancement need to percolate down to the poorest of the poor. The government commitment towards making education a fundamental right is a step in the right direction. What is required is speedy implementation of policy.

Sarva Shiksha Abhiyan (SSA)

In the last year of the Ninth Plan the Government of India launched the Sarva Shiksha Abhiyan which is the key programme through which the goals of elementary education are going to be met. This is the first programme for Universalisation of Elementary Education (UEE) covering the entire country. It is a significant step towards achieving the long cherished goal of UEE through a time bound integrated approach to be implemented in mission mode in partnership with states. The specific objectives of SSA are:

- All children in school, Education Guarantee Centre, Alternate School, Back-to-school camp by 2003.
- All children complete five years of primary schooling by 2007.
- All children complete eight years of elementary schooling by 2010.
- Focus on elementary education of satisfactory quality with emphasis on education for life.
- Bridge all gender and social category gaps at primary stage by 2007 and at elementary education level by 2010, and
- Universal retention by 2010.

It is important to make adequate provision of funds by the Centre for the fulfillment of the objectives of SSA. The programme cannot succeed without proper utilization of the available funds. Effective methods have to be evolved to transfer responsibility in terms of funds.

Systematic mobilization of the community and creating of effective system of decentralized decision-making are essential pre-requisites for the achievement of the objectives of SSA. This involves the cooperation of the stakeholders viz., the Central Government, States, Local Government bodies, teachers, parents, NGOs, the academic institutions and the children themselves. There is also a need for capacity build-up at all levels to make the programme self-sustainable.

Tenth Plan—Objective, Key Issues and Focus

The key issues during the Tenth Plan would be a greatest focus an improving access reducing disparities by emphasizing upon the common school system: renewal of vocationalization and employment oriented courses expansion and diversification of the open learning system reorganization of teacher training and greater use of new information and communication technologies, particularly computers.

The Central/State Government propose to take a number of steps to increase the access of secondary schools, to remove regional and sectional imbalance. A new scheme, Access and Equity, has been launched in the tenth plan which will increase the spread of secondary schools all over the country. The strategies under the scheme include (*a*) providing seed money/one-time grant to reputed private organization NGOs, missionaries to start school (*b*) to encourage NOS to open study centers in existing schools (*c*) improving hostel facilities for girl student (*d*) to start double shift in existing schools.

Conclusion

It is upon the youth of the world that the future of humanity depends, and the future of youth in turn depends on the sort of education that we impart to them. Creative innovations are required not only in the methodology but also in the content of educational systems around the world. With the new technology, distance education is becoming increasingly important. The computer has transformed the whole concept of learning and it is essential that this tool should be utilized to maximum advantage, particularly in reaching the vast rural areas of Asia and Africa where there is still large-scale deprivation, economic as well as educational. All this represents a tremendous challenge to educationists around the world.

In the final analysis it is upon the texture and content of our educational systems around the world that the future consciousness of the human race will crystallize. All of us involved in the field of education bear a heavy responsibility, not only towards the existing younger generations but to generations yet unborn, to provide them with a holistic, human race has passed for thousands of years, we can at last emerge into the sunlight of a sane and secure global society.

Suggestions

In the tenth plan tempting quality education at all stages of education and the pursuit of excellence is the key theme. In Secondary Education, the ongoing efforts in revision of curricula, so as to make it more relevant in the current context, would continue. The convergence of centrally sponsored schemes will help in imparting science, mathematics and, computer education: environment and value education; in a more focused manner. Following strategies which would improve the Higher Education system:

(*a*) Consolidation and Expansion of Institutions.
(*b*) Development of Autonomous Colleges and Departments.
(*c*) Redesigning of Courses.
(*d*) Training of Teachers.
(*e*) Strengthening of Research.
(*f*) Improvement in Efficiency.
(*g*) Review and Monitoring etc.

Higher education, general and technical must have links with all industrial and societal endeavours. Towards this end, a large number of centres for excellence, to turn out quality manpower in areas relevant to industry and society, need to be established with triangular partnership of academia, industry and government. These institutes of excellence are essential to make India a 'Knowledge Super Power' and would help in retaining our competitive edge in the global economy.

Modernization of syllabi, examination reforms and greater attention to issues of governance of universities and colleges, all require urgent attention.

The emphasis would be on conferring autonomous status to more college, provision of the means to interact across geographical boundaries of institutions, better infrastructure more rationalized funding of research, integration of teaching, research and evaluation, networking, mutual collaboration and cooperation among universities for optimum utilization of available resources. There is a crying need to improve the management and governance of universities to better enforce financial and administrative discipline. Decentralization of the university system, greater powers to faculty/departments and student nomination to university bodies of the basis of merit/excellence are issues, which would receive attention. The accreditation process should be made more transparent, time-bound and be progressively freed of Government regulation and control leading to a situation when the whole procedure would be based on a system of public appraisal/acceptance.

REFERENCES

Ansari, M.M., "Open Learning in the Context of Globalization", *Yojna,* Vol. 47, September, 2003, No. 9

Jayanti, C., "Role of Education and Social Change", *Yojna,* Vol. 47, March, 2003, No. 3.

Karan Singh, "Education for Youth in the Global Society," *Yojna,* Vol. 47, September, 2003, No. 9.

Kulkarni, Vijay, "Universalization of Education: A Challenge", *Yojna,* Vol. 47, March, 2003, No. 3.

Laxmi Ratan, V., "Education in Last Fifty Years", *Yojna,* Vol. 47, May, 2003, No. 5.

Myron, Weiner (1991), *The Child and the State in India—Child Labour and Education Policy in Comparative Perspective,* Oxford University Press, Delhi, Mumbai, Kolkata and Channai.

Ramachandran, Vimala (2003), "Backward and Forward Linkages that Strengthen Primary Education", *Economic and Political Weekly,* March 8-14, 2003, Vol. XXXVIII, No. 10.

Ramachandran, Vimala (1999), *"The Visible but Unreached"*, Seminar, February, New Delhi.

Uther, M.M., "Vocational Education For Development of Rural India", *Yojna,* Vol. 47, September, 2003, No. 9.

Wednesday, March 28, 2001; C. Rammanohar Reddy, "Puzzling Patterns in Census 2001", *The Hindu,* Chennai.

Yerankar, S.K., "Peace Education", *Yojna,* Vol. 47, September, 2003, No. 9.

7

Ups and Downs of Education in the Present Era of Economic Reforms

SARITA JAIN

Education is a major scheme of the social sector. Education is a system. It is a spectrum. Education is a human right, literacy provides access to knowledge, development of skills and thereby brings about the awareness of rights and responsibility in every individual and the community as a whole. In the 21st century countries will be measured by the education and health status of their population and not by GDPs and GNPs. In short development of any country depends on the developments of human resources. The bulk of the education system in our country is in the public sector. In the last few years, more so after the 1991 Reforms, there has been inundation of the district headquarters with institutions imparting professional education. Large cities are flooded with the subsidiaries and affiliates of foreign universities, led by those from the US and the UK. With the emphasis laid on IT these have enlisted a fresh lease of life.

A well-educated work-force is essential for garnering the fullest benefit of extended economic freedoms. People having different kinds of education and qualifications are now requisitioned in this age of IT.

According to the World Employment Report (1998-99) of the ILO, India had not done enough in the field of education, even though it had made considerable progress in moving towards industrialization. Less than 10 per cent of the new entrants to the labour-force possessed any formal education. In 1992 the main years of schooling of population over 25 years came to 2.4 years. From 1990-91 to 1997-98 the professional colleges preparing doctors and engineers and trained teachers had the highest percentage. Hopefully talent and brainpower has no extrinsic dearth in our country.

Education combines within itself two values—one instructive value and the other instrumental value. The former signifies desire for education for its own sake because it opens up a vast world of opportunities and ideas to the educated person; and in that manner it has a consumption effect on the person, whereas the latter has a nexus with growth and development and control of population and in that manner it has a production or income-earning effect. Expected life-time earnings are a multiple of the investment made in education.

There is greater educational inequality in our country. This is more serious problem than income inequality. Inequality is measured by economists with the help of a yardstick called the Ginni Coefficient, which ranges from 0 to 1, 0 denotes total equality and 1 denotes total inequality.

According to Parikh, India's educational Ginni Coefficient had declined very slowly from 0.76 in 1970 to 0.69 in 1990. The gap in the median years of schooling between the richest and the poorest 40 per cent of the population was 10 years in India.

Primary education, which has, by the Constitution, a free and compulsory status, could be free only in name and is to be compulsorily enforced by the 83rd Constitutional Amendment Bill, the high incidence of poverty has uptill now turn the children of the school-going age-group into child labour, which is helping their parents in eking out their existing somehow or any how, thereby compounding the illiteracy rate.

Dr. Swarup Singh, an Ex-Vice-Chancellor of Delhi University, acknowledged the public accusation that there had occurred a tremendous decline in the standards of teaching, as reported in TOI, 14th December, 1999, which addressing a university assemblage, he had criticised teachers for holding protest marches and staging dharnas. He had commented on the malpractices in the appointment of teachers. But the exponents of the teachers had rebutted his remarks by insinuating that 90 per cent of the teachers who did not teach were on the best terms with their principals and Vice-Chancellor or, in the refusal of the authorities to listen to the teacher. Conditions in most other universities were still far worse.

In many status universities had degenerated into the subordinate offices of the Education Department. The bureaucracy control of the universities was most in evidence. The bureaucrats interfered so much that those in the universities suffered indignities and humiliations at their hands. Even Vice-Chancellors were indicated as being tactless and sacked unceremoniously for their failure to trifle with the laws and thereby oblige the ruling politicians and their henchmen who professed to act at their pleasure, having been armed with unqualified powers in the University Acts.

India's performance in education over five decades has been mixed impressive achievements on the one hand and conspicuous failure on the other. There are various reasons for this.

1. The Indian education system is characterized with the severe degree of under-investment. Developing countries spend more public money on education than in India. Table 7.1 shows the difference.

Table 7.1

Countries	*Per cent of Public Money Spend on Education*
Sweden	8.4
Zimbabwe	8.3
Maldives	8.1
Canada	7.6
New Zealand	7.3
Kenya	6.8
Australia	6.6
France	5.8
U.K.	5.4
India	3.6

2. In Indian economy educational expenditure had increased gradually. In 1951 it was 0.68 per cent of GDP and it was 4.39 per cent of GDP in 1990. Dr.V.R. Panchamukhi has calculated the average growth rate of per pupil expenditure in education in the pre-reform and post-reform period.

Table 7.2: Average Annual Growth Rate of Per Pupil Expenditure in Education

Education Level	*Pre-Reform Period*	*Post-Reform Period*
Elementary Education	6.9	1.2
Secondary Education	5.0	0.0
University Education	0.2	–4.4

Source: *EPW*, March 4-10-2000, p. 839.

The Table 7.2 shows that there has been a serious deterioration in per pupil expenditure in education in all sectors of education. In the field of elementary education, the annual average growth rate of expenditure came down from 6.9 per cent in the pre-reform period nearly 1.2 per cent during post-reform period. In secondary education, the growth rate was zero and in university education it became negative to the extent of 4.4 per cent in the post-reform period.

In absolute terms, the increase in expenditure on education in India during the 50 years of independence is impressive. The real increase in expenditure for the student has been rather very modest. There has been increase in the allocation for education in the 1990s, but at the same time, this has been curved by economic policies of stabilising and structural adjustment, that seemed to have very seriously affected the allocation of education. Plan expenditure on different sectors of education shows ups and downs in expenditure on different sectors of education.

Table 7.3

Sectors of Education	*Plan Period*										
	I	*II*	*III*	*Plan Holiday*	*IV*	*V*	*VI*	*VII*	*1990-92*	*VIII*	*IX*
Elementary	56	35	34	24	30	35	33	37	37	47	58
Secondary	13	19	18	16	18	17	21	24	22	18	13
Adult	–	–	–	–	–	–	9	6	9	9	3
Higher	9	18	15	24	25	22	22	16	12	8	12
Technical	13	18	21	25	13	12	11	14	17	14	12
Other	9	10	12	11	14	14	4	3	2	4	2
Total	100	100	100	100	100	100	100	100	100	100	100

Source: Various Issues of Economic Survey and National Account Statistics of India.

Suggestions for Improvement

1. There should be strong support from the policy makers and chief administration for globalization, to make Indian education as a major source of foreign exchange, to improve quality of Indian education to spread Indian culture and value.
2. Steps should be taken to make the parents of school going children aware of the importance of education. In all states, the mid-day meal programme must be implemented in full vigour, and then only, the aim of universal education can easily be achieved.
3. Higher education is paramount importance for economic and social development institutions of higher education should have the main responsibility for equipping individuals with advanced knowledge and skills required for position of responsibility in government, business and the professions.
4. State and society perceive higher education not as burden on federal budgets but as long-term domestic investment in order to increase economic competitiveness, culture development and social cohesion.
5. A minimum level of learning is required for creating awareness about goods/services available in the international market.
6. The entire educational system has progressively come under the government regulation and control as a result the system has lost flexibility, initiative and invectiveness. So essential in the fast changing world of today the process of liberalization of education should begin.
7. The share of expenditure on education should be raised, and then only the educational sector can avail all the facilities required for quality education.
8. New financing techniques should be encouraged to correct the unacceptable decline in allocation for higher education in the plan. In the case of higher education, the network of IITs, IIMs, IISs, NCST etc. should be expanded and present intake of these institutions should be increased to cater the needs of the economy.

The syllabus in schools and colleges should be restructured to impart to students to each stage of education the ability to forge on his own self-employment schemes. The allocation of investment in primary, secondary and higher education should be such as to socially optimize the rate of return on the investment.

8

The Role of Education in India

DR. R.C. AGRAWAL AND MISS ROONA

Education is a major scheme/programme of the social sector, or it is one of the social sectors. In significance elementary education and adult education have topped the list. Education is a system. It is a spectrum. The bulk of the education system in our country is in the public sector. In the last few years, more so after the 1991 Reform, there has been inundation of the district headquarters with institutions imparting professional education. Large cities are flooded with the subsidiaries and affiliates of foreign universities, led by those from the US and the UK. With the emphasis laid on IT these have enlisted a fresh lease of life. But older and more popular, numerically, has been the growth of a whole, parallel education economy/system along the fringes of our formal and liberal education system, "coaching" students for all levels and all types of examinations. Generally, teachers employed elsewhere teach in them and earn an enormous amount of largely unaccounted income, and the administration is lukewarm in initiating disciplinary action against them because of their political and other connections.

Broadly speaking, human capital stands for stoke of educated workers. Aristotle's dictum was that the educated were as superior to the uneducated as the living are to the dead. Education brings with it knowledge and improvement in the quality of life. It inculcated the right values (given the right men to impart it). It comments different sections of society (assuming there are not men determined to divide it). If skills are acquired from training, then it is the key to success amidst competition as are hard work and noble values.

A well-educated work-force is essential for garnering the fullest benefit of extended economic freedoms. People having different kinds of education and qualifications are now requisitioned in this age of IT. A very convenient development in recent times has been that skills can be acquired through learning-by-doing, by training on the job itself. For sustaining higher rates of overall economic growth in an increasingly integrated world economy, the long-run success of the education system is crucial, nay, its very backbone.

According to the World Employment Report (1998-99) of the ILO, India had not done enough in the field of education even though it had made considerable progress in moving towards industrialization. Less than 10 per cent of the new entrants to the labour-force possessed any formal education. In 1992 the main years of schooling of population over 25 years came to 2.4 years.

Another snag/pitfall is that labour-force and skill development are not distributed between regions according to their requirements.

Add to this is the absence of proper education which prepares citizens to participate in economic activity.

We have the statistical backing of the contention often made that India has one of the world's largest stocks of the highly educated and capable persons; also, that during 1990-91 to 1997-98 the professional colleges preparing doctors and engineers and trained teachers had the highest percentage increase of all, that is, by 234 per cent. Hopefully talent and brain-power has no extrinsic dearth in our country.

Between 1991 and 1996 there was good progress in the number of professional graduates, as brought out. More engineers than doctors, commerce degree-holders in more numbers than science or arts degree-holders, more nursing personnel than physicians, this was the trend.

Between 1990-91 and 1997-98 enrolment in the primary institutions rose by the lowest percentage, and in the High/Higher Secondary institutions it rose by the highest percentage. Enrolment rose by a higher percentage in middle institutions than in the primary ones. Enrolment of girls was better in primary as well as middle institutions than that of boys.

There was a general recognition of the fact that better education (here in the quantitative sense) in India had meant more purchasing power and had augmented income and hence its growth rate. Were we to accept the statement in the UNESCO charter that a value system was pivotal to education, then we would at best only make the comment that the decision on the value system was under critical scrutiny having become outmoded after independence and more so after the transformation brought about by Science and Technology and IT?

Education combines within itself two values—one instructive value and the other instrumental value. The former signifies desire for education for its own sake because it opens up a vast world of opportunities and ideas to the educated person, and in that manner it has a consumption effect on the person, whereas the latter has a nexus with growth and development and control of population (as revealed in the health effect, life expectancy, empowerment, etc.) and in that manner it has a production or income-earning effect (see K.S. Parikh). Expected life-time earning are a multiple of the investment made in education.

But educational inequality is a far more serious problem than income inequality, which is measured by inequality in years of schooling between different income groups, or alternatively, by the average number of years of schooling of the youngsters between ages of 15 to 19 years.

Inequality is measured by economists with the help of a yardstick called the Gini Coefficient, which ranges from zero (0), which connotes total equality of unity, 1, which denotes total inequality.

According to Parikh, India's educational Gini Coefficient had declined very slowly from 0.76 in 1970 to 0.69 in 1990. The gap in the median years of schooling between the richest and the poorest 40 per cent of the population was 10 years in India.

Because primary education, which has, by the Constitution, a free and compulsory status, could be free only in name and is to be compulsorily enforced by the 83rd Constitutional Amendment Bill, the high incidence of poverty has uptill now turn the children of the school-going age-group into child labour, which is helping their parents in eking out their existence somehow or any how, thereby compounding the illiteracy rate, which, in its turn, has taken a heavy toll of the teeming millions' awareness of their fundamental rights and the State's Directive Principles, but positively assisted growth of caste and religious feeling which their social and political leaders have inculcated in them, right and left, most of all in choice of candidates for elections to the Panchayats, State legislatures and the Parliament, which took their predominance as the most acceptable criterion for this choice. High incidence of illiteracy has paid those who thrive in politics and business by misleading the illiterate masses. In Laloo Parsad Yadav's meteoric rise, Bihar's occupying to first place in the number of illiterates was one of the most striking factors, for illiteracy is amenable to and succumbs to the caste sentiment.

According to a report published in TOI on 12th September, 2000, in the backwaters of Bihar the villages government primary school was virtually defunct. The primary school had two teachers. Each drew a fat salary of over Rs. 10,000 per month, but both were always absent from their work.

The Higher Education institutions were in no better condition. A report published in TOI in 10th September, 2000 spoke scathingly of the state of affairs in the capital of the country thus: In the colleges of Delhi teachers often regarded their jobs as a sine-cure which they could hang on to while freelancing as private tutors and, in some extreme cases, as real estate agents. Students showed no interest in studied and skipped classes at the drop of a hat.

Dr. Swarup Singh, an ex-Vice-Chancellor of Delhi University, acknowledged the public accusation that there had occurred a tremendous decline in the standards of teaching, as reported in TOI, 14 December, 1999, while addressing a university assemblage. He had criticized teachers for holding protest marches and staging *dharnas*. He had commented on the malpractices in the appointment of teachers. But the exponents of the teachers had rebutted his remarks by insinuating that 90 per cent of the teachers who did not teach were on the best terms with their Principals and Vice-Chancellors or, in the alternative, that such behaviour was necessitated by the refusal of the authorities to listen to the teachers. Conditions in most other universities were still far worse.

In many States universities had degenerated into the subordinate offices of the Education Department. The bureaucratic control of the universities was most in evidence. The bureaucrats interfered so much that those in the universities suffered indignities and humiliations at their hands. Even Vice-Chancellors were indicted as being tactless and sacked unceremoniously for their failure to trifle with the laws and thereby oblige the ruling politicians and their henchmen who preferred to act at their pleasure, having been armed with unqualified powers in the university Acts.

The case of Bihar was unique. If all academic institutions set up by the caste leaders were political outfits. They produced caste-tainted students, who always got record marks but eventually ended up as petty office clerks or kidnappers or assassins or dacoits. The exceptional ones who ploughed their lonely furrows by putting up with inhuman treatment did better career-wise but even in this their success was a function of the backing they enjoyed from the caste members of the State legislature or the Parliament. In fact, in that State opportunities were distributed in strict conformity with the numerical strength of the castes represented in the State legislature, the Parliament, the Service Commission, the Selection or Recruitment Boards, etc.

It is not that only those academic institutions wearing the caste labels are playing a part in manufacturing caste-minded products; even in other such institutions, without any caste tag, caste-minded products are being produced on an increasing scale, and hardly anything is being done to arrest this tendency, which is always to the advantage of many who eventually benefit directly and indirectly, although merit is constantly the first casualty of this regime.

If teaching is on sufferance, the examination system is in tatters and, all in all, the entire education system is in an awful mess. Neither knowledge is imparted nor character is formed (exceptions allowed) of which those who are partners in running the system could be genuinely proud of it, as used to be the case in the good old days. Public acceptance with little important resentment or stir is its silent proof.

In the early 1950s, 15 to 20 per cent of total expenditure of universities was met from fees; by 1992-93 the percentage had dwindled to 2 to 3 per cent. Fees formed less than 14 per cent of the total education in Britain, less than 4 per cent in France, and less than 15 per cent in public institutions in the US (in the private ones, 40 per cent). In the US, higher education was subsidized by both public and private bodies.

In 1964-65, the Kothari Commission had recommended that 6 per cent of GNP should be disbursed on over-all education.

A look at Table 98 would show how during the first thirty

years of planning, the relative contribution of the governments to education finances had risen, while that of the private sector had fallen. Table 99 furnishes statistics on Plan and Non-Plan expenditures on education by the governments, Central and State, during the first to seventh Plan. Whereas Plan expenditure by the Central Government, the non-Plan expenditure by the State governments was an increasing proportion of these Plan expenditure by them. The case of the Central Government was the reverse of it.

In respect of both types of expenditure, Plan and non-Plan, the range increased between 1990-91 and 1999-2000, but as proportion to GDP, the range increased in respect of Plan expenditure on education but decreased in respect of non-Plan expenditure on education. Proportionally more came to be spent on education, as the 1990s passed, out of the total budget earmarked for public expenditure, but there was no change in the proportion of GDP spent on education (Table 100).

A different source gives 6 per cent of GDP as expenditure on education in 1998.

In 1990-91, non-Plan expenditure on academic administration in JNU was the highest and the lowest in Hyderabad University. Enrolment of students was 1720 in Hyderabad University, 14784 in Delhi University, 13074 in BHU and 10891 in AMU. The cost per student per annum was Rs. 22,965 in Hyderabad University, Rs. 19,000 in AMU, Rs. 22,965 in Hyderabad University, Rs. 19,000 in AMU, Rs. 13,850 in BHU, Rs. 12,370 in Delhi University. The weighted mean was Rs. 17,000 per student.

In 1996 another study gave the following information: Per child per year cost of primary education and health needs Rs. 65, cost of building a drinking water well in rural areas Rs. 3258. The Rs. 65 crore Hawala scam was one-fourth of the 1994-95 Government irrigation budget. Two wells could serve one village. Per information school for the pre-primary children the cost was Rs. 1,083. Per grassroots development project the cost came to Rs. 1,805.

In October, 2000 total education budget was 6 per cent of GDP (in developed countries the figure was 6 to 10 per cent). Pranab Mukherjee estimated that 10 per cent of GDP in 2000 was needed to eradicate illiteracy and attain cent per cent primary education in India. On the other hand, Parikh calculated the cost of making primary education universal and compulsory, the cost of making primary education universal and compulsory at about 2.8 per cent of GDP per year. At present the outlay was 1.5 per cent of GDP.

In addition to legislating the 83rd Constitutional Amendment Bill to make schooling compulsory, and incurring the needed public expenditure every year, the teachers as well as parents of the school-going children should be properly motivated.

But the impending issue is not easily tackled. One section wants relatively more spent on higher education, while another section wants relatively more spent on primary education. If primary education is claimed to be fundamental to the nation by one body of thinkers, higher education is claimed to be the determinant of the economic and technological progress the nation could make by another body.

At present our education system is lopesided, skewed. Institutions in the private sector are, by investing money, spinning money. We may take those institutions which are teaching computer science today. The minority institutions are alleged to be abusing their powers and fleecing the parents of their students.

All sections of education in the public sector (including the unaffiliated institutions, preceding their affiliation and grant of government aid) are at present encountering problems relating to the availability and adequacy of funds. In the primary, middle and secondary schools teacher's absenteeism and deficiencies exist in an accentuated form. Teachers and non-teachers are made to do the private work of the legislators and members of the Parliament representing their constituencies (as reported).

Critics allege that our education and training systems are beset with rigidity and unawareness of the needs of our economy.

Towards the fag-end of the last decade of the last century the Human Resource Development (HRD) Ministry wanted cost of higher education and professional education to be raised by 7 per cent, at the rate of one per cent in each succeeding year, subject to the condition that Government had taken the position that the students were paying less for their higher education, while funds were not enough for primary education, which could not be made compulsory due to the resource barrier.

The Government is thinking of linking one-third of its own and the UGC's grants given to the universities to their performance. It wants value to result from the money that was invested in higher education. It wants quality consciousness infused into higher education.

The criteria for judging the performance of the educational system would be: (1) Timely examination (but not without covering the prescribed courses of studies) and results. (2) Number of teaching days. (3) Number of hours spent by teachers on the campus by providing them sitting and study and research rooms/ facilities. (4) Number of research papers/works published by them. (5) The Sababaticals undertaken by them. (6) Number of working days lost on account of strikes by teachers, non-teaching staff and students. A part from these, accountability of the employees must be ensured, subjectivity avoidance is a condition imposed, evaluation of success of students in national-level competitive examinations: fixing teacher-student ratio, show of social concerns, participation in sports and cultural events, and participation, outreach and continuing teaching programmes. The idea of Adjunct Faculties has been breached, according to which people from industry would teach in the universities for limited periods, and *vice-versa*, i.e., people from universities would learn things by going to factories and firms for short periods.

In April, 2000 some top industrialists in a report submitted to the Prime Minister suggested the following: (1) Making the higher education system competitive by withdrawing the Government support from it, thereby making it self-financing or privatizing it, the goal being full-cost recovery, and market-oriented education. (2) As a by-product, improving the quality of higher education. The public funding for the universities would be progressively reduced and they would be made to adopt the route of self-sufficiency. A Private University Bill should be legislated in order to encourage the establishment of new private universities in the field of science and technology. Others are: (3) Allowing FDI in education. (4) A ban on all forms of political activity on the campuses of the universities and educational institutions. (5) Making Primary and Secondary Education compulsory. (6) Introducing a compulsory vocational training in an intensive manner from the secondary level onwards.

In a nutshell, the Government should focus strongly on Primary and Secondary Education and leave Higher Education and Professional Education to the private sector which would charge the fees to the students in accordance with the User Pays Principle.

Suggested in the Memorandum by the top industrialists were three mutually reinforcing methods, viz., (1) To recover the public cost of higher education and reallocate government spending on primary and secondary education. (2) To develop a credit market for education. (3) To foster expansion of private and community supported schools.

The university teacher's sharp reaction to the above was that education was not a commodity and the university was not a market place which gave warrant to the state to shy away but the state could not shy away from its responsibility whether it was higher education the Government would be limiting access to those who were meritorious but lacked resources for the purpose of prosecuting their studies at the higher and professional levels. The result would be commercialization of education.

REFERENCES

1. Sigliz, Joseph E. (2002), *Globalization and Its Discontents*, W.W. Norton and Company, New York.
2. *World Bank Report* (2002), Constructing Knowledge Societies: New Challenges for Tertiary Education (Draft).
3. Hayword, Fred (2002) on overview of Higher Education and GATS, *Draft Document for the American Council on Education* in July.
4. Kigotho, Wachira (2001), Academics "Emigration said to Hurt Africa, *The Chronicle of Higher Education*, 2 November, 2001.

9

Role of Education: With Special Reference to Health Status

DR. UPASNA SHARMA

About 500 years before Christ, a Chinese philosopher, Khan Tzu (551-479 B.C.) very rightly declared, "If you plan for a year, plant a seed, if for ten years, plant a tree, if for two hundred years, teach the people." When you saw a seed once, you will reap a single harvest; when you teach people, you will reap a hundred harvests. We looking at the world can claim that the nations and cultures committed to education and training have made greater stride in both intellectual and economic growth.

Education plays a vital role in shaping our lives and life-styles. It is an established fact that education is a catalyst of socio-economic transformation. In many countries including India, education is provided by the state as a matter of right to all its citizens. The term 'education' is derived from the Latin word 'educate' which means bringing up a child, both physically and mentally. In a broader sense, education is conceived as a group process by which culture or the knowledge storehouse is transmitted from one generation to another.

According to UNESCO, "Education is organized and sustained instruction to communicate a combination of knowledge, skills and undertaking valuable for all activities of life."

In the words of the eminent French sociologist Emile Durkheim who is called, "The Father of Sociology of Education", Education is the influence exercised by adult generations on those that are not yet ready for social life...education is the socialization of the younger generation...it is the means by which society perhaps within the children, the essential conditions for its very existence.... Education creates a new being."

Aderemi Olutola describes education as "a process of socialization, of change and innovation, of preservation and dissemination of societal values and of the total development of an individual from birth to death." Education has a great bearing on societal structure, mode of living, thought and behaviour patterns and the personality structure of the individuals.

Education broadly defined to all those activities which aim at educating and preparing the child for the rational and norm-oriented participation in the community. Two types of education which community may provide to an individual are:

(*a*) Education for socialization or socializing of the individual; and
(*b*) Formal or academic education.

It can be said that the education is the most powerful tool in shaping our future. We expect education to help build-up a qualified and creative workforce that can adopt to new technologies and to advance knowledge in such a way that economic development goes hand in hand with responsible management of the physical, human and cultural environment. Education also adopts new trends in society to prepare our future generations for change.

Education works in so many different ways and has so many different meaning that one cannot risk making a flat statement about its nature and role.

J. Krishnamurthy, analyzing education as a process with complex social ramifications, says that modern education has made a significant contribution to conflicts at all levels. To understand this interface, we need to distinguish the historical role of education from its normative meaning and function.

It is rightly believed by most people that education will provide necessary knowledge, training in skills and occupational roles and this will produce the needed competent personnel for manning different specialized jobs in modern industry, business, educational and research institutions, bureaus (offices) etc. It is also widely expected that modern education can mould people into enlightened, empathetic, risk-taking, skilled, industrious and mobile personalities. That education will be of immense help in bringing about democratization, secularism, national integration in the given society, is yet another expectation of all leaders and enlightened citizens. It is expected that the axe of education can cut down the thick roots of superstitions, deadwood of tradition, ignorance, backwardness, parochialism (narrow-mindedness) etc. Education can help people in knowing their weakness, faults, shortcomings or gaps in knowledge and enabling them to rectify them in order to achieve progress in all walks of life in a consistent manner. Education is an eye-opener, it illumines like a torch or candle, it helps in finding our ways in the dark and thick forest or in might.

Education develops basic skills and abilities, and thereby boosts productivity. It also fastens a value system conducive to the national development goals and preserves and promotes the cultural ethos of the country. The main aim of education is to preserve, transfer and enrich the culture.

The significance of education was realized even during the national movement and stress was laid on the need to provide a quality of education which was commensurate with the economic aspirations as well as social and cultural milieu of India. The resolution on 'National Policy on Education' adopted in 1968, therefore, emphasized the need for a radical reconstruction of the educational system in India. The resolution stressed the need:

(*i*) To transform the educational system so as to relate it more closely to the life of the people.
(*ii*) To make continuous effort for expanding educational opportunities.
(*iii*) To make sustained efforts for raising the quality of education at all levels.
(*iv*) To give a special emphasis on the development of science and technology.
(*v*) To promote and cultivate moral and social values.

Table 9.1 shows that expenditure on education has multiplied 377 times during last 46 years but its ratio with GDP has not increased much. In 1950-51, it was 1.27 per cent of GDP, which increased to 4.14 per cent in 1990-91. But higher values of economic indices thereafter the ratio has declined and the latest data available for 2003-04 reveals that it is 3.74 per cent of GDP.

Table 9.1: Expenditure on Education in India

Year	*GDP at Factor Cost (at current price) (Rs. in crores)*	*Expenditure on Education (Rs. in crores)*	*% of GDP*
1950-51	8979	114	1.27
1960-61	15254	344	2.26
1970-71	39708	1118	2.82
1980-81	122427	3859	3.15
1990-91	477814	19791	4.14
1996-97	1285259	43026	3.35
2003-04	NA	NA	3.74

The education sector grew at an average rate of 6.2 per cent per annum in phase 1 from 1950-51 to 1979-80. It continued to grow at around the same rate in Phase II B from 1980-81 to 1991-92. Growth has accelerated sharply to an average rate of 9.0 per cent per annum during sub-phase II B from 1992-93 to 2001-02. This has happened despite:

(*a*) Government expenditure on education and training declaration from an average growth (1993-94 prices) of 11.7 per cent per annum in Phase I to 6.4 per cent per annum in Sub-Phase II B (till 2001).

(*b*) Severe constraint on private provision of education. The Supreme Court had interpreted the constitutional provisions to enjoin the state to provide education to its citizens, as prohibiting private provision of "basic" education (schooling; B.A./B.Sc., M.A./M.Sc.).

With reforms the rate of growth of the sector could be doubled and its quality improved manifold without an excessive strain on limited government revenues. The education sector in India can be transformed within a span of 3 to 5 years given the right mix of policy, regulation and reorientation of government expenditure. This is in turn can have a profound impact on the quality of output in all sectors of the economy and the competitiveness of Indian industry, services and agriculture.

Public health is yet another important factor to bring socio-economic changes in Indian society. A health condition too is an equally vital input for economic development and a pre-requisite for making manpower more desirable to national needs. It is closely related to the education. The role of education in health matter is very important.

Health is real wealth. A healthy person is an asset to himself, to his family and to his community. On the other hand an ailing person is a burden on all. He is a danger for coming generations because heredity plays an important part in this respect.

Health cannot be achieved merely by taking one or two pills everyday nor by observing a few restrictions. It can be achieved only by understanding what health is, on what it depends and then applying this knowledge in everyday life. The care of the body regarding food, cleanliness, exercise, rest and protection against disease, are essential for the preservation of sound health. Life is for living. Without health, life is deprived of not only much of its usefulness but also its joys and pleasures. The stream of life will be rich and lasting in proportion to the sources which nourish it. These sources belong to every person. They are food, exercise, proper posture care of bodily functions and wholesome mental and emotional attitudes.

National and International Needs in Health Statistics

By and large, the purpose of vital and health statistics is to contribute to social and economic progress. Existing levels of health and demographic problems have to be studied in relation to the conditions factual knowledge is essential. The more advanced a country, the more precise and penetrating are the studies it has to undertake.

Once public health services have been successful in reducing epidemic diseases and death rates, the need arises for precise data on the relative importance of various residual causes of sickness and death. Indeed it is on the basis of such careful security that the importance of accidents in childhood and of degenerative diseases in adult life and old age in advanced countries is not being brought out.

It has been truly said that health is individual. This is especially apparent when epidemic sweep from one country to another and cover more than one continent. Recent example is the spread of anthrax in 2003. Each country has, therefore, to be constantly on the look out for what is happening epidemiologically throughout the world.

However, from the international point of view, while the special needs of individual nations are still paramount. International co-operation has to be secured so that national health statistical services will produce data in a form that is useful not only to themselves but to the world at large. Moreover, certain health problems affecting groups of countries have to be studied statistically from an international stand point statistics are also important in connection with the help given by WHO to various countries in the implementation of their health programmes and introduction of modern techniques in health work. With the assistance of WHO and UNICEF, various national activities such as maternal and child health service, school health work and dental health are being expanded.

Quality of human effort can be greatly improved and its productivity enhanced by investment in human capital i.e. by expenditure on health, education and the like. Human resources development is a key factor in the process of growth and development. The success of any development strategy depends largely on the extent to which human resources are developed in terms of skills, education, health and well-being. Large stock of population in India can be a precious asset on the provision that it possesses reasonable levels of health and is trained and educated on sound lines.

Health in a way is an important asset of welfare. Because health is considered to be that part of the human welfare, which depends on the normal, functioning of the body. According to F.S. Williams—"Health is the quality of life that ensures the individual lives longer and serves best." It is a state of "complete physical, mental and social well-being and not merely the absence of disease" (World Health Organisation).

Importance of Health

Good health as people know from their own experience is a crucial point of well-being but spending on health can also be justified on purely economic grounds. Health increases the enrolment of children in school, makes them better to learn and use resources that would otherwise have to be spent on treating illness could be used for alternative uses.

Good health starts from the very infancy. It is here that

protection and care is needed, so that each organ functions well, each organ develops naturally, and there are no deformities, disabilities and diseases but often the health of children remain neglected, with the result that they grow unhealthily and that affects their education as well.

A healthy child develops into a healthy adult. In case the child does not properly, and the remains handicapped in some way; his ill-health spoils his adult life. He cannot join any active service; he cannot be a successful professional, nor can he live his life happily.

The health status of a population is determined by various factors like, per capita income, nutrition, water supply, sanitation, housing amenities, health service available to the community, response of people in availing the facility, morbidity rate, climate, percentage of Population Below Poverty Line (PBPL), structure of the economy, number of personnel and household characteristics, etc.

Standard indicators of health status are IMR or LEB. Link between income and health status is not a deterministic one. Therefore poor countries with relatively high health status e.g. in Sri Lanka, and rich countries with poor health status, e.g., Saudi Arabia. Moreover as Perston has argued, the relations between national income and health status are shifting over time as a result of improvements in medical science, technology and public education. There is a strong assumption that the increase in social inputs such as health status, education, nutrition, water supply, sanitation and health services of people will improve to enable a higher rate of economic growth to be achieved.

The health of the population is a matter of serious national concern. It is highly correlated with overall development of the country. A healthy population is a developmental goal by itself though it is also a necessary ingredient for the other wider goals of social and economic development. India's health system seems to be currently at cross roads with major changes occurring in the morbidity and mortality patterns. Some of these changes are consequent to the demographic transition, which is accompanied by changes in the age structure of the population but most of the changes are due to the control of the health conditions and the composition of the health sector and simultaneously major transportation have occurred in knowledge and technology, as well as in the political and economic environment.

During colonial rule, the development and growth of health care was based on the demands made by defense and civil administration and consequently some data pertaining to public health and communicable diseases emerged. The Bhore Committee realised the deficiencies of database on health and created a benchmark for a variety of health related information in its report submitted in 1946. This committee provided the first organised set of health care data for the country as a whole, prior to which records and reports of the public health department and census were the only source of any health related information. The recommendation of this committee for Setting up sub-Centres (SCs), primary health centres. Increased access to quality health care services has been one of the thrust areas of the social development programmes being undertaken in the country. Technological advances and the extension in the infrastructure network have resulted in decline in mortality. There are centrally sponsored disease control programmes for the control of Malaria, Tuberculosis, Leprosy, AIDS, Blindness, pulse polio immunization, anti-malaria programme smallpox eradication schemes etc. on the other hand preventive measures like availability of safe drinking water supply, central rural sanitation programme, minimum needs programme etc. to cater requirements for pollution free environment on the other.

Table 9.2: Expenditure on Education, Health and Social Security

Year	*Education*		*Health*		*Social Security*	
	Total (in crores)	*Per Capita*	*Total (in crores)*	*Per Capita*	*Total (in crores)*	*Per Capita*
1980-81	3859	57	943	14	756	1
1985-86	8812	117	2225	29	2008	27
1990-91	19791	236	4508	54	4873	58
1995-96	37096	400	7879	85	10569	114
1996-97	43026	456	9170	97	11495	122
2005-06	NA	NA	NA	NA	NA	NA

The Table 9.2 shows:

(*i*) Government expenditure on education is doubling in about four years and in a span of 17 years it has multiplied by 11 times. But the per capita expenditure has increased from Rs. 57 to Rs. 456. Thus it multiplied eight times.

(*ii*) The expenditure on health has multiplied by 9.7 times during 1980-81 to 1996-97. But the per capita expenditure on health has multiplied by less than seven times.

(*iii*) Social security expenditure of Government of India has multiplied by 15 times. But per capita expenditure on social security has increased by 11 times during 1980-81 to 1996-97.

It is observed that government allocation on education, health and social security is rapidly rising yet per capita allocation is miserably poor and resource crunch is a major hurdle in improving the lot of the masses. It needs no emphasis to mention here that for the development of the country's vast human resource and improvement in the quality of life, health care and education are necessary inputs.

Need for Health Education

The health standard are efficient administered and maintained only when adequate knowledge and information about personal and environmental hygiene and sanitation; awareness of various diseases and their remedial treatment, at least at the just aid level; available utilization of resources, facilities and technical information at various primary health centers upward, is disseminated by means of a mass health education programme. These programmes are launched to create general awareness of health and nourishment of the population at different levels and stages of the development of an individual and other contingencies, by means of health education. Health, therefore, is the primary task of any government so as to harness the optimal human resource development of a country and should be accorded necessary and suitable priority at all levels. It is all the more important during the period of growth and development of a child. Healthy child, healthy nation.

Consisting of awareness programmes health education aims at improving general conditions at the individual and community levels by encouraging people to change community levels by encouraging people to change their behavioural pattern, habits and life-style to achieve necessary standard of health. It must be remembered that physical development and maturation are essential for a child's overall growth and development in such other areas as mental, emotional and social growth and development "Healthy mind in a healthy body" is the age old slogan and ideal of any civilized society.

"Health education is the sum total of all those experiences derived from the school and other environmental situations that influenced health habits and attitudes of an individual, community and society."

It is evident that child education aims at developing awareness towards the rules and practice of child health care.

Principles of Health Education

For the successful implementation of the school health service, the following principles are enunciated:

1. Cooperation of community and parents.
2. Simple and usable health education should consist of simple and pragmatic practices and activities.
3. Care of the health of an individual.
4. For total implementation of health care programme necessary and suitable priority should be accorded to health education by its school administration and management.
5. Healthy teachers.
6. Healthy habits.
7. Knowledge of the human body.
8. Physical exercise.
9. Mid-day meal.
10. Periodic medical check-up.

India is signatory to Alma Ata declaration thereby it is committed to achieve "Health for all by 2000 A.D." Health care and medical facilities programmes, initiated and executed since the advent of planning, have been helpful in bringing down considerably the incidence of communicable disease. Imbalances in the growth of health-care infrastructure, particularly between the rural and urban areas have been one of the notables backwards of the health care programmes. However after the adoption of National Health Policy and Rural Health Programme is being restructured and there is shift in priorities. Expansion and extension of rural health facilities through a network of community health centres, primary health centres and availability.

The results indicate that mere growth of per capita income in India has no significant effect on the health status of the population. However we cannot say that per capita income need not be given importance. We can only say that apart from per capita income importance for social service may also be given. The significance of other variables strengthens the view that the government should raise female literacy, per capita expenditure on health, poverty alleviation programmes, the nutritional status of children, reducing morbidity by improving health, sanitation, and water supply by vaccination. Hence, it is expected that if the governments take serious steps in strengthening the above mentioned social sector variables, faster economic development may be achieved.

Health programmes increase the number of people in the working force as well as the quality of labour product. The people added to the work force provide a direct measurement for the units of the labour resulting from improving in health status (Muskin, 1962).

Active community participation is considered to be one of the most important supportive activities for successful implementation of the health programmes. Therefore, a larger allocation of funds be made by local governments, by state and by central government for public health. However the role of NGOs needs to be promoted to replace existing public health machinery of the government.

The country today needs to invest in primary education, primary health and stop compromising on standard and quality. The public institution must own respect and the youth address themselves for building a country, which cherishes secular democracy.

REFERENCES

1. Agrawal, A.N.; Verma, H.O. and Gupta, R.C., *India Economic Information Year Book 1991-92*, National Publishing House, New Delhi, 1992.

2. Das, Debendra Kumar, "*Social Sector and Development, Experiences and Challenges*", Deep and Deep Publications, New Delhi, 1999.
3. *India 2002* (A Reference Manual) compiled and edited by Research, Reference and Training Division, Publication Division, Ministry of Information and Broadcasting, Government of India.
4. Kumar, Krishna, "Recasting Education", *The Times of India*, New Delhi, 16 October, 2004.
5. *Report of the National Statistical Commission*, Vol. II, Chander Press, Delhi, August 2001.
6. *Report of the National Statistical Commission*, Vol. II, Chander Press, Delhi, August 2001.
7. Ruhela, S.P., *Education in Emerging Indian Society*, International Publishing House, Meerut, 2006.
8. Selected Socio-Economic Statistics, India 1998, Central Statistical Organisation, Development of Statistics, Ministry of Planning and Programme Implementation, Government of India, New Delhi.
9. Singh, Paramjeet and Bal, Gurpreet, *Strategies of Social Change in India*, M.D. Publications Pvt. Ltd., New Delhi, 1996.
10. Singh, Yash Pal and Agrawal, Anju, "Role of Education for Economic Development and Social Transformation", *Employment News*, 19-25 January, 2002.
11. *Statistical Abstract, India 1992*, Central Statistical Organisation, Development of Statistics, Ministry of Planning and Programme Implementation, Government of India, New Delhi.

10

Education of Different Religions, Philosophy and Culture for Value Based Social Life and Spiritual Development: A Study in Perspective of Secularism in India

DR. H.M. MITTAL

We have a vast and diverse ancient country historically, geographically and socially. Traditions are different; the ways of thinking and living are also different. But there are certain common elements which unite the country in its diversity. This country has a long tradition. Here from ancient times, there have been great saints and thinkers from different religions and sects who have talked about some eternal values. These values are to be inculcated by our young generation.

In ancient times in **Gurukuls,** emphasis used to be primarily on building the character of a student. Today right from the schools upto the professional colleges, emphasis is on acquiring techniques and not values. We seem to have forgotten that skills acquired on computers tend to become outdated after some time but values remain forever. In other words, present day education is nothing but an information transmission process. Our educational system aims at only information based knowledge and the holistic views turning the student into a perfect human being and a useful member of society has been completely set aside. Swami Vivekananda aptly said:

"Education is not the amount of information that is put in

your brain and runs riot there, undigested, all your life. We must have life-building, man making, character making, assimilation of ideas. If education is identical with information, libraries are the greatest sages of the world and encyclopedias are rishis." (See para 7 of Aruan Roy's case)

Truth (*Satya*), Righteous Conduct (*Dharma*), Peace (*Shanti*), Love (*Prema*) and Non-Violence (*Ahimsa*) are the core universal values which can be identified as the foundation stone on which the value based education programme can be built up. These five are indeed universal values and respectively represent the five domains of human personality, intellectual, physical, emotional, psychological and spiritual. They also are correspondingly co-related with the five major objectives of education, namely knowledge, skill, balance, vision and identity.

Primary school stage is the period in child's life when seed of value education can be implanted in his/her impressionable mind in a very subtle way. If this seed is nurtured by the capable hands of dedicated teachers in school, if they insert values at appropriate intervals during a child's school life, it can be easily said that half the battle in building up national character has been won.

It is very essential that at the school level right from primary stage, deliberate, planned and sustained efforts are made to inculcate basic human values among the students. Values are best initiated by a mother to her small child under her small child under her tender care in the secure atmosphere of home. However, now-a-days, children are enrolled in school as early as at the age of four. At this impressionable stage, values like respect for parents, elders and teachers, truth, punctuality, cleanliness and courtesy can be easily inculcated in small children. They can also be sensitized regarding gender equality.

In view of the diverse, character of our country, it is essential that certain national values are also imbibed by our young students. They should be acquainted with the history of India's freedom struggle, cultural heritage, constitutional obligations and the features comprising our national identity.

Education should aim at multi-faceted development of a human being—his intellectual, physical, spiritual and ethical development. Youth is the mirror in which future of a nation is fully reflected in order to preserve, maintain and advance the position of our country in the world. It is imperative that there should be a comprehensive programme of value-education starting from the pre-primary level, embracing the entire spectrum of educational process. The minds, hearts and hands of children are to be engaged in forming their own character to know what is 'good', 'love good', and 'do good'.[1]

Values are principles which are consistence and universal and which direct our action and activities. They are in-built in our society, common to not only all the communities but also to all religions at all times. Values are, in other words, virtues in an individual. These values, if deteriorated, will hasten or accelerate the breakdown of family, society and nation as a whole. India has age-old tradition of values interwoven in the national fabric. Although there has been great advancement in science and technology, there has been a gradual erosion of values, which is reflected, in the day-to-day life of a large section of our present society. Our young generation under the growing influence of negative aspects of Western culture is stranded on the cross-roads, not able to decide which direction to take.[2]

The past five decades after independence have witnessed constant erosion of the essential social, moral and spiritual values and an increase in cynicism at all levels. Although schools are not isolated islands untouched by the prevailing mood of indifference and even disregard for the entire value system, their potential for the role in the task of guiding the national psyche cannot be underestimated. Schools can and must strive to restore and sustain the universal and eternal values oriented towards the unity and integration of the people, their moral and spiritual growth enabling them to realize who they are and what is the ultimate purpose of human life. Self-recognition would come to them through proper value education that would facilitate their spiritual march from the level of sub-consciousness to that of super consciousness through the different intermediary stages. Value-based education would help the nation fight against all kinds of fanaticism, dishonesty, avarice, corruption, exploitation and drug abuse.[3]

We are heading for a materialistic society disregarding the entire value based social system. None can also dispute that in secular society, moral values are of utmost importance. Society where there are no moral values, there would neither be social order nor secularism. Bereft of moral values secular society or democracy may not survive. Values are virtues in an individual and if these values deteriorate, it will hasten or accelerate the breakdown of the family, society and nation as a whole. In a society where there is constant evaporation of social and moral values for getting property, power or port—is it not advisable to have solid social foundation from base level so that a grown up person would fight against all kinds of fanaticism, ill-will, violence, dishonesty, corruption and exploitation? Answer would obviously be 'yes'.

The National Policy on Education (1986) lays emphasis on equity and social justice in education to promote the country's unique socio-cultural identity and to contribute to national cohesion, promoting tolerance, scientific temper and the concerns enshrined in the Indian Constitution. The recommendations of the **Justice J.S. Verma Committee on Fundamental Duties** of citizens pave the way for strong commitment to basic human values and social justice.

The school curriculum in 1988 was designed to enable the learner to acquire knowledge to develop concepts and inculcate values commensurate with social, cultural, economic and environmental realities at the national and international levels. The social values aimed at were friendliness co-operativeness, compassion, self discipline, courage, love for social justice, etc. Truth, righteous conduct, peace, love and non-violence are the core universal values that can become the foundation for building the value-based education programme as per the recommendations of the **S.B. Chavan Committee Report submitted to the Indian Parliament in February, 1999**. These five universal values represent the five domains of the human personality—intellectual, physical, emotional, psychological and spiritual—are "correlated with the five major objectives of education, namely knowledge, skill, balance vision and identity"(81st Report on Value-based Education presented to Rajya Sabha on 26th February, 1999, Item No. 8).

Besides, curriculum in schools has to develop the key qualities like regularity and punctuality, cleanliness, self-control, industriousness, sense of serve responsibility to greater equality, fraternity democratic attitude and sense of obligation to environmental protection.[4]

Religion and Values Generation

Although religion is not the only source of essential values. It certainly is a major source of value generation. What is required today is not religious education but education about religions, their basics, the values inherent therein and also a comparative study of the philosophy of all religions. These need to be included at appropriate stages in education right from the primary years. Students have to be given the awareness that the essence of every religion is common, only the practices differ. The students should also be led to believe that differences of opinion in certain areas are also to be respected. The Chavan Committee (1999) strongly urges education about religions as an instrument of social cohesion and social and religious harmony. The UNESCO Department for Intercultural Dialogue and Pluralism for a Culture of Peace pleads for "Spiritual Convergence" and proposes to promote dialogue among the different religious and spiritual traditions in a world where intra and inter-religious conflicts have become the order of the day. It observed that it is from early childhood that children should be introduced to the discovery of 'otherness', and to the values of tolerance, respect, and confidence in the 'other' that will bring about a change of behaviour and attitudes towards others. The introduction of specific teaching of inter-cultural and inter-religious dialogue, through the adequate pedagogical tools, is conceived as a means to foster reciprocal knowledge of shared values contained in the message issued by religious and spiritual traditions which can be considered as a common spiritual and cultural heritage.

However, a word of caution is required here. Education about religions must be handled with extreme care. All steps must be taken in advance to ensure that no personal prejudice or narrow-minded perceptions are allowed to distort the real purpose of this venture and no rituals, dogmas and superstitions are propagated in the name of education about religions. All religions therefore have to be treated with equal respect (Sarva Dharma Sambhav) and that there has to be no discrimination on the ground of any religion (Panthnirapekshta).[5]

From the aforesaid paragraph, it can be culled out:

(*i*) that the object for values based education is to have national fight against all kinds of fanaticism, ill-will, violence, dishonesty, corruption, exploitation and drug abuses;

(*ii*) National Policy on Education (1986) also lays down emphasis on equity and social justice in education and to promote the country's unique, socio-cultural identity and to contribute to national cohesion, promoting tolerance;

(*iii*) Enable the learner to acquire knowledge to develop concepts and inculcate values commensurate with social values aimed at friendliness, co-operativeness, compassion, self-discipline, courage, love for social justice, truth, righteous conduct and non-violence;

(*iv*) For religion, it is stated that students have to be give the awareness that the essence of every religion is common, only practices differ; and

(*v*) As a matter of caution it provides that all steps should be taken in advance to ensure that no personal prejudices or narrow-minded perceptions are allowed to distort the real purpose of imparting education on religions; no righteous dogmas and superstitions should be promoted to propagate in the name of education about religions.

Religion is the most misused and misunderstood concept. The process of making the students acquainted with the basics of all religions, the values inherent therein and also a comparative study of the philosophy of all religions should begin at the middle stage in schools and continue upto the University level. Students have to be made aware that the basic concept behind every religion is common. Only the practices differ. Even if there are differences of opinion in certain areas, people have to learn to co-exist and carry no hatred against any religion.

One should never forget that all the values are derived from ultimate reality—supreme power of self-consciousness—to which man orients himself. Once faith in that reality is lost, then values lose their meaning. To believe that we have the divide spark in each one of us is the most important eternal value to be inculcated by the small children even before starting their school life. It is acknowledged now the world over that ultimate goal of education is realization of the treasure within.

For controlling wild animal instinct in human beings and for having civilized cultural society, it appears that religions have come into existence. Religion is the foundation for value base survival of human beings in a civilized society. The force and sanction behind civilized society depends upon moral values. Philosophy of co-existence and how to co-exist is thought over by the Saints all over the world which is revealed by various philosophers. How to co-exist, not only with human beings but all living beings on the earth, may be animals, vegetation and environment including air and water, is thought over and discussed by Saints and leaders all over the world which is reflected in religious, if that is taught, it cannot be objected as it is neither violative of constitutional or legal rights nor it offends moral values.

The process of making the students acquainted with basics of all religions, the values inherited therein and also a comparative study of the philosophy of all religions should begin; students have to be made aware that the basic concept behind every religion is common, only the practices differ.

In **Aruna Roy *v.* Union of India,**[6] under a Public Interest Litigation Petition it was contended that giving education about religions would be violative of Article 28 and also it would be violative of Article 28 and also it would offend the basic structure of the Constitution, namely, Secularism.

Learned Solicitor General submitted that for challenging the policy framed by NCRET, petitioners have picked up some sentences out of the context. The national curriculum is prepared on the basis of report submitted to the Parliament on 22nd January, 1999 by the S.B. Chavan Committee which was appointed by the Parliament in 1996. Paliament is supreme and policies have to be framed and approved by the Parliament. Parliament had constituted CABE and NCERT and if Central Advisory Board (CABE) has any objection to the National Curriculum nothing prevented it from expressing its opinion accordingly. The Apex Court held that it is ultimately for the Parliament to take a decision on the National Education Policy one way or the other. Thus, the contention of the learned Senior Council for the petitioners that as CABE is not consulted or its approval is not sought by the government before framing the National Curriculum for School Education (NCFSE, 2000) the said policy requires to be set aside, cannot be accepted.

The Court observed that it appears to be totally wrong presumption and contention that knowledge of different religions would bring disharmony in the society. On the contrary, knowledge of various religious philosophies is material for bringing communal harmony as ignorance breeds hatred because of wrong notions, assumption, preaching and propagandas by misguided interested persons.

In **Santosh Kumar and Others *v.* Secretary, Ministry of Human Resources Development and Another (1994) 6 SCC 579**, the Court negatived the contention that teaching of Sanskrit language as an elective subject would act against secularism as accepted by nine-Judge Bench of this Court in **S.R. Bommai *v.* Union of India (1994) 3SCC 1** and held thus:

"16..........para 147 of the Justice Sawant's report what Shri **M.C. Setalvad** had stated on secularism in his Patel Memorial Lectures, 1965. One of the observations made by Setalvad was that a secular state is not hostile to religion but holds itself neutral in matters of religion. The further observation in para 148 is that the state's tolerance of religion does not make it either a religious or a theocratic State. Ramaswami, J stated in para 179 that secularism represents faiths born out of the exercise of rational faculties and it enables to see the imperative requirements for human progress in all aspects and cultural and social advancement and indeed for human survival itself.

It would be profitable to note that according to Justice H.R. Khanna secularism is neither anti-God nor pro-God: it treats alike the devout, the agnostic and the atheist. According to him, secularism is not antithesis of religious devoutness. He would like to dispel the impression that if a person is devout Hindu or devout Muslim he ceases to be secular.

Religion and Dharma—Difference

In **A.S. Narayana Deekshitulu *v.* State of A.P. and Others (1996) 9SCC 548** in a concurring judgment Justice Hansaria aptly pointed out difference between 'religion' and 'dharma' and observed thus:

"143. Our dharma is said to be 'sanatana' i.e. one which has eternal values; one which is neither time-bound nor spacebound. It is because of this that Rig Veda has referred to the existence 'Sanatan Dharmani'. The concept of 'dharma', therefore has been with us for time immemorial. The word is derived from the root 'Dh.r'—which denotes: 'upholding', 'sustaining'. It is because of this that in Karna Parva of the Mahabharata. Verse 58 in Chapter 69 says:

> "Dharma is for the stability of the society, the maintenance of social order and the general well-being and progress of human kind. Whatever conduces to the fulfilment of these objects is Dharama: that is definite."[7]

It is crystal clear, that the word "religion" has different shades and colours. Important shade is dharma (duty). That is to say, duty towards the society and the soul.

The English word 'religion' does not fully convey the Indian concept of religion. Hindus believe in Vedas. The word 'dharma' has a very wide meaning. One meaning of it is the 'moral' values or ethics on which the life is naturally regulated Dharma or righteousness is elemental and fundamental in all nations, periods and times...Religion, in wide sense, therefore, is those fundamental principles which sustain life and without which the life will not survive. Rig Veda describes Dharma as Athodharmani Dharyan. In this concept of religion or Dharma, different faiths, sects and schools of thoughts merely are different ways of knowing truth which is one. The various sects or religious groups are understood as Panth or Sampradaya. In Western world particularly in Britain, religious education has been understood as nearly identical with the religious instructions. India which is wedded to a secular philosophy by its constitution: 'Religious education' to distinguish it from 'religious instructions' can mean approach in the many religions of the world with an attitude of understanding and trying to convey that attitude to children. This distinction between 'religious instructions' and 'religious education' has to be maintained while introducing a curriculum of religious education and implementing it.

Dharma is Identical with Truth

The Brhadaranyakopnishad identified dharma with truth, and declared its supreme stauts thus:

> "There is nothing higher than dharma. Even a very weak man hopes to prevail over a very strong man on the strength of

dharma, just as (he prevails over a wrongdoer) with the help of the King. So, what is called dharma is really truth. Therefore people say about a man who declares the truth that he did declaring dharma and about one who declares dharma they say he speaks the truth. These two (dharma and truth) are this."[8]

The essential aspect of our ancient thought concerning law was the clear recognition of the supremacy of dharma and the clear articulation of the status of 'dharma' which is somewhat akin to the modern concept of the rule of law, i.e. of all being sustained and regulated by it.

In Versa 9 of Chapter 5 in the Ashram Vasika Parva of the Mahabharata, Dhritrashtra states to Yudhisthira: "The state can only be preserved by dharma—under the rule of law."

Ashoka mentioned about victory of dharma in his rock edict at Kalsi which proclaimed his achievement in terms of the moral and ethical imperatives of dharma, and exemplified the ancient dictum i.e. where there is law, there is victory.

The perennial truths, rules and laws that help maintain peace and harmony in one's individual and in the community life constitute dharma. It applies for all times and in all places. Social laws and even national constitutions devoid of such a dharma will lead a society towards an inevitable decline.

What are the signs and symptoms of dharma? The answer is that which has no room for narrow-mindedness, sectarianism, blind faith and dogma. The purity of dharma, therefore, cannot be compromised with sectarianism. A sectarian religion is open to a limited group of people whereas dharma embraces all the excludes one. This is the core of our dharma, our psyche.

Conclusions

Religious education, if permitted to be imparted should consist of "understanding the child as he is without imposing upon him an ideal of what we think he should be". However, highly educated, one may be but without deep integration of thought and feeling, his life is incomplete, contradictory and torn with many fears; and as long as education does not cultivate an integrated outlook on life, it has very little significance.

To educate the student rightly is to help him to understand the total process of himself; for it is only that there is integration of the mind and heart in everyday action that there can be intelligence and inward transformation.

A great philosopher, social reformer and religious man of our times, **Vinobha Bhave** who studied all the religions of India and some of other countries. He quotes the following lines of Rig Vedas—'Ekam Sat Bahuda Vadanti'. Truth everywhere is same; the devotees worship it in different forms. Therefore, according to him, different religious thoughts can be assimilated and synthesized for creating religious harmony. The author is of the view that this approach should be adopted by all Indians.

The real meaning of 'Secularism' in the language of Gandhi is Sarva—Dharma—Sambhav meaning equal treatment and respect for all religions.

The word **'secularism'** used in the preamble of the Constitution is reflected in Article 25 to 30 and Part IV added to the Constitution containing Article 51-A prescribing Fundamental Duties of the citizens. Secularism is susceptible to a positive meaning that is developing understanding and respect toward different religions, because 56 years experience of the working of the Constitution reveals that complete neutrality towards religion and apathy for all kinds of religious teachings in institutions of the State have not helped in removing mutual misunderstanding and intolerance inter se between sections of people of different religions, faiths and beliefs. The essence of the secularism is non-discrimination of people by the State on the basis of religious differences. Article 28(1), therefore, does not prohibit introduction of study of religions in the State educational institutions including those wholly or partly aided by the States. **As a matter of fact, study of religions has been considered necessary for the unity and integrity of India.**

REFERENCES

1. See S.B. Chavan Committee's Report Point No. 2 in *Aruna Roy v. Union of India,* AIR 2002 SC 3176 at p. 3187 in Para 32.
2. *Ibid.,* Point No. 1.
3. See National Council for School Education at 1.4.7, *Education for Value Development* in Aruna Roy's Case, AIR 2002, SC at p. 3185.

4. *Ibid.* at p. 3186.
5. *Ibid.* at p. 3186, Para 27.
6. AIR 2002 SC 3176, Para 29.
7. See Aruna Roy's Case (Supra), Para 38.
8. *Ibid.*, English translation of the verse as finding place in the Convocation Address by Dr. Shankar Dayal Sharma.

11

Role of Extension Training in the Upliftment of Rural People

DR. BABITA AGRAWAL, MRS. RAKHI MITTAL AND MS. SARIKA

Training means to educate a person so as to be fitted, qualified, and proficient in doing some job. For an extension worker, training includes education, which aims at bringing a desirable change in the behaviour of the trainee, or the learner. This change requires a change in his knowledge, skills, attitudes, values, beliefs and understanding, so that the fits in his job and become qualified and proficient in communicating the desirable knowledge to his client system, i.e., the farmers, animal breeders homemakers etc.

Training of employees has been defined by Milton Hall as "the process of aiding employees to gain effectiveness in their present or future work the development of appropriate habits of thought and action, skill, knowledge and attitudes." It consists of mainly of telling, showing and guiding people in the performance of tasks and then in checking the results. Training is not only the idea of knowledge received, but that of such knowledge digested through application, drill and discipline. It means getting a man to do a job correctly, effectively and conscientiously—correctly, so that he can do or apply what he has learnt effectively, so that he can produce the desired results, conscientiously so that his underlying attitudes, convictions and enthusiasms provide the discipline he need to keep on doing the right things in the right way and thus contribute to the welfare of the organization.

According to Collins, training must include the instruction, and other learning experiences, which purport to fit the worker into the service so that he competently meets the demands of his job, as determined by the changing leadership needs of people. It has the characteristics of: (*a*) concern with skill; (*b*) concern with whole learning, (*c*) concern with practice, and (*d*) concern with safe experimentation.

It is an overt process, a sequence of experiences, a series of opportunities to learn, in which the trainee is exposed in some more or less systematic way to certain materials or events. Training is what done to the trainee and it exits to bring about learning in the training.

Lynton and Pareek discussed the relationship of training to other related areas such as education and learning. According to them, education is primarily concerned with opening out the world to the student so that he can choose his interests and mode of living and also his career. Training on the other hand is primarily concerned with preparing the participant for certain lines of action which are delineated by technology and by the organization in which he works and which also improves his performance in it. Education deals mostly with knowledge and understanding whereas training deals mostly with understanding and skill.

Importance of Training

The per acre yields, or per mulch animal milk production or egg laying per poultry layer is the lowest in India as compared to other countries. This is because there is a large gap in the latest technology known and the technology being used by the farmers, animal raisers and poultry keepers, etc. The same is true regarding Home Science, health and sanitation; our resources are not being utilized properly because our people in the villages are ignorant about many scientific innovations. The communication of the desired knowledge requires trained personnel, who have knowledge of the techniques, are interested in doing their job efficiently and know the ways of imparting this knowledge to the people who need it. To raise 60 quintals of paddy or wheat per hectare in place of 51 quintals per hectare requires the assistance of properly trained extension workers. These proper or appropriate training requires: (1) Relating the contents of the syllabus at the colleges or training centres to the needs of extension agents; (2) The teaching of manual skill; and

(3) Teaching for developing desirable attitudes for working with villagers, kitchen gardeners or poultry keepers in the rural as well as urban areas.

In other words it can be said that the training needs to communicate: (1) What to extend, i.e., the knowledge of technical subject—how to grow crops scientifically, how to raise better animals, better birds, what crops to grow, what to feed animals, how to control pests and diseases, and (2) How to extend, i.e., knowledge of extension, including methods extension, or communication, programme planning, administration in extension; rural sociology, rural social system, rural organization, Planned Social Changes etc.

Without such knowledge the extension workers cannot do this job effectively. Even if he has sound knowledge of a technical subject, e.g., in crop raising and does not know how to communicate this knowledge effectively he can do his job properly. This is like knowing the mechanism of a motor car but not knowing how to drive it. Because of the lack of knowledge of extension methods, the extension service of the State Departments of Agriculture before 1952 could not do its job effectively. Before 1953 our country did not realize that there could be a subject like extension education. Graduate trained in Extension Education and Rural Sociology was available to the extension service after 1959 and this marks a turning point in India's extension service. The technology was there, the agricultural colleges existed in India since 1905, but they did not know "How to Extend". Because of the lack of this knowledge most of our technology remained in the files of plants breeders, entomologists and crop specialists. The gap between the research institutes and the farmers continued because of this missing link. The integration of the teaching, research and extension, and the training of the extension workers were responsible for the Green Revolution. The history of the development of agriculture in the USA, Taiwan, Japan, Israel shows that it was because of trained extension personnel and in-service training of the extension workers that the gap between the technology known and the technology used by the farmers could be removed. So the earlier we are able to provide trained personnel who passed the technology and know the job of educating the farmers, the faster will be our rates of adoption and growth rates.

Need for Training

It is felt that a young person entering a career will have to train for two or three professions in the span of their active lines of work. This is because many new developments will render much of today's knowledge obsolete.

Man's knowledge, like machines, can rapidly become obsolescent. "Training is means to reduce the obsolescence among people and organizations in the face of relentless technological innovation."

The professional workers must keep abreast of the latest development in his field; otherwise he will soon be working far below his potential and capacities.

Training improves a person's skill his power of intelligence and develops in him the desired attitudes and values required for his work. Training helps the new entrants to acquire occupational work-skills and the latest knowledge, makes him familiar with the objectives of the organization to which he belongs and helps to make his potential contribution in promoting the goals of his organization. Training also makes up for any deficiencies in the new recruits and maintains or boosts up the morale of the staff. It is conductive to cohesion in regard to methods of work and approach to problems.

Training has special significance in the field of agricultural development and in the context of community development extension since the very essence of these programmes is to train rural people to solve most of their problems individually or in groups. The success of the extension worker can be judged ultimately by the extent to which he has been able to make the village people self-reliant, in getting them to do things by themselves without relying on outside help.

Ensminger has stated that it is not enough to agree that all staff-administrators, specialists, and village extension workers should be trained in the methods of extension education. To be trained in extension for community development means, according to him, first to understand the philosophy and objectives of community development; second, to understand what is meant by extension; third, to know what can be expected from the correct use of extension; fourth, to know how to apply extension methods and finally to know how to evaluate the effectiveness of the extension methods used.

It has been pointed out that extension involves not only educating the rural people in determining their problems and methods of solving them, but also inspiring them towards positive action. It is, therefore, of the highest importance for this task that personnel of the right types are obtained that will take to their work with zeal and enthusiasm.

The role of the extension workers, discussed earlier, indicates clearly the need for a new kind of worker. The planners and administrators of rural development programmes have recognized this. This type of worker should be able to get on well with the common people, know their way of life, have sympathy with their hopes and aspirations and possess a genuine desire to help them. In contrast to the past, Government servants must approach the villager as a friend—one who wants to and will help the villagers learn how to make decisions and achieve for himself and his family a better way of life.

Types of Training for Extension Workers

The training of extension workers can be classified as follows:

Pre-Service Training

Pre-Service Training, i.e., the training the extension worker receives before joining the actual job. This includes his education at a High School or Higher Secondary School, a general college or professional college, namely: Agricultural University, Agricultural College, Veterinary College, College of Agricultural Engineering. Home Science College, Engineering College, Medical College from where the extension workers receive degrees of B.Sc./B. Sc. (Agri.), B.V.Sc., B.Sc., B.Sc. Agri. Engg., B.Tech/B.E., and the specific training as in case of a village level workers at the VLW Training Centre, for nurses at Nurses' Training Centre in Medical Science or Family Planning.

In-Service Training

This is for improving the ability of the extension workers, or keeping him abreast of the latest knowledge, or giving him some special training in the new job he is required to do. This may be (*a*) Orienting new worker after he joins the job, or orienting an old worker with the new job he is required to do; (*b*) Induction training; (*c*) Job training; (*d*) Short range courses; (*e*) Periodical meetings and conferences, seminars, workshops, etc.

Orientation of New Entrants

The worker when he joins the job needs to be oriented to the organizational setup where he has to work, the philosophy behind the organization, the code of conduct, e.g., the extension and C.D. workers have to have training in the correct approach to the farmers, his relationship, the way of doing things, facilities he will get reports he is to submit, broad principles of extension work, etc. For this job, there are some orientation and study centres.

Induction Training

Some institutions have been designed where extension workers can be given the knowledge of the working and organization of community development and extension service, his place of work and his place in the work-team. The orientation centres do this job.

Short-Range Courses

The Directorate of Extension in the Ministry of Food and Agriculture and Community Development through the State Agriculture and Veterinary Departments and Agricultural Colleges and Universities organizes 45 days training at Agricultural and Veterinary Colleges. About 35 AEOs are deputed for such training and are paid Rs. 75 per month in addition to their pay and travelling allowance, etc. They are given training in technical subjects like latest varieties and cultural practices, plant protection, use of fertilizers, horticulture and extension methods. Similar training is given to Veterinary Extension Officers also.

Job Training

If the extension workers are required to do some job like soil conservation or landscaping, they may be deputed to get this special training being given at some specially designed centres. In solid conservation it may be at Dehradun Forest Research Institute in Uttaranchal or at Kota in Rajasthan, etc.

Periodical Meetings and Conference

Agricultural Universities, now organize such training in collaboration with State Agricultural and Veterinary Department for extension officers, working at District level or above. Rabi and Kharif meetings are held to work out the package of practices for various districts for the coming crop seasons. At such meetings the research staff and the subject-matter specialists of the university or colleges are also invited. There may be some special workshops on information and communication, viz., Soyabean Conference, Minor Irrigation and Water use, etc. These are held to refresh the extension workers. Similar courses of about three months are organized for village level workers at VLW training centres and also for other extension personnel.

Training Process

Lynton and Pareek divided the process of training into three phases: Pre-Training, Training and Post-Training.

In case of pre-service and induction training, no previous experience is needed for the trainee as he is a fresher, and hence he usually accepts whatever he is offered as his need. But in case of in-service training, the participant may feel the need for more skill in a particular job so as to qualify for its, or to understand particular things or events, so as to continue to grow as a person. Here the participant's motivation and point of view will determine his focus of attention and learning. Sometimes the general reputation of the course, and the institution running it, the ways people are selected for it, and its cost, all play a part in the personal calculation that each prospective participant makes for himself before he is even sent for training.

Training phase: In addition to his work experience, the in-service training participant brings to the programmes his expectations and explores in the training situation the subjects 'hat interest him. The training institution's basic task is to provide the necessary opportunities to solve the job problems, and meet his expectation. Having explored, the participant tries out some new behaviour. If the participant finds the new behaviour useful, he incorporates the new item into his habitual behaviour in the training situation. If he does not find it useful, he discards it or tries an alternative one. This intricate selection goes on continuously.

After the training phase, the in-service trainee goes back to his work. He goes prepared with some anticipations of the encounter he will face. When he actually arrives he finds a changed situation and there begins a process of adjustment. For instance the newly learned skills undergo modification to fit in with the work situation. The participant may find his organization encouraging and helping him to use his training and also offering him the additional support of continuing contact with the training institutions. At worst the colleagues, the organization, the family members, will let the returning participant know they resented his absence and the extra burden in puts on those who stayed behind, that his holiday is now over, and that he better get back to work to make up for lost time. In that case, contact with the training institutions is broken off. Thus, the preparation of the trainee prior to coming to the training institution and his behaviour after the actual training in his own organization should also be considered for effective training.

Principles of Extension Training

Some of the basic principal of training is briefly discussed below:

1. Motivation is basic to good training. Good trainers must start his work by creating a feeling of need or want in the trainee since the actual willingness and desire to learn come from within the person. Basic needs, wants, desires, motives, incentives or urges have been classified broadly in four ways:
   (*i*) The desire for security—economic, social, psychological and spiritual security.
   (*ii*) The desire for new experience—adventure, new interests, new ideas, new friends and new ways of doing things.
   (*iii*) The desire for affection and response—

companionship, gregariousness and social mindedness; the need for a feeling of belonging.

(*iv*) The desire for recognition—status, prestige, achievement and being looked upto. There are all powerful motivating forces for learning.

2. Good training requires specific and clearly defined objectives. The different aspect of the training objectives, namely the persons to be trained, the behavioural changes to be developed in them, the content or subject-matter to which the behaviour in related and the real situation in which the changes are to take place must be clearly spelled out in the training objectives.
3. Good training must accomplish certain kinds of educational changes in relation to the subject-matter learned. These may be change in knowledge, or things known; changes in skills or ability to do new things, including mental skills and manual or physical skills; and changes in attitudes or feelings for or against things and issues, points of view etc., including changes in interest, and changes in understanding.
4. Good training should require an effective learning situation, which includes five major elements, viz., Teacher, Learner, Subject-matter, Teaching Aids and Facilities or Environment.
5. Good training should provide effective learning experiences to the trainers.
6. Good training requires usually a combination of training techniques. Training should involve appropriate activities engaging the maximum number of senses and a combination of techniques such as oral, visual, audio-visual and doing things.
7. Training should be challenging and satisfying. To be challenging, subject-matter must be presented in the form of problems for which the training should be encouraged to find solutions. Appropriate a timely recognition should be given to the trainees' achievements. Fear and ridicule have no place in the training process and their uses in a training programme are usually an adverse reflection on the ability of the trainer.
8. Good training requires careful evaluation of results.

Name of Training

The nature of training depends upon the training needs of extension work.

Training needs can be determined by finding out the difference between what is being done now and what ought to be done in near future. The gap gives clues to the kind and amount of training needed.

The training needs may be those of an individual or of a group; needed immediately or some time in the future; call for formal or informal activities; and the organization can meet it by itself or meet through outside resources.

There are different ways of determining the training needs. Each may meet a specific situation and they can be used singly or in combination. Some methods of ascertaining training needs are:

(*i*) Analysis of jobs performed by extension personnel;
(*ii*) Analysis of equipment used in the job;
(*iii*) Analysis of problems faced by the workers;
(*iv*) Analysis of behaviour of the workers; and
(*v*) Analysis of organization; and appraisal of performance of the personnel.

Problems and Prospects of Training

It has been clearly understood that the main objectives of a training programme is to bring about a desirable changes in the trainee. According to R.L. Ebel, this change if it is important must make an observable difference in the behaviour, i.e., under some circumstances, a person who has more of training must behave differently from a person who has less of it, or not had it at all.

Thus, the main problem is the problem of making training effective. That sometimes it is not due to the following sub-problems:

1. What is taught to trainees is often not relevant to their work or situation.
2. The trainers do not know the techniques of transferring their knowledge to trainees.
3. Lack of clear concept about training and wrong attitudes of the trainers and trainees.

4. Lack of proper motivation and incentives.
5. Reasonable methods of assessing effectiveness of training are absent.
6. Problems in recruiting the right kind of trainers and trainees.
7. Disparities of socio-psycho-economic status of trainees in a group.
8. Information overloading, i.e., to much information in too short time.
9. Training process does not correspond to the operations and timings.
10. Lack of training about utilization of available resources and inputs. No linking of training to the available inputs.
11. Lack of communication and feedback in the post-training phase.
12. Lack of media support and non-coordination among agencies to support an integrated training programme.
13. Non-availability of resource persons and clashes between their timings and training schedules.
14. Rare pre-post surveys of training effectiveness by the institutions.
15. Non-utilisation of available research findings in shaping an effective, need-based and useful training programme.

Training of Villagers and Professional in Technical Things

This covers the training of farmers, farmers' sons, auxiliary courses for poultry keepers, dairymen, kitchen gardeners and fruit preservation etc., for village people as well as urban people.

Training of the Farmers

Besides the national demonstrations, maximisation demonstrations and other activities of the extension workers in the villages, there is a regular Farmers Training Programme in all Agricultural Universities. There are training centers for young farmers. In some states they also arrange short courses for the farmers. The training includes crop raising, animal feeding and management, plant protection. For such training, the following points should be considered.

Time of Holding the Training

It should be at the convenience of the farmers, i.e., when they are comparatively free from the rush of agricultural operations. This will differ according to the seasons and climate, for example in M.P., U.P., Punjab and Haryana the months from January to March for Kharif crop training and August to September for Rabi crop are more suitable for courses in general agriculture.

Duration of Course

For farmers who are engaged in farming, a one-week course is sufficient. On some special topics, such as, use of irrigation facilities and water management, operating some implements, plant protection, etc., it may be two or three days' duration.

Venue of Course

Besides physical facilities, the appropriate environment under which the course is to be conducted, i.e., where the farmers can see the actual crop, method demonstrations, operations with some machines and implements, or some treatments, such as the application of fertilizers, use of plant protection methods, etc. is to be given due consideration.

Production-cum-Demonstration Camps and Discussion Group of the Farmers

These should be arranged in the villages because the farmers cannot afford to remain away from their farms and homes. The duration should be 1-2 days only, and the trainees or participants should be from the same village or groups of nearby villages, so that the farmers can walk back to their home the same evening. This will provide technical knowledge to the farmers right in their villages, and the topics can be related to their local problems. This can be organized before each main crop season.

Training for Farmers' Sons

In each State there are two or three Farmers' Sons Training Centres.

In Madhya Pradesh there are four such training centers at Rewa (Kuthalia Farm), Gwalior, Raipur and Jabalpur. The last two were established in July 1970 and 1971. The procedure for such training is:

1. The applicant who wants to receive training should himself be a farmer and should not be interested in service. His age should be 16-32 years. He should be able to understand simple Hindi and should be able to write and read it.
2. He is given free boarding and lodging and second class railway or bus fare both ways.
3. The duration of the course is five weeks, and four such courses are run in a year: (*a*) 16th January to end of February; (*b*) 17th April to 31st May; (*c*) August 1st to 14th September; (*d*) 17th November to 31 December. The last dates for receipt of applications are: 31st December, 1st March, 1st July and 1st October for each course respectively.

The application is to be submitted to the Principal, Young Farmers Training Centre with details of land possessed, area under crops, number of wells, etc. The Young Farmers Association of India, New Delhi runs some of these centers.

Punjab Agricultural University runs a school for farmers' sons. Haryana also has a similar training school for farmers' sons. These can very well be utilized for farmers training also.

The efforts made in the past by various departments/agencies in this sphere are summarized below:

Ministry of Agriculture and Irrigation

The Rural Youth Programmes of the Ministry of Agriculture are being implemented by the Directorate of Extension, People's Action for Development India, Indian Council of Agricultural Research and Department of Rural Development.

Directorate of Extension (Department of Agriculture)

The directorates of extension have taken up the following programmes for farm youth:

Pilot Young Farmers Clubs Around Extension Training Centres

With the start of the Community Development Programme in India, the Directorate of Extension took up the responsibility of training the Gram Sewaks (village level workers) in rural youth activities, so that after training they could organize these programmes in the development blocks. In order to provide them project oriented training in this aspect, ten pilot young farmers' clubs were organized in selected villages in each of the development blocks attached to the Extension Training Centres. The staff and trainers of the Extension Training Centres organize training for the club members in leadership development, organizational aspects, skill development in the field of agriculture, and project activities. After training, a regular follow-up is done to provide continuing education and guidance.

There are separate clubs for boys and girls. The membership varies with the age group of 15 to 25 years. The members of the clubs have taken up economic projects relating to crop production, grain storage, horticulture animal husbandry, home science and fisheries etc. Recreational activities are also taken up to sustain the interest of club members. There are individual as well as group projects and are guided by voluntary leaders and extension workers, so that the participants can acquire necessary skills and knowledge relating to that work. In addition, it also helps the members to earn while they learn through the project work.

Training-cum-demonstration camps of one to two days duration are organized before each cropping season in the villages where the Young Farmers Clubs have been formed, with a view to training the club members in the recommended package of practices for the crops so that they can adopt them. In addition, short duration institutional courses on leadership development and project activities are also organized at the extension training centers in which youth leaders are being trained.

Training of Young Farmers in Districts

A massive programme of Farmers' Training and Education have taken up in one hundred selected districts, with a view to training the farm family, i.e., farmer, farm women and farm youth in modern farming technology. The young farmers, within the age of 20 to 30 years, participate in programmes like demonstration-cum-training camps, short duration training courses and discussion groups. Special courses of three months duration were previously organized for young farmers, but later on they were discontinued as the courses become of longer duration. It is now planned to organize short of a specialized nature and to follow it up regularly through discussion groups.

Training of Young Farmers in Districts

National Level Farmers Voluntary Organisations are being encouraged to take up training programme for the benefit of young farmers by organizing short duration training courses, seminars and exchange visits. Financial assistance is being provided to the six national level organizations by the Directorate of Extension to enable them to undertake programmes relating to agricultural production. These organizations have branches at the State and district level and they work through them.

One of these organizations is the Young Farmers' Association of India, which has set up Young Farmers' Training Centres at Rakhra and Visakhapatnam to provide institutional training facilities in various disciplines of Agriculture and Animal Husbandry. They have also been organizing youth activities in selected areas and are operating a Young Farmers' Exchange Programme.

International Farm Youth Exchange Programme with the USA

The Directorate of Extension has taken up this programme in collaboration with the National 4-H Club Foundation of the USA with a view to providing an opportunity to promising farm boys and girls to visit the USA to study modern methods of agricultural production, the rural youth programme and leadership development. So far 291 Indian farm youth have visited the USA and in exchange, 150 farm youth from USA visited India. The returned Indian I.F.Y.Es have utilized their experience in improving their own farming and organizing demonstrations on their farms to provide training and education to other young farmers in their locality.

International Young Farmers Exchange Programme with Countries Other than the USA

Considering the utility of the International Farm Youth Exchange Programme with the USA it was decided to extend these programmes to cover other countries so that our young farmers could take advantage of the developments taking place in those countries. Similarly, it is proposed to invite the young farmers from the developing countries to visit India so that the experience gained by us could be shared with those countries. So far Sri Lanka has agreed to participate in this programme. The programme with other counties is being processed through our embassies abroad.

Exchange of Farmers within the Country

The scheme of exchange of farmers within the country is being implemented through the national level farmers voluntary organisations. Under this scheme young farmers from one area being encouraged to visit other areas where considerable progress in the field of agriculture and animal husbandry has been made, and to see for themselves how the young farmers have taken up such programmes. The farmers' voluntary organizations are being given financial assistance to take up this programme.

Regional Rural Youth Staff and Leaders Training Workshop

In order to provide training in Rural Youth Development to the trainers of the Extension Training/Farmers' Training Centres and Voluntary Youth Leaders, a national workshop in collaboration with FAO was organized earlier. Based on this experience regional workshops are now being organized every year to meet this objective.

People's Action for Development in India (PADI) (Department of Agriculture)

The people's action for development in India receive aid from FAO and other donor countries to provide assistance to voluntary organizations and training institutions for taking up programme for rural youth development and young farmers training. Some of the projects which were financed under this programme, are: (*a*) Kitchen Garden Competition among Rural Youth Clubs around selected Extension Training Centres; (*b*) Development of Village Youth Clubs in Districts Agra (UP) and Udaipur (Rajasthan); (*c*) Poultry Development Programme through youth clubs in selected villages near Narendrapur (West Bengal); and (*d*) Establishment of Young Farmers Training Centres at Visakhapatnam (AP) and Rakhra (Punjab).

Role of Indian Council of Agricultural Research (ICAR) in Training

ICAR is an apex body involved in training at levels. It has 31 research institutes and helps 22 Agricultural Universities functioning in the country. Some of these institutes and universities have taken up research studies on the Rural Youth Development Programme while others have taken up rural youth field projects in selected villages. In addition ICAR has established Krishi Vigyan Kendras.

Krishi Vigyan Kendra (Farm Science Centres)

In pursuance of the recommendations of the Education Commission (1964-66) to establish institutions for providing vocational education in agriculture at the pre and post-matriculate level, the Indian Council of Agricultural Research has started a scheme to establish Krishi Vigyan Kendras (Farm Science Centres) in the country. The National Commission on Agriculture and the Planning Commission have strongly recommended its implementation.

To work out the details for the establishment of the Krishi Vigyan Kendras, a committee under the chairmanship of Dr. Mohan Sinha Mehta was constituted by the ICAR in the year 1973. The main objectives of the Krishi Vigyan Kendras are as follows:

1. The Kendras will impart learning through work experience and hence will be concerned with technical literacy, the acquisition of which does not necessarily require as a precondition the ability to read and write.
2. The Kendras will impart training only to those extension

workers who are already employed, or to practising farmers and fishermen. In other words, who wish cater the needs of those who are already employed or those who wish to be self-employed.

3. There will be no uniform syllabus for the kendras. The syllabus and programmers of each kendra will be tailored according to the felt needs, natural resources and the potential for agricultural growth in that particular area.

Training Programmes

The in-service courses envisaged at a Krishi Vigyan Kendra will be mostly of short duration (1-3 months) and only field level extension staff village level workers will be trained at the Kendras. Courses in the Krishi Vigyan Kendras will be tailored to the needs of the areas served and will be for both men and women. The following types of courses might be provided; cultivation of local crops, application of package of practices; farm planning and plant protection; care and feeding of animals; poultry keeping; tubewell operation, irrigation and water control; nutrition, cooking and hygiene; food processing and cooking, marketing of agricultural--products, catching and marketing of fish, etc.

The success of these Kendras will be ensured if the programme is made as flexible as possible, both in vertical and horizontal dimensions and is attuned specifically to the needs of the area of its location. The keynote of these Kendras should be to involve the local community in skills according to the stages of development in agriculture and the density of population, as to enable it to improve the economic conditions for the better living standards of its members.

Women play an important role in agricultural production, production, particularly in post-harvest operations. Therefore, women's training programmes to increase their efficiency in agricultural operations, and to improve family living are also important. Since Krishi Vigyan Kendras will be an innovative institution, developing training programmes to suit the expanding needs of agricultural development, they will function as autonomous units insofar as their academic programmes and internal administration are concerned. The training programmes should mostly have need-based courses of a few weeks duration, a few months or even of a longer duration of one or two years. There may be part-time and full-time educational courses. Some of them could be correspondence courses. There could be detailed courses of sufficiently long duration, even one or two years. Evaluation will be a built in component of the programmes, to review and improve the courses according to the needs of the region, clientele and the general development programmes.

Organisation Aspects

In the staffing pattern, emphasis will be on recruiting a core staff, well-experienced and specialized persons. Some of expert craft teachers may be hired for short periods, whenever required for specific courses. At the Krishi Vigyan Kendras, some of the progressive farmers may serve as very practical teachers.

An advisory committee on Krishi Vigyan Kendras was constituted by the council with a view to developing operational criteria and guidelines for the establishment of the Krishi Vigyan Kendras, and for screening the proposals, which were received by the council from different parts of the country. It was pointed out by the committee that in view of the importance of such a scheme as the Krishi Vigyan Kendra, every taluka in the country should ultimately have one Krishi Vigyan Kendra. It has been decided that the agencies, which could be entrusted with the responsibility of running the Krishi Vigyan Kendras, would be:

(*a*) Agricultural Universities and ICAR Institutes.
(*b*) Voluntary organizations with a good record of serving the rural communities, especially backward areas, tribal areas or hilly areas etc.
(*c*) Institutes of Science and Technology who wish to organize agro-based industries.
(*d*) State government agencies, if the above institutions or agencies are not available.

It was insisted that after the Kendra has been identified and approved by the function. This detailed survey would serve as bench-maker and also will provide back ground information for formulating different kinds of training programmes based on the felt needs of the farming communities. The staff that is likely to be involved in the Krishi Vigyan Kendra Programme, either directly or indirectly, should do this survey, as a matter of fact. This will provide occasion to the staff members to understand the farmers' problems in detail, not necessarily through the collected data alone but also through their own observations based on the interaction with the farmers.

The budget provision will be around Rs. 10 lakh for the Fifth Five Year Plan period. The stress will be more on a humble beginning with quality training for the farmers, rather than a heavy investment in the establishment of the kendras. Regarding the jurisdiction of the Krishi Vigyan Kendra for training the local farmers, it was felt that it should not be very large. A large area would mean varied types to training programmes involving more and more staff resulting in large institutions, which may follow in the footsteps of the traditional institutions.

In 1976-77, 18 Krishi Vigyan Kendras were established; this means that the States and the Union Territories has been covered. The initial effort is to cover each of the States and Unoin Territories in the phase, and more such centres can be started after having established these first ones successfully. This scheme is of vital importance, for it is intended to provide problematic and field-oriented training which can have direct bearing on the agricultural and allied production.

As it has been explained, the training envisaged in the Krishi Vigyan Kendra Programme will be problem and field-oriented, with due follow-up measures. This will have direct bearing in raising agricultural production. The programme further intends to cover the backward areas, weaker sections and tribes and the hill farmers on a priority basis. This class of farmers deserves our immediate attention.

Staff Development Programme

The teachers of the Krishi Vigyan Kendras will be initially given 4-5 months' training in the Trainers Training Centres established by the ICAR in its specialized institutions. Besides, the Krishi Vigyan Kendras will also have in-service training in Institutional Management at the Central Staff for Agriculture for about a week or so. Based on the felt-needs, higher training will be arranged for the Krishi Vigyan Kendra staff. In fact, staff development will be a continuous process for keeping them abreast of the latest agricultural innovation, and doing an effective job of training the farmers.

Trainers' Training Centres

Since the Krishi Vigyan Kendras are going to be innovative institutions for imparting practical and skill-oriented to the farmers and fishermen, the ICAR has decided to establish seven Trainers' Training Centres in different parts of the country to provide specialized training to the teachers of the Krishi Vigyan Kendras as also to other in-service staff and teachers who are involved in vocational agriculture in different institutions. The main objectives of the Trainers Training Centres are as follows:

(*a*) To impart training to the teachers of the Krishi Vigyan Kendras both in agricultural technology as well as in pedagogy with a view to improve their subject-matter background in agriculture, home economics and the skills necessary for the teaching-learning process and techniques.

(*b*) To train the teachers who are, likely to be, engaged in teaching or work-experience in agriculture and home economics in high schools and vocational courses at the plus 2 level under the new pattern of education of 10 plus 2 plus 3.

(*c*) To train trainers of the Gram Sevika/Gram Sevak Extension Training Centres of the Region, specially in the latest Agriculture and Home Economics technologies so that their training programmes at the Extension Centres can be enriched.

(*d*) To organize vocational training programmes in agriculture and e-economics, as and when required, for the teachers and social workers of the voluntary organizations who are committed to rural development.

(*e*) To organize and conduct other short or long-term vocational courses for teachers/trainers as and when required by the Government and agricultural and home science institutions.

Organisational Aspects

Initially seven Trainers' Training Centres were established at:

1. Chettali (Coorg) in Horticulture, as an integral part of the Indian Institute of Horticultural Research, Bangalore.
2. Hyatnagar, Hyderabad in Dryland Farming, with the All India Coordinated Research Project on Dryland Agriculture.
3. Karnal, National Dairy Research Institute in Dairying.
4. Dhauli (Bhubaneshwar) in Fishers, under the Central Inland Fisheries Research Institute, Barrackpore (West Bengal).
5. Bhopal in Agricultural Engineering, with the Central Institute of Agricultural Engineering.
6. Indore (Madhya Pradesh) for the women teachers in-service staff.
7. One in the North Eastern Hilly Region areas for women teachers as well as in-service women staff of the State Departments. As a part of the plan with each Trainers' Training Centre, a Krishi Vigyan Kendra will also be established to serve as a training laboratory for, i.e., Trainers' Training Centre's trainees.

The Trainers' Training Centre will have a core staff of 5-6 specialists headed by a Chief Training Organiser. Wherever necessary, training organizers and training associates/assistants will also be provided. In addition, guest/specialists/visiting specialists will be invited for a specified period of time, depending upon the duration of the training courses.

It may be stressed that the Krishi Vigyan Kendras and Trainers' Training Centres are both innovative and institutions for practical training for the farmers and in-service personnel and hence more investment will be required. The staff of the Trainers' Training Centre will be provided short and long-term training depending upon their needs in their respective fields.

Department of Rural Development

The Department of Rural Development took up the Rural Youth

Programme with the inception of the Community Development Programme in the country. The Rural Youth Clubs organized under this programme are known as 'Yuvak Mandals' and are open to both boys and girls within the age group of 15-30 years. There are about 5000 blocks in the country and the average number of Yuvak Mandals in each block is reported to be about 20. The basic objective of these clubs is to provide a training ground for the youth club members to become better farmers, better homemakers, better citizens and better leaders. For this purpose, they take up economic, social, cultural and recreational projects. Their activities aim, on the one hand at developing civic sense and civic responsibility and on the other provide channels for dissemination of new knowledge and essential skills and techniques in agriculture and the allied fields. The project activities include agriculture, horticulture, dairying, poultry, pisciculture, piggery, home management, spinning, tailoring, embroidery and food preservation etc.

The village level worker helps in organizing these clubs and provides necessary leadership in helping the club to take up project activities. The subject-matter extension officers in the block provide technical guidance for organizing the various programmes.

In order to strengthen these clubs, the Department of Rural Development is providing financial support to 2,500 selected Yuvak Mandals in the 500 blocks. The clubs will also be federated at the block level and suitable grants will be provided to meet their expenses. The office-bearers of the Yuvak Mandals are also imparted training in organizational aspects and project activities. The training is organized at selected Extension Training Centres for duration of five days.

Ministry of Education and Social Welfare

Department of Education—Youth Services Wing

The Department of Education has set up a youth services wing to look after the development of youth programme in the country. The following programmes have been taken up by them:

Nehru Yuvak Kendras

The programme visualized the establishment of youth centres

called Nehru Yuvak Kendras—one in each district, by the end of Fifth Plan period. The scheme was initiated in the year 1972, and so far, 225 centres have been established. These centres are primarily designed to provide a forum for the non-student youth, particularly in rural areas, with a view to giving them the opportunities to participate in the development process. The main activities visualized are:

(*a*) Non-formal education including functional literacy and education in agriculture, health, family life and community living.
(*b*) Opportunities for self-employment through appropriate training in productive skills and assistance in setting up small scale industries and other enterprises.
(*c*) Social service including cleanliness campaigns, vaccination, inoculation and other health service.
(*d*) Cultural activities like participation in the performing arts including community singing and theatre.
(*e*) Promotion of sports and games particularly those which have the possibility of mass participation.

It is proprosed to set up a network of youth services in the villages which will be the focal point for development and recreational activities. The programme is being guided from the district level by the youth coordinator supported by a professional coach for organizing sports and games etc. The scheme is fully financed by the Central Government, and the State Governments are closely associated with the implementation, programme and activities. In order to provide proper coordination at various levels, organizing committees have been formed at the National, State and District levels.

National Service Scheme

The National Service Scheme was launched in 1969 and at present it is being implemented in almost all the universities in India. It provides for utilization of leisure time of the students in various items of social work and national development activities. As a part of the constructive involvement, large of student youth during their vacation period, certain large scale camping programmes are also being organized under the NSS, in the course of which some aspects of rural youth are being covered. The major programmes taken so far are Youth Against Famine in 1973 and Youth for Afforestation and Tree Plantation in 1974-75. Similar programmes are proposed to be taken up in the future also. Special emphasis is also being laid on a literacy campaign. Each university has a National Service Scheme Coordinator to arrange programmes and special campaigns.

Department of Social Welfare

The Department of Social Welfare has taken up rural youth programmes as far as it relates to pre-vocational training programmes for school dropouts in the age group of 10-15 years. Pre-vocational training centres have been established with a view to provide training in the mechanical engineering trades, besides general education to children who are able to continue their education at middle school level due to social and economic reasons.

Ministry of Labour

The Minisry of Labour has taken up a scheme for providing craftsmanship training to rural youth in various fields, including agro-industries, at their vocational training/centres. The scheme is meant for rural youth of the 15-25 age group.

Constraints on Development of Rural Youth Programme

There is a lack of clear-cut national policy regarding rural youth development programmes, particularly in relation to the agricultural sector. The programme needs to be coordinated, guided and channeled properly at all levels so that the benefit could percolate to the farm youth. Since these programmes mostly relates to agriculture, the Ministry of Agriculture should go in a big way to take up farm youth development work, of course, in close partnership with other sister ministries and voluntary organizations.

There is inadequate staff for implementing the farm youth programme. At village level, the village level worker hardly gets time for youth work. At the block level in some states, there is one extension officer for social education in the panchayat to look after the rural youth programme. He is generally entrusted with many other jobs and the real objective of the programme remains unrealized. In many states, this post has been abolished. Besides, in some states there are no special officers at district and state levels to ensure proper implementation of the rural youth programme.

Youth development does not form a regular part of agricultural extension education. What is being done in the name of rural youth at many places are cultural type of activities which neither sustain the interest of the youth at many places are cultural type of activities which neither sustain the interest of the youth, or of the parents, as it has no scope for economic or professional advancement on a long-term basis.

The agricultural extension worker has poor knowledge or experience to provide the type of service and support necessary to enable the farm youth to assume the role of an enlightened farmer, in due course of time. The job chart of the agricultural extension worker does not include providing service to this important section of the farm family.

There is no financial provision in the Development Block's budget to cater the education and training requirements of farm youth. As a result, this dynamic sector of the farming population, which could become an effective instrument for dissemination of modern technology, remains unexploited by the extension machinery. The mass of idle manpower leads to unproductive and sometimes even destructive actions, as energetic youth, by nature, cannot keep quiet.

The agricultural and veterinary institutions have so far offered attractive programmes to the rural youth to sustain interest in rural areas nor have they suggested action plans to build up their knowledge and skill to take farming as a profitable and interesting enterprise.

A number of educational type of programmes launched for youth by different organization (official and non-official) are not designed according to the needs of specific age groups. Such education can be beneficial only if their state of physical and mental development is taken into consideration.

The voluntary organizations/institutions engaged in rural

youth service are not self-sufficient. They have not developed enough so as to be able to render free service to farm youth. Apart from due encouragement from Government, they need to become popular amongst youth and build goodwill confidence by working among the rural masses.

Mobilisation of Rural Youth in Agricultural Production and Other Development Programmes

Some of the rural youth go for higher education, and after graduation return to their villages to take up farming as their occupation. Among these, some are agricultural graduates, and their services could be utilised to act as demonstrator farmers for the area and provide consultancy services to other young farmers. The nationalized banks are coming forward in a big way to give financial help to such agricultural graduates to purchase agricultural machinery, etc., and to settle on the farm. Such young farmers can provide custom—hire service to other small farmers and consultancy service to other farmers in matters relating to modern agriculture.

The remaining education rural youth in the villages could be trained to act as voluntary leaders to provide guidance and leadership to other young people in taking up various development activities. They could also function as conveners of Radio/T.V. discussion groups and help people in discussing and understanding the programmes relayed by Radio/Television.

The rural youth can be mobilized for participation in the community programmes relating to agricultural production and rural development. While initiating such programmes, care has to be taken to provide proper incentives to the participants. Secondly the programme should be of interest to rural youth and its duration should not be too long, otherwise they will not have a sustained interest. The jobs, which are of a challenging nature, would attract a larger number of youth as compared to those, which are labour-oriented. Some of the agricultural development programmes that could be of interest to them are listed below:

(*a*) Mass spraying, dusting and control of crop diseases and pests including baiting against rates.

(*b*) Afforestation, raising of community orchards, nurseries, etc.

(*c*) Maintenance, repair and clearing of irrigation channels, village roads, etc.
(*d*) Maintenance and decoration of community buildings like panchayat ghar, village school, temple, etc.

It would be observed that rural youth, if organized properly and provided adequate training, supervision and incentives, could undertake a number of programmes not only for their individual benefit but also for the development of the community as a whole. The programme could also help in developing necessary skills and leadership qualities among the rural youth to become progressive farmers and help in agricultural production and rural development programmes.

Workshop Wings

To train carpenters and blacksmiths there are 23 workshops in the country run by the Ministry of Community Development. They are at: (1) Rajendra Nagar (Hyderabad, A.P.), (2) Samalkot (A.P.), (3) Jarhot (Assam), (4) Muzaffarpur (Bihar), (5) Junagarh (Gujarat), (6) Mashobra (H.P.), (7) Kottarakara (Kerala), (8) Antri (M.P.), (9) Obedullaganj (M.P.), (10) Nowgong (M.P.), (11) Powerkhere (M.P.), (12) Manjri (Maharashtra), (13) Shindhewahi (Maharashtra), (14) Kullapatri (Tamil Nadu), (15) Kuggi (Mysore), (16) Bolangir (Orissa), (17) Nabha (Punjab), (18) Nilokheri (Hissar), (19) Bakshi Ka Talab (Lucknow, UP), (20) Ghazipur (UP), (21) Fulia (Bengal), (22) Burdwan (Bengal).

Khadi Gram Udyog Vidyalaya

Such training centres are being run to help the weavers. These are located at: (1) Gandhi Niketan Ashram, Kallupati, (2) Wardha, (3) Sadakat Ashram, Patna, (4) Duewani Nagar, Bangalore (5) Himayat Nagar, Hyderabad, (6) Nilokheri, Haryana.

Auxiliary Courses

Courses in Poultry-keeping, Livestock Management, Fruit Preservation, Kitchen Gardening, Home Management, Use of Soybean in Human Diet and the recipes from it, etc., are being organized by the Agricultural Universities and some Agricultural Colleges. Some such universities are organizing flower, fruit and vegetable shows each year and encourage urban people to take advantage of such facilities. Some special courses for military personnel, retired persons etc., are also organized.

Conclusion

India is predominantly an agricultural country and it is through effective training, useful research as well as solution-oriented extension education that attach can be made or problems affecting the welfare of the rural people. Extension Training provides a stable base for economic and mental security other than the directive of increasing yields and improvement of personal and village wealth.

12

Importance of Distance Education in Developing Countries with Special Reference to India

MRS. RAKHI MITTAL

Education has a desirable controlling influence over development of the individual family, community and society, leading to reduce poverty, income equity and controlled employment. There are significant social and economic differences between developed and developing countries causes of history of the development of such nations and include social cultural and economic variables, historical and political elements, international relations and geographical factors. The differences in the scientific and technological infrastructure and in the popularization of science and technology in the two groups of countries are the most important causes of differential social, economical levels. An essential prerequisite to a country's technological progress in early recognition of necessity of a good educational system. The best implementation of science and technology can be best observed in the process of Distance Education.

The emergence of distance education can be seen in correspondence programme. Distance Education is more with reference to geographical boundaries. Distance Education is a method of indirect instruction, implying geographical and emotional separation of teacher and taught whereas, in mainstream education, the relationship between a teacher and student in classroom is based upon social norms, in distance education, it is based upon technological rules.

In National Education Policy 1986, it is stated—"lifelong

education is a cherished goal of the educational process. This presuppose universal literacy, opportunities will be provided to youth housewives agricultural and industrial workers and professional to continue the education of their choice, at the pace, suited to them. The future thrust will be in the direction of open and distance learning. This statement reflects over the new thinking regarding the universalisation of education lifelong education and its conceptual framework is now old enough.

The system of education in India has a great historical and cultural heritage. It has been changed from time to time because of socio-economic and cultural pressure. Many branches of knowledge and culture were the contribution of lust for it, but the concept and need of mass education have recent origin. These changes are effected by historical necessity. Since the age of Vedas there was learner motivation. Those who were interested to learn approached to Guru and stayed with him in his Gurukul for few years. There actual instructions were given and the skills were developed. This type of learner motivation was also found in Buddha's period. During this period, education of institutionalised, Nalanda, Texsila, Vikramshila and so many others were the universities where the learners from all nobles of life used to come for study. During Muslim period, there were Pathsalas for Hindus and Madrasa for Muslims. In Madrasa, Hindu who were desirous to seen the empires and Nawabs, also secured their education, the system, recognized by the state was perso-Alabic. Upward mobility was the aim of the system.

During British period, English system of education was introduced. Learners from families with some educational background thronged the schools, which were situated in towns. The purpose of education in British period was to prepare proves who might be helpful to run the administration.

Dr. Radhakrishnan Commission says in its report that education must be universalised and equal opportunities for all be given. Each and every citizen is given education irrespective of his caste or creed, social or economic status, motivation or aptitude.

Studies Related to Distance Education

Wedemeyer expressed Distance Education as an independent

study, open learning and distance education. The three terms expressed the following meanings:

Independent Study > Correspondence Courses.
Open Education > Open University.
Distance Education > Correspondent Education.

Wedemeyer has outlined this idea about "Independent Study" and its purpose:

(*i*) It consists of teaching learning arrangements, and these arrangements have various forms. The special feature of these arrangements is that, the teachers and learners stay away from each other and didactic, communication takes place in various ways.
(*ii*) Its purpose are to facilitate learning activities of both the on campus and the off campus students.

Michael Moore, expressed his views in his work "Teaching at a Distance" about Distance Education. Distance and Autonomy are the two variables of this programme. There are three phenomenon of it:

(*i*) Dialogues; (*ii*) Individualisation; and (*iii*) Structure.

Dialogue means the face-to-face communication, *Individualisation* refers curricular components—objective, methods, material and evaluation. *Structure* means that the process of instruction be maintained.

Educational Method in Distance Education

In distance education the learners has to learn apart from the teacher. There is a vast difference between traditional classroom learning and learning with distance. The innovations in education and technology have given a different way of learning as well as teaching. Writing made possible to record communication and transfer them over space and time. Printing broke down the monopoly of a single copy writing, telecommunication collapsed the dimensions of space and time, democratic philosophy broke down the monopoly of elites. Correspondence education was the result of needs and pressures. The development of programme learning and teaching machines pointed to the possibility of self-instruction and learner based education.

The main characteristic of distance study means that the learner is physically at a long distance from the teacher for much, most or even all of the time during the teaching-learning process. In distance education, there must be the autonomy of objectives; methods, materials and evaluation, and these must be decided by the institute and the teacher.

Growth of Distance Education

Distance Education is a worldwide phenomenon. In Africa, Distance Education was spread over to train teachers and to educate the masses. In North, South and Central America, application and professionally oriented courses are being offered, print and electronic media play an important role in disseminating information, knowledge and skills. In Asia, countries like India, Pakistan, Thailand, Sri Lanka, Philippines, China, South Korea, Indonesia and Japan adopted Distance Education system and courses are based mainly on print materials, which are supplemented, by electronic media and contact programme. In Australia, the university level courses are based on an integrated model—New Zealand, New Guinea and Pacific Islands promote Distance Education in a big way.

Growth of Distance Education in India

About 25 years ago, correspondence education in India was started as a pilot project in the university of Delhi. The success of this experiment encouraged other universities to take up instructions through the distance education. As a result in 1985, the Government of India decided to set up Indira Gandhi National Open University.

The Focal Points of IGNOU are as under:

1. To promote open university and distance education system.
2. To determine the standards of teaching evaluation and research in such system.

3. To allocate and disburse grants to colleges, whether admitted to its privileges or not, or to any other, university or institution of higher learning as may be specified by the Statutes.

Indira Gandhi National Open University is providing degrees in B.A., B.Sc. and B. Com., Diploma Courses in Distance Education, Creative Writing, Nutrition, Management, Local Self-Government, Library Science, Banking, etc. Separate Radio and T.V. channels have been started to broadcast and telecast the educational programmes. As a measure for implementation, the Programme of Action has also favoured and recommended Open Universities System to provide higher education through non-formal channel. The main suggestions and recommendation of this Action Programme are given as under:

(*i*) Action Programme suggested the Open University system. This should be cost-effective, flexible and innovative.
(*ii*) Indira Gandhi National Open University has been established and is running effectively.
(*iii*) Non-formal education system should be structured on modular pattern.
(*iv*) Minimum level of learning should be objectively assessed.
(*v*) Separate Radio and Television channels be used for the use of distance education.
(*vi*) Network of course be framed.
(*vii*) Quality of Programme be ensured.
(*viii*) Financial Assistance will be given very carefully.

Open University

Open University is an experiment recently introduced to universalize higher education in the world. An open university is meant for those who want to gain higher knowledge and develop higher learning skill. To universalize higher education Open University system is a unique experiment in India. Science 1958 to 1985, an individual had to go through the formal stream of education to get the entry into the gateway of university. If any person deviated from the stream, he had to face a lot of difficulties to regain the same. The first step was to give permission to the individual to appear as private candidate for university examination. Second step was—correspondence courses for the various subjects and standards. Finding increasing craze for getting higher education, India felt the need to establish Open University on the lines of England.

What is Open University?

Open University is an experiment recently introduced to universalize higher education in the world. Through this syste.n an individual wants to keep himself up-to-date in the process of emerging new knowledge. An Open University is meant for those who want to gain higher education knowledge and develop higher learning skill. Following are the main characteristics of an Open University:

(*i*) There is no need of any qualifying examination to get admission in the university.
(*ii*) There is no age limit for selecting admission.
(*iii*) Individual belonging to any State or region may seek admission.
(*iv*) There is no limit for examination.
(*v*) There is no formal campus for study.

It is to be noted that Open University has curriculum, study and examination just like traditional universities.

Development of Open Universities

The pressure is regularly increasing on the universities. To solve this problem, in 1979 the first Open University was opened in Britain. There 25,000 candidates were registered in the first year. By 1985, there 1,00,000 candidates had registered. This number is increasing day by day. This university uses 300 study centers, Radio, Television and other means of communication for conducting studies. Now-a-days, there are open universities in China, Japan, Thailand, Korea, Spain, Netherlands, Pakistan, Sri Lanka and India.

Since 1970, the efforts were made to open universities. In 1982, the first Open University was started in Andhra Pradesh; the name of this university is Annamalai University. This university imparted instruction for B.A, B.Sc., B.Com and Postgraduate degrees in various subjects as well as B. Ed., M.Ed. and LL.B.

The first Open University in India was S.N.D.T. University, Bombay. Formerly it was a university for women. Later on the structure of this university has been changed. This university through distance education is running many useful curricula for women. Seeing the achievements of open universities. Homeberg has rightly said that real study is basically an individual effort. This effort comes out through inner urges. Open universities were called Air universities. Later on, these universities renamed as open universities. Open universities are becoming popular and this experiment is quite successful. The achievements of this experiment are as follows:

(*i*) This is a successful experiment to universalize higher education.
(*ii*) There is no need of any qualifying certificate to seek admission in it.
(*iii*) Radio and television are frequently used to impart education.
(*iv*) Every individual who wants to seek admission may get opportunities for the same.
(*v*) Individual is free to select the life-style and way of progress of this media of higher education.
(*vi*) Through correspondence the teaching material along with complete instruction is sent to the candidates. They send it back to the office for evaluation.
(*vii*) This university has complete structure—Academic and Administrative. There is a central body to control over the functions of the university.
(*viii*) There are university study centers in States.
(*ix*) In each district, there is an arrangement for study center.

System of Education

In an Open University, there is a three tier system of evaluation:

(*i*) Self-education.
(*ii*) Education by the tutor.

(*iii*) Education by the university after completing three stages a certificate is awarded to the candidate.

New Education Policy and Open University

New policy of education 9816, stressed over the need of Open University. There is 4.9 per cent higher education in our country. Therefore, a policy is adopted to universalize higher education and keep the individual up-to-date with knowledge. In the policy following points have been stressed:

- Open University system has been introduced to democratize education and increasing educational opportunities for the common man.
- Indira Gandhi Open University established in 1985 will cater the needs of learners.
- The development of this powerful educational media will be done with a great care.

The strategy of an Open University is as follows:

Evaluation Structure

Evaluation will be done by the candidate himself, by the tutor and by the university.

Execution

This programme has been started since 1987 and new curriculum have also been started since 1988. A separate channel on T.V. is introduced for educational programmes. Orientation courses are being introduced for men and women. This programme is framed on the pattern of Modulus are credit system. University Grants Commission will give sufficient grant for the promotion of this programme. Courses for Agriculture, Industry and many other fields, National norms for Agriculture, Industry and many other fields. National norms for curriculum and evaluation will be developed. State Open Universities will seek guidance from the National Open University.

Indira Gandhi National Open University

In 1985, Indira Gandhi National Open University has been established through an Act passed by the Parliament. President of India is a visitor of this university and head of the university is Vice-Chancellor. For his assistance there is an Executive Council, Academic Council, Planning Board, Finance Committee and Board of Recongnition. There is Pro-Vice Chancellor and Directors for assisting Vice-Chancellor. There is a Registrar who is Administrative head and a Finance Officer. Its headquarters is at New Delhi.

Structure

There is a different structure of Open University. There is no boundary for learners. Audio-visual aids, audio equipments, Television, edited teaching material and contact programme are used in place of teacher. Guidance programme is introduced in contact place. Co-ordinators of study centers are responsible for conducting the contact programmes.

Teaching Programme

Diploma in Management, Diploma in Distance Education, Nutrition Creative Writing and B.A., B.Com., B.Sc., etc., have been started in 1987. Besides these Diplomas in Management, Studies, Local Self-Government, Bounding, Energy Resources, Horticulture, etc., have been planned. Qualifying examination for the admission is Intermediate or its equivalent. There is an admission test for those who are not intermediate.

Regional Centres

There are Regional Centres to run the programmes of university smoothly. Head of the Centre is called Director. State Governments provide this Centre building and other facilities. These centres are co-ordinating units. There are libraries and other reaching material in every centre.

Curriculum

B.A., B.Sc., B.Com, courses under three years degree scheme have been started by Indira Gandhi National Open University. The student is expected to complete this degree within eight years.

Communication technologies have come to play a vibrant role in democratizing education not only in the developed but also in the developing countries. However, in spreading the use of information and communication technology some major difficulties are felt by the policy-makers as well as the implementers. These difficulties are felt both at the growth and application stages of communication technology. Yaverbaum and Reisman highlights the importance of three aspects in the application of new information and communication technology. They are people, software and hardware. Different permutations and combinations with regard to the three variables create different implications for the growth and application of information and communication technology (James, C. Taylor, "Computer Assisted Distance Education: A Pedagogic and Professional Development Perspective"). Among these, they stated that the most difficult aspect to address would invariably be the human element. Pete Thomas and Dean Taylor state that as access to information and communication technologies become more extensive, their use is extended from the activities related to internal administrative aspects towards more of interaction with students (James, C. Taylor, "Computer Assisted Distance Education: A Pedagogic and Professional Development Perspective"). Such a scenario throws up new challenges before technologists in terms of both technical and human aspects. Hidetoshi Kato states that in the years to come communication technologies will play a major role in deciding learning outcomes.

Why Use ICT?

Information and communication technology has come to be regarded as the mainstay of all distance education methods. Dr. Ramanujam succinctly put the importance of information and communication technologies in the current scheme of distance education forward in the following words:

"The spread of Information and Communication Technology (ICT) has revolutionized the access to education in general and the Distance Open Learning (DOL) in particular. ICT's role in the expansion of DOL need not be overemphasized. It is common knowledge that every Distance Teaching Institution is fast adapting itself to technology based teaching and learning in order to keep abreast of the changes taking place in educational technology.

Educational technologists have cited many reasons as to why an education system based on ICT can more effectively result in positive pedagogic outcomes than one based only on conventional techniques. One of the prominen reasons why ICT has come to hold an important place in ODL is that distance learning is basically a Guided Didactic Conversational process (Borje Holmberg) in which the institution has to be in constant touch with the student. The high degree of interactivity exhibited by ICTs is an indispensable aspect in facilitating Guided Didactic Process. ICTs can transmit information to the students through a wide variety of media in a way that promotes informed discussion as well as provides guidance.

The autonomous learner of ODL institutes needs to be continuously attended by the Distance Learning Institute. This was termed by David Stewart as "Continuity of Concern". The ODL institutes will not be able to express their continuity of concern to their students without the appropriate use of modern ICTs. Modern ICTs like teleconferencing can reach the farthest corners of the world discounting the traditional limitations of space and topography. Such a scheme will be able to effectively tackle the problems of students at all levels and at all stages.

The use of new ICT is extremely compatible with the "Industrial Form of Learning"(Otto Peters) that is propounded by ODL institutes. The emphasis on systematization by such institutes makes it highly imperative that each stage of the learning process is associated with skill that has to be pandered to by using a different learning device. This has prompted the cognitive theorists like Skinner to propound the usage of teaching machines. Such machines greatly reinforce the stimuli provided by the learning process.

Policy Structure of the Government

The growth of any communication technology in a society and hence its applicability for Distance Education depends to a very great extent on the degree to which policy makers recognize the importance of ICTs in promoting a knowledge based society. Many developing countries like India have realized the importance of giving a boost to New Information and Communication Technologies for the general betterment of the society. The New Information Technology Act 2000 passed by the Indian Parliament is a step in the right direction. Many countries have bestowed tax incentives on communication technology based industries. Some countries that have paid relatively scarce attention to the area of information technology are lagging behind in the field of spreading education using the latest technology. The failure of Distance Education in many African countries can be attributed to this. Not only are policies important but also their implementation deserves greater attention. The road to failure is often paved with good intentions. Many structural factors make the implementation of technology a daunting task. At the planning stage the enormity of such factors are often not recognized.

Factors Affecting the Growth of Technology in Distance Education

Political Factors

The perceptions and attitudes of a political system greatly affect the acceptance and growth of technology in any society. The same holds true for all the ICTs relevant to Distance Education. A political system conscious of the payoffs of ICT for the enhancement of the educational profile of a country will frame appropriate policies for the adoption and dissemination of ICT through out the length and breadth of the country. As A.W. Bates states while talking about his criteria of Media Selection, Novelty of an ICT should be the least important criteria that should guide the political society in deciding upon the ICT that should be selected. Rather than being guided by the fashion of the day, ICT should always be selected in accordance with its end result, that is the extent to which it can bring about positive pedagogic outcomes.

"Mere 'buying' of technology will not become a policy, because any unprofessional decision at some level will be enough to buy technology. In such a case technology will become a disabling rather than an enabling tool". Technology-Pedagogy Combine: Need for Quality in Distance-Open Learning.

The growth of ICTs will be generally welcomed in a democratic society, because, ICTs are known to democratize societies through wider dissemination of information. However, in a society in which an autocratic form of government prevails, growth of ICTs may not be viewed with favour because, greater access to information may encourage interest in creating more democratic space in the society.

Economic Factors

In Distance Education, cost is an important factor that guides the adoption and growth of Communication Technology in a country. Developing countries often lack the initial allocation as well as matching funds to make feasible investments in ICTs. Many countries often acquire costly technology without making provisions for building sufficient infrastructure to run them.

Thomas (1987) states that there are four major factors that can affect the growth of Communication Technologies in a country. They are:

- Financial strength of the society;
- Attitude of policy-makers;
- Budget allocation for the technology; and
- Cost-efficiency of the technology.

(IGNOU, "Growth of Communication Technology", Communication Technology for Distance Education, ES-318, p. 34.)

Most developing countries are constrained by resource scarcities. Even where the importance of ICTs is recognized, allocation for the development of these is at best paltry. Due to this, many developing countries are forced to depend on mostly traditional means of communication. These are limited in their efficiency.

The developing countries are vitally dependent on substantial foreign assistance to ensure the development of ICTs. Often it is found that it is very difficult to invite the attention of donors on ICTs. These countries are perennially short of Foreign Exchange for acquiring latest technologies. Most of the developing countries are undergoing Structural Adjustment Programmes under the auspices of the IMF.

Cost-efficiency of an ICT is another major factor that is

important that determines its growth. Developing countries have to ensure that such a technology is adopted that is easily accessible to the target group and also fulfills all the functions that are expected of it. Such a scenario essentially implies that a costly technology need not always be the best technology. However, it is often seen that developing countries often invest in the latest technologies without considering whether the target audience is effectively reached or whether the target audience is interested in the technology. The latter is the case of UGC's countrywide classroom scheme whose utilization rate is as low as 10 per cent.

Cultural Factors

Contractor, Fulk, Monge and Singhal (1986) state that culture is a complex whole that includes knowledge, beliefs, arts, morals, laws, customs and any other capability and habit acquired by a human being as a member of the society (IGNOU, "Growth of Communication Technology", Communication Technology for Distance Education.

Language

Language is one of the major factors that hinder the easy assimilation of ICTs by many developing countries. This hinders transfer of technology. The radio and TV programmes, computer software and the printed texts are produced in different countries bearing different cultural backgrounds. As such, such tools may fail to impress students of another country. For example, a zoology text can safely give the example of a koala in Australia, but the same cannot be replicated in India.

With regard to cultural patterns there are two groups of policy makers. Policy makers can be pro-implementation or anti-implementation. It is precisely the cultural moorings of a society that makes people either in favour of implementing technology or to reject it. Japanese have over the years built up a reputation of being quick to adapt and implement new technology. This can be linked to the way in which a new culture of receptivity to new ideas was built up after centuries of stagnation when commodore Perry forced the Japanese to open up their society. Again, in recent times it has been seen that the culture of classroom teaching and learning has been so strongly built into the psyche of the teaching community that they often exhibit resistance in the way of implementing technological change that forces a change in the role of the teacher from being a store house of all learning to a manager of the teaching-learning process.

Technological Factors

Very often, technology becomes the determining factor in the growth of ICT in any society. One would be justified in applying the Bates criteria for media selection as an appropriate parameter for selecting appropriate technology for educational purposes.

Bates Criteria for Media Selection

Bates states that the following are the major criterion that have to be taken into consideration while selecting appropriate media for educational purposes:

A — Access to the Media.
C — Cost of the Proposed Media.
T — Teaching Functions of the Media in Relation to Learning Goals.
I — Interactiveness and User-Friendliness.
O — Organisational Issues.
N — Novelty of the Media.
S — Speed with which Change can be Brought About in the Media.

The Relative Successes and Failures of Various Types of TV and Radio in the Indian Context

Radio

Radio broadcasts in India for educational purposes has taken the form of school broadcasts, adult education and community development projects, farm and home broadcasts, university broadcasts and language learning projects.

Among school broadcasts, the programmes aired by the Central Institute of Educational Technology for primary classes was one of the best programmes of the genre. Among the adult education and community development projects the "Radio-forums" that were tried out in 144 villages around Poona with the help of UNESCO. The programme was tried out in groups of 20 members each. These forums were expected to listen to thirty-minute radio programmes on agriculture and community development.

Farm and Home Broadcasts were initiated in a big way in 1966. The topics covered in these were related to agriculture and allied topics. The aim was to educate the farmers and to provide them information in innovative practices in their field. These programmes were very effective.

University Broadcasts in India have traditionally been of two types—'general' and 'enrichment' oriented. The former includes topics of public interest while the latter is used to support correspondence education of various institutes. The University of Delhi works out details in association with AIR Delhi for providing education through radio. Again many open universities in the country also use radio broadcasts. Even the CIEFL, Hyderabad is engaged in offers modules through radio mode.

Language learning projects are also a popular form of using the medium of radio. The most prominent example of the same is called the "Radio-pilot project" aimed at covering 500 primary schools of Jaipur and Ajmer in order to teach Hindi language. These projects were successful in improving the vocabulary of students by a very large measure. Later on such an experiment was also repeated in Hoshangabad district of Madhya Pradesh (IGNOU, ES-318, Communication Technology for Distance Education, 2000, pp. 42-44). Gyanvani project was launched by IGNOU is offered in FM channels in 40 cities around the country for the purpose of educational development. EMPC is the nodal agency for implementing the project. The EMPC is currently studying the possibilities of creating a global Gyanvani.

Interactive Radio Counselling is a recent conception in Indian Distance Education scheme. In this scheme various experts at AIR stations provide live counselling across the country. They are conducted at 189 radio stations on Sundays for an hour. Reflecting on the Interactive Radio Counselling mechanism as adopted in IGNOU, S.S. Chaudhary, *et al.*, reported that IRC was an effective input to accomplish course objectives (Bansal, Kiron and Chaudhary, Sonvir, S., 1999, "Interactive radio for supporting distance education: An evaluative study", Indian Journal of open learning). Again, B. Sukumar states that IRCs provide a major forum on which the students, especially from the remote areas can interact with the teaching end and can get their doubts clarified. The study revealed that even though IRC is well accepted by the students, there needs to be more attention given to its various aspects to make it really effective.

Radio as an information and communication technology is by far the most successful of all ICTs in India.

Television

Experiment with television as a medium began very early in India. The major programmes of significance in this regard were Secondary School TV programme, Delhi Agricultural Television Project: Krishi Darshan, Satellite Instructional TV Experiment (SITE), Indian National Satellite Project (INSAT); UGC's Higher Educational Television Project (HETV) and Gyan Darshan (TDCC).

Secondary School TV Programme

This programme was started in Delhi on an experimental basis in October 1961 to impart lectures in Physics, Chemistry; English and Hindi for Class XI.These were basically syllabus-based programmes. The aim of the programme was also to enable students without laboratory facilities to have a feel of the same in a detached environment (for science programmes).

Delhi Agricultural Television Project

This project was initiated on 26 January, 1966 for providing information related to agriculture to farmers. It was provided in 80 villages in and around Delhi. The programme attained a fair degree of success.

Satellite Instructional TV Experiment (SITE)

This experiment was started in the year 1975, initially for a period of one year. The telecast concentrated on the broadcast of two types of programmes—1. Development related programmes featuring health, agriculture etc.; and 2. School programmes in Hindi, Kannada, Telugu and Oriya.

Indian National Satellite Project (INSAT)

The INSAT series of satellites were a landmark in the history of Indian Educational Technology. Educational television broadcasts were inaugurated through the INSAT series of satellites on 15th August, 1982 in Orissa and Andhra Pradesh. Later on it was extended to AP, Bihar, Gujarat, Maharashtra, Orissa and UP. The cover of the INSAT spans the whole of the country in today's date. One of the avowed objectives of the INSAT scheme was to bring the rural population into the national mainstream. The areas covered include most of the areas of interest to these populations.

UGC's Higher Educational Television Project (HETV)

The UGC's countrywide classroom programme was inaugurated in 1984.The production of programmes under this scheme is undertaken by the Electronic Media Research Centres (EMRC) located at various spots in the country. Some of the programmes are also imported from other countries too. The aim of UGC through its CWC was to upgrade the quality of education in the country.

The Gyan Darshan Experiment

A collaborative effort between the MHRD and IGNOU, the Gyan Darshan channel has come to stay as a major innovation in educational television. The EMPC is the coordinating and transmitting agency for the programmes. Regular transmission of programmes from EMPC started on 10 January, 2000. Cable operators are being encouraged to make available the programmes of Gyan Darshan to all their customers. This was for ensuring a countrywide reach. Currently Gyan Darshan is available for viewing both in India and abroad.

Human and Administrative Factors

Human and Administrative Factors can play a major role in the growth of ICTs in the third world. It is seen that if all sections of people do not have access to the technology being implemented then it will result in the creation of two classes of people—'haves' and 'have-nots'. This may result in a sense of deprivation among the 'have-nots'. It may also result in many administrative problems. Implementation is a major issue. When new technologies like computers are implemented, resistance from ground level staff is a real possibility. Far more important than technological resistance is the attitude of the people towards the use of technology for educational purposes. Sonvir Choudhary and Shyam Behari in their Modasa experiment state that developing countries do not lag behind advanced countries in the use of technology for entertainment. With a little change in perception the same technologies can be used for education too. The authors proved this fact through their experiment at Modasa, a village in Gujarat. (Choudhary, Sonvir and Behari, Shyam (1994), Modasa Experiment: Distance teaching through cable TV network system, Indian Journal of Open Learning 3(1), pp. 24-28.

Equipment Related Factors

Equipment Related Factors are a major hurdle in the growth and application of communication technologies. The main aspect in this pertains to the import of various equipments. In many cases, maintenance of the same requires foreign technicians. In the case of dual use technologies, there may emerge many import restrictions. A major case in view is the import restrictions imposed on the export of cryogenics related rocket technology to India by USA in recent times.

The Human Element is also of major importance in the growth and application of new ICT. In many cases, it is seen that the teachers act as a major roadblock against the implementation of new technology. They are not ready to accept any change in their role. With the advent of new ICT teachers are no longer the storehouse of all knowledge, but are more of managers of education.

Communication policies of various countries also play a major role in deciding the application of various communication technologies. These policies are a product of social pressure. Policy formulations are based on the kind of role the political elite want that media to play in the process of development of the country.

In the educational field policies should be formulated in such a way that the inter-regional disparities as well as the inter-strata disparities are overcome and equal access is made available to all the segments in their quest for education.

Advantages of Distance Education

Distance Education is a very continuing education. Rather to say is an effective media of lifelong education. National Education Policy of Education (1986) has rightly explained the life-long education—It is a cherished goal of educational process. This presupposes universal literacy. Opportunities will be provided to the youth, housewife, agricultural and industrial workers and professionals to continue the education of their choice, at the pace suited to them. The future thrust will be in the direction of open and distance learning. National Education Policy 1986 has rightly stressed that Distance Education will provide many opportunities for education and will lessen the burden of formal education. The advantages of Distance Education are as under:

Reliable

Distance education is reliable. It has the cost-effective alternative and new means of communication.

Education at Learners' Door

Distance education is the only way which provide the education to the learner at his door. It provides equal educational opportunities even to those who used to live in remote areas.

Beneficial to Adults

Distance education provides many benefits to adults. They may up-to-date themselves for the development of skills and knowledge.

Variety of Programme

Distance education provides variety programmes according to the needs of the learners.

Co-ordination

Distance education is the co-ordination of various educational factors, i.e., general, basic, professional, technical, lifelong, in-service and expansion.

Minimising Pressures

Distance education minimizes the educational pressures caused by the explosion on population.

Educational Needs

Distance education fulfills the need of society through variety of educational programmes.

Learner Centred

Distance education is learner. A learner learns according to his needs, conditions and facility.

Lust for Knowledge

Distance education provides the opportunities to gain knowledge to those who are really thirsty for it.

The Opportunities Offered in Distance Education

Globalisation of distance education provides many opportunities for developing countries for the realisation of the systemic goals of which the following are crucial:

More Access

The MBA programmes offered by institutions in America, Canada, Australia, Britain etc., are now available in most parts of the developing countries. This is true of many other programmes offered by developed countries, which are available in many developing countries. The learners in developing countries have access to education and training programmes offered by many developed countries. The 'foreign degrees', can be acquired now without the learners going to foreign countries. Many developing countries with limited educational resources can have wider access to the world educational and training resources to supplement and complement their efforts to provide education to large numbers. The satellite technologies are extensively used by developed countries to beam their educational programmes to remote areas in countries like India. There are more responses to the market demands to meet the educational and training needs in technical and professional areas like management, computer applications, education, multi-media etc. The list of foreign institutions offering distance education programmes in India is very large, varied and impressive. This has certainly resulted in widening the access to foreign education to people in India.

Learning from Others' Experience

The instant connectivity of resource persons and the easy accessibility of resource materials in distance education made possible by the communication technologies, help in learning from others expertise and experience. The different methods adopted by distance education institutions in the development, production and delivery of materials is easily available to others through database systems. The information technology has made the distance education processes and the products more open enabling others to use and build on the existing knowledge and practices. Globalisation in this sense further facilitates the process of learning from others' experiences.

Partnerships for Enrichment

The saying "Two is better than one" is as true in distance education as in many other areas. The partnership arrangements between the players located in different countries, make it possible again through technologies, and can contribute to providing services, which are beyond the capacity of any one institution. The partnership in developing the distance education materials in certain areas of global concerns like environment, gender equality, human rights etc., will certainly complement the expertise and resources and facilitating the production of better learning materials. The partnership between the Commonwealth of Learning (COL), Canada and Indira Gandhi National Open University, India in offering the Masters Programme in Distance Education (MPDE) under the Rajiv Gandhi Fellowship scheme is one such example of international partnership activity facilitated by the process of globalisation. The European Union activities in the promotion of distance education are also influenced by a wider processes of globalisation (John Field, 1995). The educational needs of small developing countries can be met effectively by the partnership arrangements particularly in the development of learning materials, which is a very capital-intensive activity in distance education.

Competitive Environment

The wider access also may result in heightening the competitive environment. For example, as mentioned earlier, some of the world's best management and computer programmes developed in certain advanced countries are available to many in other countries, including the developing ones. This, it is hoped, will ignite the spirit of competition among the local institutions. The breaking up of borders [sic] by technology may threaten the survival [sic] of mediocre institutions/programmes. The exposure to the best may motivate others to improve their own performance. The free market may reject the non-performers. The globalised distance education programmes of institutions with a spirit of performance, may bring competitiveness in the working of local distance education institutions. This process may result in better institutional performance.

The Challenges of Distance Education

The globalisation of distance education should be approached from the perspectives of its impact on the developing countries that are mostly at the receiving end. Some of the challenges and dilemmas faced by these countries are:

Globalisation and Neo-Colonialism

In situation of uneven development the information

superhighways may be used more for 'invasion' than for access. More access may result in the danger of certain sets of countries dominating the educational scene of countries with less resource. Terry Evans rightly observes that "globalisation presents nations with a dilemma: they access the world, but the world invades them" (Terry Evans, 1995). The access is also driven by market demands, which need not necessarily reflect the national needs of countries at the receiving end. Added to this the access to global programmes, is mostly restricted to more affluent sections of society in view of the costs involved. This may further accentuate the educational inequalities in developing countries. In the highly differentiated world, the virtual world has not shrunk uniformly. So the access also is not uniform within a country and among the countries. To some of the countries in the developed world globalisation may only mean liberal access to the markets of developing nations. The unequal competition may result in small fish being swallowed by big fish. Those of us who feel exited about information superhighways, should also be aware of limitations of the use of superhighways in developing countries since so far it has been mostly a one way traffic highway—from developed countries to developing countries. The partnership arrangements may result in assigning a secondary role to institutions for the developing countries loosing [sic] their initiative and self-identity. These fears persuade many to consider globalisation as another form of neo-colonialism.

Globalisation Versus Localisation

The paradox of globalisation is that it is also accompanied by a strong urge for localisation (John Field, 1995). The development of distance education materials programmes for the world may be an impossible task. At present the materials developed in one context are mostly used in a wider context. Developing relevant curriculum for the international context is a difficult task. More difficult is getting the educational materials developed in a particular cultural context to suit a different cultural context. The generic materials in distance education that may be global in nature may have to be supplemented by national/region specific materials to make the global distance education programmes more relevant. This is also one of the lessons offered by the experience of IGNOU in offering the MADE programme internationally. Localisation also emphasises the importance of bringing cultural sensitivities into global materials. Learning is a cultural activity, after all. The globalised learning materials and the delivery systems should take into account the diversity of the world cultural context. The learners' needs may also vary accordingly (Janet Jenkins, 1996). Even though it is said that a global distance educator should "think globally and act locally", we can also observe a contradictory trend operating here "thinking locally and acting globally". Developing the materials/programmes keeping in view one's own context, and offering the programmes internationally more to cash in on the market demands is what we mean by "thinking locally and acting globally".

Global Vision Versus Market Vision

Globalisation should have a vision of using global resources for human development. Globalisation will then, help in entering into collaborative arrangements for pooling of world resources to realise the shared vision of 'one world'. The alternative possibility is that the more resource-endowed countries to create and exploit the market demands in developing countries for profit making may take the globalisation process. This profit making drive of collaborative arrangements may distort the social priorities of education. In this situation the international partnership arrangements will be driven more by profit motives, favouring developed countries and allowing a few visits to foreign lands by 'educationists' of developing countries. The partnership arrangements in an unfair competitive situation may not bring any substantial benefits to learners in developing countries.

Infrastructural Deficiencies

Even though the information superhighways provide opportunities of global transfer of knowledge, the developing countries are not yet properly equipped [sic] with necessary exportable goods (knowledge) and vehicles (technology) to use the superhighways. The outdated telecom facilities, high costs of connection, low levels of technological awareness and bureaucratic interference in using the technology may inhibit the countries like

India to actively participate in the global provision of distance education programmes. The inability to use modem communication systems and resultant delay in communication is one of the problems faced by IGNOU in operationalising one of its international programmes in developing countries.

The Response

Globalisation is of course, a reality of the modem world. The flow of information across the world is now effectively beyond the control of national governments. We cannot wish away the trends of globalisation in distance education on the pleas of neo-colonialism, cultural sensitivity, lack of social relevance etc. The critique in the earlier sections of this chapter should be viewed more in the perspective of self-understanding of limitations in order to overcome them. We may have to properly equip developing countries to live with globalisation with honour and purpose. Some of the measures that may help in this direction are:

Selective Approach

The international collaborative arrangements should be based on national priorities as identified by appropriate authorities at the national level. In defining the rules of competition, the nation concerned should use its privilege of regulation to protect its national interest. The selective approach should also emphasise more on accessability [sic] and transfer of knowhow of distance education than on materials and programmes. This would strengthen the self-sustainability of institutions in developing countries.

Value Addition

The local institutions, as partners in the international collaboration, can play an effective and critical role only when they are capable of making value addition to the process. This value addition should take care of localisation of materials and services, adaptation of materials, sensitisation of the processes to the local cultures etc. This type of contribution will neutralise the possible dominance [sic] of resource rich outside agencies.

State Intervention

The nation state may have to actively intervene to minimise the distortions of globalisation processes. The state should subsidise and support the learners from the weaker sections of society to use the opportunities of global distance education programmes. The state can also play an important role in building the necessary information technology infrastructure for enabling the distance education institutions in developing countries to participate as equal partners in global distance education programmes.

Role of International Agencies

The international agencies like COL, Asian Development Bank, UNESCO, World Bank etc. can play a very important level playing role in the promotion of globalisation of distance education. The international agencies can strengthen the competencies of distance education institutions in the developing countries to cooperate and collaborate with institutions in the developed countries on equal terms. The COL is making efforts in this direction by building databank on reliable and comprehensive information on distance education, Commonwealth Credit Bank for transfer of programmer and credits etc. (Gajaraj Dhanarajan, 1996). The other international agencies also should develop norms and guidelines for global distance education programmes to ensure the elimination of unfair competitive practices.

Concluding Remarks

It is not enough if we merely log on to world trends; we must also build the capacities to do so on our terms. This is the common and basic challenge faced by developing countries in the globalisation of distance education particularly in the context of uneven world development. Globalisation as in other fields, in the field of distance education is also not an unmied [sic] blessing. There are opportunities and limitations. The Mahatma Gandhi's dictum that let all the windows be open and the wind blow from all the directions, but one should not loose one's feet firmly rooted in one's own soil should guide the approach of distance education institutions in the developing countries responding to the globalisation processes.

Homeberg has rightly said that this system influenced the outlook and perspective of the learner. This system is made them a critic and remove their doubts. The feeling of co-ordination is developed. There is a solution to remove unemployment by providing them up-to-date knowledge and skill, fine behaviour and impressionistic discipline.

Open University is a vital organization to meet the demand of the growing higher levels of learners. Those who have not enjoyed any opportunities, may get the chance to filfil their ambitions. The persons, who are working on the basis of old knowledge and skill may also keep themselves up-to-date.

Open Universities are trying their best to minimize pressures of the regular system of higher education by using the means of communication. In new education policy, it is said that modern technology of communication has controlled over the time and space. This technology has opened new dimensions in the field of teaching, learning and national development. To improve the quality of teachers training, in-service programmes, consciousness towards art and culture, developing permanent human values, this system will be a boon.

It is hoped that Open Universities, to be opened under new education policy will cater the need and aspirations of the masses. The objective of new policy is to prepare the manpower for national development; such type of manpower who is not merely the dehree earner but in real sense curious and thinkers. We need such type of education which cater the real knowledge and skill among the learners instead of spoon feeding by the teachers. There must be development of thoughtful-process which is responsible for the exposition of the inner self. India is committed for the exchange of knowledge and national development; therefore it is necessary to provide the maximum opportunities of fastly growing and emerging knowledge to the citizens of India.

REFERENCES

1. Gajaraj Dhanarajan, *Response to Tony Pritchard,* Open Praxis, Vol. 1, 1996.
2. Janet Jenkins, *Response to Tony Pritchard,* Open Praxis, Vol. 1, 1996.
3. John Field, *Globalisation, Consumption and the Learning Business, Distance Education,* Vol. 16, No. 2, 1995.

4. K.B. Pawar, Information Technology and Higher Education: The Indian Context, *Universities News*, 25 November, 1996.
5. Kiran Karnik, Emerging Communication Scenario, Mainstream, August 24, 1996.
6. Richard Edwards, *Different Discourses, Discourses of Difference: Globalisation, Distance Education and Open Learning, Distance Education*, Vol. 16, No. 2, 1995.
7. Richard Edwards, *From a Distance? Globalisation, Space-time, Compression and Distance Education, Open Learning*, November, 1994.
8. Terry Evans, Globalisation, Post-fordism and Open and Distance Education, *Distance Education*, Vol. 16, No. 2, 1995.
9. Tony Pritchard, *Globalisation of Distance Learning*, Open Praxis, Vol. 1, 1996.
10. IGNOU, "Media in Distance Education", *Communication Technology for Distance Education* (2001), ES-318.
11. Sukumar, B. (2001), IGNOU Interactive Radio Counselling: A Study, *IJOL*, 10(1), pp. 80-92.
12. Rajagopalan, T.S. and Rajan, T.N., Technology Information Base in India: A Development Perspective. In E.V. Smith and S. Keenan (eds.), *Information, Communication and Technology*, Amsterdam, Elsevier Science Publishers, pp. 441-50, 1987.
13. Salam, A., *Ideals and Realities*, Singapore: World Scientific, 1987.
14. IGNOU (2001), "Growth of Communication Technology", *Communication Technology for Distance Education*, ES-318, pp. 34-40.
15. Bansal, Kiron and Chaudhary, Sonvir, S., (1999), "Interactive Radio for Supporting Distance Education: An Evaluative Study", *Indian Journal of Open Learning*.
16. Sukumar, B. (2001), IGNOU Interactive Radio Counselling: A Study, *IJOL*, 10(1), pp. 80-92.
17. Choudhary, S.V. (1992), "Television in distance education: The Indian scenario", *Indian Journal of Open Learning*, 1(1), p. 23.
18 Choudhary, Sonvir and Behari, Shyam (1994), Modasa Experiment: Distance teaching through cable TV network system, *Indian Journal of Open Learning* 3(1), pp. 24-28.

13

Role of Education and Its Impact on Women in Developing Countries

MS. DIPTI SINGH

The literature on women in developing countries is increasingly being enriched by the research of women scholars, some of whom are not native to the geographical area of their special interest. They identify as "insiders" based on gender rather than nationality, and no longer hesitate to make international comparisons.

It is to this body of international literature that we hope to contribute, as we analyze the changing set of options and constraints.experienced by a sample of highly educated Indian women.

Women has enlarged our scientific knowledge about societies. This provides a concrete base of intellectual leaders hoping to help guide their nations in the development process. A prime example of the use of research for policy purposes is the report of the Committee on the Status of Women in India, *Towards Equality* (Government of India, 1974). The report, issued after the publication of our first book, drew upon original studies and recent literature. It reflects the concern of India and other developing nations for uplifting the masses of their women.

Male Dominance and Female Roles

In most societies of the world, women have been defined largely in terms of their functions as wives and mothers, and by cultural images of their sexuality. The rights of women to become educated and to hold jobs outside of the home have frequently been questioned; women who have had to work have tended to be of low economic and social status. Much of the early thrust of the American women's movement of the 1970's was directed toward the right of married women to be employed outside of the home and to be freed from total preoccupation with child care. Feminists tried to shatter long-held notions about "women's place" and the accepted myths about their nature and function. Women whose economic status left them no choice but to work were still faced with the dual burden of employment and household duties.

There is no doubt that many of most Indian women do accept their traditional role of dependence on male relatives. But as the possibility of economic independence, through respectable employment, becomes a reality for middle class Indian women, they may be allowed new options.

The economic, political and social changes that combine together to create innovations need to be placed in their cultural context. That such changes have occurred in the lives of a number of urban middle class Indian women is not doubted. The reformist movements of the last two centuries, the current needs and aspirations of middle class families, and the new opportunity for female education and employment, all interact to foster change.

The growth of a nation lies in its capacity to elevate the lot of the weakest section of its society. **Pandit Jawaharlal Nehru had rightly stated: "The status of women indicates the character of country."** In India the status of women has been many ups and downs since the ancient Vedic times to the present day. During the Vedic period, girls were also welcome in a family; they were given equal education; their age of marriage was after maturation and they could select the mate of their own choice—through the tradition of "Swayamvar". They had independence for decision making, enjoyed power and participated in political, cultural and literacy activities. They had control over finances, agriculture and general welfare. This period in history, could also be called a golden era. Then came to Brahmanic period and the code as given by Manu. According to **Tikoo** (1985), "In Manu Samhita, ideas about womanhood are laid down, and morality is assigned in authoritarian codes which bring down women to the level of sub-species."

In the last five years the Government of India has brought forth many amendments in law to give women an equal right and status—a full ministry of social and women's welfare has been formed in 1985. Yet women in India face some of the most heinous crimes committed against them, such as rape, flesh trade, foeticide, female infanticide, child abuse, wife battering, dowry deaths, sati, financial exploitation, sexual exploitation of working women and female students. Law is there to prevent all this, yet we find women oppressed, exploited, cheated, uneducated, financially dependents, mentally cloisted, morally run down and physically violated. A country's socio-economic growth cannot take place if half of its population is down and trodden.

A **famous Chinese** saying goes like this "if you want to plan for a year plant wheat, if you wish to plan for ten years grow trees but if you want to plan for 100 years educate your women". How true it is that if the head that is rocking the cradle is weak, psychologically depleted, what could be the future of the progeny. So much is being talked about poverty elevation programmes from socio-economic point of view, but little is being said about the individual psyche. **Pareek** (1970) defined poverty psychologically in terms of "deprivation and helplessness".

She has many frustrations and lack of recognition. As **Sinha** (1983) described that a poor man encounters failure and frustration, and due to poor academic attainments, is rendered less capable to combat his poverty, isn't this also the case with females? Failure is in-built in their rearing up practices, then cultural norms weight heavy on their shoulder, lack of education makes them more superstitious and prone to prejudicial thinking. This becomes a wending vicious circle.

Development of Self

In understanding the female psyche we have to understand the growth of herself. In the growth of self also some sex-role linked attitudes are developed. **Lenore Walker** (1977) said that the attitude of passivity in women takes a form of fatalism-learned dependency of helplessness established early in life. "It seems highly probable that girls, through their socialization in learning the traditional women's role, also learn that they have direct little control over their lives no matter what they do." A woman's self-concept revolves around the basic belief that she is the weaker sex and has always to look upon the man for her maintenance. As a concept developed by Mohan (1988) she suffers from "Hanuman

Complex"—i.e., not knowing her true strength and harping more on incapability. Somewhat similar thought is found in the work of Miller (1976) when she says, "In a situation of inequality and powerlessness, these characteristics can lead to subservience and to complex psychological problems."

Opportunity for Work

Women will have to be trained to be financially independent and self-sufficient. Financial dependency on someone, can lead to many complexes and feelings of worthlessness and sub-servience. Women have been doing household chores which itself is a full time job plus child bearing and rearing—yet for all this work, she has no financial backing.

Role Conflict

According to Mohan and Kapur (1985) though more and more women are taking up work, yet they have also faced a lot of role conflict. Earlier they were supposed to belong only to home and its responsibilities. Today the working women is torn by the conflict that if she goes to work, she is neglecting her home and children. She feels it is her responsibility to do both the jobs efficiently. In this process she develops feelings of guilt of not devoting full time to her children and home. As a result she doubles her effort. This furthering of effort tells upon her mental and physical well-being. In the cases where the wife demands the husband to share household chores, tension starts mounting and family disputes take place.

Nilanjana Mukherji (1985) writes in Femina "with inflexible standards to meet at both home and work, the working woman is thus always chasing an impossible ideal."

The women are facing a lot of conflict. To compete with men a women has to be twice as good to get half of what she deserve. If she is not all that competent then either she faces stagnation into lower jobs or she is sexually exploited by her bosses with the lure of job enhancement. Another problem arises when women doing the same amount of work are not paid the same wages. Sometimes on daily or weekly waged jobs there is again sexual exploitation.

Working women is the entry into marriage market. Even if a girl is working and earning, dowry is still to be paid. Sometimes marriage even means a sacrifice of a professional career, or if a woman is as qualified or better, than her would be, then she has to face the wrath of his insecure ego, male chauvenism, and false pride. In order to secure marriage—she sacrifices her career and promotions. Besides the tension which is thus generated takes a heavy toll of her work performance.

The process of modernisation brought many changes in the society. The change is fast in advanced countries whereas it is slow in developing countries. When modernisation takes roots in the society, it not only affects the structure of the society but also the values and attitudes that are held by the members of that society. Women are not exception to it.

The pre-modern societies encouraged dominance-dependence and obedience-loyalty relationship whereas modern societies lay emphasis on independence, individuality, equality and companionship in the relations of man and woman. This is due to the expansion of educational and employment opportunities. Women no longer believe the natural superiority of man over woman. Instead they feel that modern women would enjoy greater equality in their relations with men. A few assumptions are put forward here to measure the modernity of women employees.

In the present day, a woman may be called modern:

(*a*) If she is free to choose her husband.
(*b*) If she does not expect her first child to be a boy.
(*c*) If she believes in divorce and co-education system of education.
(*d*) If she is free from the joint family.
(*e*) If she does not believe in the natural superiority of man over woman.
(*f*) If she has a greater say in the family matters.
(*g*) If she associates herself with the activities of trade unions and associations.
(*h*) If she does not believe ritual and worship aspects of religions.

The purpose to examine whether women employees feel themselves modern, whether they possess the modern qualities or whether the modernisation of the society affected their lives or not.

Opinion on Celebration of Marriage

Due to the arranged marriage system traditional performance of marriage is being in practice in almost all the societies. Under the traditional marriage, it is believed that marriages are irrevocable and both the partners should bind together until death. Whereas under registration and under the Marriage Act of 1955 the marriages have become contractional basis where both partners can live together if they like each other or can get separated if incompatible.

Respondents' Friendliness with Male Colleagues

As the public service is dominated by men, women have to work along with male colleagues at office. The study shows that 97.3 per cent respondents are friendly with their co-workers while others are not. This also shows the attitude of men. They have accepted the fact that women are their co-workers and not as women.

The respondents who are not friendly are more in teaching department (5 %) compared to others. This can be due to the professional jealousy and politics in the educational institutions.

Similarly, Hate in her study also found that 95 per cent of the respondents have satisfactory relations with co-workers while only 3 per cent complain that this is not the case. The rest have not replied.

Continue the Job if Transfer Occurs to Either of Them

The data show that 43.1 per cent respondents are willing to do their jobs even if transfer occurs to either of them and they have to stay away from their husbands. Thirty-one per cent are not willing to stay away from their husbands. This is so because their family relations may get disturbed. However, 35.5 per cent feel that they will not face such circumstances because even if one of them is transferred, they will get a transfer to the same place after some time. They can work together at one place according to the Government Order (G.O.). Similarly, Kala Rani's study shows 57 respondents out of 150 liked to continue in jobs and 79 preferred to give up their job, if either of them is transferred and has to live alone.

Husbands Feeling Towards Respondents' Occupational Position

Husband's attitude of trustfulness towards wife's character and his attitude of pride towards her occupational or professional achievements helps her to carry out her job with pride and without tensions. Reveals that 52.2 per cent respondents husbands are neither jealous nor take pride and 36.6 per cent respondents take great pride in respondents occupational position.

That 54 per cent Class-I officers and 54.6 per cent teaching respondents husbands take pride in their wife's employment. These services are considered to be respectable hence their husbands take pride.

This was due to the fact that they felt emotionally insecure, on account of his wife's working for a job in such an environment where she comes across other men and was likely to make friends with them.

In Kala Rani's study 103 out of 150 women felt that their husbands took pride in their occupational achievement while 47 husbands do not feel so.

Describe to do the Job Even if Husband's Salary is Enough

An attempt is made to know whether women work only if their family income is inadequate. The data show that 71 per cent of the respondents have desire to do the job even if their husbands salary is enough to their family expenses. These respondents want to contribute something as a human being and do not want to waste their education. Desire to work is more in Class-I (85.7%), teaching (90.9%) and Medical (83.7%) respondents. These jobs are respectable and high income earning jobs and they do not like to leave their jobs even if their husband's salary is enough. It seems once women starts earning money, they do not feel like sitting at home idle and also do not want to lose their financial freedom.

Submission of Women to Man

The data indicate that 91.3 per cent respondents feel that women should be submissive to man but feel equal. They believe in women's liberation movement and demand that women should be treated on par with men but not inferior.

Employed women who have their own independent income will influence their status and may bring about changes in the family structure.

In Ramanamma's study 81 respondents out of 505, both married and unmarried, wanted equality in everything.

Freedom to Spend One's Earning

Though woman work as the sole supporter or additional bread winner of the family it does not mean that some maintains full control over her income. The same is put before the respondents.

Revels that 70.3 per cent of the respondents are free to spend their earnings and 7 per cent respondents do not have financial freedom, 22.7 per cent respondents are sometimes not free to spend their earnings. The married respondents in Class-I (82.7%), Class-II (77.8%), P&T (74.3%) and Medical (72.1%) services have more financial freedom than others.

The present study Goldstein found that 77 per cent of the employed women in her sample of highly educated turned over more than half of their earning to their families. The fact that women usually earn less than men does not necessarily mean that their contribution towards the basic needs of the family is also less.

This reveals that there is a link between the employment status and freedom to spend. Women in financially better positions have more freedom as compared to others. The income-earned by the employees in less paid jobs are low and the income of the wife is not necessarily the primary source and generally lower than their husbands, have less financial freedom.

Women's contribution to the family income would enable her to have a voice in the spending of that income and greater co-operation and respect from other family members. Hence, her share of authority in spending the family income has been considered as a rough approximation of the economic power of a woman in the family.

Freedom to Spend One's Earning in Relation to Age

Freedom to spend their earnings is increasing with the increase in age. Ninety per cent respondents in the age group of above 45 years are more free to spend their earnings than 20-25 (65.9%), 26-35 (69.9%) and 36-45 (71.4%) age group respondents. This is so because as the age increases their command over the family also increases.

Freedom to Spend One's Earning in Relation to Education

Freedom to spend one's earnings in increasing with the increase in education. Postgraduates (75) have more freedom to spend compared to graduates (71) and matriculates (66). Graduate respondents in Class (55.2), Class-II (66.7), Banking (50.0) and P&T (54.3%) have more financial freedom than others. Postgraduates in teaching (54.5) and medical services (32.5) have freedom to spend their earnings. This is due to their professional education.

Indicates that more the education the more is the financial freedom.

It may be said that if we wish a nation to develop, then, half of its population of females must also grow—educate her self-sufficient and have a positive self-image and development. This is also going to be a harbinger of social change for families, communities and nation. Without the all round development of individuals not much can be achieved at the national level.

14

Role of Education and Rural Women Empowerment in Developing Countries

DR. MEENU AGRAWAL AND
DR. PRATIMA KUMARI

"Education never ends. It is a series of lessons with the greatest for the last." *The Adventure of the Red circle by Arthur. C. Doyle.*

For more than 40 years, different stakeholders have partnered to support the development of basic education throughout the developing countries. Since independence, the progression achieved in education in developing countries has been remarkable. This massive expansion has been made possible by the infusion of large sums of money by the new governments who saw the expansion of education opportunity as a political necessity. Human development is partly a matter of people and communities improving their own lives and taking greater control of their destinies. Education is broadly used as an instrument for social change.

Harbison and Hanushek (1992) said that a country that is unable to develop the skills and knowledge of its people and to utilize them effectively in the national economy would be unable to develop anything else. And according to Psacharopoulos (1985, p. 5), education is widely regarded as the route to economic prosperity, the key to scientific and technological advancement, the means to combat unemployment, the foundation of social equity, and the spread of political socialization and cultural vitality. One can also make up an intricate argument in that educating all the children provides stratification costs to oneself and one's children since only in this way will one protect one's own rights. Equalizing the welfare of the individual in society is therefore an important modern desideratum.

This article discusses the issues surrounding these problems. Relevant, locally controlled educational programmes play key roles in rural development in developing nations. Education has a desirable controlling influence over development of the rural individual, family, community, and society, leading to reduced poverty, income equity, and controlled unemployment. The failure of trickle-down development and recognition of the importance of rural areas and rural people to the economic emancipation of developing countries has given education a key role in rural systems of supply, production, marketing, personnel maintenance, education, health care, and governance. Functions of education include imparting social change, improving individual social position and standard of living, activating participation in rural and cultural development, increasing critical abilities of rural people to diagnose their needs, assert their rights, and take greater control of decisions affecting their lives, providing trained manpower in rural areas, linking rural and urban sectors, providing employment and income opportunities, increasing labour force productivity, and developing leadership. Education oriented to urban rather than rural needs may do more harm than good by accelerating rural to urban migration, generating youth unemployment, and leaving students ill-equipped to succeed in a rural environment. Education contributing to rural development must be locally controlled, practical, applied, problem posing, and focused on functional specialization.

Poor women, especially from backward communities and lower castes, are mostly illiterate, untrained, and have very little social and economic status. In India, there are over 350 million such people, mainly in rural areas. The unemployed are nearly 200 million people, a great majority of them belonging to these deprived sections of the society. Without meaningful skills, social status, and economic power, they are unable to do any business on their own even with financial assistance.

In the village societies, the caste system is deeply entrenched. The lower caste colonies are ostracized and basic facilities are denied to them. Female infanticide is a common practice and women are punished socially for bearing girl children. Gender biases are very evident in the preferential treatment given to the male child. Rural women still remain a disadvantaged segment of Indian society. Statistics show that whereas 86.1 per cent females are engaged in agriculture, the figure of males is 74 per cent. But there are hardly any special programmes for enhancing women's agricultural skills. While 7.1 per cent rural females are engaged in manufacturing, the percentage for rural males is 7 i.e. less than that of females. But most of the training programmes have hardly any female participation. While rural males have opportunities in construction, trade, transport, storage, and services, these are mostly denied to rural females. Obviously, opportunities must be created to enable them to acquire the skills necessary for entering these newly emerging occupations.

In the field of primary education, the system calls for much overhaul since centralized curricula, heavy textbooks, centralized teacher recruitment, orthodox pedagogy, unsuitable school-timings and vacations, rigid and distrustful supervision and administration, have been the main hurdles in its reaching the rural masses. Besides, the primary system is traditionally connected with secondary general education. Productive skills and the cultural contexts of education are ignored. The solution now perceived by India's educational thinkers and planners is liberation of the education system through a movement for adult literacy and non-formal alternatives for meeting the urgent as well as long-term needs of the rural and tribal people, especially women. Science and technology components are visualized as essential educational elements for future-oriented education. Lifelong learning through alternatives in education, especially continuing education for diverse needs and groups, is, therefore, the main concern of Indian reformers. This article emphasizes that rural women's mindset of 'dependency' must be changed so that they become conscious of their abilities to change themselves, their families, and their community. Their empowerment would lie in becoming creative, self-dependent, individuals.

The principle of gender equality is enshrined in the Indian Constitution in its Preamble, Fundamental Rights, Fundamental Duties and Directive Principles. The Constitution not only grants equality to women, but also empowers the State to adopt measures of positive discrimination in favour of women. Women, as a separate target group, account for 407.8 million (including girl children) as per 1991 census and constitute 48.1 per cent of the country's total population are still now have-nots even among the have-nots, because historically and traditionally women are denied the vital rights of taking decision and share in her family income. Women in whichever economic class, are thus completely dependent on men, resulting in their lack of bargaining power even in matters of marriage, divorce and remarriage etc. not to speak of the absence of any rights whatsoever in matters related to land, other properties and her personal or family income. The principles of gender equality and equity and protection of women's rights have been the prime concerns in Indian thinking right from the days of independence. It is a myth or reality.

Within the framework of a democratic polity, our laws, development policies, plans and programmes have aimed at women's advancement in different spheres. From the Fifth Five Year Plan (1974-78) onwards has been a marked shift in the approach to women's issues from welfare to development. In recent years, the empowerment of women has been recognized as the central issue in determining the status of women. The National Commission for Women was set up by an Act of Parliament in 1990 to safeguard the rights and legal entitlements of women. The 73rd and 74th Amendments (1993) to the Constitution of India have provided for reservation of seats in the local bodies of Panchayats and Municipalities for women, laying a strong foundation for their participation in decision-making at the local levels.

Goal and Objectives

The goal of this policy is to bring about the advancement, development and empowerment of women. The policy will be widely disseminated so as to encourage active participation of all stakeholders for achieving its goals. Specifically, the objectives of this policy include:

(*i*) Creating an environment through positive economic and social policies for full development of women to enable them to realize their full potential.

(*ii*) The *de-jure* and *de-facto* enjoyment of all human rights and fundamental freedom by women on equal basis with men in all spheres—political, economic, social, cultural and civil.

(*iii*) Equal access to participation and decision-making of women in social, political and economic life of the nation.

(*iv*) Equal access to women to health care, quality education at all levels, career and vocational guidance, employment, equal remuneration, occupational health and safety, social security and public office etc.

(*v*) Strengthening legal systems aimed at elimination of all forms of discrimination against women.

(*vi*) Changing societal attitudes and community practices by active participation and involvement of both men and women.

(*vii*) Mainstreaming a gender perspective in the development process.

(*viii*) Elimination of discrimination and all forms of violence against women and the girl child.

(*ix*) Building and strengthening partnerships with civil society, particularly women's organizations.

Policy Prescriptions

Decision-Making

Women's equality in power sharing and active participation in decision-making, including decision-making in political process at all levels have ensured by the role of education for the achievement of the goals of empowerment. All measures will be taken to guarantee women equal access to and full participation in decision-making bodies at every level, including the legislative, executive, judicial, corporate, statutory bodies, as also the Advisory Commissions, Committees, Boards, Trusts etc. Affirmative action such as reservations/quotas, including in higher legislative bodies, will be considered whenever necessary on a time bound basis. Women-friendly personnel policies will also be drawn up to encourage women to participate effectively in the developmental process.

Economic Empowerment of Women

Poverty Eradication

Education and training play an essential role in reducing women's poverty. For reducing the poverty and the development the commission sets out some priorities for the community, namely:

- Basic education for women, in particular primary education, and women teacher training.
- Work-related training.
- Higher education for women, in particular at regional level.
- Improving school access opportunities and moving towards free and compulsory primary education for girls and women.
- Reducing existing gender-based inequalities in relation to access to education by promoting the participation of women.
- Paying greater attention to the impact of AIDS on education systems and improving the prevention of the disease through education.
- To increase education knowledge programmes for women for the development.

In spite of the vital role of basic education, it is also important to ensure balanced development of education, in other words improved education systems at all levels.

Since women comprise the majority of the population below the poverty line and are very often in situations of extreme poverty, given the harsh realities of intra-household and social discrimination, macro-economic policies and poverty eradication programmes will specifically address the needs and problems of such women. There will be improved implementation of programmes which are already women-oriented with special targets for women. Steps will be taken for mobilization of poor women and convergence of services, by offering them a range of economic and social options, along with necessary support measures to enhance their capabilities.

Micro-Credit

In order to enhance women's access to credit for consumption and production, the establishment of new, and strengthening of existing micro-credit mechanisms and micro-finance institution will be undertaken so that the outreach of credit is enhanced. Other supportive measures would be taken to ensure adequate flow of credit through extant financial institutions and banks, so that all women below poverty line have easy access to credit.

Women and Economy

Women's perspectives will be included in designing and implementing macro-economic and social policies. Their contribution to socio-economic development as producers and workers will be recognized in the formal and informal sectors (including home based workers) and appropriate policies relating to employment and to her working conditions will be drawn up. Such measures could include:

- Reinterpretation and redefinition of conventional concepts of work wherever necessary e.g. in the census records, to reflect women's contribution as producers and workers.
- Preparation of satellite and national accounts.

Globalization

Globalization has presented new challenges for the realization of the goal of women's equality, the gender impact of which has not been systematically evaluated fully. However, from the micro-level studies that were commissioned by the Department of Women and Child Development, it is evident that there is a need for re-framing policies for access to employment and quality of employment. Benefits of the growing global economy have been unevenly distributed leading to wider economic disparities, the feminization of poverty, increased gender inequality through often deteriorating working conditions and unsafe working environment especially in the informal economy and rural areas. Strategies will be designed to enhance the capacity of women and empower them to meet the negative social and economic impacts, which may flow from the globalization process.

Women and Agriculture

It is clear that education in agriculture plays an important role in preparing farmers, researchers, educators, extension staff, members of agro-businesses and others to make productive contributions. A critical issue in the 21st century will be the changes and adaptations required in agricultural education in order for it to more effectively contribute to improved food security, sustainable agricultural production and rural development.

Reduced funding for primary and secondary education in rural areas means poorer educational standards. In many developing countries, rural youth women find difficulty in obtaining a basic education of the same quality as urban youth women, and hence have difficulty in gaining entrance to higher education institutions. The result is a significant waste of human resources.

In view of the critical role of women in the agriculture and allied sectors, as producers, concentrated efforts will be made to ensure that benefits of training, extension and various programmes will reach them in proportion to their numbers. The programmes for training women in soil conservation, social forestry, dairy development and other occupations allied to agriculture like horticulture, livestock including small animal husbandry, poultry, fisheries etc. will be expanded to benefit women workers in the agriculture sector.

Gender Issues in Agricultural Education

Women play a major role in the world's agricultural production systems. In the less developed countries, an estimated one-third of all rural households are managed by women. In Sub-Saharan Africa and the Caribbean, women produce 60-80 per cent of basic foodstuffs, while in Asia they perform over 50 per cent of the labour involved in intensive rice cultivation. In recent years, there has been widespread recognition of the vital roles played by women in all areas of agriculture and the need for women to have access, through formal and non-formal training, to the knowledge and skills needed for improved agricultural production, processing and marketing. Extension agents, researchers, teachers and students all need to be educated and informed about rural women's problems, potentials and aspirations.

The 1991 FAO expert consultation urged that special efforts be made to recruit and support female students from rural areas who could become extension agents, agricultural researchers, teachers and policy-makers. One of the reasons why there are few women extension workers, researchers and other agricultural professionals is the small number of female graduates from intermediate and higher-level agricultural education institutions. Yet, there are various countries where the enrolments of women are proportionately high. On average in Africa, FAO data show that there has been a 10 per cent increase from 1983 to 1993 from about 15 to 25 per cent female enrolment in agricultural education institutions.

The question of how to attract more female students to agricultural disciplines is linked to the issue of encouraging students from rural areas to enter higher education. As noted above, the number of female students has increased over the past ten years and this trend should be supported and encouraged. Also, more role models for young women to emulate are needed, including teachers in agricultural education institutions. Raising the number of women in agricultural education, both as educators, administrators and students is important as a means of reinforcing a commitment to understanding and changing the status of women in agriculture.

Educators need to become more responsive to gender related issues by taking into account women's roles and contributions in the total agricultural industry. While there is a trend for increased enrolment of women students in agricultural sciences at the technical or higher levels, this has not resulted in the dissemination of improved technology to women farmers because few female graduates are employed in extension work. Agricultural education institutions may increasingly have gender-sensitive admittance policies, but due to traditional barriers female graduates continue to have problems finding employment in agriculture (Crowder, 1998). Strategies, curricula, and policy shifts need to emphasize and include women as role models and leaders in agriculture.

Gender-sensitive policies have, at best, resulted in training programmes in which women are treated equally with men. However, it is not only the equal treatment of women that is important, it is equal employment benefits that are important. Equal treatment does not necessarily lead to equal benefits for women; indeed, the treatment may have to be different in order to take into consideration the different needs, time constraints and productive activities of women.

Gender-sensitive educational policies should be developed

with a wide-range of stakeholders, including community leaders, politicians, potential employers and especially women themselves. Measures should be put in place to encourage young women and better prepare them to take up agricultural studies. For example, special attention should be paid to revising admissions policies that discriminate against women and to the creation of special scholarships for women to study agriculture. There is also a need to provide gender sensitisation courses for teaching staff and to eliminate stereotyping of females in agricultural studies. In some cases, professional organizations of women agriculturalists can act as pressure groups for these changes.

Women and Industry

The important role played by women in electronics, information technology and food processing and agro industry and textiles has been crucial to the development of these sectors. They would be given comprehensive support in terms of labour legislation, social security and other support services to participate in various industrial sectors. Women at present cannot work in night shift in factories even if they wish to. Suitable measures will be taken to enable women to work on the night shift in factories. This will be accompanied with support services for security, transportation etc.

Support Services

The provision of support services for women, like child care facilities, including crèches at work places and educational institutions, homes for the aged and the disabled will be expanded and improved to create an enabling environment and to ensure their full cooperation in social, political and economic life. Women-friendly personnel policies will also be drawn up to encourage women to participate effectively in the developmental process.

Social Empowerment of Women

Education

Equal access to education for women and girls will be ensured. Special measures will be taken to eliminate discrimination, universalize education, eradicate illiteracy, create a gender-sensitive educational system, increase enrolment and retention rates of girls and improve the quality of education to facilitate lifelong learning as well as development of occupation/vocation/technical skills by women. Reducing the gender gap in secondary and higher education would be a focus area. Sectoral time targets in existing policies will be achieved, with a special focus on girls and women, particularly those belonging to weaker sections including the Scheduled Castes/Scheduled Tribes/Other Backward Classes/Minorities. Gender-sensitive curricula would be developed at all levels of educational system in order to address sex stereotyping as one of the causes of gender discrimination.

Health

A holistic approach to women's health which includes both nutrition and health services will be adopted and special attention will be given to the needs of women and the girl at all stages of the life cycle. The reduction of infant mortality and maternal mortality, which are sensitive indicators of human development, is a priority concern. This policy reiterates the national demographic goals for Infant Mortality Rate (IMR), Maternal Mortality Rate (MMR) set out in the National Population Policy 2000. Women should have access to comprehensive, affordable and quality health care. Measures will be adopted that take into account the reproductive rights of women to enable them to exercise informed choices, their vulnerability to sexual and health problems together with endemic, infectious and communicable diseases such as malaria, TB, and water borne diseases as well as hypertension and cardio-pulmonary diseases. The social, developmental and health consequences of HIV/AIDS and other sexually transmitted diseases will be tackled from a gender perspective.

Environment

Women will be involved and their perspectives reflected in the policies and programmes for environment, conservation and restoration. Considering the impact of environmental factors on their livelihoods, women's participation will be ensured in the conservation of the environment and control of environmental degradation. The vast majority of rural women still depend on the locally available non-commercial sources of energy such as animal dung, crop waste and fuel wood. In order to ensure the efficient use of these energy resources in an environmental friendly manner, the policy will aim at promoting the programmes of non-conventional energy resources. Women will be involved in spreading the use of solar energy, biogas, smokeless chulahs and other rural application so as to have a visible impact of these measures in influencing eco-system and in changing the lifestyles of rural women.

Science and Technology

Science and technology are widely acknowledged to be essential components of social and economic development. Scientific knowledge and new technologies can help to tackle many of the problems developing countries are struggling with, such as healthcare, infrastructure, or safe drinking water. Through S&T a country can develop new or improved products, processes and services, thus accelerating the rise in a country's productivity, competitiveness and economic growth. Women can play a vital role in the developmental process through the use of new technology and science. Programmes will be strengthened to bring about a greater involvement of women in science and technology. These will include measures to motivate girls to take up science and technology for higher education and also ensure that development projects with scientific and technical inputs involve women fully. Efforts to develop a scientific temper and awareness will also be stepped up. Special measures would be taken for their training in areas where they have special skills like communication and information technology. Efforts to develop appropriate technologies suited to women's needs as well as to reduce their drudgery will be given a special focus too.

Women in Difficult Circumstances

In recognition of the diversity of women's situations and in acknowledgement of the needs of specially disadvantaged groups, measures and programmes will be undertaken to provide them with special assistance. These groups include women in extreme poverty, destitute women, women in conflict situations, women affected by natural calamities, women in less developed regions, the disabled widows, elderly women, single women in difficult circumstances, women heading households, those displaced from employment, migrants, women who are victims of marital violence, deserted women and prostitutes etc.

Violence Against Women

All forms of violence against women, physical and mental, whether at domestic or societal levels, including those arising from customs, traditions or accepted practices shall be dealt with effectively with a view to eliminate its incidence. Institutions and mechanisms/ schemes for assistance will be created and strengthened for prevention of such violence, including sexual harassment at work place and customs like dowry; for the rehabilitation of the victims of violence and for taking effective action against the perpetrators of such violence. A special emphasis will also be laid on programmes and measures to deal with trafficking in women and girls.

Rights of the Girl Child

All forms of discrimination against the girl child and violation of her rights shall be eliminated by undertaking strong measures both preventive and punitive within and outside the family. These would relate specifically to strict enforcement of laws against prenatal sex selection and the practices of female foeticide, female infanticide, child marriage, child abuse and child prostitution etc. Removal of discrimination in the treatment of the girl child within the family and outside and projection of a positive image of the girl child will be actively fostered. There will be special emphasis on the needs of the girl child and earmarking of substantial investments in the areas relating to food and nutrition, health and education, and in vocational education. In implementing programmes for eliminating child labour, there will be a special focus on girl children.

Mass Media

Media will be used to portray images consistent with human dignity of girls and women. The policy will specifically strive to remove demeaning, degrading and negative conventional stereotypical images of women and violence against women. Private sector partners and media networks will be involved at all levels to ensure equal access for women particularly in the area of information and communication technologies. The media would be encouraged to develop codes of conduct, professional guidelines and other self regulatory mechanisms to remove gender stereotypes and promote balanced portrayals of women and men.

Women and Land

Rural women in many developing and transitional countries are among those with no or very insecure rights to land. Increasing numbers of women in rural areas bear primary responsibility for agricultural production. Studies by both RDI and others underline the importance of women's secure access to land, with its relationship to gains in agricultural productivity, family welfare (particularly child nutrition), and women's empowerment.

Many developing and transitional countries have, in the past several decades, adopted legislation formally giving women equal, or more equal, rights to land and attempted to elevate women's status within the household. Often, however, this legislation has not been successful in achieving its stated goals. RDI's research on these issues has shown that one of the reasons recently adopted written laws have had limited effect on women's rights and access to land has been the continued prevalence of customary law in governing gender-related cultural norms and intra-household affairs. Written laws may prove ineffective due to drafters' failure to consider customary law. Indeed, in some cases customary law may offer greater protection of women's rights and access to land than new legal systems that formalize land rights, even when these systems attempt to reflect women's rights and needs.

Understanding the effects of laws—both written and customary—regarding land tenure and intra-household division of rights and responsibilities for women is critical in formulating effective policy measures to address women's secure access to land.

Rural Development Index Programme

The India programme was established by RDI Executive Director,

Tim Hanstad, who was stationed in country for two years. Following his return to the U.S. in June 2003, RDI has continued its work through a team of Indian nationals based in Delhi, Bangalore and Calcutta.

RDI is working with partners including key government actors, selected research institutions, and NGOs to study, develop, communicate, and help implement feasible legislative, policy, and administrative reforms. RDI is currently active in Karnataka, West Bengal and Andhra Pradesh and has begun the work in Madhya Pradesh, Gujarat and Uttar Pradesh. Additional states have also sought RDI's advice on land policy matters and we have dialogued with officials in numerous other states through national and state workshops. Mainly this programme had started for women.

The Problem and the Opportunity

Poverty imposes an oppressive weight on India, especially in rural areas where almost three of four Indians and close to 80 per cent of the Indian poor live. Despite decades of efforts at poverty alleviation, the absolute number of poor has doubled since Independence in 1947. India today has the largest number of poor people on the planet. India also has the greatest concentration of rural households that are totally landless—60 million households. Landlessness and rural poverty are closely linked. In fact, a recent World Bank report, *India: Achievements and Challenges in Reducing Poverty* (A World Bank Country Study, 1997), showed that *landlessness is by far the greatest predictor of poverty in India—even more so than caste or illiteracy.*

Another 250 million rural residents live in households that own less than 0.2 hectares of land. For many of these households, gaining access to more land would be an opportunity to climb out of poverty. However, land policy and the legislative and administrative framework in India present substantial obstacles to gaining greater land access and rights.

Rural women in India feel the weight of poverty the most. Females are more likely than males to die as infants and children. More than six of ten women in India are illiterate—almost double the male rate. And, most significantly, Indian women rarely have legal rights to land, despite the fact that they are often more engaged in agriculture than men.

Rural land problems in India have not gone unnoticed. In the decades following independence, many Indian states passed land reform laws aimed at broadening access to rural land. But these efforts—except for a few notable successes—were poorly designed and implemented. Measures aimed at taking significant land from larger landowners (with very little compensation) and strictly regulating the landlord-tenant relationship was difficult to administer and aroused strong opposition. They provided little relief to the rural poor and women and, in many cases, led to perverse results that stymied land access and rights for the poor. Until recently, these failures caused Indian policy-makers to conclude that land reform was not an answer to problems plaguing India's countryside.

In recent years, RDI research and advocacy has encouraged policy-makers to put land reform issues back on the agenda. Numerous government actors at both the state and national level are actively exploring a revised agenda for land reform with the continued assistance of RDI's research and comparative experience.

Operational Strategies

Women's Reservation Bill

The movement toward the empowerment of women is gathering force across the country. Parliament has passed Bills meant to protect women against domestic violence and harassment elsewhere. It has also amended the Hindu Succession Act, conferring on the girl child coparcenary rights as also of domicile. The winter session of Parliament will have, on its agenda, the Women's Reservation Bill that will ensure women representatives' form at least one-third of the members of State Legislative Assemblies, the Lok Sabha and the Rajya Sabha. The National Women's Commission is attentive to cases of women's hardships and often hauls up and reads strictures to the husband and the in-laws of the harassed woman.

Action Plans

All Central and State Ministries will draw up time bound action plans for translating the policy into a set of concrete actions, through a participatory process of consultation with Centre/State Departments of Women and Child Development and National/ State Commissions for Women. The plans will specifically include the following:

(*i*) Measurable goals to be achieved by 2010.

(*ii*) Identification and commitment of resources.

(*iii*) Responsibilities for implementation of action points.

(*iv*) Structures and mechanisms to ensure efficient monitoring, review and gender impact assessment of action points and policies.

(*v*) Introduction of a gender perspective in the budgeting process.

Institutional Mechanisms

Institutional mechanisms, to promote the advancement of women, which exist at the Central and State levels, will be strengthened. These will be through interventions as may be appropriate and will relate to, among others, provision of adequate resources, training and advocacy skills to effectively influence macro-policies, legislation, programmes etc. to achieve the empowerment of women.

National and State Councils will be formed to oversee the operationalisation of the policy on a regular basis. The National Council will be headed by the Prime Minister and the State Councils by the Chief Ministers and be broad in composition having representatives from the concerned Departments/ Ministries, National and State Commissions for Women, Social Welfare Boards, representatives of Non-Government Organizations, Women's Organizations, Corporate Sector, Trade Unions, financing institutions, academics, experts and social activists etc. These bodies will review the progress made in implementing the policy twice a year. The National Development Council will also be informed of the progress of the programme undertaken under the policy from time to time for advice and comments.

National and State Resource Centres on women will be established with mandates for collection and dissemination of information, undertaking research work, conducting surveys, implementing training and awareness generation programmes, etc.

These Centres will link up with Women's Studies Centres and other research and academic institutions through suitable information networking systems.

While institutions at the district level will be strengthened, at the grassroots, women will be helped by Government through its programmes to organize and strengthen into Self-Help Groups (SHGs) at the Anganwadi/Village/Town level. The women's groups will be helped to institutionalize themselves into registered societies and to federate at the Panchayat/Municipal level. These societies will bring about synergistic implementation of all the social and economic development programmes by drawing resources made available through Government and Non-Government channels, including banks and financial institutions and by establishing a close interface with the Panchayats/ Municipalities.

Amendment to Succession Act

Under the new legislation, a girl child enjoys coparcenary rights. That is, she is entitled to an equal share in the inherited property, exactly like a male sibling.

On the death of the father, the daughter, married or otherwise, also gets an equal share of his self-earned property, along with her brothers and mother. She also has a claim of inheritance of the property in the house she has married into.

It would appear that the drafters of the Bill have not given sufficient attention to the problems of women's property rights in the patrilocal (relating to residence with a husband's kin group or clan) society. It is still a moot point if after the death of a married woman the property inherited by her will be treated as 'streedhan'. It would appear more than probable that on her death the property inherited from the parents will go back to the parental house, to any of the surviving siblings and all nephews and nieces. There is hardly any point establishing a legal right to property and undergoing contentious litigation with members of the family of birth, if the property has to go back to where it came from.

The entanglement of women's property rights in a patrilocal society can be much better resolved by an anomaly with partnerships under the Partnership Act. Both the family of birth and the family by marriage will be treated as partnerships, in which the girl child gets an equal share, along with her siblings living at the time of her birth.

At the time of her marriage, there should be an assessment of the assets and liabilities of the family of her birth and the girl is allowed to migrate to her family by marriage with her share of the property. The married woman's share in the property of the family by marriage would be equal to the proportion between the net assets of that family and the amount the bride has brought from the parents' house. In the eventuality of a break-up of the partnership in the family by marriage, she would again get the same share of the property as on the date of the break-up—that may have expanded or shrunk since the date of the marriage.

Rural women have a further difficulty because they are not educated. They cannot maintain the accounts. Agricultural land is an immovable asset. As a consequence, the married daughter or a widowed daughter-in-law staying with her parents finds it extremely difficult to assert her right to property. For centuries, the father and the brothers of the bride have resolved the problem by making a lump-sum payment to the family by marriage and endowing jewellery on the bride.

A large number of farmer women appeared to prefer the present system. Only some of them consider that some system of converting land into equity would overcome the problem of the immovable character of agricultural land. It is rather remarkable that many rural women do not consider that the present pieces of legislation have been drafted after mature consideration.

Resource Management

Availability of adequate financial, human and market resources to implement the policy will be managed by concerned departments, financial credit institutions and banks, private sector, civil society and other connected institutions. This process will include:

- (*a*) Assessment of benefits flowing to women and resource allocation to the programmes relating to them through an exercise of gender budgeting. Appropriate changes in policies will be made to optimize benefits to women under these schemes;

(*b*) Adequate resource allocation to develop and promote the policy outlined earlier based on (*a*) above by concerned departments;
(*c*) Developing synergy between personnel of Health, Rural Development, Education and Women and Child Development Department at field level and other village level functionaries; and
(*d*) Meeting credit needs by banks and financial credit institutions through suitable policy initiatives and development of new institutions in coordination with the Department of Women and Child Development.

Gender Sensitization

Training of personnel of executive, legislative and judicial wings of the State, with a special focus on policy and programme framers, implementation and development agencies, law enforcement machinery and thc judiciary, as well as non-governmental organizations will be undertaken. Other measures will include:

(*a*) Promoting societal awareness to gender issues and women's human rights.
(*b*) Review of curriculum and educational materials to include gender education and human rights issues.
(*c*) Removal of all references derogatory to the dignity of women from all public documents and legal instruments.
(*d*) Use of different forms of mass media to communicate social messages relating to women's equality and empowerment.

Panchayati Raj Institutions

The 73rd and 74th Amendments (1993) to the Indian Constitution have served as a breakthrough towards ensuring equal access and increased participation in political power structure for women. The PRIs will play a central role in the process of enhancing women's participation in public life. The PRIs and the Local Self-Governments will be actively involved in the implementation and execution of the National Policy for Women at the grassroots level.

Women in India

Problems for Indian women begin at birth. Even today boys are considered more desirable than girls in some families, because they offer parents security in old age as the parents traditional live with the oldest son. Girls are often seen as a burden because of the family. Indian newspapers frequently report stories of female babies being killed, or women committing suicide because they have not produced a son.

The Baha'i Vocational Institute for Rural and Tribal Women living in small communications in the districts of Madhya Pradesh (M.P.). The curriculum at BVIRW teaches literacy, healthcare, environmental education and vocational skills. After six months at the institute the women return to their villages equipped with the necessary skills to start a small business. Through literacy training they become aware of their rights as citizens and are also able to take out bank loans. Through educating these tribal women the BVIRW has won the UN Role of Honour for their work in the eradication of guinea worms in Madhya Pradesh.

Similarly, the Hoysala Community Development Project works for the empowerment of women and children in seven villages around Hassan. The women's self-help groups meet weekly; the women pay a small fee, which goes into a central account. Each of the women can then borrow a lump sum to either invest in their land or small business, or pay for medical treatment for a member of their family. The literacy classed meet every evening and empower the women by making them aware of their rights and giving them new confidence. While in Hassan, I asked the husbands and fathers what they thought of their wives and daughters being empowered in this way. Response was very positive, clearly these women are not just empowering themselves; the whole community is benefiting.

Summing up

Modern science permeates every aspect of economic and social life. For this reason education, research and technology as instruments for accelerating development should receive special attention in national planning in the developing countries. One of the major factors for marginal science and technology development in the most developing countries is the lack of planning and management of these activities. Thus far, only a few developing countries have attempted to formulate and adopt a national policy. In order to make a realistic plan, not only a vision, but also scientific leadership, and investment in scientific enterprise both by government and private sectors are required. Short-term financial considerations in investment decisions that have been observed so far in developing countries will always be more costly and time consuming.

Developing countries that plan to have a rapid economic growth should first consider if they have provided ideal opportunities for their high-level scientists and nurtured their talents for the nations' well-being. Furthermore, these countries must ensure the economic and social well-being of their scientist and provide an attractive and well equipped research environment to their migration to countries with enriched scientific and social opportunities. Science and technology based industry should be identified as a major source of economic growth and a means of addressing important social problems as well. In conclusion, developing countries should be committed to retaining high-level scientists, stimulating them, and providing funds and other support to encourage and maintain their productivity.

In developing countries economic growth can mainly be enhanced by a science and technology policy. However, science and technology can play their role in development only when the integrity of the whole enterprise—research institutions, universities, publications research priorities and emphasis and the education of creative scientists, as well as those active in science is preserved. Thus, the simplest strategy in developing countries is first of all, to increase the percentage of GNP that is to be devoted to universities and research institutions so that number of educated women can increase.

Developing countries should understand the fact that perceiving investment in sciences as a time-consuming, wasteful and costly activity will bring further limitations on their economic growth. In conclusion we believe with Salam [4] that it is a political decision on the part of those who decide on the future of developing countries to take proper steps toward creating, mastering and utilizing the resources of science and technology. Due to the lack of specific implementation plans and faulty representations, local communities have not adequately accepted government and private schemes for the upliftment of women. Women have not actively participated in their own emancipation due to their lack of economic independence and lack of proper education. Therefore, the George Foundation decided to address this important issue of women's empowerment in India by raising the status of women in Hosur Taluk through economic empowerment and education.

As UN Secretary General Kofi Annan has stated, "Gender equality is more than a goal in itself. It is a precondition for meeting the challenge of reducing poverty, promoting sustainable development and building good governance." This recognition is currently missing in India. Transforming the periling social discrimination against women must become the top priority, and must happen concurrently with increased direct action to rapidly improve the social and economic status of women. In this way, synergy of progress can be achieved.

- As women receive greater education and training, they will earn more money.
- As women earn more money—as has been repeatedly shown—they spend it in the further tobacco or other women.
- As women rise in economic status, they will gain greater social standing in the household and the village, and will have greater voice.
- As women's economic power grows, it will be easier to overcome the tradition of "son preference" and thus put an end to the evil of dowry.
- As son preference declines and acceptance of violence declines, families will be more likely to educate their daughters and age of marriage will rise.
- As women are better nourished and marry later, they will be healthier more productive, and will give birth to healthier babies.

Only through action to remedy discrimination against women can the vision of India's independence—an India where all people have the chance to live healthy and productive lives—be realized. Education is likely the single most important factor in improving a woman's life; the more schooling she has, the brighter her future (Neft and Levine, 1997). Educating women is also advantageous to society. There is a positive correlation between education enrolment rates of girls and GNP per capita (Karl, 1995). Education for women in Europe and North America has never been as accessible as it is today. For almost two centuries American education, following European traditions, barred girls from academic higher learning. In the past, education was the path to professions and careers open only to men. During American colonial times women, viewed as mentally and morally inferior, were relegated to learning only domestic skills (Sadker and Sadker, 1995). The roots of these beliefs can be found in the writings of the educator Jean-Jacques Rousseau who believed that women were created for the purpose of entertaining and caring for men, and that their education should equip them for the task (Spender, 1992). Women were not allowed to learn Latin or Greek, the sign of an educated person, on the scientific grounds that their brains would burst or that they would become unfit for child-bearing (Spender, 1992). While developed countries have seen an increase in the number of women receiving education, some developing countries are still notably biased towards educating males over females. Some countries maintain policies that limit or forbid girls and women from education. The most notable example is Afghanistan where the education of girls and women has been banned (Marsden, 1998). Inherent in women's struggle for educational opportunities are issues of power and institutionalized perceptions of women's role in society.

No country can thrive in which women's voices are silenced, their rights are violated, and their potential is left unrealized. That fact will grow ever more prominent as the world's markets and opportunities continue to interconnect. Guaranteeing the human rights of women and children, including the education of girls, is fundamental to building stable, democratic, economically prosperous societies. The education gap for girls in developing countries and post-conflict societies remains a collective global task. We must continue to work together to lay the foundation for a more sustainable, secure world. Gareth Thomas, the junior international development minister, said that the government was already spending £ 240 m a year on education in India but was allocating more money over the next three years to provide extra school places in rural areas. In 2003, India accounted for a quarter of all children globally who were not in school, but rapid growth has helped reduce the number from 23 million four years ago to 13.5 million in 2005 and an estimated 10 million last year. Mr. Thomas said that the Indian Government was financing 60 per cent of the expansion of primary education itself but aid was vital to fill the gap.

> "Education is not preparation for life; education is life itself and it is a progressive discovery of our ignorance. The roots of education are bitter but the fruit is sweet that's why education is the key for developing countries. "

REFERENCES

1. Ahmed, A. & Carron, G. (1989), The Challenges of Basic Education for All, *Prospects*, 14, p. 4.
2. Bunch, Charlotte, "*The Intolerable Status Quo: Violence Against Women and Girls.* "The Progress of Nations 1997, New York: UNICEF.
3. Burney, N.A. & Irfan, M. (1991), Parental Characteristics, Supply of Schools and Child-School Enrolment in Pakistan, *The Pakistan Development Review*, 30 (1), pp. 21-62.
4. Carr, Marilyn; Chen, Martha and Jhabvala, Renana (1996), *Speaking Out: Women's Economic Empowerment in South Asia*, Southampoton Row, London: Intermediate Technology Publications Ltd.
5. Choudhary, S.V. (1992), "Television in Distance Education: The Indian Scenario", *Indian Journal of Open Learning*, 1(1), p. 23.
6. Choudhary, S.V. and Behari, Shyam (1994), Modasa Experiment: Distance Teaching Through Cable TV Network System, *Indian Journal of Open Learning* 3(1), pp. 24-28.
7. Chimombo, J.P.G. (2004), *Financing Free Primary Education: Tracing the Self-help Spirit in Malawi.* Paper presented at Hiroshima University, Center for the Study of International Cooperation in Education, Hiroshima, Japan.
8. Dalin, P.; Ayono, T.; Biazen A.; Dibaba, B.; Muntaz, J.; Miles, M. & Rojas, C. (1994), *How Schools Improve: An International Report*, London: Cassell.
9. Dall, F. (1989), *Confronting the Basic Education Crisis: The Zambian Dilemma*, Cambridge: Bridge Project, Harvard University.
10. Davison, J. & Kanyuka, M. (1990), *An Ethnographic Study of Factors Affecting the Education Girls in Southern Malawi*, Zomba: Chancellor College.

11. Dodd, W.A. (1969), *Education for Self-reliance: A Study of Its Vocational Aspects*, Columbia, New York: Teachers College Press.
12. Fuller, B. & Heyneman, S. (1989), Third World School Quality: Current Collapse Future Potential, *Educational Researcher*, 18(2), pp. 12-19.
13. Fuller, B. & Robinson, R. (Eds.) (1992), *The Political Construction of Education: State, School and School Expansion and Economic Change*, New York: Praeger.
14. Fuller, B. & Clarke, P. (1994), Raising School Effects: While Ignoring Culture, *Review of Educational Research*, 64, pp. 119-57.
15. Hallak, J. (1991), Education for All: High Expectation or False Hopes, *IIEP Contributions No. 3*, Paris: UNESCO.
16. Hallak, J. (2003), *Education the Poor*, Paris: UNESCO.
17. Hanushek, E. (1995), Interpreting Recent Research on Schooling in Developing Countries, *World Bank Research Observer*, 10(2), pp. 227-46.
18. Harbison, R. & Hanushek, E. (1992), *Education Performance of the Poor: Lessons from Northeast Brazil*, New York: Oxford University Press.
19. Havelock, R.G. & Huberman, A.M. (1977), *Solving Educational Problems: The Planning and Reality of Innovations in Developing Countries*, Paris: UNESCO.
20. IGNOU (2001), "Growth of Communication Technology", Communication Technology for Distance Education, *ES-318*, pp. 34-40.
21. IGNOU (2001), "Media in Distance Education", Communication Technology for Distance Education, *ES-318*, pp. 28-31.
22. *Modernisation and Its Impact on Indian Women* edited by S. Vats and Shakuntala Mudgal, 1999, vii, p. 216, ISBN 81-86867-21-X, Details No. 14754.
23. *Modernity, Feminism and Women Empowerment* edited by Abha Avasthi and A.K. Srivastava, Delhi, Rawat, 2001, p. 296, ISBN 81-7033-643-0, Details No. 19583.
24. *Modernizing Women: Searching Their Identities*, Kali Nath Jha, New Delhi.
25. *Modern Women and the Society*, H. Parameshwar Hegde, New Delhi, Mohit Pub., 2005, vii, p. 232, $ 26, ISBN 81-7445-338-5, Details No. 43815.
26. *Modern Working Women and the Development Debate*, edited by Kranti Rana, 1998, VI, p. 304, tables, Details No. 13397.
27. Neft, Naomi and Levine, Ann D. (197), *Where Stand: An International Reports on the Status of Women in 140 Countries*, New York: Random House.
28. Nicolae, V.; Smulders, R.H.M. and Korka, M. (1989), *Statistics on Higher Education*, Bucharest: European Centre for Higher Education.

29. Oxfam (2001), *Education: Tackling the Global Crisis,* Briefing Paper, Oxfam, UK.
30. Prakash, S. & Chaubey, P.K. (1992), Universalisation of Elementary Education, A Simple General Equilibrium Type Policy Model, *Manpower Journal,* 28(2), pp. 9-18.
31. Rawat, 2005, xii, p. 220, ISBN 81-7033-954-5, Details No. 42312.
32. Rajagopalan, T.S. and Rajan, T.N. (1987), Technology Information Base in India: A Development Perspective, in E.V. Smith and S. Keenan (eds.): *Information, Communication and Technology,* Amsterdam: Elsevier Science Publishers, pp. 441-50.
33. Ramanathan, K. (1988), Evaluating the National Science and Technology Base: A Case Study on Sri Lanka, *Science and Public Policy,* 15, p. 304.
34. *Rural Women Workforce in India,* Madhuri Nath, Delhi, B.R., 2003, xiv, p. 130, tables, ISBN 81.
35. *Rural Development and Women,* B.N. Singh, Delhi, Vista International Pub., 2006, viii, p. 274, tables, $39. ISBN 81-89652-71-0. Details No. 47813.
36. *Rural Development Through Women's Participation and Electronic Media,* edited by Sawalia Bihari Verma and Shiv Kumar Singh, Jaipur, Pointer, 2004, xvii, p. 364, tables, ISBN 81-7132-359-6, Details No. 37052.
37. *Rural Landless Women Labourers: Problems and Prospects,* A. Balakrishnan, Delhi,
38. Kalpaz, 2005, p. 256, tables, ISBN 81-7835-315-6, Details No. 38598.
39. *Rural Women Empowerment,* edited by S.B. Verma, Shiv Kumar Jiloka and Kumari Jyoti Kushwah, New Delhi, Deep & Deep, 2006, xvi, p. 400, tables, $47, ISBN 81-7629-887-5, Details No. 46765.
40. *Rural Women Empowerment and Development Banking,* N. Lalitha, 1997, v, p. 277, tables, Details No. 12576.
41. Salam, A. (1988), *Notes on Science, Technology and Science Education in the Development of the South* (Prepared for the 4th Meeting on the South Commission, 10-12 December, 1988, Kuwait). Trieste: The Third World of Academy of Sciences.
42. Schiefelbein, E. & Farrell, J. (1985), *Eight Years of their Lives; Through Schooling to Labour Market in Chile,* Ottawa: IDRC.
43. Shishido, T. (1983), Japanese Industrial Development and Policies for Science and Technology, *Weekly Science,* p. 219, 21 January, 1983.
44. *Social Movements and Women,* Raj Pruthi and Bela Rani Sharma (1995), p. 296, Details No. 10873.
45. *Social Status of Indian Women,* edited by Muniruddin Qureshi, New Delhi, *Anmol,* 2003, Vol. 3, p. 889, ISBN 81-261-1360-X, Details No. 31966.
46. *Social Status of Women,* Sunder Lal, Jaipur, ABD Pub., 2005, viii, p. 290, ISBN 81-89011-56-1, Details No. 38710.

47. *Social Status and Role of Women,* edited by S.R. Bakshi and Kiran Bala, New Delhi, 2000, v, p. 330, ISBN 81-7629-115-3, Details No. 15413.
48. *Social Status of Women in India,* Maya Majumdar, New Delhi, Dominant, 2004, xii, p. 316, ISBN 81-7888-159-4, Details No. 33804.
49. *Social Structure and Change,* Vol. 2, *Women in Indian Society,* edited by A.M. Shah, B.S. Baviskar and E.A. Ramaswamy, 1996, p. 214, tables, [Vol. 1 published earlier is available], Details No. 11387.
50. Thompson, A.R. (1981), *Education and Development in Africa,* London: Longman.
51. UNESCO (2004), *EFA Global Monitoring Report,* Paris: UNESCO.
52. Warwick, P.D.; Reimers, F. & McGinn, N.F. (1992), *The Implementation of Education Innovations: Lessons from Pakistan, International Journal of Educational Development,* 12(4), pp. 297-309.
53. Watson, K. (1988), Forty Years of Education and Development: From Optimism to Uncertainty, *Educational Review,* 40(2), pp. 137-74.
54. Williams, E. (1996), Reading in Two Languages at Year Five in African Primary Schools, *Applied Linguistics,* 17(2), pp. 182-209.
55. World Bank (1995), *Priorities and Strategies for Education: A World Bank View,* Washington DC: The World Bank.
56. *Women's Work, Health and Empowerment,* Anjali Gandhi, Delhi, Aakar Pub., 2006, p. 288, tables, figs., $42. ISBN 81-87879-71-8, Details No. 46683.
57. *Work, Income and Status of Rural Women,* edited by Thota Jyothi Rani, New Delhi, *Serials,* 2005, viii, p. 298, tables, ISBN 81-86771-93-X, Details No. 42661.

15

Education for Dignity of Human Life with Special Reference to Women's Education and Child Education in India

MS. PRABHA SINGH, MR. ARUN KUMAR SINGH AND DR. SUMAN LATA

Introduction

Education is the most important element for growth and prosperity of a nation. India is in the process of transforming itself into a developed nation by 2020. Yet we have 350 million people who need literacy and many more who have to acquire employable skills to suit the emerging modern India and the globe. Children who belong to weaker sections of our society are undernourished, and only a small percentage of them manage to complete eight years of satisfactory education. We need to think specifically for them.

According to **A.P.J. Abdul Kalam (2005),** Education in its real sense is the pursuit of truth. It is an endless journey through knowledge and enlightenment. Such a journey opens up new vistas of development of humanism.

The Indian Government has expressed a strong commitment towards education for all, however, India still has one of the lowest female literacy rates in Asia. In 1991, less than 40 per cent of the 330 million women aged 7 and over were literate, which means today there are over 200 million illiterate women in India. This low level of literacy not only has a negative impact on women's lives but also on their families' lives and on their country's economic development. Numerous studies show that illiterate women have high levels of fertility and mortality, poor nutritional status, low earning potential, and little autonomy within the household. A woman's lack of education also has a negative impact on the health and well-being of her children. For instance, a recent survey in India found that infant mortality was inversely related to mother's educational level.

Additionally, the lack of an educated population can be an impediment to the country's economic development.

The Indian Government's commitment to education is stated in its Constitution with an article promising "free and compulsory education for all children until they complete the age of 14" (The World Bank, 1997b). The National Policy on Education, which was updated in 1992, and the 1992 Programme of Action both reaffirmed the government's commitment to improving literacy levels, by providing special attention to girls and children from scheduled castes and scheduled tribes.

Literacy Levels Improving Over Time

Although literacy levels are low, there has been progress in improving educational attainment for both sexes in India over the last several decades. In 1971, only 22 per cent of women and 46 per cent of men were literate (Registrar General and Census Commissioner (RGCC), 1977. By 1991, 39 per cent of women and 64 per cent of men were literate (RGCC, 1993). Thus, there has been a large increase in the proportion of women who are literate in just 20 years. Despite the improvements in literacy, there continues to be a large gap between the literacy levels of men and of women. For India as a whole, the gender gap in literacy has been decreasing since 1981; in some states, however the disparity in literacy between the sexes has been growing.

There are dramatic differences in literacy rates by place of residence, with rates in rural areas lagging behind rates in urban areas. In 1991, the urban female literacy rate was more than twice that of the rural rate, 64 and 31 per cent, respectively (RGCC, 1993). While there have, however, been substantial increases in literacy rates in both urban and rural areas, the gap between the two sectors has not narrowed appreciably.

Large Difference in Literacy Among the States

The differences in literacy rates among the states are also extreme. Kerala has the highest female literacy rate, with over 86 per cent of women literate in 1991. The state with the second highest female literacy is Mizoram, where nearly 79 per cent of women are literate. On the other hand, there are several states that have literacy rates of less than 30 per cent, including Bihar and Uttar Pradesh, the two most populous states. Together these two states have over 63 million illiterate women. These literacy levels are highly correlated with the health status of the population. Kerala has the lowest infant mortality rates and the highest life expectancies of all the states. Conversely, Uttar Pradesh and Bihar have some of the lowest life expectancies found in India (India Registrar General (IRG), 1996; IRG, 1995). As with India as a whole, many states have large rural-urban differences in female literacy. In 6 of the 24 states, 25 per cent or less of the women in rural areas are literate. In Rajasthan, less than 12 per cent of rural women are literate.

Education is indeed a fundamental right of every Indian child. Can we allow the situation to continue in which millions of these children are forced into lifelong poverty? The requirement is that the parents should be able to go to any school nearby and admit their children and happily come back home with the confidence that their children will get a good and value-based quality education in that school. The conditions of differently-abled children require equally important attention. In view of such critical issues and their importance, and also to break out of our historical mindset, an effective and self renewing education system is therefore fundamental to the survival and growth of civilizations, therefore it is proposed to address the issues pertaining to education in some detail and suggest some solutions, which can be considered for implementation.

Let me share with you one important concern: unequal access to educational resources still exists due to a variety of reasons. For example, there exist in our villages three types of families. The fortunate ones who realize the importance of educating the young ones at any cost, guide them at all critical stages due to their economical well-being. There are those families, who might realize the importance of education, but are not aware of the opportunities in time, nor the procedures and ways to realize these opportunities for their children. There is a third category of families who are economically weak and do not realize the value of education and hence for generations together their children are neglected and continue to live in poverty.

It is essential that we enlighten and create widespread awareness of education among all sections of society particularly in rural areas and among urban poor. We should use technology for this important social purpose. It is possible for NGOs, other social and philanthropic institutions and media to focus on this area of creating awareness. We should also mobilize necessary resources for providing education to the underprivileged people. Let us elaborate the way ahead.

Mobilising Resources

Over the last 50 years, successive governments have been committed to achieving the national goal of universal education and has steadily increased the budgetary allocation for education. However, 35 per cent of our adult population is yet to achieve literacy. The expenditure on education as a percentage of our gross domestic product has a direct impact on our literacy. Today our expenditure on education in India is little more than 4 per cent of our GDP. If we have to achieve nearly 100 per cent literacy, it is necessary to increase its expenditure on education to about 6 to 7 per cent of the GDP. This 2 to 3 per cent increase has to be sustained only for a few years. Thereafter, a lower percentage of GDP allocation to education will be adequate to sustain the high degree of literacy in this country for all times to come.

According to **Krishna Kumar (2005),** educational structures themselves may be said to have ideological properties when they develop serious gaps between rhetoric and reality.

Clearly public expenditure alone from governments in the Centre and states might not able to meet the challenge of mobilizing an additional 2 to 3 per cent of GDP for the mission of education. It is here that we have to generate additional resources for this noble mission. Expenditure on education, whether in the Centre or in the states can no longer be provided only by the respective Ministries or Departments for human resource development. Indeed, every department of government must play a significant role as a partner of the human resource development organization, and contribute resources in terms of budget and infrastructure for implementing the mission of providing quality education to the whole nation.

To augment the government resources, the entire corporate sector shall emulate the example set by some corporate leaders who have focused on education to make a national difference. Different regions of the country may be adopted by the corporate sectors within an overall national mission for education. The mechanism should enable the persons to have freedom to innovate and deliver directly. The preferred school concept is arising because of differential quality and standards of teaching. There is a need to make the quality of teaching high in all schools. Also there is a need for preparatory education even in rural areas to make the child competitive when he or she joins the regular school. For running such schools in rural areas NGOs and corporate sectors can play a vital role. Also rich parents who can afford can adopt certain number of rural children for educating in preparatory schools.

Job opportunities being national, the syllabus should be structured in such a manner that it should meet the changing societal needs, fulfil the needs of the occupation and inculcate high moral values among the students in addition to learning skills. The delivery of quality education is possible only through quality teachers. The teacher has to be a committed teacher who loves teaching and children. And also the teacher has to be equipped with all the knowledge required for effective teaching. The self-esteem of the teacher must be high and the teacher must have the quality to become a role model for the children. Some element of competitive rewarding is to be done based on performance. This competency has to be built up throughout the country through a massive teachers education programme delivered through a tele-education system and continuously updated. This can be funded and implemented by a consortium of government, educational institutions with the corporate sectors providing value added services. There is an urgent need that every school should have basic amenities such as good building equipped with ventilated, lighted, airy and spacious classrooms besides library, laboratories including the latest IT tools and infrastructure, safe drinking water, clean toilets, playground. This is possible by earmarking the additional two to three per cent of GDP.

Parents have an important role in the education of the children and making them enlightened citizens. They must be aware of the need for good education of the child, male or female. Like teachers, parents also should set an example for the child in their overall behaviour and conduct. This will enable the child to develop love and respect for their parents and see them as role models.

Reducing Dropouts

It is reported that 39 per cent of children dropout from schools after studying upto 5th class and 55 per cent dropout after studying upto 8th class. This situation needs remedial action, especially since assent has been accorded for the 86th Constitution Amendment Act—Right to Education Bill for children between the age group of 5 and 14 years. But an Act alone cannot achieve the goal unless the education is delivered in a manner, which will take into account the socio-economic reality, and perception of people to whom it is addressed. Apart from attracting children to schools, the education system should be able to provide nourishment and inject creativity among the children. Also the aim of the education system should be to build character, human values, enhance the learning capacity through technology and build the confidence among children to face the future.

An education model implemented in Karnataka, provides an accelerated learning using the computer aids so that children can have a creative learning with the tools of creative animation through computers. Dropouts are identified and brought to the school. This holistic phenomenon of learning once ingrained in the primary stage where there is a happy learning process and a non-threatening evaluation, has led to voluntary learning by the participants. Recently A.P.J. Abdul Kalam have received many e-mails from children and parents regarding too many entrance examinations which the children have to appear from nursery up to plus two level for entry into schools, colleges, universities and professional courses. This is a heavy burden on the children. Also, it has led to proliferation of tuitions and coaching institutes for preparing the students for entrance examinations. For entry into universities and professional colleges, we have to devise a common all India examination to be conducted by a nominated institution of government. Also, the examination must be so designed that attending a coaching course does not provide undue advantage to privileged students. Entrance test should be more in the nature of aptitude assessment rather than creating a seniority list.

According to **Job Zachariah (2005)** that India cannot wait any it cannot let children miss education.

Examination Reforms

There is a demand for more transparent and reliable system of examination, evaluation and reporting. It is also noticed that the examination primarily tests the memory of the students. During my study in MIT, Chennai in mid 1950s, they used to conduct open book examination. This used to be one of the tough examinations for the students. The examining bodies may consider introduction of open book system of examination. This will promote creativity among the teachers in setting questions and the evaluation of the creative ability of the students. A secure examination system is the need of the hour. The examining bodies should have a reliable evaluation system and timely declaration of results. After the initial evaluation of the answer paper a centralized core group can draw random sample from each batch and carry out independent evaluation. If there is no discrepancy between the initial evaluation and the core group evaluation, and it is consistent with the performance of the students, it will be presumed that the batch marking is satisfactory. In case of a discrepancy further samples should be drawn for verification. Special training must be carried out by examining bodies for certifying the examiners in the evaluation process. In short the examining bodies must evolve very good procedures and then get ISO Certification for their evaluation system.

The recent tragedy involving school children at Kumbakonam must have rung some bells in all the educational institutions in the country. It is the responsibility of sponsoring organization to see that their schools maintain basic minimum norms both in the academic field as well as in the physical facilities which they provide on their campuses. Certain safety features must be built in our school buildings without which it should not be possible to get affiliation to these schools. And there should not be any discretion available with anyone, to waive off these conditions. Honesty in implementation is vital at all levels.

Constraints of time and space together with the rapid obsolescence of knowledge in some areas of science and technology, have created a huge demand for different courses from different institutions in the distance mode. There is a need for a working digital library system that alone can, in the long run, provide the kind of access required for a Knowledge Society. Technology Enhanced Learning is a solution. It attempts to exploit the rapid developments in Information and Communication Technology. As the communications bandwidth continues to increase and the cost of computer power continues to drop, Technology Enhanced Learning will become an economically viable solution. Virtual classrooms of the future will have students from many locations taught by a team of geographically distributed instructors through tele-education delivery system.

Three Out of Five Girls Attend School Versus Three Out of Four Boys

Although literacy rates in India are low, there has been a concerted effort to encourage girls to attend school, which should lead to higher literacy rates in the future. In 1992-93, 75 per cent of boys and 61 per cent of girls aged 6 to 10 years were attending school. As with literacy measures, there are large differences in school attendance by state. In six states, over 85 per cent of girls aged 6 to 14 were attending school. Not surprisingly, these states also had female literacy rates that were above the national average. In all states except Bihar, Rajasthan and Uttar Pradesh, more than half of the girls aged 6 to 14 were attending school. Although Bihar has the lowest enrolment for both boys and girls, there was still a large gender gap, with only 38 per cent of the girls attending school compared to 64 per cent of the boys (International Institute for Population Science, 1995).

A major educational problem facing both boys and girls in India is that although they may be enrolled at the beginning of the year they don't always remain in school. It is estimated that 45 per cent of girls and 41 per cent of boys dropout of school between grades 1 and 5. Girls are often taken out of school to help with family responsibilities such as caring for younger siblings. Girls are also likely to be taken out of school when they reach puberty as a way of protecting their honour. The data on school attendance by age show the proportion of girls attending school decreases with age while for boys it remains stable. In 1992-93, only 55 per cent of girls aged 11 to 14 were attending school compared with 61 per cent of the younger age group.

Serve Shikha Abhiyan (2005), the programme has generated considerable interest and commitment in all the states and has helped bring elementary education closer to the centerstage of the development agenda.

Although there are numerous studies demonstrating a link between education and a variety of demographic indicators, more recent studies are finding that there is a minimum threshold of education (more than 5 or 6 years) that must be achieved before there are significant improvements in female autonomy, particularly in a highly gender-stratified society such as India. Of the literate women in India, 59 per cent have only a primary education or less. This level of education may not be sufficient to meaningfully improve the status of these women. Only 41 per cent of the literate population, or 13 per cent of all Indian women, have more than a primary education.

Alternative Education

The Non-Formal Education (NFE) programme was created by the Indian Government in 1979-80 to reach children that were not in the formal education system, particularly girls and working children. Classes are held at times that are convenient for the students, and the curriculum is adapted to their needs. The teacher is a local person who has been trained to run the NFE center and the classes are held either in the teacher's home or after hours in already existing schools. In 1994, there were 255,000 centers serving 6.4 million children. Approximately 40 per cent of the centers are exclusively for girls (The World Bank, 1997b). While the NFE programme has the potential to solve many of the problems with access to education, as with any type of education programme, the quality varies from location to location (Rugh, 1994).

Barriers to Education

There are several reasons for the low levels of literacy in India, not the least of which is the high level of poverty. Over one-third of the population is estimated to be living below the poverty line (The World Bank, 1997a). Although school attendance is free, the costs of books, uniforms, and transportation to school can be too much for poor families. Poor families are also more likely to keep girls at home to care for younger siblings or to work in family enterprises. If a family has to choose between educating a son or a daughter because of financial restrictions, typically the son will be chosen. Negative parental attitudes toward educating daughters can also be a barrier to a girl's education. Many parents view educating sons as an investment because the sons will be responsible for caring for aging parents. On the other hand, parents may see the education of daughters a waste of money. Daughters will eventually live with their husbands' families, and the parents will not benefit directly from their education. Also, daughters with higher levels of education will likely have higher dowry expenses as they will want a comparably educated husband. However, education sometimes lowers the dowry for a girl because it is viewed as an asset by the husband's family.

Inadequate School Facilities

Another barrier to education in India is the lack of adequate school facilities. Many states simply do not have enough classrooms to accommodate all of the school-age children. Furthermore, the classrooms that are available often lack basic necessities such as sanitary facilities or water. In Uttar Pradesh, a recent survey found that 54 per cent of schools did not have a water supply and 80 per cent did not have latrines (The World Bank, 1997b). Lack of latrines can be particularly detrimental to girls' school attendance. In some states, the inadequate supply of classrooms is further compounded by the large increase in the number of school-age children due to high population growth rates. For instance, in 1993, Uttar Pradesh needed to build 284,000 additional classrooms to achieve full enrolment of children age 6 to 10. The need for new classrooms will persist as the population continues to grow. On the other hand, in states where population growth rates are low, the number of primary-age children is beginning to decline and state governments can focus on improving the quality of education rather than increasing the supply of classrooms.

India has a Shortage of Female Teachers

Lack of female teachers is another potential barrier to girls' education. Girls are more likely to attend school and have higher academic achievement if they have female teachers. This is particularly true in highly gender-segregated societies such as India. Currently, women account for only 29 per cent of teachers at the primary level. The proportion of teachers who are female is even lower at the university level, 22 per cent of instructors. These proportions reflect the historic paucity of women with the educational qualifications to be teachers. However, the proportions are likely to change in the future as women currently account for nearly half of those being trained as teachers. Again there are differences among the states; the states with the highest literacy rates are also the states with the highest proportion of female teachers.

Conclusion

Ultimately, education in its real sense is the pursuit of truth. It is an endless journey through knowledge and enlightenment. Such a journey opens up new vistas of development of humanism where there is no scope nor room for pettiness, disharmony, jealousy, hatred or enmity. It transforms a human being into a wholesome whole, a noble soul and an asset to the universe. Universal brotherhood in its true sense becomes the sheet anchor for such education. Real education enhances the dignity of a human being and increases his or her self-respect. If only the real sense of education could be realized by each individual, and carried forward in every field of human activity the world will be so much a better place to live in. Mission of education by Government at Centre or States or the combination is the foundation to ensure the creation of enlightened citizens who will make a prosperous, happy and strong nation.

REFERENCES

A. Jalal (2006), Emerging Trends in Education in the Global Era, *Kurukshetra,* Published by Ministry of Rural Development, New Delhi, p. 18.

A.P.J. Abdul Kalam's address to the Independence Day (2004), *Yojana*, published by the Ministry of Information and Broadcasting, p. 2.

Charulata Singh (2005), Value of Education, *Yojana*, published by the Ministry of Information Broadcasting, p. 45.

Job Zachariah (2005), Universal Elementary Education, *Yojana*, published by the Ministry of Information Broadcasting, p. 15.

Krishna Kumar (2005), Politics of Change, *Yojana*, published by the Ministry of Information and Broadcasting, p. 5.

Pratiyogita Darpan (2007), *Education and Business*, published by Partiyogita Darpan Swadesh, Bima Nagar, Agra, p. 55.

16

Education and Women Empowerment: Developments in India

DR. PRAVESH

Empowerment is an ongoing and dynamic process, which enhances women's and any other, marginalized and alienated group's abilities to change the structures and ideologies that keep them subordinate. It is a process of making present power structure more inclusive including all women and men, senior citizens, dalits, indigenous people and people with disabilities [Bhasin & Dhar 1998]. Present time women empowerment is a global issue. Women empowerment is very broad term.

Empowerment of women involves many things, economic opportunity, property rights, political representation, social equality, personal rights and so on. Historically the world over, either by law or by custom, the status of women is undermined by asymmetrical power relationship in decision-making, personal and social rights, access to resources and entitlement. Women in many countries still lack rights to inherit property, own land, get education, obtain credit, earn income or work outside home, control their fertility; they are still widely under-represented in decision-making at the household or social level. Empowerment by means of modest income-generation projects is clearly insufficient to ameliorate the prospects for a high quality of life for women.

Empowerment is considered a collective process. Process and collectivity are central to empowerment. Certain type of experiences will lead to feelings of self-confidence and this self-confidence can generate more courage for women to venture into previously foreign arenas where they can exert pressure or challenge social situation that create difficulties for them.

Achievement of positive results from such an endeavour is reflective of an empowering process. But individual efforts to effect change in one's life or environment, though important, are limited in scope. They also provide contexts in which empowerment is more actively and energetically pursued. Collective action has the potential to create a stronger voice and sustain a more powerful challenge to discriminatory structures, and to elicit a more adequate response. Experiences of a collective nature can be more dynamic and achieve greater results in empowering the participants and effecting positive social change.

Noble Laureate Prof. Amartya Sen said that the fundamentals of decentralization were information, autonomy, incentives, competition and empowerment of women. (International Seminar on 'Decentralization, Devolution and Participation' at Calcutta on 28 December, 1998). Women Empowerment can be viewed as a continuum of several interrelated and mutually reinforcing components.

- Awareness building about women's situation discrimination, rights and opportunities as a step towards gender equality. Collective awareness building provides a sense of group identity and power of working as a group.
- Capacity building and skills development especially the ability to plan make decisions, organize, manage and carry out activities to deal with people and institution in the world around them.
- Participation and greater control and decision making power in the home community and society.
- Action to bring about greater equality between men and women.

In short, empowerment is a process of awareness and capacity building leading to greater participation to greater decision-making, power and control and to transformative action.

Women Empowerment: Why

The term of "Empowerment" has been overused in the mid 1980s in the field of development especially in reference to women. India is a developing country which depends very much on its vast potential of human resources, if these resources are properly tapped the country is bound to progress efficiently, effectively and rapidly. Women form the most important part of the human resources of the nation and they may contribute very substantially in building a strong powerful and affluent nation.

Women Empowerment is very necessary from the grassroots of social development. There are several cogent and pressing reasons for evaluating, promoting and monitoring the level of women's empowerment in India not the least of which is that household health and nutrition is generally in the hands of women, and their empowerment is necessary for ensuring not just there own welfare but also the well being of the entire household. Empowerment of women is also critical for the very development of India. Since it will enhance both the quality and the quantity of human resources available for development. Further the success of development efforts depends on the fruits of development reaching men and women, boys and girls equally. The extent to which this happiness, however, depends critically on gender relations within the society that set the worth of one sex relative to the other. A final but one of the most fundamental reasons for promoting the empowerment of women is that failing to empower women as well as the mean to reach their full potential is a violation of their basic human rights.

Seminars, conference and demonstrations by women's organizations marked the International Women's Day in the Capital few years ago. Addressing a conference on "Development of Women in Fifty Years of Independence", the (then) first Lady, Mrs. Usha Narayanan, said that very little had changed for the majority of women living in rural areas. She underlined the need for greater co-ordination and interaction between governmental policy at the national level to tie with the concerns and matters raised by women at the local government level. The conference was jointly organized by the National Commission for Women (NCW), Department of Women and Child Development and Central Social Welfare Board. Mrs. Narayanan said that the women need to be empowered to take their rightful place on an equal footing with men. "They need to be liberated from discrimination and exploitation." She also said that since Independence women have taken more and more initiatives to improve their conditions by actively participating in non-governmental organizations and cooperatives. For instance, she said that village level Mahila Mandals have taken up cudgels against rape, alcohol abuse by men and wife battering. Speaking on the occasion, the chairperson of NCW, Mrs V. Mohini Giri, said that the concept of gender equality has become a crucial input to solve national and local problems. She maintained that special attention was given by NCW to the condition of Scheduled Castes and Scheduled Tribes who were ignored so far. She informed that four reports released by the commission to mark the occasion, were related to tribal development. She said that the NCW has undertaken special efforts to support the handicapped and disabled women. She said that the NCW forwarded a number of recommendations to the government to amend the discriminatory provisions in various laws relating to women. Several women freedom fighters were honoured at the function. A special stamp to commemorate fifty years of universal declaration of human rights was also released.

Meanwhile, Pragateesheel Mahila Sangathan, a women's organization, staged a demonstration at Ferozshah Kotla ground.

The activists of the organization also staged street plays to highlight the plight of the rural women. They also raised slogans against the Government's apathy to meet the basic requirements of the downtrodden.

Relationship between Education and Empowerment

There is a close relation between education and women empowerment. Women education helps to improve their awareness and ability, to evaluate and choose the proper alternative education. Education has been regarded as the most important instrument for changing women's subjugated position in the society. It not only develops the personality and rationality of individuals but also makes them qualified to fulfill certain economic, political and cultural functions and thereby improve their socio-economic status. One of the direct expectations from educational development in a society is the reduction in the inequality among individuals and that is why education was included as the basic right of every human being in the universal declaration of human rights.

Education is the milestone for women empowerment because its enables them to respond to opportunities to challenge their traditional role and to change their lives. Similar ideas were supported in international conference in 1994—"Education is on of the most important tool of empowering women with the knowledge skills and self-confidence...educating women benefits the whole society. It has more significant impact on poverty and development than men's education."

Education is necessary for women, the Constitution of UNESCO also directs its efforts to achieve the ideal of equality of educational opportunity without regard to race, sex or any distinction, economic and social, for the first time UNESCO conference in 1962 underlined the importance of the access of girls and women to technical and vocational education for economic and social development. In free India the education of women is more important than that of men. The Radhakrishan University Education Commission says, "There cannot be educated people without educated women, if general education had to be limited to men or to women, the opportunity should be given to women, for them it would more surely be passed on to the next generation." Pandit Jawaharlal Nehru also remarked, "Education of a boy is the education of one person but education of a girl is the education of the entire family", realizing the need of women's education the national policy of education states "the education of women should receive emphasis not only on grounds of social justice, but also because it accelerates social transformation".

The National Policy on Education (NPE), 1986 has given very important recommendations for women education. The major recommendation was education would be used as an agent of basic change in status of women in order to neutralize. The National Policy of Education (NPE) specifically emphasised the necessity of reorienting education to promote women's equality, and envisioned education playing a positive interventionist role in the empowerment of women. The policy recommended revision of textbooks to eliminate gender bias and stereotyping, and the training of teachers towards greater gender sensitivity. The NPE, 1986 was a radical policy intervention in that it placed gender equality through education as a social and political commitment of the state and it has continued to advocate efforts for women's education. However, even this major intervention at the policy level was limited by the fact the education and school education in particular had remained marginal to knowledge building within the women's movement and women's studies.

Thus, the NPE Review Committee (NPERE) in its critique of the 1986 policy, noted that gender was markedly absent in the chapter of "Content and Process of School Education except for a mention that equality of the sexes also pointed out that the task of addressing gender is fraught with complexity.

Education is a powerful tool in the empowerment of women. The movements of empowerment of women's status all over the world have emphasised the important role of education. Education should include not only formal education but also skills, training and functional literacy because girl and women are not only housewife and mother but they are also "workers" in the economic sense. They should be educated to perform an indispensable role in the home and in the household economic life as well for bringing enlightenment and emancipation. Empowerment of women through education will develop.

1. Education provides the information relating to women's right and helps them participate more strongly in community and political affairs.
2. Education should make women aware of the various legal social, economic and political rights available to them and way they can take advantages of them for their advancement.
3. Education gives women the moral support and knowledge, increases their awareness of injustice, social evils and wrong doers.
4. Education gives personal benefits for the individual in terms of self-confidence leading to motivation and interest in society.
5. It helps them develop the ability to think critically by strengthening their organization and networking.
6. It should aim at providing women with education and vocational guidance in order to release them from dependent and unequal status. Improvement of their employment opportunities and earning power has to be given priority to enable them to self-reliance and economic independence such as doctor, scientist, administrator and educator. They should not sacrifice their talent in home making and family life alone.
7. Education has increased the women's decision making power and choosing the proper alternative.

8. Social interaction is easier when persons are capable of reading a newspaper about social and political issues in the community and the rest of the world.
9. Education helped the women to become more balanced and lead a regulated good life. The development of natural virtues and latent capabilities and aimed at all round development of their character and personality.
10. It should aim to include suitable habits of health care, mental application, management of time and conservation of physical mental and emotional energies.

Education is the key that opens the door of life, develops humanity and promotes national development. Education has improved the position of women through its indirect effect as well. Education give not only modern outlook and rational perspective but it also protects individual from insularism and dogmatism. It is clear that the education plays the important role in the process of overall empowerment of women.

Indian Constitution on Women Empowerment

India adopted its Constitution on 26 November, 1949. The Constitution gave full and equal right to women as compared to men. Thereafter we are witnessing a strong, persistent and unrelenting struggle for the emancipation, empowerment and dignity led by women activists, enlightened political leaders, educationists and social reformers.

The Constitution of India has granted equal rights and equal participation in political process of the country along with equal opportunity and right in education and employment. A number of laws have been passed to ensure equality and improvement in the lives of women like the Hindu Succession Act, 1956; Hindu Marriage Act, 1955; Dowry Act, 1961 etc. Besides the social legislation, the planned change played an important role in creating awareness amongst women. A full-fledged Department of Women and Child Development under the Ministry of Human Resources Development for Women was set up by an Act of the Parliament.

The Constitution has also made some other provisions:

(Article 14) of the Constitution provides equality before law to all citizens and forbids discrimination (Article 15). The state is further obliged provision for women and children and for children within the age 6-14 education is now a fundamental right through a constitutional amendment (93rd Constitutional Amendment 2001). International Assertions have been backed by national policies of education, which have linked women's right to education with empowerment.

Article 16: Constitution guarantees equality or opportunity.

Article 19: Protection of certain rights regarding freedom of speech.

Articles 23, 24: Right against exploitation.

Article 39d: That there is equal pay for equal work for both man and woman.

Article 42: Provision for just and human condition of work and maternity relief.

Article 47: Duty of the state to raise the level of nutrition and the standard of living and to improve public health.

Article 243: 73rd and 74th Amendments of the Constitution. Amendment reserves one third of total seats for women in all elected offices of local bodies in rural areas and urban areas.

Conclusions

From the foregoing analysis it is clear that empowerment of women is a complicated and uphill task. Empowerment is very broad term—the empowerment of women by increased participation in all aspects of political and economic life has become one of the major goals of demarcate and participatory movements as well as women's organizations and processes which enables women to realize their full identity and power in all spheres of life.

Education is a powerful tool in the process of overall development to bring about awareness of women's rights and responsibilities and help them participate in the development process. The greater exposure of women to education and other development processes would increase their role in family responsibilities and participation in the social and political activities. Education gives moral support, knowledge and self-confidence; and develops new productive social relations through their learning groups. An educated and economically independent woman takes all decisions concerning various aspects for of the life. Education help her them understand problems better and guides her in the right direction. Education will be used as an agent of basic change in the status of women.

Though present Indian constitutional safeguards that determine women's right to education also guarantee equality and special protection of women: for example Equality before Law, (Article 14), Forbid Discrimination (Article 15), Guarantee Equality of Opportunity (Article 16), Right Against Exploitation (Articles 13, 24), Equal Pay for Equal Work for both men and women (Article 39 d), etc.

Government is very much aware of the need of providing education and other special protection to the women of the country.

From the fore going analysis, it is not enough if women empower themselves through education or constitutional provision of women. The present measures of empowering women are only symptoms but not the disease:

Even after fifty years of independence women suffer from ignorance, family violence, wife battering, dowry death, ghunghat phenomenon, prostitution, burden of domestic labour, etc. It is because there are some basic problems in our society that are caused by:

(*i*) Gender Inequality.
(*ii*) Inactive Administration.

The following are some suggestions regarding the changes:

A new movement in this direction is the need of the hour, radical change in value system, the principles of gender equality and re-establishing the principal of gender equality and gender justice will be able to achieve women equality and ensure honourable co-existence of women with men in society.

Parents must change their attitudes to their children and provide them the parenting that reflects equality to daughters; they must be given opportunities to develop their decision making skills and leading capacities and sons must be taught to respect their sisters as equals. In particular, daughter must have equal access to the same quantity, quality and type of education as sons. The education system must be transformed to ensure that the content and process of education reflects gender equality. A new movement in this direction is the need of the hour in a democracy and this should be initiated at the political level and administrative level. Everyone who is committed to women's freedom and equality must join hands and the work together to promote awareness to mobilise action to draw the attention of decision makers, to break social barriers and to ensure justice. Woman leaders at every level must be supported to build their capacities to function effectively and advance women's interest. Necessary steps should be taken in the form of training male members in their attitude buildings. Empowerment process requires social changes by organizing and enabling the women groups for struggle. If we are able to change value, it will be a great contribution in empowerment of women at national development.

REFERENCES

1. *Economic and Political Weekly*, Vol. XL, Nos. 44, 29, October-November, 2005, p. 4720.
2. Chandrashakharam, *Empowerment of Women*, p. 107.
3. Schuler, Margaret A. and Sakuntala Kadirgamar Rajisingham (eds.) *Legal Literacy: A Tool for Women Empowerment*, Washington D.C. off International, 2004.
4. Kabeer Naila, *Reversed Realities Gender Hierarchies in Development Thought*, London, Verso, 1994.
5. Panchayati Raj UPDATE Institute of Social Science, New Delhi, 1998.
6. Apte, J.S. "Education and Women's Empowerment", in the *Indian Journal of Public Administration*, Vol. XI-III, No. 3, July-September, 1997.
7. *Economic and Political Weekly*, Vol. XXXIX, No. 7, February 14-20, 2004, p. 694.
8. Vani, Prabhakar, *Women in Rural India*, Dominant Publishers and Distributors, New Delhi, pp. 271-72.
9. *Ibid.*, pp. 271-72.
10. B.N. Das, *Trends and Issues in India Education*, Vol. II, Dominant Publisher and Distributor, p. 422.
11. *Ibid.*
12. Maya Majumdar, *Social Status of Women in India*, Dominant Publisher and Distributor, p. 35.

13. *Economic and Political Weekly*, 2003, October 25-31, Vol. XXXVIII, No. 43, p. 4578.
14. N.V. Paranjpay, *Criminology and Criminal Administration Pub.*, Central Law Publisher, p. 463.
15. Buch, Nirmala, *Panchayants and Women's Status of Panchayati Raj in the State and Union Territories in India*, Concept Publishing Company, New Delhi, 2000, pp. 34-41.
16. S. Sarkar and J.J. Munir, *The Constitution of India*, Article 14, p. 4.
17. *Ibid.*, Article 15, p. 5.
18. *Indian Journal of Gender Studies*, Vol. 11, No. 3, September, December 2004, p. 267.
19. S. Sarkar and J.J. Munir, The Constitution of India, Article 16, p. 5.
20. *Ibid.*, Article 19, p. 6.
21. *Ibid.*, Articles 23-24, p. 10.
22. *Ibid.*, Article 39(d), p. 16.
23. *Ibid.*, Article 42, p. 17.
24. *Ibid.*, Article 47, p. 17.
25. *Ibid.*, Article 243 (d, t.), pp. 90, 96.

17

Child Labour and Role of Education to Eliminate it

DR. (MRS.) ANUPAM SHARMA

As a developing country, India is faced with a multitude of social problems. One such problem is, child labour has is graced the entire subcontinent giving it the distinction of having the largest number of child labours in the world. Child labour, however, is the opposite of child work. Child labour hampers the normal physical, intellectual, emotional and moral development of a child. Children who are in the growing process can permanently distort or disable their bodies when they carry heavy loads or are forced to adopt unnatural positions at work for long hours. Children are less resistant to diseases and suffer more readily from chemical hazards and radiation than adults. UNICEF classifies the hazards of child labour into three categories, namely (*i*) physical; (*ii*) cognitive; and (*iii*) emotional, social and moral.

Physical Hazards

There are jobs that are hazardous in themselves and affect child labours immediately. They affect the overall health, coordination, strength, vision and hearing of children. One study indicates that hard physical labour over a period of years stunts a child's physical stature by upto 30 per cent of their biological potential. Working in mines, quarries, construction sites, and carrying heavy loads are some of the activities that put children directly at risk physically. Jobs in the glass and brassware industry in India, where children are exposed to high temperatures while rotating the wheel furnace and use heavy and sharp tools, are clearly physically hazardous to them.

Cognitive Hazards

Education helps a child to develop cognitively, emotionally and socially, and needless to say, education is often gravely reduced by child labour. Cognitive development includes literacy, numeracy and the acquisition of knowledge necessary to normal life. Work may take so much of a child's time that it becomes impossible for them to attend school; even if they do attend, they may be too tired to be attentive and follow the lessons.

Emotional, Social and Moral Hazards

There are jobs that may jeopardise a child's psychological and social growth more than physical growth. For example, a domestic job can involve relatively 'light' work. However, long hours of work, and the physical, psychological and sexual abuse to which the child domestic labours are exposed make the work hazardous. Studies show that several domestic servants in India on average work for twenty hours a day with small intervals. According to a UNICEF survey, about 90 per cent of employers of domestic workers in India preferred children of 12 to 15 years of age. This is mostly because they can be easily dominated and obliged to work for long hours and can be paid less than what would have to be paid to an adult worker. Moral hazards generally refer dangers arising for children in activities in which they are used for illegal activities, such as trafficking of drugs, the sex trade, and for the production of pornographic materials.

The Extent and General Pattern of Child Labour and Its Hazards in India

Researchers give a range of incidence of child labour in India from about 14 million to about 100 million. Some studies show every fourth child in the age group of 5-15 is employed. It is estimated that over 20 per cent of the country's GNP is contributed by child labour. The figures released by the non-governmental agencies are much higher than those of the State. UNICEF cites figures from various resources that put child labour in India at between seventy-five to ninety million. For some observers, the exact number of child labours in India could be as high as 150 million. In brief, India is the largest producer of child labour and illiteracy on this earth. According to at least one study, a quarter of the world's total number of child labours are in India and every third household in that country has a child at work.

Children in India are employed in almost all the activities of the non-formal sector. However, most of them are employed in the agricultural sector or in jobs closely related to agriculture, as is the pattern in many developing countries. A unique factor in India is that a significant number of these children are bonded labours.

Bonded Child Labour

Slave labour or bonded labour is one of the worst forms of labour not only for children but also for adults. In India, bonded labour has been illegal since 1976 when Parliament enacted the Bonded Labour System (Abolition) Act. However, the practice is still widespread. Even conservative estimates suggest that there are at least 10 million adult bonded labours in India. 89 per cent of adults in debt bondage belong to scheduled castes and tribes and 89 per cent of those who control them are agricultural landlords. Most of the work carried out by bonded labours is hard manual labour in the fields or brick kilns. Children or adults are bonded in order to pay off debts that they or members of their families have incurred. They toil all their lives and endure physical attacks that often amount to torture.

There are thousands of bonded child labours in India. They are also mostly the children of parents who belong to scheduled castes and tribes. Young children are sold to employers by their parents to pay back small loans that they have borrowed. Such children are made to work for many hours a day over several years. According to one study, there are about 10 million bonded child labours working as house servants in Indian families. Varandani recently estimated that there were nearly 55 million children in India working as bonded labours in agriculture, mining, brick-kilns, construction work, fishing activities, carpet weaving, fireworks, matches, glass moulding, bidi-making (cigarettes), gem-cutting and polishing work, electroplating, dyeing, washing and domestic work. About 20 per cent of these bonded child labours were sold to cover some small debts obtained by their parents, usually for some social celebration like a wedding in the family.

The Agricultural Sector

A recent ILO report states that in some developing countries nearly one third of the agricultural workforce is comprised children. According to a survey of 1989, about 82 per cent of the 6.1 million fully economically active children in Bangladesh worked in agriculture. Similarly, in India about 80 per cent of child labours are employed in agriculture and allied occupations. Studies also reveal that about 86 per cent of bonded labour is found in India's agricultural sector.

Street Work

There are thousands of children who live and work in the city streets of India. According to a study conducted among the street children in the city of Chennai (Madras), about 90 per cent of them live with their parents in the streets. The same study also revealed that the largest group of street children in Chennai work as coolies (22%). About 10.4 per cent of them work in hotels (small restaurants and snack bars), 9.6 per cent do rag picking, 8 per cent pull rickshaws, and 7.1 per cent sell flowers. A smaller percentage of children are employed in other areas of work, including prostitution (0.3%). They work for 10-12 hours a day and at the end of the day what they earn is barely enough for their survival. About 32 per cent of them receive less than 100 rupees (about 2.5 U.S. dollars) per month as wages.

Contrary to the general conception that many street children are delinquents, the study revealed that only 6.6 per cent of the total sample had served time in juvenile homes or correctional institutions. Studies in a few other Indian cities showed that the majority of the street children were doing rag picking for their living. Usually, these children are unable to submit references or pay deposits to their employers to obtain any work. They choose rag picking as it is the most convenient way of earning something for their living that does not require much experience and investment.

Scavenging is the work that faces children with the most extreme risk. As many of them work with bare feet, they get cuts; they are also exposed to extreme weather conditions, sunstroke, pneumonia, influenza and malaria. They have to carry heavy loads, which stunts their physical growth. They face digestive disorders and food poisoning as they eat thrown away or left over food.

Some Other of Most Hazardous Form of Child Labour in the Manufacturing Sector of India

Glass Factories

Children are used in all the various phases of bangle making and glass blowing. About 85 per cent of them are employed in carrying molten glass on a seven-foot iron rod called *labya* from the furnace to the adult worker and back to the furnace. They sit in front of furnaces where the temperature is said to be 700 degrees centigrade. Children, as they are small in stature have, to go close to the fire when they collect molten glass from the furnace.

Match Factories

The total labour force in this industry is estimated to be 200,000, with about 35 per cent being children. Some of these children are bonded child labours. Respiratory diseases, eye infection, and exposure to chemical agents are the major health hazards in the match and fireworks industries. Researchers accuse the employers of not taking any precaution for fire safety in such workshops where even a small crack could start a fire. They found several children with burn scars on their hands, thighs and legs and 80 per cent of the children interviewed in such workshops reported cases of accidents.

Carpet Industry

An ILO study estimates that there could be 420,000 child labours in India employed in the carpet industry. According to some NGOs, between 1979 and 1993 the value of export earnings in the hand-knotted carpet industry in India grew tenfold. They also claim that the number of children working at the looms has increased from 100,000 in 1975 to 300,000 in 1990. The Indian 'carpet belt' is found mostly in Uttar Pradesh stretching over a vast area. There are usually about 20 or so loom sheds in each village. Some children work as bonded labours; others are kidnapped from their poverty-stricken home villages, including villages in Bihar, the neighbouring state.

Brass Industry

Children in the brass industry are employed in different sectors. Moulding is one of the activities, which is very hazardous and dangerous both to adults and children. More than 15000 children are employed in this sector. If the child is a new recruit, he is given the work of rotating the wheel that fans the underground furnace. Other children in the moulding section must heat the oblong ingot on top of the furnace, break it into small pieces with a hammer and then melt the required amount of brass. When the molten brass is ready, they have to pass the graphite crucible with the raw material to an adult worker holding it with long tongs. Sometimes they themselves have to pour the brass into the moulds and replace the crucible into the furnace the adult worker to remove the hot moulded metal from the moulds.

Lock Industry

Studies reveal that more than 60 per cent of the workers in this sector are children less than 14 years of age. Children do polishing, electro-plating, spray painting and working on hand presses. They cut different components of locks for nearly 12-14 hours a day with hand presses. Exhaustion causes accidents; many lose the tips of their fingers, which get caught in the machines.

The most hazardous job for children in the lock industry is polishing. The boys who do polishing stand close to the buffing machines. The buffing machines that run on electric power have emery powder coated on bobs. While polishing the locks, they inhale emery powder with metal dust and almost all polishers suffer from respiratory disorders and tuberculosis. In the small units, about 70 per cent of the polishers are children.

Similarly, electroplating is another extremely hazardous process in which more than 70 per cent of workers are children below the age of 14 years. Children work with naked hands in dangerous chemicals such as potassium cyanide, sodium phosphate, sodium silicate, hydroelectric acid, sulphuric acid, sodium hydroxide, chromic acid, barium hydroxide, etc. Children, besides being affected by the usual consequences of chemical substances, are also at risk of shocks as these substances also produce electricity and the floors are usually wet. The children have their hands in these solutions for the better part of the twelve-hour-day. Some cases of electrocution have been due to illegal electric connections obtained by some of these units from streetlights.

Role of Education

Children are working everywhere in India and are doing all activities. Now the question arises that how can we eliminate this problem from the society. The data of last decade shows that which states have higher literacy rate, those have less child problem while other states which have low literacy have great problem of child labour. It indicates that education play crucial role in reducing the problem of child labour.

Education is linked to child labour in many different ways. The education system can contribute to the recruitment of children into the labour market by not providing enough school places for the children in school-going age, by not providing schools where the children live, by providing education where the private costs exclude some groups, or by providing education of insufficient quality or relevance.

On the other hand, education can play a key role in prevention. Provision of free, accessible, universal education of quality for all will always be a very important contribution to a sustainable solution to the child labour problem. In addition, if education is made compulsory, the education system can provide a low cost monitoring system to ensure that children continue to be in school and not at work.

Reducing the dropout rate, creating school environments where children at risk feel welcome, and taking into consideration the factors that keep girls away from school, are all important contributions to ensuring that the education system also caters for the children most at risk.

Education can help to educate children and their families about the dangers and risks involved in child labour in relation to their health, safety and development is important. They need to learn about their basic rights, the laws that exist in their country for their protection, who they can turn to for help when they are at risk and when they are being exploited. The education of children about their rights and child labour problems should be integrated within the curriculum of all formal and non-formal education. It is important to draw upon the children's and families' own life experiences and to make them feel safe and comfortable to engage in dialogue with teachers about these topics. Education involves teaching children about their responsibilities to themselves and to others; it involves helping them to become productive citizens of their own communities. This implies the need to invest in teacher training and the production of teaching materials on the problems related to child labour and on child rights.

The availability of free, compulsory, and quality education is widely regarded as the single most important factor in the fight against child labour. The correlation between illiteracy and child labours are as low as 5 per cent. Article of the Indian Constitution commits the state to "endeavour to provide, within a period of ten years from the commencement of the Constitution, for free and compulsory education for all children until they complete the age of fourteen years." The Constitution came into force in 1950. Recognizing the central importance of education, India's leading non-governmental organizations have called for the implementation of universal, free and compulsory education. Among them are: The Child Labour Action Network (CLAN), the Campaign Against Child Labour (CACL), the Centre for Rural Education and Development Action (CREDA) and the Bonded Labour Liberation Front (BLLF). UNICEF India and Anti-Slavery International have likewise called on the Indian Government to implement education for all at the same time, alternate efforts to at least minimally educate bonded children are already underway in a few areas. CREDA in the carpet-belt, the MV Foundation in Andhra Pradesh, and the Indian Council Welfare (ICW) in North Arcot, are all involved in non-formal education initiatives. Some of these programmes utilize modest financial support to attraction children, including small cash stipends and periodic grain allowances. In addition to classic schooling, children on the verge of adulthood may benefit from concrete skills training as well.

The MVF (Andhra Pradesh) aims to eliminate child labour through the universalization of quality education. It started by organizing evening classes for working children but soon developed an innovative strategy to remove children from work and enrol them into formal schools. During the first phase, literate youth from the area carry out surveys to identify the numbers of children at work and out of school and motivate the parents to enrol their children into non-formal education activities. During the second phase, summer camps are organized for the children for three months in schools during the regular formal school summer holidays. The children start to learn the "3 Rs" in a creative learning environment. The children form committees and become responsible for running several camp activities.

The third phase involves the transition from the camp to a hostel and full-time formal education, utilizing the existing government facilities for children from disadvantaged and poor classes. MVF teachers and volunteers are attached to the hostels to guide the children in the transition to formal schools.

The MVF model has been most effective in removing children from work and mainstreaming them into formal schools. Over 10,000 children, have so far benefited from this programme. This model should be implemented everywhere in the country to combat the problem of child labour.

REFERENCES

Burra, Neera, *Born to Work, Child Labour in India,* Oxford University Press, Oxford, New Delhi, 1995, p. xiii.

Burra, Neera, *Born to Work, Child Labour in India,* p. 168.

Burra, Neera, *Born to Work, Child Labour in India,* pp. 42-43.

Child Labour Cell, *Child Labour in the Lock Industry of Aligargh,* p. 10.

Child Labour Cell, *Child Labour in the Match Industry of Sivakasi,* National Labour Institute, Noida, India, p. 1.

Child Labour Cell, *Child Labour in the Match Industry of Sivakasi,* p. 12.

Child Labour Cell, *Street Children of Madras—A Situational Analysis* (Study conducted by Joe Arimpoor), National Labour Institute, Noida, Ghaziabad, U.P., 1992, p. 9.

Dr. G. Varandani, *Child Labour and Women Workers,* p. 42.

Dr. Narendra Prasad, "Child Labour in India", *Yojana,* Vol. 34, No. 8, May 1-15, 1990, pp. 12-13, 19.

Human Rights Watch, *The Small Hands of Slavery—Bonded Child Labour in India,* Human Rights Watch, New York, 1996, p. 122.

ILO, *Child Labour Targeting the Intolerable,* International Labour Office, Geneva, 1996, p. 7.

Mahbub-ul-Haq, *Human Development* 7, Human Development Centre, Oxford University Press, Karachi, Pakistan, 1997, p. 19.

Nazir Ahmad Shah, *Child Labour in India,* Anmol Publications, New Delhi, 1992 (Reprint 1997), p. 12.

S.N. Tripathy, *Migrant Child Labour in India,* Mohit Publications, New Delhi, 1997, p. 2.

UNICEF, *The State of the World's Children* 1997, p. 25.

UNICEF, *The State of the World's Children,* 1997, p. 38.

UNICEF, *The State of the World's Children,* 1997, p. 68.

UNICEF, *The State of the World's Children,* pp. 32-33.

18

Educational Development of Rural Girl in India

DR. UPASNA SHARMA AND DR. J.C. PANT

Education: Foundation for Rural Girl Development

Education is a basic human right, vital to personal and societal development and well-being. Education enhances lives. It ends generation cycle of poverty and disease and provides the means for sustainable development. A quality basic education will better equip girls and boys with knowledge and skills needed to adopt healthy lifestyles, to protect themselves from HIV/AIDS and other sexually transmitted diseases, and to take an active role in social, economic and political decision-making as they transit to adherence and adulthood. As educated adults, they are more likely to have few children, to be informed about appropriate child-rearing practices, and to ensure their children start school on time and are ready to learn.

UNICEF advocates quality basic education for all children—girls and boys—with an emphasis on gender equality and eliminating disparities of all kinds. In promoting equality, UNICEF focused on the most disadvantaged children through a range of innovative programmes and initiatives in education.

Many countries still do not have equality of education. There are many reasons for this including limited economic opportunities for girls; religious societal and financial constraints; and parental concern for girl's safety arising from cultural traditions. Parents see the cost of their son's education as an investment because they will care for them in their old age.

Nearly three-fourth of India's population lives in rural areas. Education for rural people is a subject that requires serious thought from the central and state government and civil society as key component of actions and initiatives aiming at achievement of the goals of development by 2020. Education and training are two of the most powerful weapons to fight against rural poverty and achieve sustainable. Unfortunately, these are also among neglected aspects of rural development initiatives taken by central and state governments.

Despite the fact that education is basic right in itself and an essential prerequisite for reducing poverty, improving the living conditions of rural people and building a self-sufficient society, access to education in rural areas is still much lower as compared to urban areas and the quality of education is poor. Non-attendance in school, early dropout of students, adult literacy and gender inequality in education are found very high in rural areas. Educational activities and training needs have to be linked to the specific requirements of the rural community. Focusing on skills and capacities useful for rural people would generate economic opportunities, improve livelihood and enhance the standard of living. A multi-layered educational approach involving all ages, formal, non-formal and informal education and training needs is necessary.

Of the three pillars of rural development viz. the village school, the village panchayat and the village co-operative, the school is the most vital component of human development, the most enduring tool of rural change. Education holds the key to the stability of the democracy are best tested in the field of education where our investments are next only to defense. Starting from being an educationally backward country as a result of 150 years of colonial rule India today is the largest educational system in terms of students, teachers and educational institutions. In rural India of ancient times there was a proverb: If you are planning for a year, plant coconut, if you are planning for five years, cultivate rice but if you are planning for future, send your child to the school.

Those countries that have lagged in promoting girls' education have also lagged developmentally. It is expensive—both politically and financially to eliminate gender gaps in school enrolment. But if developing countries wish to improve their living standards and catch up with the industrialized world, not educating one's girls to the same extent as boys will surely prove even more expensive.

The conventional view of illiteracy is that it is closely linked to poverty. While that is certainly true, there are numerous other factors responsible for the low level of literacy especially among females.

Factors Responsible for Illiteracy Among Rural Girls

1. Inadequate school facilities.
2. Lack of qualified female teachers.
3. Lack of transport facilities.
4. Lack of hostel facilities for girls.
5. Fear of sexual harassment.
6. Fixed schooling hours.

These factors combine to produce unattractive environments in which girls must run the gauntlet of difficulties to remain in schools, as a result of which their learning is severely compromised even if they do remain. Countries that provided education for girls as well as boys experienced higher economic growth rates than those did not. Gender inequality in education also produced a moderate negative effect on economic growth and provision for basic needs.

Educational Status of Rural Girl Child

Presently, India has the second largest educational system in the world after China, with 6,26,737 primary, 1,90,166 upper primary, 79,648 high schools, 28,487 higher secondary schools. Table 18.1 presents the growth of primary, upper primary, secondary and

Table 18.1: Growth of Recognised Educational Institutions in Rural Areas

Years	*Primary*	*Upper Primary*	*Secondary/Hr. Sec/ Inter/Pre-Degree*
1950-51	175999	10413	2827
1980-81	444752	94249	34668
1990-91	482628	117279	50415
2002-03	573085	193864	87380

higher secondary schools in rural India. During this period the number of primary schools increased by more than 3 times, while the upper primary schools and secondary/higher secondary schools increased by about 19 and 31 times respectively.

Enrolments in Rural Areas

Enrolment by category of schools in rural areas is presented in Table 18.2. It is evident that in all stages boys are enrolled more than girls. However this difference is higher towards the higher stages.

Table 18.2: Enrolment by Category of Schools in Rural Areas (In Million)

Year	*Primary*			*Middle Upper Primary*			*Secondary/Hr. Sec.*		
	Boys	*Girls*	*Total*	*Boys*	*Girls*	*Total*	*Boys*	*Girls*	*Total*
1965-66	25.09	13.06	38.15	4.71	1.19	5.90	1.88	0.33	2.21
1973-74	30.18	16.86	47.04	6.27	2.13	8.40	2.96	0.69	3.65
1978-79	33.14	18.79	51.93	7.91	3.05	10.96	3.26	0.90	4.16
1986-87	39.82	25.98	65.80	12.08	5.64	17.72	5.71	2.08	7.79
1993-94	42.06	30.14	72.47	14.19	7.28	21.47	7.17	3.33	10.50
2002-03	42.28	38.09	80.37	29.83	24.31	54.14	37.71	28.59	66.30

Girls Enrolment

The participation of girls at all stages of education has been increasing steadily through the years as may be seen from Table 18.3. Since 1950-51 girls' participation has increased manifold in Primary, Middle Sec./Hr. Sec. stages and Higher Education levels from 28.1 per cent to 46.8 per cent, from 16.1 per cent to 43.9 per cent from 13.3 per cent to 41.3 per cent, and from 10.0 per cent to 40.1 per cent respectively. However, the girl's participation is still below 50 per cent at all stages of education.

School Dropouts Among Rural Girls

It is evident from Table 18.4 that school dropout rates among girls are higher than boys. But if we look at the figure, we find that over the year it has gone down at different stages of school education (from 1960-61 to 2001-02).

Table 18.3: Percentage of Girls Enrolment to Total Enrolment by Stages

Year	*Primary*	*Middle*	*Sec./Hr. Sec./Intermediate (IX-XII)*	*Hr. Education (Degree & above level)*
1950-51	28.1	16.1	13.3	10.0
1960-61	32.6	23.9	20.5	16.0
1970-71	37.4	29.3	25.0	20.0
1980-81	38.6	32.9	29.6	26.7
1990-91	41.5	36.7	32.9	33.3
2000-01	43.7	40.9	38.6	39.4
2002-03	46.8	43.9	41.3	40.1

Table 18.4: Dropout Rates (%) at Different Stages of School Education from 1960-61 to 2001-02

Year	*Primary (IV)*			*Elementary (I-VIII Classes)*			*Secondary (I-X Classes)*		
	Boys	*Girls*	*Total*	*Boys*	*Girls*	*Total*	*Boys*	*Girls*	*Total*
1960-61	61.7	70.9	64.9	75.0	85.0	78.3	N.A	N.A	N.A
1970-71	64.5	70.9	67.0	74.6	83.4	77.9	N.A	N.A	N.A
1980-81	56.2	62.5	58.7	68.0	79.4	72.7	79.8	86.6	82.5
1990-91	40.1	46.0	42.6	59.1	65.1	60.9	67.5	76.9	71.3
1992-93	43.8	46.7	45.0	58.2	65.2	61.1	70.0	77.3	72.9
1999-2000	38.7	42.3	40.3	52.0	58.0	54.5	66.6	70.6	68.3
2001-2002	38.4	39.9	39.0	52.9	56.9	54.6	64.2	68.8	6.0

Reasons for School Dropouts Among Rural Girls

Various reasons of school dropouts amongst girls in rural areas. One of the major reasons for children being kept out-of-school was the lack of education of parents. The public report on basic education sought to find reasons for both dropouts and never—enrolment of children in five states (Rajasthan, Himachal Pradesh, Uttar Pradesh, Madhya Pradesh and Bihar). It was found that parents' attitude towards education have a major effect on education. It seems that when either of the parents is literate or especially when women are literate, they are more willing to send their children, especially girls, to the school. "The huge dropout rates, however, indicate that children, girls more often than boys, are needed for other activities such as looking after other siblings, domestic work and help with farm work. Parents play a crucial role in keeping young people in school. The degree and nature of family support are determined by such factors as a stressful/ unstable home life, socio-economic status, minority membership, siblings, completion of high school, single parent household, poor education of parents and primary language other than English.

Prof. Nidhi Kotwal and Dr. Neelima Gupta in their study stated that the main causes of dropping out of girls from the school in rural areas were reluctance of parents and participation in domestic activities. Another major reason was problem of financial constraints. The parent's educational status was poor and they did not gave much importance to the education of girls as they did to their sons. They perceived that sons support them in their old age.

Main reasons for school dropout are presented in Table 18.5. It can be inferred from the table that majority of the girls left the school because they required for household work, sibling care etc.

Table 18.5: Main Reasons for Dropout: 1998-99

	Rural		*Urban*		*Total*	
	Male	*Female*	*Male*	*Female*	*Male*	*Female*
School too far away	1.0	5.9	0.2	1.0	0.8	4.8
Transport not available	0.4	1.6	0.1	0.2	0.3	1.3
Further education not considered necessary	2.3	4.3	2.4	5.4	2.4	4.5
Required for household work	8/7	17.3	5.7	14.7	8.0	16.7
Required for work on farm/ family business	9.2	2.9	4.7	1.6	8.0	2.6
Required for outside work for payment in cash or kind	9.9	3.7	11.3	3.0	10.3	3.5
Cost too much	13.3	11.4	15.2	17.0	13.8	12.6
No proper school facilities for girls	0.0	3.5	0.0	1.2	0.0	3.0
Required for care of siblings	0.6	2.3	0.2	1.5	0.5	2.2
Not interested in studies	40.0	24.8	42.5	30.2	46.6	26.0
Repeated failures	5.3	3.7	6.0	6.1	5.5	4.2
Got married	0.2	8.5	0.1	4.9	0.2	7.7
Other	5.3	6.2	5.8	8.2	5.5	6.6
Don't know	3.8	4.0	5.7	5.1	4.2	4.2
Total per cent	**100.0**	**100.0**	**100.0**	**100.00**	**100.0**	**100.0**
Number of children	**5475**	**61221**	**1852**	**1747**	**7327**	**7868**

Hurdles to Girls Education

Girls and boys both have hurdles to overcome. For girls the hurdles are, for the most part, higher and more frequent—simply because they are girls. Family poverty is also a barrier to education. Sending children to school may result in the loss of their income or help at home. The school may charge fees that the family knows it cannot meet or require a uniform that a family cannot afford. Many of the parents directly questioned the objective of educating their girl child. They stated that "Kudi Ne Padhiye Ke Karna." And often, when a choice is to be made between sending a girl or a boy to school, the family will put its scarce resources into the education of the boys, believing that it is a better long-term investment.

Compulsory and for "free" education laws may not exist, or may not be enforced. Early marriage and pregnancy are widespread in many countries, yet most have laws and policies that prohibit pregnant girls from attending school or returning to school after the birth of their child. Worldwide, an estimated 50 million children are not registered at birth, and the majority are female. In many countries, the lack of a birth certificate can prevent admission to school or block eligibility to take examinations.

The international goals connected to girls education are the ensuring that by 2015 all children—particularly girls, children in difficult circumstances and those belonging to ethnic minorities have access to and complete free and compulsory primary education of good quality. Eliminating gender disparities in primary and secondary education by 2015, with a focus on ensuring girls, full and equal access to and achievement in basic education of good quality.

It can be concluded that despite government and NGO initiatives the progress is not up to the mark. Although there is a considerable increase in the spread of educational institutions in rural areas but school dropout among girls has still witnessed substantially. However, participation of girls at all stages of education has been steadily increasing over the years, but in all stages (Primary, Middle, Upper Primary, Secondary/Hr. Secondary) boys are enrolled more than girls and this difference is higher towards the higher stages.

Although both girls and boys have hurdles to overcome but it is in case of girls especially in rural areas. To overcome gender inequality in education by 2015, we have to eliminate gender disparities in primary and secondary education.

It is now recognized that the girls' education is a cornerstone of development. Educated mothers invest more in their children's schooling, thus improving both families and societies' development prospects. They are also likely to have fewer children. Having fewer children allows families to invest more in the health and education of each child, thereby raising the productivity of future generations.

Promoting girls' education, therefore, involves changing attitudes across society as well as spending money on increasing the number of school places available to girls. Donors providing funds for education can help by insisting that their funds are used to educate girls as well as boys. New means of engaging policy makers perhaps through a bottom-up approach, where pressure is applied by civil society, or through better use of evidence to show the benefits of girls schooling may also reap rewards. Religious leaders also need convincing, as do men in general, who are usually the main decision-makers within households. Changing cultural attitudes toward women is a slow and difficult process. In nations that have succeeded, such changes have typically required strong political will as well as leadership.

REFERENCES

1. Das, Debendra Kumar (1991), *Social Sector and Development, Experiences and Challenges,* Deep and Deep Publications, New Delhi.
2. Kaushal, M.P. and Kaushal, M.P. (1973), *Dynamics of Planned Social Change,* Bee Kay Publications, Ludhiana (India).
3. Kotwal, Nidhi and Gupta, Neelima, "Reasons for School Dropouts Among Rural Girls", *Kurukshetra,* The Monthly Journal, Ministry of Rural Development, Vol. 55, No. 1, November, 2006.
4. Kumar, Krishna, "Recasting Education", *The Times of India,* New Delhi, 16 October, 2004.
5. Ruhela, S.P. (2006), *Education in Emerging Indian Society,* International Publishing House, Meerut.
6. Sharma, Sheetal, "Education: Foundation for Rural Development", *Kurukshetra,* The Monthly Journal, Ministry of Rural Development, Vol. 55, No. 1, November, 2006.
7. Singh, Paramjit, Bal, Gurpreet (1996), *Strategies of Social Change in India,* M.D. Publications Pvt. Ltd., New Delhi.

19

Gender Disparities in Education: A Study of Uttar Pradesh

DR. (MRS.) DEEPA RAWAT, SHELENDRA KUMAR,
DR. VIKRAM SINGH AND GUNJAN AGARWAL

Introduction

In India, after independence, it was widely recognized that without the effective participation of all sections of people, democracy or meaningful development is not possible, because quasi or partial democracy denies equal opportunity to the underprivileged to participate in governance at all levels. The Constitution of India guaranteed the right of equality to all its citizens irrespective of their sex, caste, creed and religion. Indian democracy, after being proclaimed a Republic, has been thriving on this basic principle and has continued in the same direction for the last five decades. Strengthening the weaker sections and marginalized communities through reservation system was implicit in the democratic system of the country.

The national movement under the leadership of Mahatma Gandhi was one of the first attempts to draw Indian women out of the restricted circles of domestic life into equal role with men. Writing in 'Young India' in 1918, Gandhiji said, "Woman is the companion of man gifted with equal mental capacities. She has the right to participate in the minutest details of the activities of man. She has the same right of freedom and liberty as he."

The Tenth Plan (2002-07) approach aims at empowering women through translating the National Policy for Empowerment of Women into action and ensuring survival, protection and development of women and children through Rights Based

Approach. Empowerment is a multi-dimensional process, which should enable the individuals or a group of individuals to realize their full identity and powers in all spheres of life. It consists of greater access to knowledge and resources, greater autonomy in decision-making to enable them to have greater ability to plan their lives, or have greater control over circumstances that influence their lives and free them from the shackles imposed on them by custom, belief and practice.

Empowerment of women also means equal status of women. Empowering women socio-economically through increased awareness of their rights and duties as well as access to resources is a decisive step towards greater security for them. Empowerment includes higher literacy level and education for women, better health care for women and children, equal ownership of productive resources, increased participation in economic and commercial sectors, awareness of their rights and responsibilities, improved standards of living and acquiring self-reliance, self-esteem and self-confidence (Shanthi, 1998).

All round development of women has been the focal point of planning process in India. The Indian Government's programme for women development began as early as 1954, but the actual participation began only in 1974. The vast majority of the people in India live in rural areas and are engaged in agriculture earning a subsistence wage. Development, which has been focused on them, seems to have just passed them by. Rural population involves women folk also who make almost half of it. However rural women have acquired a secondary status in social life, economic activities and decision-making among their families. Their role in work productivity, employment generation and income oriented activities are hindered by many socio-economic constraints. The position of women in the socio-economic sphere is evident from the following statistics.

Of the world's 1.3 billion poor, nearly 70 per cent are women. Between 75-80 per cent of the world's 27 million refugees are women and children. Only 24 women have been elected as heads of governments in the last century. Women hold only 10.5 per cent of the seats in world's parliament. Of the world's one billion illiterate, two thirds are women. Two thirds of 130 million children world-wide, who are not in school, are girls. In most countries, women work approximately twice the unpaid time men do. Rural women produce more than 55 per cent of all food grown in developing countries. The value of women's unpaid house work and community work in estimated at 35 per cent of GDP world-wide. HIV is increasingly affecting women. Today, about 42 per cent of the estimated cases are those of women. 20 million unsafe abortions are performed every year resulting in the deaths of 70,000 women.

In India women both urban and rural are subjected to some hindrances, which impose limitations on their potential to play their role effectively. Women are said to have equal status in the society, but when it comes to the actual decision-making, men have final say while the women have to accept a subservient status. In particular, rural women have lcw level literacy, which in turn affects the attitude of women to be socially moved. Education, no doubt widens the individual's mental horizon and releases him/her from the clutches of ignorance and superstitions.

Excessive illiteracy among rural women has given them a primary role in home making and in household activities. It is known that household work is unrecognized and unpaid, consuming more than half of their energy and time. It is estimated that the household work done by rural women in developed countries constitutes about 35 per cent of Gross National Product (GNP) while the work of the rural women in developing countries are not being accounted for. Besides attending to their routine household activities, rural women are involved in agricultural and allied activities like livestock rearing, food processing etc.

Due to this dismal condition of women in India especially in rural areas, the issue of gender disparity is of vital significance. In this chapter we have focused on the status of women, the problem of gender differences in literacy especially in Uttar Pradesh, the need for empowerment and finally suggestions to improve the status of female literacy in Uttar Pradesh and India in general.

Status of Female Literacy

Women are often subjected to the double burden of earning for the family and caring for the children and they are also often excluded from education. In India, most of the women living in rural areas are illiterate and trapped in a vicious cycle of poverty and deprivation. The proportion of women is high among the poor and illiterate persons, which is retarding the efforts to expedite rural development. A situational analysis of the status of women indicates that they occupy a low position in society and the Indian educational gender gap is the greatest among the poorest countries. Recent studies have shown a strong link between education and development, particularly in the case of developing countries, as education is vital to rural development.

The purpose of providing education to women is to make them play a positive role on their own in the development of the nation. It is evident from empirical research that educational discrimination against women hinders the process of rural development. Expanding educational opportunities for women is desirable for increasing productivity on the farm, greater labour force participation, late marriage, lower fertility, child health and nutrition. Since females constitute a major proportion of the rural labour, it is essential that improved education and skill formation become crucial for better development process.

The expansion of educational opportunities for women at all levels can have an important impact on breaking the vicious cycle of poverty by creating a more productive labour force and endowing it with increased knowledge and skills (Sivaramayya, 1983). At the same time, women education can influence the future shape and direction of society in a number of ways. Finally, educating women has been shown to be a critical ingredient in breaking the vicious multi generational cycle of poor child health, low educational performance, low income, high fertility and poor maternal health (Chatterji, 1990). It is no exaggeration to say that the keynote of India's progress lies in the education of her women. It is, therefore, realised that women have to be provided with the vital educational inputs, if they are to become a powerful force in the society and gain a foothold in the developmental processes. Giving education to women will reduce their dependency and enhance their status. It will also reduce fertility and slow population growth; improve child survival; increase the share of family income allocated to food and health care for children and raise household income, especially in families below the poverty line.

Particularly after independence, literacy has been viewed as the essential component of the overall architecture of development planning in India. The government has recognized the role of women in the process of rural development.

Table 19.1: Literacy Rate in India: 1951-2001

(In percentage)

Census Year	*Persons*	*Males*	*Females*	*Male-Female Gap in Literacy Rate*
1951	18.33	27.16	8.86	18.30
1961	28.30	40.40	15.35	25.05
1971	34.45	45.96	21.97	23.98
1981	43.57	56.38	29.76	26.62
1991	52.21	64.13	39.29	24.84
2001	65.38	75.85	54.16	21.70

Source: *Census of India*, Part III, 2001.

With the phenomenal expansion of the formal educational system since independence, there has been noticeable progress in literacy rate of the general population. Table 19.1 shows that literacy rate has increased from 18.33 per cent in 1951 to 65.38 per cent in 2001. Male literacy rate has increased from 27.16 per cent in 1951 to 75.85 per cent in 2001 whereas female literacy rate has increased from 8.86 per cent in 1951 to 54.16 per cent in 2001. There has been a continuous progress in total male and female literacy rates in the previous decades. It is evident from the above table that though male and female literacy rates have increased over the period there is an undesirable continuance of gender disparity. There is a long and wide gap i.e. 21.70 per cent in 2001 census between male and female literacy rates, which is serious enough to cause concern. The gap should be brought down from 21.70 per cent to 10 per cent.

Ours is a value based system of education from primary level onwards which needs a market approach in modern times. According to Article 29 of the "Rights of Child" the education of the child should be directed to the all round personality development. The Government of India has invested huge funds for development of primary education with certain goals. One of the goals is that all children within the age group of 6-14 must complete primary schooling (Behera and Tripathy, 2005). Official entry age for primary school in India is 6 years and the country is also committed to give free education for all children upto the age of 14 years. However, how far these goals are achieved is for all to see. Several indicators can help assess the real situation at the primary level. The most important indicator pointing to the participation of children in schooling is the enrolment ratio. Table 19.2 presents the Gross Enrolment Ratios (GER), which represents school enrolment as a ratio of the total population in the age group of 6-14 years.

Table 19.2: Gross Enrolment Ratio-National

Years	*I-V Primary (6-11 years)*			*VI-VIII Upper Primary (11-14 years)*		
	Boys	*Girls*	*Total*	*Boys*	*Girls*	*Total*
1991	98.12	75.89	87.28	79.82	54.62	67.87
1992	95.0	73.46	84.6	72.5	48.94	67.5
1996	98.7	81.9	90.6	70.9	52.8	62.4
2001	98.5	81.5	90.3	66.5	49.5	58.5

Source: Growth of School Enrolment 1950-93, MHRD, Government of India, *Selected Educational Statistics 2000-01* of MHRD, GOI.

Gross enrolment ratios have remained relatively static during the last decade. This is particularly true of the figures for boys at the primary stage (6-11 years). Corresponding figures for girls show an increase of about 6 percentage points. However, the figures indicate a decline with respect to enrolment at the upper primary stage. This is possibly due to several factors. One of these is the fact that children are not enrolled exactly at the official age specified by the state which also varies from one state to another. As revealed by the figures related to proportion of official age children in Class I, the spread is quite large. While in the states of Kerala and Tamil Nadu, more than 60 per cent children are enrolled in Class I when they are five-year-old, the level of enrolment is highest at six years in most of the states, and is quite high even for the seven-year-old category. This could be due to lack of school readiness and the fact that the number of first generation learners is very large in educationally backward states. Further, special enrolment drives carried out to bring even older children into the primary schools have also influenced the age composition of the school going population (Government of India, 2001). Table 19.3 gives the current GER and NER figures for different states.

Table 19.3: State-wise gross Enrolment/Net Enrolment Ratio (2003-04)

	Gross Enrolment Ratio			*Net Enrolment Ratio*		
	Total	*Boys*	*Girls*	*Total*	*Boys*	*Girls*
Andhra Pradesh	79.20	79.80	78.58	68.6	71.1	66.1
Arunachal Pradesh	93.29	98.68	87.64	69.3	81.7	58.4
Assam	79.23	80.10	78.32	98.4	102.5	94.2
Bihar	55.82	62.37	48.50	75.9	90.9	59.4
Goa	99.26	102.07	96.31	61.2	68.3	55.2
Gujarat	97.23	104.19	89.38	86.4	87.7	84.7
Haryana	71.51	71.53	71.49	73.4	72.5	74.4
Himachal Pradesh	103.13	103.62	101.61	68.1	74.3	62.9
Jammu & Kashamir	73.21	78.77	67.31	55.2	68.1	43.7
Karnataka	95.89	97.95	93.76	88.6	94.2	82.8
Kerala	95.58	96.61	94.51	71.5	72.5	70.4
Madhya Pradesh	90.44	96.89	83.43	88.1	97.4	78.2
Maharashtra	99.56	100.71	98.31	84.4	86.2	82.5
Manipur	116.77	118.85	114.60	67.8	77.7	59.5
Meghalaya	89.16	88.01	90.34	50.3	54.5	46.8
Mizoram	103.51	105.10	101.86	72.6	77.7	67.6
Nagaland	66.30	66.11	66.50	58.5	64.0	53.6
Orissa	89.65	93.28	85.86	69.7	81.0	58.0
Punjab	68.22	66.52	70.25	70.60	68.8	72.7
Rajasthan	95.87	103.65	87.19	71.6	82.6	59.3
Sikkim	92.68	90.63	94.77	61.4	63.4	59.3
Tamil Nadu	110.26	111.57	108.88	84.6	85.7	83.6
Tripura	102.27	105.01	99.41	79.5	92.0	68.6
Uttar Pradesh	78.16	81.09	74.86	46.8	56.0	36.4
West Bengal	90.90	91.57	90.20	55.6	59.2	51.8
A & N Islands	107.92	111.27	104.47	63.8	72.1	56.7
Chandigarh	70.71	70.95	70.42	60.1	65.1	55.2
D&N Haveli	110.30	120.14	99.86	70.2	79.0	61.4
Daman & Diu	106.36	107.76	104.81	74.2	81.6	67.8
Delhi	88.30	88.26	88.33	67.6	74.0	61.7
Lakshadweep	102.56	108.51	96.38	72.8	77.2	68.4
Pondicherry	120.09	121.92	118.18	73.6	83.4	56.2
INDIA	84.91	88.02	81.51	71.1	77.7	64.0

Source: *Selected Educational Statistics 2003-04*, MHRD, Government of India.

On the whole, as against a GER of 84.91 per cent (88.02% boys and 81.51% girls) in primary education, the NER comes to only 71.1 per cent (boys: 77.7% and girls: 64%) 17 States/UTs have a lower NER than the country's average while fifteen States/UTs have a higher NER than the national average. The enrolment ratios indicate the major challenge that the country faces in bringing all children to school. Seen from another angle, one could say that since 1990s the GERs both for boys and girls at primary stage are getting stabilised.

Table 19.4 shows the dropout rate among boys and girls. It shows that the dropout rate has improved over the years, but still, the gender disparity is markedly present. At the primary level, the dropout rate of boys in 1980-81 was 56.2 per cent which has been reduced to 38.7 per cent in 1999-2000. In the same time period the drop-out rate of girls has decreased by 20.2 per cent i.e. from 62.5 per cent in 1980-81, it has come down to 42.3 per cent in 1999-2000. In the year 1980-81, 1990-99 and 1999-2000 the drop-out rate among girls at the primary level was 6.3, 5.9 and 3.6 per cent higher than the boys respectively. Almost same situation is evident at the middle level (Raghav, 2006).

Besides the overall grim situation, there are also wide regional and state disparities. Some states like Kerela do not have a gender bias whereas in states like Uttar Pradesh and Bihar, the situation is very dismal.

Uttar Pradesh Scenario

Female literacy situation in Uttar Pradesh is dismal. Only one out of four in the 7+ age group was able to read and write in 1991. This figure went down to 19 per cent for rural areas, 11 per cent for the scheduled castes, 8 per cent for scheduled tribe in rural areas and 8 per cent for the entire rural population in the most educationally backward districts. The 1981 census figures suggest that in UP the crude female literacy rate among scheduled castes in rural UP was below 18 per cent in 18 out of UP's 56 districts and below 25 per cent in a majority of districts (Department of Education, Uttar Pradesh Government).

In terms of more demanding educational attainment (the completion of primary or secondary education), in 1992-93 only 50 per cent of literate males and 40 per cent of literate females could complete the cycle of eight years of schooling involved in the primary and middle stages. One other notable feature of the Uttar Pradesh education system is the persistence of high levels of illiteracy in the younger age group. Within that age group, illiteracy was endemic in the rural areas. In the late 1980s, the incidence of illiteracy in the 10-14 age group was as high as 32 per cent for rural males and 61 per cent for rural females, and more than two-thirds of all rural girls in the 12-14 age group never went to school (Jean Dreze and Gazdar, 1997).

Table 19.4: Dropout Rate in Girls (1980-81—1999-2000)

Year	Primary				Middle (6 to 8)			
	Sum	*Girls*	*Boys*	*Male-Female Gap in Drop-out Rate (Column 3, 4)*	*Sum*	*Girls*	*Boys*	*Male-Female Gap in Drop-out Rate (Column 3, 4)*
1980-81	58.7	62.5	56.2	6.3	72.7	79.4	68.0	11.4
1990-91	42.6	46.0	40.1	5.9	60.9	65.1	59.0	6.0
99-2000	40.3	42.3	38.7	3.6	54.6	58.0	52.0	6.0
Difference between 80-81 and 99-00	58.7–40.3 = 18.4	62.5–42.3 = 20.2	56.2–38.7 = 17.5	6.2–3.6 = 2.7	72.7–54.6 = 18.1	79.4–58.0 = 21.4	68.0–52.0 = 16.0	11.4–6.0 = 5.4

Source: Education Department, Ministry of Human Resources and Development, Government of India, New Delhi, 2000.

The problems of education system are exacting. Due to public apathy the schools are in disarray. While privately run schools (including those run by Christian missionaries) are functional, they are beyond the reach of ordinary people. The state government is trying to take steps to make the population totally literate. There are special programmes like the World Bank aided DEDP. Steps are being taken with the help of NGOs and other organizations to raise participation. As a result some progress in adult education has been made and the census of 2001 indicates a male literacy rate of 70.23 per cent and a female literacy rate of 42.98 per cent.

Prior to 1972, the primary and upper primary schools in Uttar Pradesh were run, maintained and controlled by District Boards and municipalities including municipal corporations etc. The schools were constituted under various Acts related to management of local bodies i.e.

U.P. Kshetra Samiti and Zila Parishad Adhiniyam, 1961.
U.P. Municipalities Act, 1916.
U.P. Nagar Mahapalika Adhiniyam, 1959.

Considering urgent need to improve literacy in the state, it was felt that education needed planned interventions from the state government. In this background, the government of Uttar Pradesh passed the Uttar Pradesh Basic Education Act, 1972 (U.P. Act No. 34 of 1972).

The main objective of this Act was to organise, co-ordinate and control imparting of basic education in schools other than high schools or intermediate colleges. By this Act, an autonomous body named "Uttar Pradesh Board of Basic Education" was constituted under chairmanship of the Director, Basic Education. All schools which were managed and controlled by local bodies have since then been transferred to the Board. The Board of Basic Education controls appointment, transfer and posting of basic school teachers, determines school timings and gives recognition to private schools imparting basic education in the state.

Uttar Pradesh Board of Basic Education Act, 1972 has been amended in year 2000, incorporating principle of devolution of powers to the village community and management of education has been decentralised for empowering grassroots participatory agencies. Other Acts relating to basic education were also amended one of the most crucial one has been United Provinces Panchayati Raj Act, 1947 wherein there is a committee for each village or group of villages called Gram Shiksha Samiti.

The Gram Shiksha Samiti establishes, controls and plans basic schools in its panchayat areas. It prepares plans for development and improvement of the schools. Major functions also include giving advice regarding building and other improvement plans to Zila Panchayat.

Table 19.5: Educational Indicators of Uttar Pradesh

Number of primacy schools (Govt.+ Private recognised)	135112
Number of upper primary schools (Govt.+ Private recognised)	41595
Number of regular teachers in Parisadiya Primary Schools	20207.;
Number of Shiksha Mitras in Parisadiya Primary Schools	
Number of Regular Teachers in Parisadiya Upper Primary Schools	70200
Teacher-Pupil Ratio at Primary level	1: 45
Teacher-Pupil Ratio at Upper Primary Level	1: 39
EMIS	2005-06
Student-Classrom Ratio	1: 64
Repetition Rate (%)	1.59
Transition rate for class V to VI (%)	73
% of girls in primary enrolment	48
% of girls in upper primary enrolment	46
% of SC in primary enrolment	28
% of SC in upper primary enrolment	28
% of Female Teacher Ratio	30

Source: *National Human Development Report 2001*, Government of India.

Table 19.5 gives the overall situation of education in Uttar Pradesh. Though the number of primary schools is quite large— 135112, yet they are insufficient and unable to bring all children in the age group 6-11 years under their fold. Also the gender disparity is quite evident in the percentage of girls in primary enrolment (48%) and in the female teacher ratio (30%). Education of girls, especially those belonging to the scheduled castes and scheduled tribes, is the primary focus in Sarva Shiksha Abhiyan in different states including Uttar Pradesh. Efforts are being made to mainstream gender concerns in all the activities under the Sarva Shiksha Abhiyan programme. Mobilization at the habitation/ village/urban slum level, recruitment of teachers, upgradation of primary into upper primary schools, incentives like midday meals, uniforms, scholarships, educational provision like textbooks and stationery, all takes into account the gender focus. Every activity under the programme will be judged in terms of its gender component. Besides mainstreaming, special efforts like the Mahila Samakhya type of mobilization and organization, back-to-school camps for adolescent girls, large-scale process based constitution on Mahila Samoohs, are also being attempted. The selection criteria takes into account the low female literacy among the scheduled caste and scheduled tribe women.

The Sarva Shiksha Abhiyan recognizes the need for special efforts to bring the out-of-school girls, especially from disadvantaged sections, to school. This requires a proper identification of girls who are out of school in the course of microplanning. It also calls for involving women through participatory processes in the effective management of schools. Experiences across the states under Mahila Samakhya and under the District Primary Education Programme have suggested the need for a clear perspective on women's issues. The provision for girls' education would have to be situated in the local contexts and interventions designed to suit the specific community needs in this regard. Special interventions need to be designed to address learning needs of girls and relating education to their life. The Sarva Shiksha Abhiyan is committed to making these interventions possible.

Conclusion and Suggestions

Although the National Policy on Education (1986) emphasized elimination of disparities in the educational system and provision of greater facilities through qualitative programme interventions, the problem of women's illiteracy has still not received concerted attention in educational planning. There have been many special drives in respect of literacy promotion like Farmer's Functional Literacy Programme, National Adult Education Programme, Mass Programme of Fundamental Literacy, Total Literacy Campaign of the National Literacy Mission, Operation Black Board etc. all giving emphasis to women as the priority group among others. As a result of these efforts, the literacy rates have progressed over the period. However, the absolute number of illiterates has also gone up among women. The following are some suggestions to remove gender bias and to improve literacy rate among women.

- Special support services that reduce costs to parents and create incentives for them to enroll their daughters.
- Appointment of women teachers.
- Involving women's group like Self-Help Groups in promoting women's literacy.
- Appointing more girl child promoters at the village level.
- Providing free and compulsory education for all girls up to 20 years.
- Establishment of more number of primary schools to meet the demand.
- Effective implementation of mid-day meals programme.
- Removing misconceptions about girls' education and bringing changes in the attitudes of parents and society.
- Involving academic institutions and NGOs in implementing literacy programmes.
- Effective implementation of follow-up programmes including vocational training and skill development courses especially for girls in school curriculum.

In recent years, momentum has been gathering not only in India but all over the world, demanding gender equality and push for equal representation of women in all spheres of activity. Literacy for women may impart knowledge and skills, which enable poor women to improve their earning potential and address their survival needs. It is, therefore, realised that women have to be provided with the vital educational inputs, if they are to become a powerful force in the process of development. Thus literacy for poor women is a tool for rural development.

The greatest hindrance, to the progress of India and eradication of many social evils of her people is illiteracy of the masses. While lack of education is one of the prominent causes of poverty, the poverty of the people is one of the most common causes of illiteracy. The efforts for the rural development must go together with educational progress especially or particularly in women education. Efforts have been made to link women's education to larger social and economic development that impinges upon their education. It is against this background of the general neglect of educating illiterate women that we need to examine salient issues pertaining to gender equity in literacy in India and Uttar Pradesh in particular.

Literacy for poor women is a tool for empowerment in a wider struggle against inequality and injustice in society. Literacy for women can impart knowledge and skills, which enable poor women to improve their earning potential and address their survival needs.

In recent years, empowerment of women has been recognized as a central issue in determining the status of women. Empowerment covers aspects such as women's control over material and intellectual resources. It is a process, not an event, which challenges traditional power equations and relations. Abolition of gender-based discrimination in all institutions and structures of the society and participation of women in policy and decision-making processes at domestic and public levels are few dimensions of women empowerment and this can be achieved only, when female literacy rate is increased and gender disparities are removed in India and especially in gender biased states like Uttar Pradesh.

REFERENCES

Behera and Tripathi, Bamadeba, Primary Education: An Overview, *Kurukshetra*, Vol. 53, No. 11, September, 2005.

Chatterji, Angana, Women in Search of Human Equality, *Social Action*, Vol. 40, 46-56, 1990.

Department of Education, *Government of Uttar Pradesh*, Lucknow, India, 2004.

Jean Dreze and Haris Gazdar (1997), Uttar Pradesh, *The Burden of Inertia, India Development: Selected Regional Perspectives*.

Ministry of Human Resource Management, Government of India, Education Department, New Delhi, 2000.

Raghav, V.S., *Success of Sarv Siksha Abiyan*, September, 2006.

Shanti, K. (Ed.) (1998), *Empowerment of Women*, Anmol Publication Pvt. Ltd., 1998.

Sivaramayya, B. (1983), Status of Women and Social Change, *Journal of Indian Law Institute*, Vol. 25, 1983.

20

Education and Gender Justice in Bihar

PROF. R.N. THAKUR

In 1985, there became 'The international women's conference' at Nairobi which opened the eyes of the women to conceive the concept, 'empowerment of women' as a redistribution of social power and control of resources in favour of under-privileged (including women). The 'programming of action 1992' has broadly conferred the following measurements of empowerment for them. Those are:

(*a*) To enhance self-esteem and self-confidence in women.
(*b*) To develop in them an ability to think critically.
(*c*) To foster decision-making and action through collective process.
(*d*) To ensure equal participation in the development process.
(*e*) To provide information, knowledge and skill for economic independence.
(*f*) To enhance access to legal literacy and information to their right and entitlement in the society with a view to increase their participation on equal footings in all areas.

These parameters of empowerment are multi-facets and multidimensional for the real upliftment of the downtrodden and weaker sections of the society, particularly women. There are many aspects of women's empowerment viz. economic, social, political, academic and psychological etc.

Table 20.1: Sex-Ratio in Bihar and India 1901-2001

Census Year	*Sex-Ratio in Bihar*	*Sex-Ratio in India*
1901	1061	972
1911	1051	964
1921	1020	955
1931	995	950
1941	1002	945
1951	1000	946
1961	1005	941
1971	957	930
1981	948	934
1991	907	927
2001	921	933

Source: *Economic Survey*, 2001-02, Government of India, Census of India 2001, Series II, Bihar Provisional Population Totals, Delhi.

Table 20.2: District-wise Sex-Ratio of Bihar State

District	*Sex-Ratio*	
	1991	*2001*
Bihar	907	921
W. Champaran	877	901
E. Champaran	883	898
Sheohar	876	896
Sitamarhi	884	893
Madhubani	932	943
Supaul	904	920
Araria	907	916
Kishanganj	933	940
Purnia	903	916
Katihar	909	919
Madhepura	885	915
Saharsa	884	910
Darbhanga	911	914
Muzaffarpur	904	928
Gopalganj	968	1005
Siwan	1017	1033
Saran	963	965
Vaishali	921	921
Samastipur	926	927
Begusarai	989	911
Khagaria	968	890

(*Contd.*)

District	*Sex-Ratio*	
	1991	*2001*
Bhagalpur	864	878
Banka	893	908
Munger	856	878
Lakhisarai	880	923
Sheikhpura	896	920
Nalanda	898	915
Patna	867	873
Bhojpur	904	900
Buxar	884	884
Kaimur (Bhabhua)	• 884	907
Rohtas	894	909
Jahanabad	919	928
Aurangabad	915	936
Gaya	922	927
Nawada	903	917

Source: Computed from Census 1991 and 2001.

Education and Gender Justice in Bihar

Women had been kept in the margin or they lead their lives in isolation and thus everywhere women are left alone. Thus it is seen that women are going behind the scenario. The state shows a rising masculinity with the proportion of women in the total population gradually falling. This is very shocking and alarming for the process of economic development.

Table 20.3: Low Literacy Rate

Census	*Bihar*	*Percentage*
1991	Persons	37.49
	Male	51.37
	Female	21.99
2001	Persons	47.53
	Male	60.32
	Female	33.57

Table 20.4: Trends of Sex-Ratio and Literacy in Bihar (2001)

Districts	*%age of Child Population*	*Child Population, Sex-Ratio Literacy*				
		Sex-Ratio		*%age Literacy Rate*		
		Total	*Child*	*Total*	*Male*	*Female*
Bihar	10.47	921	938	47.53	60.32	33.57
W. Champaran	10.17	901	942	39.63	51.91	25.85
E. Champaran	6.39	998	934	38.14	50.14	24.65
Sheohar	4.15	896	919	37.01	45.54	27.43
Sitamarhi	5.74	893	986	39.38	51.02	26.35
Madhubani	3.48	943	938	42.35	57.26	26.56
Supaul	5.40	920	921	37.80	53.23	21.02
Araria	6.24	916	967	34.94	46.50	22.14
Kishanganj	9.97	940	941	31.02	42.80	18.49
Purnia	8.75	916	968	35.51	46.16	23.72
Katihar	9.13	919	966	35.29	45.51	24.03
Madhepura	4.46	915	918	36.19	48.87	22.31
Saharsa	8.23	910	900	39.28	52.04	25.31
Darbhanga	8.12	914	883	44.32	57.18	30.35
Muzaffarpur	9.30	928	925	48.15	60.19	35.20
Gopalganj	6.07	1005	961	48.19	63.81	32.81
Siwan	5.45	1033	927	52.01	67.67	37.26
Saran	9.17	965	941	52.01	67.81	35.74
Vaishali	6.88	921	933	51.63	64.00	38.14
Samastipur	3.62	927	945	45.76	57.83	32.69
Begusarai	4.58	911	940	48.55	59.71	36.21
Khagaria	5.97	890	942	41.56	52.02	29.62
Bhagalpur	18.59	878	966	50.28	60.11	38.63
Banka	3.50	908	938	43.40	56.28	29.10
Munger	27.88	878	915	60.11	70.68	47.97
Lakhisarai	14.68	923	955	48.21	60.97	34.26
Sheikhpura	15.48	920	959	49.01	62.56	34.13
Nalanda	14.92	915	941	53.64	66.94	39.03
Patna	41.80	873	948	63.82	73.81	52.17
Bhojpur	13.98	900	938	59.71	74.78	42.81
Buxar	9.18	901	926	57.49	72.82	40.36
Kaimur (Bhabhua)	2.23	907	940	55.57	70.57	38.90
Rohtas	13.34	909	947	62.36	76.54	46.62
Jahanabad	7.40	927	909	56.03	70.90	40.08
Gaya	13.71	937	958	51.07	63.81	37.40
Aurangabad	8.42	936	932	57.50	71.99	42.04
Nawada	7.66	948	974	47.36	61.22	32.64
Jamui	7.38	917	964	42.74	57.10	26.92

Source: Census of India, 2001 series—Bihar: Provisional population Totals, Paper-2 of 2002: Rural-Urban distribution of population, Director of Census Operations, Bihar, Annexure 3 to 5, pp. 75-112.

Table 20.5: State-wise Literacy Rate in India

States	2001	1991
	Literacy Rate (%)	
Andhra Pradesh	61.1(51.2)	44.1
Assam	64.3(56.0)	52.9
Bihar	47.5(33.6)	37.5
Delhi	81.8(75.0)	75.3
Goa	82.3(75.5)	75.5
Gujarat	70.0(58.6)	61.3
Haryana	68.6(56.3)	55.9
Himachal Pradesh	77.1(68.1)	63.9
Jammu Kashmir	54.5(41.8)	NA
Karnataka	67.0(57.5)	56.0
Kerala	90.9(87.9)	89.8
Madhya Pradesh	64.1(50.3)	44.2
Maharashtra	77.3(67.5)	64.9
Manipur	68.9(59.7)	59.9
Meghalaya	63.3(60.4)	49.1
Nagaland	67.1(61.9)	61.7
Orissa	63.6(51.0)	49.1
Punjab	70.0(63.6)	58.5
Rajasthan	61.0(44.3)	38.6
Tamil Nadu	73.5(64.6)	62.7
Tripura	73.7(65.4)	60.4
U.P.	57.4(43.0)	40.7
W. Bengal	69.2(60.2)	57.7
All India (Incl. others)•	54.9(54.3)	51.6#(27.8)
	25.7(54.3)	65.4 (51.6) #

- Figures relate to population aged seven years and above. Figures in brackets show female literacy rate.

\# Exclude J&K.

Source: Statistical Outline of India, 2003-04.

Table 20.6: Percentage of Literates Among Persons Aged 7+ Based on 2001 Census

State	Persons	Male	Female	Rural	Urban
H.P.	77.13	86.02	68.08	74.38	89.59
Punjab	69.95	75.63	63.55	65.16	79.13
Haryana	68.59	79.25	56.31	63.82	79.89
Rajasthan	61.03	76.46	44.34	55.92	76.89
U.P.	57.36	70.23	42.98	53.68	70.64
Bihar	47.53	60.32	33.57	44.42	72.71
Assam	64.28	71.93	56.03	60.92	85.76
W. Bengal	69.22	77.58	60.22	64.06	81.63
Orissa	63.61	75.95	50.97	60.44	80.95

(Contd.)

State	Persons	Male	Female	Rural	Urban
M.P.	64.09	76.74	50.29	58.13	79.68
Gujarat	69.97	80.50	58.60	58.53	79.25
Maharashtra	77.27	86.27	67.51	70.84	85.76
Andhra Pradesh	61.11	70.85	51.17	55.33	76.39
Karnataka	67.04	76.29	57.45	59.68	81.05
Goa	82.32	88.88	75.51	79.65	85.03
Kerala	90.92	94.20	87.86	90.05	93.38
Tamil Nadu	73.47	82.33	64.55	66.68	82.07
All India	65.37	75.85	54.16	59.21	80.07

Source: *Sarvekshana*, October 2001, March 2001.

Table 20.7: Literacy Rate in Bihar (1951-2001) in % age

Census Years	Persons	Male	Female
1951	13.49	22.68	4.22
1961	21.95	35.85	8.11
1971	23.17	35.86	9.86
1981	32.32	47.11	16.61
1991	37.49	51.37	21.99
2001	47.53	60.32	33.57

Source: Census of India, 2001 series—Bihar: Provisional population Totals, Sahitya Bhawan, Agra.

Table 20.8: District-wise Literacy Rate of Bihar State

(Literacy Rate in %age)

Districts	1991			2001		
	Persons	Males	Females	Persons	Males	Females
Bihar	7.49	51.37	21.99	47.53	60.32	33.57
W. Champaran	27.99	39.65	14.41	39.63	51.91	25.85
E. Champaran	27.59	39.65	13.69	38.14	50.14	24.65
Sheohar	26.18	36.36	14.34	37.01	45.54	27.45
Sitamarhi	28.49	39.86	15.49	39.38	51.02	26.35
Madhubani	33.22	48.49	16.75	42.35	47.26	26.56
Supaul	28.11	40.96	13.74	37.80	53.23	21.02
Araria	26.19	36.99	14.01	34.94	46.50	22.14
Kishanganj	22.22	33.12	10.38	21.02	42.80	18.49
Purnia	28.52	38.92	16.80	35.51	46.16	23.72
Katihar	28.70	39.24	16.88	35.29	45.51	24.03
Madhepura	27.72	39.31	14.41	36.19	48.87	22.31
Saharsa	29.98	42.37	15.83	39.28	52.04	25.31
Darbhanga	34.94	48.31	20.09	44.32	57.18	30.35
Muzaffarpur	36.11	48.44	22.33	48.15	60.19	35.20

(Contd.)

Districts	1991			2001		
	Persons	*Males*	*Females*	*Persons*	*Males*	*Females*
Gopalganj	34.96	51.62	17.75	48.19	63.81	32.81
Siwan	39.13	57.51	21.33	52.01	67.67	37.26
Saran	41.79	60.18	22.71	52.01	67.81	35.74
Vaishali	40.56	55.62	24.08	51.63	64.00	38.14
Samastipur	36.37	50.39	21.17	45.76	57.83	32.69
Begusarai	36.88	48.66	23.52	48.55	59.71	36.21
Khagaria	32.33	42.97	19.79	41.56	52.02	29.62
Bhagalpur	41.84	53.41	28.11	50.28	60.11	38.83
Banka	34.55	48.17	18.99	43.40	56.28	29.10
Munger	52.27	64.95	37.07	60.11	70.68	47.97
Lakhisarai	39.40	53.12	23.48	48.21	60.97	34.26
Sheikhpura	40.92	55.43	24.41	49.01	62.56	34.13
Nalanda	46.95	61.95		53.64	66.94	39.03
Patna	56.33	69.07	41.35	63.82	73.81	52.17
Bhojpur	48.18	66.35	27.95	59.71	74.78	42.81
Buxar	45.54	62.94	25.74	57.49	72.89	40.36
Kaimur (Bhabhua)	39.35	55.68	20.69	55.57	70.57	38.90
Rohtas	48.52	64.50	30.29	62.36	76.54	46.62
Jehanabad	45.83	63.11	26.81	56.03	70.90	40.08
Aurangabad	45.14	61.80	26.67	57.50	71.99	42.04
Gaya	40.47	55.22	24.20	51.07	63.81	27.40
Nawada	39.86	54.85	21.82	47.36	61.22	32.64
Jamui	33.41	48.48	16.41	42.74	57.10	26.92

Literacy Rate in Bihar

Literacy is such parameter which indicates the index of economic development and human development of the state or country. Bihar is on the last ladder of the literacy rate of parameter as well as female literacy rate parameter in the country. In 2001 the literacy rate in Bihar remained 47.53 per cent (against 65.38% at all India level) and female literacy rate 33.57 (male literacy 60.32%) against 54.3 per cent at all India level. Kerala is on the peak where literacy rate is 90.9 per cent whereas female literacy is 87.9 per cent. No state in India records neither lower literacy rate nor lower female literacy rate than Bihar. The most disturbing feature of population growth trend in Bihar is its low level of literacy. This lowest social infrastructure in Bihar keeps the women on the lowest place in the field of empowerment.

Table 20.9: Female Literacy in Percentage

	1991	*2001*
All India	39.3	54.2
Bihar	22.9	33.6
M.P.	28.8	50.3
Rajasthan	24.4	44.3
U.P.	25.3	43.0
Kerala	86.7	89.4
Punjab	50.4	68.1
Jharkhand		39.4

The Table 20.9 shows that only about 13.5 per cent people were literate in Bihar in 1951. Since 1951 the rate of literacy has been continuously increasing. But this is not a matter of great happiness for us. We have entered 21st century but even now more than 52 per cent. Biharis use their thumb-impressions or they are merely thumb-printers. What a sorry figure it is. The condition of women class is the worst in this regard because 67 per cent of our women don't know even how to read and write. The problem becomes more heart-painting when we compare the literacy rate of Bihar with those of other states and the national average.

Female Literacy and Population

The increase of population of the country is also a great problem. Due to lower literacy rate and particularly of female the population of country is adversely affected. Due to this it increases very rapidly and vice-versa. Its remedy is also possible through the expansion and extension of literacy and education. In India those states, which have higher level of female literacy and education, have so higher fertility rate. It is evident that Bihar is at the top in this respect (having female literacy rate at the bottom). But those states, which have higher level of literacy and education have lower fertility rate. Bihar, U.P. and Rajasthan having least female literacy rate are in the category of such states having most fertility rate. Kerala, T.N. and W. Bengal have higher female literacy rate, thus those states have less fertility rate. The present union UPA government has assured in its manifesto that it will increase the education expenditure upto 6 per cent of GDP increasing from 3.2 per cent. In 2003-04 the total GDP of the country was more than Rs. 25 lakh crore of which 6 per cent become Rs. 1.5 lakh crore. When the Union and State Government made expenditure over education Rs. 80,779 crore only being combined together. It means if the Union Government executes its promise to education, it has to spend on education at least Rs. 70,000 crore additional expenditure.

In 2001 census literacy rate of India is 65.4 whereas female literacy rate is 54.3 per cent. In 1991 census literacy rate of India was 51.6 per cent whereas female literacy rate was 39.3 per cent. In Bihar 1991 census recorded 37.49 per cent literacy rate whereas male literacy rate was 51.37 per cent and female literacy was 21.99 per cent only. But in 2001 census, literacy rate is 47.53 per cent, male literacy rate is 60.32 per cent and female literacy rate is 33.57 per cent only. Thus it is seen that in 2001 census difference between male literacy (60.32 %) and female literacy (33.57 %) is much higher. It is almost double. So it is evident that female literacy rate is very low in Bihar in respect of male literacy rate. It is also the lowest in respect of female literacy rates of all the states of India. There is one encouraging fact that rate of female literacy in Bihar during the period 1991-2001 increased more rapidly than that of increase of male literacy rate. But in spite of that female literacy rate of Bihar is far behind the male literacy rate.

In Bihar 17 districts are such which record more female literacy rates in respect of its state level rate i.e. 33.57 per cent. Those districts are following viz. Patna (52.7 %), Munger (47.97), Rohtas (46.62), Bhojpur (42.81), Aurangabad (42.04), Buxar (40.36), Jehanabad (40.08), Nalanda (39.03), Kaimur (Bhabhua) 38.90, Bhagalpur (38.83), Vaishali (38.14), Siwan (37.26), Begusarai (37.21), Saran (35.74), Muzaffarpur (35.20), Lakhisarai (35.36) and Sheikhpura (34.13 %).

Kishanganj district records the lowest female literacy rate i.e. 18.49 per cent. This district records the lowest literacy rate (person) 21.02 and male literacy rate 42.80 per cent also. This district is Muslim majority district. Thus the Muslim populated district has the least rate of literacy both in male and female. In this way the academic and educational empowerment of women in Bihar is in the bottom in the graph of development.

Student Enrolment Rate

Performance of Bihar state with regard to enrolment and literacy is not satisfactory in comparison to the states of Maharshtra, Tamil Nadu, West Bengal, Andhra Pradesh, Madhya Pradesh, Gujarat and Karnatka. Primary education in Bihar requires massive expansion and public co-opération so that enrolment rate may be increased. Its seems that the Government of India has never done equal role with Bihar.

Table 20.10: Female Literacy and Fertility Rate

States having Least Female Literacy	*Adult Female Literacy Rate (2001)*	*Total Fertility Rate*	*States having Maximum Female Literacy*	*Adult Female Literacy Rate (2001)*	*Total Fertility Rate*
Bihar	33.6	4.28	Kerala	87.9	1.80
U.P.	43.0	7.73	T.N.	64.9	1.96
Rajasthan	44.3	4.13	W. Bengal	60.2	2.44

The recently conducted mid-term Assembly Survey of Learners Achievement on All India basis reveals that the learners attainment in Grade-4 across the country is far below than expectations. Therefore, in the last alternative, if children of Grade-5 are considered literate and total enrolment in Grade-5 is obtained, it comes out to be 153.72 million. This is 75 per cent of the total literates produced between the period 1991-2001 by assuming Grade-5 students as literates, we assume that children have completed Grade-4, survived and retained themselves in the system atleast upto the Grade-5. However, it would be better and safe to consider primary graduate as literate but completion rates required to know graduates are not available. It may, however, be noted that Gaj Raj (UNESCO, 1992) considered Grade-4 student as literate. By adopting the same methodology, state specific average enrolment in Grade-4 and 5 between the period 1991-2001 is also calculated. In case of most of the states and union territories, large chunks of literates come from enrolment in Grade-4/5, which is more than 70 per cent of the total literates, produced between 1991-2001.

So far, the case of Bihar is concerned that 27 lakh children of Bihar are out of primary education who couldn't be enrolled in the school. It is pertinent to mention here that there are roughly 81 lakhs children in India who couldn't be enrolled in the school for primary education and out of that number 27 lakhs (6-14 years) non-school going children are only from Bihar.

Dropout Rate of Students

It is harsh reality that children in India particularly in poor states like Bihar dropout rate is the greatest obstacle in the path of literacy. A large no. of researches suggest that completion of at least 5 to 6 years of schooling is a critical threshold for sustainable mastery of basic competencies such as literacy and numeracy. In less than 5 to 6 years of schooling children remain functionally illiterate for the rest of their life. It is also interesting to note that among the lowest income group of people the dropout rate is very high.

In the comparison of dropout rate the rate of the female children is higher than that of male children. In India, among the several sections of the population such as SCs and STs, there is a dramatic disparity in the school completion rate. On account of heavy dropouts, largely on account of economic reasons. In those sections also dropout of girls is more than that of boys.

It is visible that dropout rate in rural areas is more pitiable at every stage i.e. primary, middle and secondary school level. It is also necessary to point out here that dropout rate among boys students are seen more in comparison to the girls students in the rural areas while the situation is different in the urban areas.

Table 20.11: Dropout Rate of Students in Bihar (5-24 Years)

Rural/Urban Boys/ Girls	*Period of Dropout (Percentage)*			
	At Any Stage	*Primary*	*Middle*	*Secondary*
Rural	43.0	41.0	27.3	16.0
Boys	47.5	41.1	26.5	17.8
Girls	36.0	40.8	29.2	12.4
Urban	27.9	27.7	19.4	17.9
Boys	30.2	14.9	17.4	19.2
Girls	24.9	32.1	22.6	15.8

Source: Bihar Insight/03/2005, p. 91.

Chart 20.1 presents a comparative study of dropout rate (school level) of students among different states including Bihar. This chart shows the Dropout rate of students ranging from class 1 to 10 which clearly indicates that neighbour state of Bihar like W. Bengal is having less dropout rate (78.52%) compare to Bihar (82.87%). When we compare the dropout situation between Bihar (82.87%)

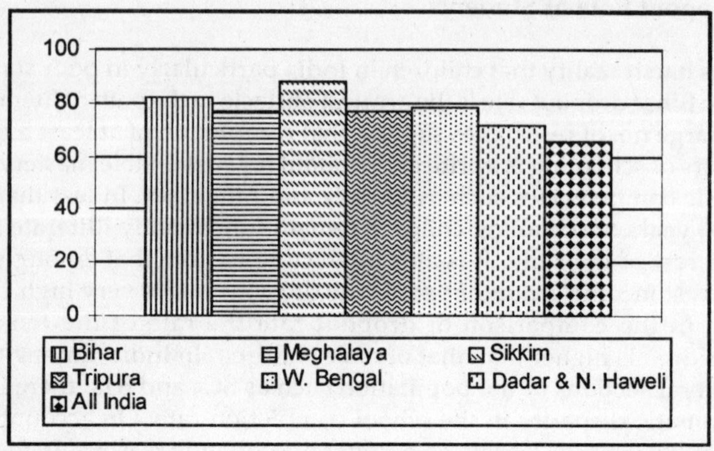

Chart 20.1: Dropout Rate of Students (Classes 1-10), Years 2001-02.

Source: *Hindustan*, Newspaper, Patna, 09, Sept., 2005.

and all India (66.04%), we find a vast gap of dropout between these two data. So, we find that at both stages percentage of dropout rate in Bihar is maximum which requires a strict measure to check the growing dropout rate. This situation needs an urgent attention of both governments—Bihar and India. A mega state like Bihar alone cannot be able to check this problem because the problem contains several kinds of social and economic issues which can be overcome by the joint efforts of state and central governments.

Absence Rate of Teachers

Bihar is the only state where absence rate of teacher has been found the highest in India i.e. 38.3 per cent. Although absence rate in Jharkhand is 39.3 per cent, but previously this state has been the part of Bihar only a few years back. So this absence rate in Jharkhand will also be attributed to Bihar state. It is also necessary to mention here that in the neighbouring state of Bihar i.e. W. Bengal the absence rate is only 24.8 per cent which is almost equal to all India level (24.5%). There are many states like Maharashtra, Madhya Pradesh and Gujarat which observe a very little percentage of absence rate of only is 14.5 per cent, 16.5 per cent and 17 per cent respectively. One can imagine the real position of state of Bihar with regard to its educational environment in light of absence rate of teachers. Primary education is the pillar of higher and technical education, but when the pillar is weak, every part of structure will be broken. We can understand the reality of fact from Chart 20.2. It is worth mentioning here that in Bihar most of the teachers are deputed on non-teaching government work such as census, election duty etc. which paralyse the teaching works in the schools.

The Gender Disparity

There has become the vast gender disparity in the male and female literacy, enrolment, dropout and the rate of higher education in Bihar. In higher education the rate of enrolment is 10 per cent at all India level, it is only 6 per cent in Bihar and percentage of female enrolment is only 3 per cent. The efforts made by the government since last five decades have reduced disparities, but the overall picture is gloomy yet now.

The percentage of female students has steadily increased since independence. In the case of general higher education it has risen from 10.77 per cent in 1947 to 44.71 per cent in 2002. In case of professional and specialised education this has been risen from 9.21 per cent in 1947 to 32.83 per cent in 2002. However, growth appears to be largely within the upper and middle classes of the open segment of population. Amongst dalits, the female students constitute 31.21 per cent in general higher education and 21.12 per cent in professional and specialised education by the end of 2002.

In accordance with demographic pattern, the percentage of the students belonging to the dalits should be about 23 per cent and keeping in view the need to encourage their access 15 per cent reservation for them in academic institutions. Yet, these communities have remained very much under-represented in higher education throughout the last five decades. In fact the percentage of students of these communities in general higher educational has fallen from 13.76 per cent in 1957 to 12.68 per cent in 2002. In the case of professional and higher education there has been a marginal increase from 7.93 per cent in 1957 to 12.35 per cent in 2002.

Higher Education and Human Development

Bihar and Jharkhand (formerly United Bihar) have the significance of higher education as paramount for overall development. They are the two faces of same coin. There are nine universities in Bihar and three in Jharkhand. There has been much enquiry and discussions on the scenario of higher education in these two states. The result is miserable. The growing population of Bihar and Jharkhand has had an inevitable effect on the problems of access to the education system. Not only is access problem at the primary and secondary school level but in Bihar and Jharkhand are extremely poor at the level of higher education with only about 6 per cent of the relevant age group of 17 to 23 enrolled. In spite of it there has been a contradictory perception that there is greater outlay for higher education than other levels of education.

With a view to the issue of access, a number of scholars have undertaken studies related to status of the under-privileged classes which could be improved. For example, the case of dalits and backward classes may be considered because without their considerable progress on the economic and social horizon, Bihar and Jharkhand have been lagging far behind and therefore, has been at the lowest ladder in terms of social development or human development. Reservations have been provided for them and they are also financially supported. Yet the enrolment today is unsatisfactory and they have a very high dropout rate. This attributes to social, cultural and economic disparities and the elitist culture and curriculum of the universities.

In comparison of the share of dalits in Bihar of 15 per cent and share of STs in Jharkhand of 30 per cent. The enrolment of them in higher education merely touches 5 per cent and 8 per cent respectively. It is, however, encouraging to note that share in general education has increased as compared to the non-dalit and non-tribal population. The enrolment of dalits in Bihar in general education increased from 5.5 per cent in 1970-71 to 17.89 in 2000-2002 and professional education from 4.3 per cent in 1980-81 to 11.21 per cent during the same period. On the other hand the increase in the share of scheduled tribe enrolment to total enrolment was only from 5.2 per cent in 1980-81 to 17 per cent to 2001-02.

To the extent of the male-female disparities are concerned, it may be noted that there has been substantial increase in female enrolment in higher education. In Bihar the share of women in total enrolment has increased from 18.2 per cent in 1980-81 to 38.2 per cent in 2001-02 and while in Jharkhand it has risen to 34.2 per cent in 2001-02. In spite of this increase the ratio of male and female students in higher education is as disparate as 3:1. The relative deprivation of women in the field of higher education is particularly significant because it underlines all other attributes of deprivation in both states. The human development in Bihar and Jharkhand in terms of the access, equity and quality in higher education has not improved in comparison to other developed states like Punjab, Kerala and Maharashtra. The most noteworthy feature is that percentage of passing students in higher education is not mounting. It has to be pleaded for separate culture for dalits and backward classes and for courses with content relevant to the communities. It can be pointed out that the institutions of higher education have poor infrastructure facilities. There is poor government support in Bihar and Jharkhand in motivating the students of these communities to enroll for higher education. The rural areas of Bihar still face severe problems concerned with higher education progress. It is necessary to ensure that a much larger number of young aspirants and especially those belonging to the under-privileged classes, or those living in rural areas, get the benefit of higher education. Different facilities and amenities should be provided for elimination of gap between male and female students. Otherwise there is the denser of an increased socio-economic stratification with the gap between the 'haves' and 'have-nots', as well as male and female increasing. In order to promote equity, it may be necessary to substitute the word 'merit' by 'minimum merit', while dealing with applications from the extremely under-privileged classes. Immediate requirement is to raise the enrolment ratio to at least 20 per cent for satisfactory social equity and justice.

Human Development Challenge

The challenge of development in Bihar is enormous due to persistent poverty, complex social satisfaction, unsatisfactory infrastructure and weak governance problems. The present Bihar which constitutes 3 per cent of the geographical area of India and about 8 per cent of its population (i.e. 8.29 crores as per 2001 census), is the third most populous state of the country and is frequently characterised as the 'most backward state of India'. Bihar has lowest literacy rate and highest percentage of people living below the poverty line, except that of Orissa. The state has the lowest PCI among the major states of India. Moreover, the state ranks among the slowest growing regions of India and GDP growth rate during the 1990s has been very slow. It was just 2.7 per cent per annum from 1991-92 to 1997-98 as against about 6 per cent for all the major states of the country (Ahluwalia, 2000). On the other hand, population growth rate of Bihar, which was 23.4 per cent during 1980s, increased to 28.4 per cent during 1990s, while in case of India as a whole population growth rate declined from 23.9 per cent during 1980s to 21.3 per cent during 1990s. Consequently, population density of Bihar stands at a phenomenally high level of 880 as against 324 for the country as a whole. Presently Bihar is least urbanised state of India with an urban population of just about 10 per cent. The agriculture sector, employing about 73 per cent of the work force in the state, is very backward with low productivity. The per capita agricultural income of Bihar is about half that of India as a whole and about one-fifth that of Punjab. Whatever few industry were there in the state such as sugar, jute etc. have collapsed in recent years. Thus, the state's performance has been dismal in respect of various social and economic indicators.

The socio-economic and political institutions of the state too have shown considerable degeneration. The academic institutions have more or less collapsed and the administrative machinery is in complete disarray. The post-independence era has witnessed a dismal failure of the state government in ushering in the necessary changes needed to accelerate economic development as well as bringing about a fair and equitable social structure. This can be traced to the very nature of the power structure in Bihar. Ownership of land and other assets, cast dominance, political power structure, all overlap in away is by no means unique to Bihar. However, this does not mean that the state has been static. There have been technological developments, which had a significant impact, with parts of the state experiencing a modest spurt in agricultural growth during 1980s after a long period of stagnation. But in the absence of an effective transformation of the underlying structures, these changes do not appear to be sustainable (Sharma, 2005).

One of the most important element of the human development for any country is the education. Education serves as the basic source of economic, social, technical and cultural changes. It influences almost all the demographic variables in different ways. It develops basic skills and abilities and thereby boosts productivity. However, Bihar has the lowest literacy rate among all the states and union territories of India accounting only 47.53 per cent as against the national average of 65.38 per cent and that of Kerala's 90.92 per cent.

In Bihar 52.47 per cent people were illiterates, in which female illiteracy as high as 66.43 per cent in comparison with male illiteracy of 39.68 per cent during 2001. Due to high illiteracy in the state, the position of unemployment, poverty and inequality in the opportunities of jobs is growing by leaps and bounds. Moreover, the gross enrolment ratio in classes I-V and classes I-VIII are not very bad in the state. The gross enrolment ratio in classes I-V was 78.70 per cent, while it was 59.69 per cent for I-VIII classes during 2001-02.

The First World Conference on Women held in Mexico City in 1975, the International Women's Year identified three key objectives that formed the basis of United Nations work on women. These were (*i*) Gender equality and elimination of gender discrimination, (*ii*) Integration and participation of women in development and (*iii*) Increase contribution of women to world peace and 1976-85 was declared the United Nations decades, for women.

The Convention on the Elimination of all forms of Discrimination Against Women (CEDAW) held in 1979 articulated the bill of rights of women. But it didn't take long for the world community to realise that mere confirment of legal status to various rights of women doesn't ensure women's ability to exercise those rights. The Second World Conference at Copenhagen in 1980 identified equal access to education, employment opportunities and health care services to be the basic factors. The third conference at Nairobi in 1985 and fourth conference in Beizing in 1995 marked a shift of focus from women to the concept of gender. For women to be fully empowered to take their rightful place as equal partner with men in all respect of life, entire structure of the society and all relation between men and women within it had to be reevaluated. The Beizing declaration and plan for action was an agenda for women empowerment. It identified, the following twelve critical areas posing the major obstacles to women advancement. Women and poverty, education and training of women, women and health, violence against women, women and armed conflict, women and economy, women and decision-making power, institutional mechanism for the advancement of women, human right of women, women and media, women and environment and the girl child.

Literacy Trend of Male and Female

According to the census 1951, the average general literacy rate was 18.33 with male 27.16 and female 8.86 per cent. The gap between male and female is 18.30. As per census 2001 the general literacy rate is 65.38 per cent with male 75.85 and female 54.16 per cent. This achievement in terms of general literacy growth is quite impressive, but when we compare the gap between male and female, it is contrary to the progress made in general literacy. It has increased from 18.32 to 21.70 per cent, which in ideal situation should have been reduced. Even though the national average is relatively better, when we compare with states in India, there is a large variation. In progressive states like Kerala male and female literacy rate are 94.2 and 87.6 per cent respectively the gap is only 634 per cent. But in Bihar this gap is enormous in respect of all the states. There was total literacy rate is 60.32 per cent and that of female is only 33.57 per cent. Thus the gap remains of 26.75 per cent.

Development of Women in Five Year Plans

Development of women remained focal point in different plan periods. The First Plan (1951-56) treated it as welfare subjects, in Second Plan (1956-79) reflected the welfare approach. Besides giving priority to women education and launching measures to improve maternal and child health service. The shift and approach from welfare to development of women could take place only in the Sixth Plan (1980-85) which adopted a multi-disciplinary approach with special thrust on health, education and employment. In the Seventh Plan (1985-90), the development programmes continued with the major objective of raising their economic and social status. The Eighth Plan (1990-95) made two significant changes in conceptual strategy of planning for women. Firstly empowerment of women became one of the nine primary objectives of the plan period. Secondly, it directed both the centre and states to adopt a special strategy of 'Women's Component Plan' (WCP) through which not less than 30 per cent of funds flow to women from all development sectors. The Tenth Plan (2002-07) adopted a sector-specific 3-fold strategy for empowerment of women, based on the transcription of national policy for empowerment of women which included.

Table 20.12: General Literacy Rate Since Independence with Gender-Gap

Census Year	*Persons %*	*Male %*	*Female %*	*Gap in Literacy Rate %*
1951	18.33	27.16	8.66	18.30
1961	28.30	40.40	15.35	25.05
1971	34.45	45.96	21.97	23.98
1981	43.57	56.80	29.76	26.62
1991	52.21	64.13	39.29	24.84
2001	65.38	75.85	54.16	21.70

Source: Census of India, 2001.

Table 20.13: State-wise Variation

Literacy Rate (States)	*Male %*	*Female %*	*Gap %*
Kerala	94.2	87.86	6.34
Mizoram	90.69	86.13	4.56
Lakshadeep	93.15	81.56	11.59
Bihar	60.32	33.57	26.25
Jharkhand	67.94	39.38	28.56

Source: Census of India, 2001.

Social Empowerment

To create an enabling environment through various affirmative development policies and programme for the development of women besides providing them easy and equal access to all the basic minimum services so as to enable them to realise their full potential.

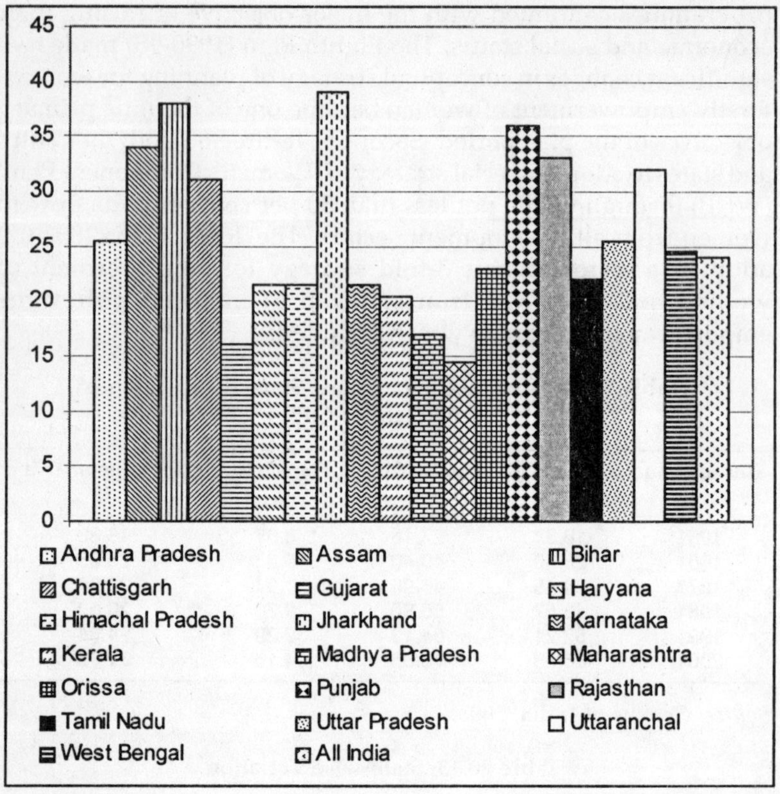

Chart 20.2: Absence Rate of Teachers.

Economic Empowerment

To ensure provision of training, employment and income generation activities with both backward and forward linkage with unlimited objectives of making all potential women economically independent and self-reliant.

Gender Justice

To eliminate all forms of gender discriminations and thus allow woman to enjoy not only de-jure but also the de-facto rights and fundamental freedom on par with men in all spheres of life.

So the gender justice is the main parameter for the real social justice and empowerment of women, particularly academic empowerment which becomes the root cause of empowerment. Honourable Nitish Kumar, the new C.M. of Bihar has appointed a commission for 'Equal Education System' in Bihar, first of all in India, which may eliminate the discrepancy in future.

Legally and politically women had achieved the goal to the larger extent and they have established the milestone. The C.M. of Bihar granting 50 per cent reservation to the women has made his name written in the golden letters of history. Women have been granted 50 per cent reservation in the Panchayati Raj Election in 2006. There have won more than 50 per cent seats on the post of mukhiya, sarpanch, panchayat samiti sadasya and zila parishad sadasya etc. formally, under 8463 gram panchayats and 2.60 lakh posts of representatives in Bihar and thus the position of women has become not only equal level but the equal plus in de-jure. But in de-facto the situation is quite different for them.

Informally they are still only the puppets in the hands of their supremo men. This is only because they are illiterate, unconscious, ignorant, orthodox, superstitious and men-fearing. They do not know and having no experience what posts they have won and what power they are assigned and granted. Lack of literacy and education is only the bottle-neck in the way of their rights and powers. This problem can be solved only by gaining education and skill, when the awareness may be enshrined in them. Without the proper awakening and awareness they cannot be able to understand and dispose of their rights and powers in future. But this right (reservation to women) endowed to them is praiseworthy and will act as pillars for gaining the real success in future. This will raise awakening and consciousness in them step by step. Today as the puppets in another's hand, they will be real decision-makers and rulers in future. It is evident that rural women were far away with their urban counterparts in comparison of consciousness, literacy and education. But this thing will lead them also to step forward smoothly.

REFERENCES

1. Census (1991), *Provisional Population Totals*, Govt. of India.

2. Census (2001), *Provisional Population Totals*, Govt. of India.
3. *Economic Survey* (2001-02), *Provisional Population Totals*, Govt. of India.
4. Bose, Asis (1991), *"Population of India"*, pp. 57-66.
5. *"Economic and Political Weekly"* (2002), No. 34, August, 24-30s.
6. *Statistical Outline of India* (2003-2004).
7. Thakur, R.N. (2004), "Empowerment of Poor People under Panchayati Raj in Bihar", *Bihar Economic Journal*, Lecture held at P.K. Roy Memorial College, Dhanbad.
8. Thakur, R.N. (2004), *"Economy of UP—The Glorious Past and Gloomy Present"*, 87th Annual Conference Spl. Lecture, IEA, BHU, Varanasi.
9. Thakur, R.N. (2002), *"Economy of Kerala: Human Development, Social Progress and Economic Crisis"*, 85th Annual Conference, IEA, Spl. Lecture, Trivandrum.
10. Thakur, R.N. (2002), *"Empowerment of Indian Women: Challenges to Development"*, Spl. Lecture in National Seminar in T.M. Bhagalpur University, Bhagalpur.
11. Thakur, R.N. (2000), *"Education and Political Status of Indian Women: Key to Economic Development, Women and Development"*, Ed. A. Banergy and R.K. Sen, Deep and Deep Publishers, New Delhi.
12. Thakur, R.N. (2002), "Women and Employment Strategy in India", *Women and Technology*, Ed. S. Murthy, RBSA Pub, Jaipur.
13. Thakur, R.N. (2005), "Empowerment of Women in Bihar", IXth Annual Conference of EAB—Conference Volume, Lecture held at A.N. College, Patna.
14. Thakur, R.N. (2002), *"Education and Women's Empowerment"*, Resource Person Lecture, National Seminar on "Empowerment of Women", Govt. PG College, Shivajinagar, Bhopal.
15. Thakur, R.N. (2006), *"Weaker Section and Women's Empowerment under Panchayati Raj in Bihar"*, National Conference on "Role and Relevance of Local Self Government in Democracy", R.N.A.R. College, Samastipur.

21

The Need for Higher Education in Developing Economies with Special Reference to India

MRS. MEENAKSHI MADAN

Introduction

In this chapter, I assess predictions about BRIC countries' economic development, focusing mainly on India and China, in terms of one key element in the growth process—human capital, especially higher-end human capital. I will argue that in the new information economy, university educated labour is crucial to economic development. Although all of these economies have other strengths (cheap labour, large internal markets, high levels of industrialization, and in the case of Russia, enormous reserves of natural resources), much of their possibilities for sustained growth in the medium and longer run depend on whether they can develop and utilize high level human capital for the organization and innovation required in today's (and tomorrow's) global information economy.

It is particularly useful to assess economic development prospects comparatively. The four societies we are discussing are very different, even though they share a common characteristic of large geographic size and large populations. The variation allows us to discuss a number of different factors that might contribute positively or negatively to future economic development, so allows us to understand better what is important in the economic development process.

I begin the chapter with the first section, a discussion of why these societies' higher education policies are so important for their future. The second section compares the educational investment patterns in the four countries over the past thirty years and their current higher educational policy. The third section focuses on the main problems facing the higher education systems in each country and their implications for future economic development.

Education and Economic Growth

Individuals are interested in taking more schooling partly because they can earn more and get better jobs, on average, with more schooling. For many, more schooling can be a source of social mobility. Similarly, nation-states and regions are interested in raising the average level of schooling in their population because they think that doing so will improve productivity, increase economic growth, raise the quality of jobs in the economy, and reduce poverty and inequality.

Some of the earliest work in the economics of education argued that a major effect of more education is to improve labour's capacity to produce. Because more highly educated workers are more literate and numerate, they should be easier to train to do more complex tasks. Further, they should have better work habits, particularly a greater awareness of time and more internalized norms that would make them more dependable.

Nations with more educated labour forces are characterized by higher output per worker, but typically these nations also have more physical capital per worker. Exactly how education increases productivity, how important it is, and in what ways it is important are difficult questions which economists have been unable to answer definitively. Controversy also surrounds the kind of education that contributes most to growth—general schooling, technical formal training, or on-the-job training—or what level of education contributes most to growth—primary, secondary, or higher education, although I will argue that the case for higher education as a key factor in economic growth has grown stronger in recent years.

One of the clues that education does contribute to growth and how much it may contribute is that countries with higher levels of economic growth have labour forces with higher levels of formal schooling. Such a macroeconomic approach to the relation between education and economic growth emphasizes the correlation between the stock of human capital and the increase in economic output per capita. This may just indicate that as individuals earn more income, they purchase more schooling for their children, just as they would buy a refrigerator or a family automobile. In that case schooling would be primarily a consumption good, not an investment good like a machine or a computer system. However, economists have been able to show that, on average, countries that have sustained high levels of economic growth are also those who have higher levels of literacy and have invested steadily in raising the education of their labour force.

With the shift to an information economy, globalization, and flexible organizations of production, economists have taken these arguments about human capital in the production process a step farther. Theories of development now argue that developing nations have a better chance of catching up with the more advanced economies when they have a stock of labour who have the skills to develop new technologies themselves or to adopt and use foreign technology.

The claim that educated workers adjust more effectively to rapid change in opportunities and technology implies that in today's more rapidly changing and more competitive markets, the payoff to education should rise. The growth of science-based industries—chemicals, biotechnology, telecommunications, information systems—also means that economic development depends increasingly on highly educated and scientifically trained labour. Yet, more than simply increasing the demand for scientifically trained labour, economists argue that the new types of production reward innovation and learning-by doing on a broader scale, even among non-scientifically-oriented workers.

In this kind of model, more education in the labour force increases output in two ways: (*a*) education adds skills to labour, increasing the capacity of labour to produce more output; and (*b*) education increases the worker's capacity to innovate (learn new ways of using existing technology and creating new technology) in ways that increase his or her own productivity and the productivity of other workers.

The first of these emphasizes the human capital aspect of education (education improves the quality of labour as a factor of production and permits technological development); the second places human capital at the core of the economic process and assumes that the externalities generated by human capital are the source of self-sustaining economic growth process—human capital not only produces higher productivity for more educated workers but for most other labour as well.

This second model sees innovation and learning-by-doing as endogenous to the production process itself. It assumes that productivity increases are a self-generating process inside firms and economies (Lucas, 1988; Romer, 1990). Such learning-by-doing and innovation as part of the work process are facilitated in firms and societies that foster greater participation and decision-making by workers, since those are the firms and societies in which more educated workers will have the greatest opportunities to express their creative capacity.

The model of endogenous innovation and learning-by-doing has major implications for the economic value of education. The value of higher educated labour, particular highly skilled scientific and management labour—those who are able to create the most valuable innovations—increases relative to other levels and kinds of educated labour.

More important, the economic value of education is generated by a much more complex set of relations between the potential of human capacity to produce more economic output and its realization through organizations of work that are both geared to realize that capacity and to innovate using their human capacity. Thus, the value of education is not just a function of the jobs that workers with more education can get in the labour market. Instead, information, ideology, political power, property rights, citizenship rights in the workplace, and the willingness of organizations to innovate all condition the economic value of education.

The fact that individuals with more education have higher earnings is another indication that education contributes to growth. The education-higher earnings connection reflects a microeconomic approach to the relation between education and economic growth. Greater earnings for the more educated in this approach represent higher productivity—hence, an increase in educated labour in the economy is associated with increased economic output and higher growth rates. Higher earnings for the more educated may just represent a political reward that elites give their members—a payoff for being part of the dominant social class. However, it would be difficult to sustain an economic system over the long-term if those who actually produced more were not rewarded for their higher productivity, and those who simply had political power got all the rewards.

The positive economic payoff to individuals with more education in the form of higher earnings suggests that their economic value to the society is higher than those who have lower education. Economists estimate the payoff to more education relative to the cost of that education just like they would estimate the payoff to any investment. They calculate what the amount invested in education yields in higher earnings over the the lifetime of those with more education. This rate of return to the investment in education is generally positive in almost every country. In Europe, rates of return to education are about 7-8 per cent, but in many developing countries, they can be much higher. In Brazil, for example, the overall rate of return to the investment in education is more than 12-14 per cent. A positive rate of return to education suggests that investing in education contributes to economic growth. The higher the rate of return, the more likely that investment in education contributes to growth. And those levels of education associated with higher rates of return should be the levels in which additional investment produces the greater contribution to economic growth.

Macroeconomic Approaches to the Education—Economic Growth Relation

The first macroeconomic analysis of growth appeared at the end of the 1980s, within a convergence model framework. Traditional convergence analysis did not do a very good job of explaining wealth disparities between countries, so economists were interested in the initial conditions that could determine the long-term level towards which economies converge. At the same time, they wanted to explain why the variations in wealth were maintained when countries did not have similar initial economic conditions. The level of education of the labour force appeared to be one aspect of this conditional convergence.

Barro (1990) was the first to show that for a given level of wealth, the economic growth rate was positively related to the initial human capital level of a country, whereas for a given level of human capital, the growth rate was negatively related to the initial level of GDP per capita. Macroeconomic convergence, therefore, appears to be strongly conditioned by the initial level of education.

Azariadis and Drazen (1990) followed Barro's analysis by assuming that economic development is not a linear process, but goes through successive stages, in which the stock of physical and human capital enable a country to reach a given growth level. Their results showed that initial literacy rate plays a different role in predicting growth rates at different levels of development. Literacy is correlated with the variations of growth in the least advanced countries, but it does not seem to be related to most developed countries' growth.

These different studies show that the variations of growth rates among countries can be explained partly by the initial level of human capital. But does a higher level of investment in education affect the growth path?

In short, the initial level of education (especially if it is relatively high) may be a strong correlate of later economic development (the countries which had a higher level of education in 1960 experienced stronger growth rates). However, it is much more uncertain that investment in education is followed by an increase in the economic growth rate.

In the 1990s, new econometric tools integrated a temporal dimension into cross-country estimates. These allowed for better control of omitted variables and helped modify estimates of the role of education in growth.

Between 1960 and 1985, access to secondary education was strongly democratized in many developing countries, without any impact on their level of wealth. However the impact is not homogeneous and the investment in human capital seems to be more efficient in open economies and where public infrastructures are relatively well developed.

Despite these somewhat conflicting results, it appears that the contribution of higher levels of education to growth is consistently positive. For example, in addition to the studies cited above, in her review of a number of econometric models that test the impact of average education levels in the population on economic growth for a sample of developing countries in the Middle East and Asia, Boutrolle (2003) finds that only the number of graduates of tertiary education seems to have a positive and significant relation to growth.

She also finds that the effect of different levels of education varies according to the economy's level of development. Increases in the number of primary school graduates are only correlated with the growth of GDP in the least developed countries. This result confirms many analyses which show how the acquisition of literacy, numeracy, and other, higher level basic skills can have a positive effect on productivity in the agricultural sector, and on the reduction of mortality and fertility rates. The generalization of primary education seems to be an important condition for transition from the agricultural to the industrial economy.

An increased fraction of tertiary level graduates in the labor force seems to have a different relationship to growth at different stages of economic development. At low levels of development, those economies with a relatively high fraction of university-trained people in the population or labor force appear to have lower economic growth.

According to Pritchett (1996), the absence of a positive relation between the higher education graduates and economic growth is explained as a rent seeking phenomenon, where educated people look for jobs that are not directly productive. But when the economy enters its second, industrialization stage of development, these graduates take part in the productive dynamics of the country.

The positive role of very educated workers on GDP is greatest in the developed countries. Indeed, according to models developed by Sorensen (1999) and Funke and Strulik (2000), when a country reaches an advanced development level, the role of human capital on economic growth moves from a direct impact on labour productivity to an indirect impact through increasing the capacity of the labour force as a whole to manage innovation and technical progress.

A number of studies in India and China support the notion that education plays a key role in economic development, but these studies are mostly based on production function estimates of education's contribution to economic productivity rather than growth models. Even so, studies in the early 1970s suggested that the contribution of education to economic growth increased from 5 per cent of the growth rate in the 1950s to 10 per cent in the 1960s, and that later studies found these estimates much too low, raising them to 27-30 per cent (Tilak, 2005, p. 37).

To summarize, education appears to contribute to long-term growth. Countries with higher stocks of education in the past seemed to have had higher rates of economic growth 20 and 30 years later. At the same time, the research suggests that higher levels of education in the labour force were most likely to contribute to growth, especially as economies reached higher levels of development.

Microeconomic research on the relation between earnings and education provides a second lens through which to view the education growth issue. We would expect that the higher the rate of return to a level of education, the more likely the investment in that level would contribute to economic growth. For many years, the World Bank promulgated the view that the highest rates of return were to primary education and the lowest to university (and that this pattern was invariate over time), so nations should focus their investment on expanding and improving elementary schooling to maximize economic growth (Psacharopoulos, 1973, 1993). If that were the case, investing public funds in higher education would be a low yield strategy.

But this is not the case. Although rates of return to education vary among countries, a dominant tendency worldwide in the past thirty years is for rates of return to investment in lower levels of schooling to fall, and for rates of return to investment in higher levels of schooling to rise (Carnoy, 1972; Carnoy, 1995). By the 1990s, in many developing countries and most developed countries, rates of return to higher education were greater than to secondary and to primary. The private rates represent the return to individuals investing in various levels of education (however, they are generally not corrected for the increased income taxes that individuals pay when they earn higher incomes); the social rates represent the private returns but include both private and public costs—the latter are not borne by private individuals. The general tendency has been for rates of return to investment in higher education to rise relative to rates of return to lower levels of schooling. Rates in the Middle East tend to be the lowest, and rates in East Asia and Latin America tend to be higher.

The payoff to higher education in Brazil in the 1980s conformed to this pattern.

Given the increased openness of Brazil's economy and increased emphasis on high value exports since the late 1980s, there is no reason to believe that the rates to higher education have declined since.

Rates of return to education have also been estimated for China and India. These vary considerably from study to study. Hossain's estimates for the World Bank show lower rates of return to higher education than to primary. The 1993 private rates are estimated as 18 per cent to primary school, 13 per cent to secondary and 15 per cent to higher education.

The problem with estimating the payoff to education in China using earnings or wages as a measure of the benefits of education—at least in the past—was that although wages or monthly earnings may have represented fairly what an individual can realize as a return to his or her investment in education, they probably under estimated the productivity increases associated with higher levels of education.

The question is whether these rates derived from total factor productivity are "truer" estimates of the payoff to higher education than those based on income estimates. In China in the 1990s, given that most workers were still employed by the State, this may have well been the case.

The estimated private rates of return to education in India since the 1960s are much higher than in China. As in most countries, payoffs to higher education in India appear to be rising over time relative to the payoffs to lower levels of schooling, although the overall rates to college do not appear to be as high as to lower secondary school.

Tilak (2003) has recently re-estimated private (Mincer) rates of return to various levels of education in India as a whole in 1983, 1993, and 1999, for both regular wage workers and casual wage workers. These show rates falling over time to primary, middle, and secondary school, and rising to investment in university. The rate is consistently higher to university in each of the three years (Tilak, 2003). Tilak estimates the private rate to higher education as 10 per cent per year in 1999.

This suggests that workers with higher education, who tend to have more access to high income jobs have seen their income rise relative to those with lower levels of schooling. Thus, the transition to the market economy in Russia has apparently created a major shift in the wages paid to workers with different capacities to take advantage of the new labour market conditions. Thus, rising rates of return to higher education in those countries appears to be driven by increasing relative demand for higher educated labour relative to the supply.

How is Higher Education Changing in the BRIC Economies?

The data we have just reviewed on the potential contribution of higher education to economic growth would suggest that higher education should be expanding, that individuals should be increasingly willing to invest in higher education, and that governments should be increasingly willing to support the higher education sector to ensure that university faculties whose graduates are likely to create social externalities would have adequate resources to train students into those fields. Is this the case?

If we observed higher education in these four countries in the 1990s, we would find that three of them—Brazil, China and India—had low rates of enrolment as a proportion of the age cohort, and Russia had very high rates of enrolment. In 1990, only about 12 per cent of the age cohort in Brazil attended higher education institutions, and in India, the proportion was less than 10 per cent.

The Expansion of Enrolment

In the past fifteen years, higher education has expanded in the BRIC economies, especially in China. Brazilian higher education now includes about 20 per cent of the age. The number of students in Russian higher education institutions fell between 1989 to 1993-94 from about 3 million to 2.6 million, then rose rapidly to 4.7 million by the year 2000 (Drougov, 2001). Since the size of the age cohort did not change significantly in that period, this represents a very large increase in gross enrolment. China's gross enrolment ratio has jumped even more, from 4 to 16 per cent in about eight years. India has made more modest gains in gross enrolment. It only increased from about 8 per cent in 1990 to 12 per cent in 2003, even though this represents 4.2 million more students attending higher education institutions (Kapur and Mehta, 2004).

Given our discussion of the relation between the stock of higher educated labour and economic growth, it is interesting that China, with very small stocks of high level human capital, were able to manage very rapid growth rates throughout the 1990s. Brazil also has had rapid economic growth in the 1970s, the late 1980s, and in the 1990s, with relatively low stocks of higher educated labour. Russia, on the other hand, with its highly educated labour force, was unable to sustain economic growth in the 1970s and 1980s, and today, Russia's economic growth is almost totally explained by the fact that it is hugely rich in natural resources at a time in history when commodity prices are soaring, and unlike many resource rich states, it has enormous human resources developed over many years of investing heavily in education.

As Belton Fleischer has suggested (Fleischer, 2002), the lesson to be learned from China's experience is not that economic growth is independent of high level human capital, but rather that China could have probably achieved even higher economic growth with a better educated labour force, and that now that China is expanding higher education, it should actually experience higher growth than in the past. Similarly, Brazil has long underinvested in higher educated human capital, and so has India. Both macro and microeconomic approaches suggest that expanding Brazilian higher education should contribute positively to economic growth. In India's case, however, it is unclear whether low investment in higher education had a negative impact on economic growth, because until the past 10 years, there were relatively few opportunities for employment of higher educated Indians in high productivity sectors—most waited for jobs as government bureaucrats.

The Changing Financing of Higher Education

All four of the BRIC economies at one time financed higher education almost totally with public funds, either from the Central Government or from State Governments.

In other words, almost every student who was accepted at a higher education institution was, other than his or her earnings foregone and direct private expenses, fully subsidized by the State to attend post-secondary education. In many cases, the student also received a stipend to offset part of his or her earnings foregone.

In that financing model, higher education was defined as a

pure public good, implicitly yielding high externalities. In addition, it was argued that, like in primary and secondary education, charging fees to cover the costs of (much more expensive) higher education would produce under investment due to imperfect capital markets. These arguments aside, since higher education was generally accessible only to middle class families already able to invest time and money to provide their children with high quality primary and secondary education, free higher education was a measure to assuage a relatively powerful and vocal political group, the professional class/government bureaucracy that wanted to assure the social mobility of their children. Eventually, everybody (meaning lower income urban and even rural classes) bought into the model, on the assumption that ultimately their children would also benefit from this "free" good.

Today, however, all four countries have, in one way or another, either implemented cost share financing (tuition fees) in public universities, or allowed higher education to become "privatized". The way each country has made this shift or allowed it to happen has important implications for the efficiency (providing the right incentives to students in terms of their course of study, for example) and equity aspects of the higher education system.

This strategy makes sense in terms of economic growth optimization if higher income students from eastern Chinese cities and provinces are academically more able and are likely to contribute more in social benefits (externalities) than lower income, lower-scoring students entering less elite, lower cost universities. A plan of public subsidies that favours enrolment of the best and the brightest in faculties and universities that produce high externalities should contribute to greater innovation and higher economic growth. It is generally assumed that externalities to investing in very smart students in certain fields of study—such as research science or teaching—are large because the activities that these students engage in once they are working great social benefits greater than the additional earnings they realize.

If the higher income students tend to study in faculties and universities that have high private rates of return but low externalities, a student loan programme would be the more cost-effective policy in terms of maximizing economic growth. A scheme of market rate education loans would help overcome barriers of entry resulting from undeveloped capital markets for educational investment but would leave students and their families responsible for paying a substantial share of the costs of high private payoff education.

Brazil has followed a completely different strategy. Rather than charging fees to the overwhelmingly middle and upper middle class students who attend the high cost public universities, the Brazilian military put in place a higher education policy in the late 1960s that promoted the expansion of private proprietary universities to absorb a growing demand for higher education among those whose entrance examination scores did not qualify them for admission to the free public universities. By 2004, 72 per cent of all Brazilian higher education students attended this type of university, most paying high tuition fees. On average, the students attending private universities come from lower income families than those attending public universities. In effect, then, Brazil provides incentives to higher social class students (more than 50 per cent of them attend private, fee-charging primary and secondary schools) to enter any field they choose (depending on their test scores and high school grades) in fully subsidized public universities, whether or not those fields are characterized by externalities. Meanwhile, other students are pushed mainly into what they perceive to be high private rate of return fields of study, since those students have to pay fees to attend a higher education institution.

Since public spending on education in Russia went through a major decline in the early 1990s, and has not recovered, both cost sharing in public universities and the growth of enrolment in private universities has necessarily increased.

In India, the situation is different again. The Indian Government has steadily reduced the emphasis it places on higher education in its Central Government budget (Tilak, 2005; Kapur and Mehta, 2004). According to Kapur and Mehta, the proportion of expenditure on higher education to total expenditure on education "ironically declined from an average of 15 per cent during the 1980s to an average of 10 per cent in the 1990s" (p. 9). This, he contends, has provoked a flight by the middle class to private education.

According to NSS data, the government's share in overall education expenditure has been declining steadily, from 80 per cent in 1983 to 67 per cent in 1999. For states like Kerala, the decline is steep, from 75 to 48 per cent, while for Madhya Pradesh it is from 84 per cent to 68 per cent. Indeed, while private expenditure on education has risen 10.8 times in the last 16 years, that for the poor rose even faster, by 12.4 times. Many students who formally enrol in publicly funded colleges and universities, barely attend classes there. Instead, they pay considerable sums to the burgeoning private sector vocational IT training firms such as NIIT and the Aptech (Kapur and Mehta, 2004, p. 5).

Besides this unusual trend to enrol in public colleges and simultaneously in private vocational training programmes (financed by government backed student loans), professional education, namely engineering, business, and medicine has been marked by a major increase in private providers. Kapur and Mehta (2004, pp. 5-6) used data from 19 important states in India to estimate the percentage of student places in engineering and medicine in private versus public universities. He finds that private engineering colleges accounted for 15 per cent of seats in 1960 and accounted for 86 per cent of seats in 2003.

In medicine, the increase was from 6.8 per cent in 1960 to 41 per cent in 2003. He also estimates that about 90 per cent of the seats in business schools are private. Although the percentage of privatized places varies from state to state, with more in the South and less in Bihar and West Bengal, the general trend even in West Bengal is to cut down support for teachers in private institutions, thus reducing overall spending on higher education.

Thus, in contrast to Brazil, which allowed the expansion of private education to absorb the "overflow" from relatively well-supported and free public institutions that serve largely middle and upper middle class students, India has allowed the public (free) higher education system to deteriorate financially after a period in which it pushed through affirmative action for scheduled castes and "democratized" the university. This, according to Kapur and Mehta, has pushed the Indian middle class, and many lower class Indians, to invest in private higher education, particularly in fields of study with relatively high private rates of return. So the public university is increasingly a place where arts and social science majors take their training. There still exist a number of elite public universities that train high quality professionals. But the public university as such is no longer a place of elite formation.

Critics of the Indian system argue that privatization is driven more by government financial "exhaustion" and lack of a concrete strategy for the education sector than by any systematic reliance on market valuation of professions or a financing scheme that attempts to maximize growth. In many ways, the Russian system could be subject to the same criticism.

The Quality of Higher Education

The last issue I would like to introduce is that of "quality" in the higher educational system. One way to measure quality change over time is to estimate the amount spent per student in higher education. If we only deal with government budgets, this can be misleading if a higher fraction of students attend private universities or pay tuition to public universities, since their spending would not be counted in the public budget allocated to higher education. In Brazil, public spending per university student increased between 1980 and 2000 from about $4,000 to $5,500 PPP US dollars (WB Indicators). It appears that spending per student has gone up in China as well, from 13,000 Yuan in 1999 to 20,000 Yuan in 2002, with tuition fees rising from 17 per cent to 27 per cent of that amount (author's estimates based on Wenli Li's research (2005). It also appears that India increased public spending per student from about 1,000 PPP dollars in 1990 and 1995 to 1,300 PPP dollars in 2000-01. We have no estimates for the Russian Federation. So, three of the countries seem to be investing more public funds per student in higher education. At least in those terms, the quality of higher education may be increasing there, or at least not declining.

In all four countries (as in the United States and Europe), the quality of education taken by higher education students varies enormously among institutions. There are two important questions to ask: how high is the quality of training in the top 10-20 per cent of higher education institutions in each country, and how much below that level is the quality of training in the bottom quarter (or even bottom half) of the institutions in each country.

The reason it is important to know the quality level at the high end is that this benchmark tells us whether such institutions are producing leaders and innovators with the critical thinking skills needed to continue to achieve rapid growth once these countries move out of the industrial and lower level services phase of their development process. We have all read about the Indian Institutes of Technology, with their incredibly difficult admission process and high-level curriculum. Are these representative of the top flight of Indian university training across fields? How deep is such high quality training? Does China have similar high-level training in science and engineering? What about Brazil and Russia? If so, how deep does it go?

The reason it is important to know about the quality at the bottom one-fourth and the bottom one-half is that a high fraction of professionals in each country get their training in such institutions. These staff engineering and management jobs in production, many jobs in government, work in financial and medical services, and in teaching. If they have very poor training, they will likely produce low levels of externalities despite, in at least three of the countries, being partly to heavily subsidized by government funding of their education. One reason that rates of return to higher education may begin to decline as enrolment expands is that the quality of higher education drops off quickly as the system expands, and that it drops of quickly from levels at the bottom half that are already quite low.

What kind of changes are taking place in each country that might make us believe that quality will increase? If one believes that privatization of the higher education system tends to improve quality, then we would expect that the quality of education in Brazil is higher today than it would have been had the government strategy been to expand public universities and to charge fees to pay for the expansion. This is not a very convincing argument given the low quality of most of Brazil's private universities.

Similarly, the gradual decline in government support in India and Russia for public universities could be leading to improved quality of higher education. This needs to be investigated. Much depends on how the private tier develops. Will the present trend produce elite private research universities, or merely proprietary schools whose claim to excellence is that they cater to higher social class students?

Some of the best Chinese universities are "importing" faculty from abroad to serve as examples for local faculty in how and what to teach in various subjects.

Conclusions

What are the chances for these countries to achieve the growth predicted for them given their higher education policies? Obviously, many factors will affect growth rates, including how well they are governed and the strength of their organizational structures (including their juridical systems) that develop as their economies grow. Yet, higher education is also key to realizing sustained high rates of economic growth.

As we have shown, economists have focused mainly on the quantitative aspects of higher education—the number of graduates in the labour force—in assessing whether an economy is allocating resources for maximum growth. In these terms, Russia is in a favourable position, with a large stock of highly educated people available for its current and future labour force. China is expanding its higher education system the most rapidly, and India, the least rapidly. Although many analysts believe that India has sufficient absolute numbers of engineers and scientists and has advantages over China in moving towards an information-based advanced service economy, Tilak (2005) and others have pointed out that proportionately, India (and we might add, Brazil) has proportionately very few highly educated technical and service personnel.

There are potentially serious problems in all four countries concerning the quality of university education for all but the small percentage of university graduates who attended elite institutions, specializing in programmes that might be considered world class.

Large numbers of graduates with university first degrees from these elite institutions get into graduate programmes in the developed countries, and many never go back, especially from India and China.

Although numbers of graduates are important, the issue of critical thinking and innovativeness, which would be fostered by college teachers who know how to develop and nurture such skills in students, and higher education institutions that provide incentives for such teaching, may be even more important in the future. Are institutions moving in this direction?

Policy makers may believe that privatization speaks to this issue, providing higher quality university education and also reducing the need for increased public funding.

However, private universities and professional schools are just as likely as public universities not to develop the higher order thinking skills needed for the information economy.

REFERENCES

Allen, J. (2001), *Effects of a Country's Economic and Social Context on the Rates of Return to Education: A Global Meta-Analysis*, School of Education, Stanford University.

Asaoka, H. (2006), "Investing in Education in India: Inferences from and Analysis of the Rates of Return to Education Across Indian States", Unpublished Ph.D. Dissertation, Stanford University School of Education.

Avakov, G. (1987), Education, *Progrès Technique, Industrialisation: Expérience des Pays Socialistes*, UNESCO, IIEP .

Barro, R.J. and Lee J.W. (1996), "International Measures of Schooling Years and Schooling quality", *American Economic Review*, Vol. 86, No. 2 , pp. 218-23.

Bassanini, A. and Scarpetta, S. (2001), *Does Human Capital Matter for Growth in OECD Countries? Evidence from Pooled-mean-group Estimates*, OECD Economic Department Working Papers, p. 282.

Blaug, M.; P.R.G. Layard and M. Woodhall (1969), *The Causes of Graduate Unemployment in India*, London: Allen Lane the Penguin.

Carnoy, M. (1972), *The Political Economy of Education*, in T. Labelle (ed.) *Education and Development* in Latin America and the Caribbean, Los Angeles, CA: UCLA Latin American Center.

Chen, B. and Y. Fang (2000), "Determinants of Economic Growth in China: Private Enterprise, Education and Openness", *China Economic Review* 11(1): 1-15.

Cresur (2004), Las Lecciones de la Reforma Educativa en el Cono Sur Latinoamericano (eds.) Martin Carnoy, Gustavo Cosse, Cristian Cox, and Enrique Martinez. Buenos Aires.

Démurger, S. (2001), "Infrastructure and Economic Growth: An Explanation for Regional Disparities in China", *Journal of Comparative Economics*, 29: 95-117.

Dessus, S. (2001), *Human Capital and Growth: The Recovered Role of Educational Systems*, World Bank, Middle-East and North Africa Working Paper Series No. 22.

Drougov, M. (2001), *Higher Education Expansion in Russia: What Stands Behind*? Moscow: New Economic School, Working Paper #BSP/01/048.

Duraisamy, P. (2002), "Changes in Returns to Education in India, 1983-94:

By Gender, Age-Cohort and Location", *Economics of Education Review,* Vol. 21(6), pp. 609-22.

Fleischer, B. (2002), *Higher Education in China: A Growth Paradox?* Department of Economics, Ohio State University (mimeo).

Fleischer, B. and Chen, J. (1997), "The Coast—Non-coast Income Gap, Productivity and Regional Economic Policy in China", *Journal of Comparative Economics,* 25, pp. 220-36.

Fleischer, B.M. and Yang, D.T. (2004), "China's Labor Market." In N. Hope (Ed.), *Market Reforms in China,* Stanford, CA: Stanford University Press.

Funke, M. and Strulik, H. (2000), "On Endogenous Growth with Physical Capital, Human Capital and Product Variety", *European Economic Review,* Vol. 44, pp. 491-515.

Goel, S.C. (1975), *Education and Economic Growth,* Delhi: Macmillan.

Judson, R. (1995), *"Do Low Human Capital Coefficients Make Sense? A Puzzle and Some Answers"*, Federal Reserve Board Working Paper.

Kapur, D. and Mehta, P.B. (2004), *Indian Higher Education Reform: From Half-Baked Socialism to Half-Baked Capitalism,* Cambridge, MA: Harvard University, Center for International Development, Working Paper No. 108, September.

Kothari, V.N. (1970), "Disparities in Relative Earnings Among Different Countries", *Economic Journal,* 80 (September): 605-16.

Kyriacou, G. (1991), *Level and Growth Effects of Human Capital,* Working Paper, 91-26, C.V. Starr Center.

Lau, L.; Jamison, D. and Louat, F. (1991), "Education and Productivity in Developing Countries: An Aggregate Production Function Approach", World Bank, *WPS* 612.

LI, H. (2001), *Economic Transition and Returns to Education in China,* School of Economics, Georgia Institute of Technology.

LI, W. (2005), *Private Expenditures, Family Contributions and Financial Aid in Chinese Higher Education,* Beijing: Beijing University, Economics of Education Institute.

Lucas, R.E. (1988), "On the Mechanics of Economic Development", *Journal of Monetary Economics* 22(1): 3-42.

Pandit, H.N. (1972), *Effectiveness and Financing of Investment in Education in India 1950-51 to 1965-66,* Delhi: Delhi University, unpublished doctoral thesis.

Pritchett, L. (1996), *"Where Has all the Education Gone?"*, World Bank Working Paper, No. 1581.

Psacharopoulos, G. (1973), *Returns to Education: An International Comparison,* San Francisco, CA, Jossey-Bass.

Psacharopoulos, G. (1993), *"Returns to Investment in Education: A Global Update"*, World Bank Policy Research Working Paper, No. 1067.

Rao, M.J. and R.C. Datta (1989), "Rates of Return in the Indian Private Sector", *Economics Letters* 30: 373-78.

Romer, P. (1990), "Endogenous Technological Change", *Journal of Political Economy*, Vol. 98, No. 5, pp. 71-102.

Sorensen, A. (1999), "R & D, Learning and Phases of Economic Growth", *Journal of Economic Growth*, Vol. 4, pp. 429-45.

Tilak, J.B.G. (1987), *Economics of Inequality in Education*, New Delhi, Sage. http://scid.stanford.edu/events/PanAsia/Papers/Carnoy.pdf

Wilson, D. and R. Purushothaman (2003), *Dreaming with BRICs: The Path to 2050*, Goldman Sachs, Global Economics, Paper No. 99, October 1.

22

Role of Higher Education in Developing Country Like India: Identifying Worry Spots

DR. BIRENDRA KUMAR JHA

Qualitative aspects of population are of great importance from the point of view of the development of a nation and the welfare of the people. No inquiry into the poverty of nations could hope to be complete without a study of the quality of men's lives. And the two basic elements in this are health and education. In our premise of the interlocking circles of development, we hold that to improve his economic and social life a man, must also improve his health and his education" (Gunnar Myrdal, 1972). Although "neither health nor education can be dealt with in insulation" (Gunnar Myrdal, 1972) as both are equally important means to development and simultaneously they are also the ends of development. Yet "education has reigned supreme as its most reliable surrogate" (G.K. Chadha, 2003). Although a child's ability to take full advantage of the schooling provided to him depends on his health and an adult ability to use the knowledge and skills he has acquired depends on his mental and physical fitness but the extent to which health conditions can be improved depends on people's knowledge of and attitude towards hygiene and so there is a new approach stressing the importance of education as a basic ingredient of human capital base in this age of knowledge economy. "Countries which have accorded high priority to human capital formation have performed relatively better in terms of economic growth, employment reduction in income inequalities and alleviation of poverty" (Rangarajan). The Nobel Laureate

Amartya Sen has also repeatedly pointed out that no country has developed with an illiterate and unhealthy population. Thus, human capital is of prime importance because it motivates and applies both natural and physical capital and its core component is education which plays a crucial role in the economic development of a nation.

During the past two decades or so, our perspective of the goals of development has changed substantially in favour of human capital formation through toning up educational and health status or say quality of life of the people. "The process of development is no more conditioned by Harrod-Domar's technical coefficients and rate of growth of physical alone Human Capital (HC) is already surging ahead to replace physical capital as the sole mover of the growth process. In the age of knowledge Revolution, a worker's intellectual capabilities are no less important than the quality of machines installed or the quality of raw material processed or any combination of the two" (G.K. Chadha, 2003). The paradigm of development in recent years has been shifted from PCGDP or PCGNP to human well being. In this concern HDR, 1966 may be quoted. According to this report human development/human capital formation is the end and economic growth is the means, so the purpose of growth should be to enrich people's lives. In India in the Seventh Five Year Plan it has been boldly accepted that "a narrow view of resource mobilisation limiting to the financial sphere, fails to do justice to the complexity of the development process in which the human factor plays the most-significant past. Without adequate development of human resources in the widest sense, we cannot avoid setbacks to the process of development itself." The issues relating to human development have come to the fore in the last few decades because of the fact that the benefits of economic growth donot necessarily accrue to all sections of the community automatically as our planners have dreamed earlier (Jha, B.K., 2006). Moreover, the World Bank evidences indicate that as much as 64 per cent of growth is explained by human capital alone while the shares of physical and natural are much lower recording 16 per cent and 20 per cent respectively. Dension (1967) estimated that 40 per cent growth in real national income during the period 1948-63 in the United States could be attributed to improvements in human capital. Many countries of the World like Germany, Australia, U.S.A. etc. have developed themselves due to proper human capital formation.

The idea that investment in human capital formation promotes economic growth dates back to the time of Adam Smith and the early classical economists but the contribution of human capital to the economic growth has been more explicitly explored by Schultz (1961), Dension (1962) and Becker (1964). With globalisation qualitative aspects of population are of great importance from the point of view of the development of a nation and the welfare of the people because as a result of the heightened competition and economic changes, developing countries like India are facing tough challenges in maintaining the employability of large segments of their labour force. Simultaneously, though not correspondingly, competition and economic changes also have been providing some opportunities for economic growth and employment expansion but to take advantage of these opportunities which are likely to be initiated by globalisation one of the critical factors is the possession of quality and relevant skill by labour force. Moreover, rapid technological changes and transition to a more open economy as a result of globalisation entails social costs, which can be restricted only through equally rapid upgradation of the capabilities in people. It is the most considerable fact that wastage of human resources can be most detrimental to any society. Any imbalance between the creation of capabilities in people which is what human development aims to achieve and the absorption of these capabilities in productive activities which is what economic growth can result in, can create social upheaval" (C. Rangarajan, 1999). For avoiding this social upheaval, upgradation of quality aspect of our people has become a must. Globalisation and rapid technological change have made knowledge a critical determinant of competitiveness in the world economy and this is reason behind an increasing institutional awareness of the importance of knowledge for economic growth and rapidly growing economies depend more on the creation, acquisition, distribution, and use of knowledge. It is needless to say that knowledge has been the key driver of economic development for centuries but in the global era it is considered to play a critical role mainstream development theories seem to have undergone change in integrating knowledge as critical input and understanding how knowledge itself is produced to influence economic development. In knowledge economy which is ability to create and disseminate knowledge and use it for economic growth and improved standard of living, therefore, human resource endowed with education and skill is considered important as knowledge can only be produced by human resources who can then transform knowledge into tangible products technology and goods and services for the market. A country, therefore, rich in educated and skilled workforce has great potentials to produce, disseminate, and adapt knowledge to enhance growth (S. Bhushan, 2005). Here lies the importance of education in the present scenario. It is heartening to take down that the Prime Minister of India has launched a National Knowledge Commission on August 2, 2005, which will give advice to him on how India can promote excellence in the education system to meet the knowledge challenges of the 21st century and increase India's competitive advantage in fields of knowledge.

It is well known how important invention and innovation are for long-term economic prosperity and how critical higher education is for the promotion of both. Although primary education is fundamental to the nation, higher education determines its entire development including academic and technological progress along with presiding over the all round social and cultural advancement of the people of our populous country. While it is mandatory that the nation achieve universal elementary education and total literacy, at the same time, we cannot afford to neglect and relegate to a neglected position our quest to achieve global standards of higher education. Higher education is likely to play the crucial role as we move from a century, which focused on the development of material resources to one, which focuses on a knowledge and information based society where the development of our human resources will be of vital importance. Although in early development phases many rural activities require only low levels of schooling and a negative relationship between level of education and traditional occupations like toddy tapers, rickshaw pullers, basket makers, barbers, cloth washing, shepherds, tailors, quarry workers, potters, carpenters, goldsmiths, gunny bag makers etc. but we expect a positive relationship between the level of education and modern occupations like mechanical repairs of tractors, services, modern textiles, jute, plywood factories etc. There is no denying the fact that people, who are trained for skilled occupations, will generally have better opportunities of employment and their productivity is said to be higher which in turn is reflected in their relatively higher earnings. The positive contribution of education to economic growth was supported by several studies conducted both in developed and developing countries (Blaug, Layard and Woodhall, 1969, Woodhall, 1987, Wheeler, 1980, Kothari and Panchamukhi, 1980, Dasgupta and Tilak, 1983, Psacharopoulos and Woodhall, 1985, Tilak 1987, Psacharopoulos, 1994, Gemmel, 1996, Psacharopoulos and Patrinos, 2002, Chadha, 2004). Of course, there is now an increasing demand for skilled labour on account of reasons such as globalisation, changes in technology, and changes in work process as but in India about 44 per cent of the workforce above the age of 15 in 1999-2000 was illiterate and if one includes those with primary level of education, the percentage is 66 or two-thirds of the work force. We cannot deny this stark truth what people knew affected what they did and so the quality of workers now matters everywhere. The quality of workforce is now indisputably tagged with per worker productivity, at the micro level, and the course of growth trajectory, at the macro level. This is no less true of agriculture as of industry, of production as of service sectors, of rural as of urban economies, and of the informal as of the formal sector. Understandably, the challenge is far more daunting in sectors/activities directly engaged in exports. But then, the onslaught of imports, in the age of open world trade, can be absorbed only if the production regime directed to domestic market also firms up its efficiency frontiers (G.K. Chadha, 2003). The growth trends in India during the last decades received a major push upward as the percentage of literates jumped from 42.9 to 65.2 registering nearly 22 per cent point change but this is not sufficient enough. Education in general and higher education in particular, which ensures availability of manpower of right quantity and quality for all activities has to be the equalizer in an otherwise efficiency driven market economy. "The externalities of education, including the dynamic externalities of higher education are indeed immense and they have profound positive effect on economic growth" (Tilak, 2005).

Higher Education at the Cross Roads

The education has become a pivot for development and so each nation strives to build sound educational system. Indian higher educational system has not only to pass the test of time but also it needs to be ready to venture into new challenges that are emerging in the global era. The new challenges have direct link with the social aspirations of the masses, which demand clever approaches for meeting the larger number of students. A UNESCO document of the international commission for the twentyfirst century, titled learning: The Treasure within states: "Higher education is at one and the same time one of the driving forces of economic development and the focal point of learning in a society. It is both repository and creator of knowledge. Moreover, it is the principal instrument for passing on the accumulated experience, cultural and scientific, of humanity. In a world where resources of knowledge will increasingly predominate over material resources as factors in development, the importance of higher education and of higher education institutions can only grow. Moreover, the effect of innovation and technological progress means that economies will increasingly demand competencies that require higher-level studies" (Delors, 1996, p. 130). There is an emerging desire or say compulsion to catch up with the world which is fast changing. Our capacity to meet the challenge will depend on how best and fast we respond to these changes. This is both an opportunity and a challenge. Strategies and development policies will have to be interwoven into a pattern which fits into the world trends and, at the same time, tackle problems unique to India where a large population has not even had the fruits of development although the growth trend for the last three years i.e. 8.5 per cent, 7.5 per cent and 8.1 per cent in 2003-04, 2004-05 and 2005-06 respectively, appears to indicate the beginning of a new phase of cyclical upswing in the economy from 2003-04. Even our president APJ Abdul Kalam, while inaugurating the concluding function of the Golden Jubilee Year of the UGC held at Vigyan Bhawan, New Delhi on the 28th December, 2006 has given an indication in this regard in these words "Higher education needs to be backed by employment opportunities the universities should become a facilitator for creating this entrepreneurship scheme through the support of the banking and the marketing system. This is one way of reducing the employment gap leading to upliftment of the 260 million people living below the poverty line." The changing character of new technologies requires workers who can learn and adapt to these changes quickly and efficiently. Although the skill itself may not be higher, the ability to master it quickly and use it productively calls for a high level of confidence and familiarity that favours the higher skilled (ILO, 1997-98, p. 46). This requirement focuses on the desirability of higher education particularly technical education. For fulfilling the dream of the then Finance Minister Yashwant Sinha who asserted in his budget speech on the 29th February, 2000. "The next 10 years will be India's decade of development", there needs to have a sound human capital base that cannot be possible without sound higher education system in the country. Even the ancient scripts such as Arthashastra by Kautilya can be seen as a treatise of human development as it discusses systems of governance that can ensure certain welfare standards to all sections of population. We need to take lesson from China, which is far ahead, and behind the phenomenal economic might of China is its human resource with adequate skills and commitment to hard work. In India the maladjustment between the education system and the socio-economic needs of our developing economy results in an increase in the number of educated unemployed side by side with the shortage of trained personnel. "Education is generally taken to be a means of wage-paid employment, especially in government offices and public sector undertakings. The most common perception, that invariably operates on ground as well, is that education is not a pre-requisite for starting self-employing small and tiny enterprises, especially those in which outside resources including hired labour are not involved, for example in a recent survey of such enterprises in Haryana, Maharashtra and West Bengal, nearly one-half of self-employing family workers had education only upto middle-level of schooling"(Chadha, 2003). Ironically, in this perception, no attention is spared for productivity levels which are many times lower than those in other enterprises which are larger in size and employ workers with higher levels of education and training. It is needless to say that per worker productivity is invariably higher, in all fields of economic activities, among the educated group of workers than among the illiterates or lowly educated ones. Although educational facilities in the country did witness a tremendous expansion during the preceding decades, yet millions of children and adolescents, most markedly in the rural areas, have had no education and a very small number of highly educated and a very small number of highly educated and professionally trained persons, hailing nearly exclusively from the urban areas, who are progressively becoming a part of the international labour market or the highly lucrative segment of the domestic market, undoubtedly, they are the product of a few top-class educational institutions. Training systems suffer from limited flexibility, poor curricula and weak links with industry and skill upgradation, which has become most desirable when the Indian economy opened itself to the world outside, is particularly weak. This weakness can be reflected from the fact that only about 5 per cent of secondary school level students were found to opt for vocational stream against a target of 25 per cent set during the eighth plan (Government of India, 1999, p. 122).

No doubt, in the opened economy, foreign education provides students in our country access to modern education and training programmes in diverse disciplines which may not be available domestically but the system exacerbates disparity in educational attainment between the rich and the poor, the urban and the rural students resulting in inequalities in earning capabilities. Globalisation of educational services creates a scenario in which higher educational institutions have to grow and to rise to world standards. Moreover, higher education provided by foreign institutions enables the developed countries to make inroads into the social and cultural fabric of the recipient country. Under the impact of globalisation domestic institutions of higher education, except for the few get marginalized in the process in the developing country like India where the majority of institutions of higher education suffer from lack of infrastructure and starved of funds. The curriculum, standards, faculty and requirements will all be determined by the sponsoring institution and may not always serve the needs of the recipient country (N. Ahmad, 2005).

Present Scenario of Higher Education in India

According to UNDP's Global Human Development Report (HDR) for 2005, India holds a rank of 127 out of 177 countries of world in terms of composite HDI for 2003. No doubt in absolute values, HDI showed improvement for India but its ranking maintained more or less at the same level both in 2000 (124) and 2003 (127) in HDI and the striking feature to be noted is that Sri Lanka, China and Indonesia are at a higher level than India both in 2000 and 2003. In July 2006, Adrian white, Analytic Social Psychologist at the University of Leicester, United Kingdom, announced that as per the World Map of happiness prepared by him, Denmark in Europe is the happiest country and Burundi in Africa is the most unhappy country in the world. Happiness according to Mr. White is found to be most closely associated with health followed by wealth and education. Switzerland, Austria and Ireland follow Denmark while China holds a rank of 82, Japan 90, India 125 and Russia 167; the study concluded that larger population is not associated with happy countries. The U.S. secured 23rd rank, U.K. 41st and France 62nd.

There has been substantial growth in higher education after Independence with respect to number of institutions, teachers as well as student enrolments. However, the percentage of students enrolled in higher education in India is only 8, which is less than percentage of enrolled students in other developing countries like Thailand, Philippines, Indonesia, Mexico and Brazil having 20.1 per cent, 27.4 per cent, 11.1 per cent, 14.8 per cent and 11.3 per cent respectively. Due to lack of facility for effective vocational education at the school level, there has been overcrowding of higher education institutions, despite the fact that it had little relevance for the job market, which requires mainly skilled labour force. Overall status of vocational and technical education is low in the country resulting in abysmally low level of human capital base in comparison to many countries.

The colonial era ended by leaving the masses of people mostly untouched by any formal education. This holds true particularly for the largest countries in the region, India, Pakistan and Indonesia. They entered their time of Independence with a very low rate of literacy, probably far below one fifth of the adult population (Gunnar Myrdal, 1979). At the time of Independence India had 20 universities and 500 colleges. On the eve of India Golden Jubilee of its Independence, that is by 1995-96 there were 228 universities of which, there are 15 central universities set up by the Acts of Parliament 164 state universities set up by Acts of state legislatures, and 39 deemed to be universities set up under the UGC Act. These 228 universities include 8 open universities and 33 agricultural universities and the remaining institutions of national importance and 4 other independent institutions. The total number of universities have risen from 184 in 1990-91 and 228 in 1995-96 to 232 by 1998 which further increased to 261 in 2001-02 and later on the total number of universities touché the figure of 350.

Table 22.1: College Education

No. of Institutions	2001-02	2000-01	1999-00	1990-91
General education colleges	8361	7834	7782	4862
Professional colleges	2340	2169	2124	886
Universities	261	251	244	184

Source: Statistical Outline of India, 2003-04.

Table 22.2: Estimated Stock of Manpower by Major Categories

	2001	2000	1991	1981
Graduates				
Arts	8769.0	8392.8	5501.9	3242.6
Science	4024.9	3837.7	2430.3	1434.6
Commerce	4853.1	4573.6	2468.0	1054.2
Post Graduates				
Arts	3917.3	3718.4	2185.3	1113.6
Science	805.0	767.1	482.1	292.4
Commerce	902.5	841.7	403.5	148.3

Source: Statistical Outline of India, 2003-04.

Table 22.3: Technical Education

	2001	2000	1991	1981
Engineers				
Degree holders	1024.4	969.5	519.6	304.9
Diploma holders	1531	1456.5	859.3	425.8
Graduates				
Medicine	391.9	380.5	296.4	219.5
Dentistry	24.0	22.9	13.9	8.0
Agri-Science	238.6	231.2	168.4	109.8
Veterinary Science	46.5	46.3	34.4	24.4

Source: Statistical Outline of India, 2003-04.

It is needless to say that the largest number of colleges is in humanities, social sciences, science and commerce although quantitative growth of technical institutions is also remarkable.

Table 22.4: Growth of Degree Diploma Institutions and Sanctioned Intake in Engineering in Post Independence Era

Year	*Degree*	*No of Institutions Intake*	*Diploma*	*No. of Institutions Intake*
1950	50	3700	46	4200
1960	110	16000	195	26500
1970	145	18200	309	43500
1980	158	28500	332	49200
1990	337	66600	879	122000
2000	776	185753	1215	211894
2003	1203	359721	1197	242698

Source: (*i*) Technical Education in Independent India, 1947-97.
(*ii*) The AICTE Annual Reports. Thus, the disturbing feature has been the proliferation of universities and colleges, especially for general education, which do not prepare for a career while a majority terminate at the bachelor's degree level. Moreover, the degree holders have little knowledge or skill, they remain unemployable thus adding to the growing mismatch between the educational system and the employment market and exacerbating the phenomenon of educated unemployment.

Warning Bells

Gunnar Myrdal has rightly observed that "the main reforms needed in education in all underdeveloped countries are of a qualitative nature" (G. Myrdal, 1970) and India is not exception. There exist a number of subviable institutions and as many as almost 50 per cent of the 9703 affiliated colleges (in 1997-98) are not eligible for the UGC assistance as they either donot fulfil the conditions for recognition under our Act (2f) or even if recognized, donot come under our grant (12B) for want of minimum requirements. There are, approximately 9703 colleges of which 4935 are recognized for development grants as of 1997-98. Thus, the most worrisome fact has been the proliferation of the universities and colleges, mainly for general education "it is estimated that one college is established everyday, sometimes with the possible exception of Sundays, and one university is established every three or four months" (A.S. Desai, 1999) providing the bachelor's degree to a majority of the student's (85%) who expect to find a job, but suffer only frustration. The U.R. Rao Committee, which has reviewed the performance of all technical education draws attention to the unsustainable expansion of technical education and makes far reaching recommendations to achieve excellence in this sector. In his report he has observed "a serious situation has arisen in recent years because of the mushrooming of a large number of private technical institutions and polytechnics. Barring some exceptions, there is scant regard for maintenance of standards." For instance there are 1208 engineering degree colleges in which 986 are in the private sector with a total sanctioned intake of over 0.36 million students. Further there are 1006 Master of Computer Applications (MCA) and 930 Master of Business Administrations, with an intake of about 53000 and 64000 students respectively. Obviously, this is occurring at the expense of quality. Hereby it is worthnoting that in the global era employment opportunities have become more sensitive to the quality of employment seekers.

Unfortunately, the massification of education has occurred in India at the lower levels of education, which feed into higher education. Of course, the quality of preparation at lower levels impacts on the students who enter the educational system at higher levels. Increasing access and decrease in quality have been major issues confronting higher education especially in all developing countries like India. Unfortunately much education in these countries is now even plain miseducation and apt to raise impediments for development (G. Myrdal, 1970). In Swami Vivekananda's vision it is not a man-making education, it is merely and entirely a negative education.... The child is taken to school, and the first thing he learns is that his father is a fool, the second thing that his grandfather is a lunatic, the third thing that all his teachers are hypocrites, the fourth, that all the sacred books are lies! By the time he is sixteen he is a mass of negation.... It would be better if the people got a little technical education so that they might find work and earn their bread, instead of dawdling about crying for services (Swami Vivekananda, 1985). It is painful that India which was well reputed for its good quality educational system, where students outside of our country came to get such education had gradually lost such prestigious status in this concern with an adoption of Macaulay's model of education designed to serve the interest of British Raj. For revival of our lost prestige, it is desirable that education is all about creativity and creativity is all about commitment. Without commitment you cannot have good education, which has more to do with quality than with quantity (which is also important) (Arun Kumar, 2005). The educational system that was introduced in the country never addressed the real problems of education resulting in wide educational disparity between rural and urban areas that impact the quality of education in the country. In the rural areas, generally only public institutions prevail in education, no one else is interested in spreading education in the rural areas and these institutions where children of low income groups families still come to read, remain uncared because there is no pressure groups to care for such institutions. All those who formed these pressure groups have migrated to the urban areas and are sending their children to English medium schools. As a growing number of students enter from the publicly supported system of school education, it also impacts on the quality of the higher education system with problems in maintaining necessary standards without providing the infrastructure for remedying the past educational deficits.

For quality improvement at the higher educational level it is required to attract the best human resources to teaching for which teaching at the higher education level needs to be more lucrative in comparison to other services as found at one time but it has lost its attraction as a most desirable profession. On the contrary, at least Bihar remained such a state where all the measures for humiliating teachers at higher education level were taken by the government and teaching in such level lost its prestigious value. Is it not true that college teacher had to face demotion instead of promotion in their career in the last decade of the last century? The UGC norms of staying 5 or 6 hours at colleges particularly colleges in rural areas where infrastructure is too poor to imagine, may prove waste of time of college teachers and cannot be helpful in improving quality of education and there is need of having sound infrastructure even in such institutions. In most institutions, there is a serious shortage of faculty and teaching loads are high so neither is research feasible and nor is an upgradation of skills possible. The decrease in infrastructure resources to the higher education system has affected the academic environment for serious pursuit of teaching and research. "It is a tragedy that while we need to generate more knowledge, our public university system, which was doing some good research, is in a deep crisis because of inadequate funding. So, many public universities are hardly doing any research because of financial crises and the private universities which are mushrooming all over are doing little or no research because they only wish to make high profits" (Arun Kumar, 2005).

In the global era such type of scenario in education has emerged which has adverse repercussion on the quality of education. What we expect from a temporary lecturer who is appointed at salary less than that of a peon. We should remember that commercialization is lowering the standards of education. It is but true that permanent faculty is being encouraged to go in for projects and consultancies to generate funds with the result that their commitment to basic teaching and research has weakened. Thus, the major challenge confronting higher education in today's global era is knowledge generation. Indeed in many countries building a work force with higher order skills is an important part of improving the climate for investment, acquiring a competitive edge and generally maintaining an engine of growth (*World Development Report*, 2007).

Identifying Worry Spots

The Director of Council of Scientific and Industrial Research, Dr. R.A. Mashekhar has stated that India will be among the world's three biggest economies by the year 2050 and we will be there much earlier if we can master the economics of knowledge (Raghavan, V.P. 2006) which provides the pathway for future progress and prosperity and the source of knowledge is education particularly higher education. Of course, higher education is so important that any point of time, weakening of higher education sector would weaken the forces of competitiveness and efficiency in the functioning of different sectors of economy (*Panchamukhi*, 2002) and indeed, among the developing countries of the world, India can be proud of its achievements in higher education. "From just three universities in 1860's, we now have about 350 universities with 17,000 colleges affiliated to them some ten million students are enrolled in these institutions. This, however, is not enough to meet the demands of social justice, equally, human development and finally the projected rates of economic growth" (K.C. Reddy, 2006).

No doubt, the Indian system of higher education has

undergone rapid development in the post Independence era. Despite this, the fact remains that the system has not been able to accomplish the goals of higher education. It is but true that the number of higher education institutions have increased by leaps and bounds, the quantitative expansion has been accompanied by qualitative deterioration, most probably because infrastructures in the institutions of higher education have been limited and stretched to tearing points. We cannot hesitate to realize the fact that the new global scenario poses challenges for the higher education system, which cannot be faced without improving quality of higher education. The UGC in its Sixth Plan document, gives an indication of these challenges in these words... "the need of reconciling the new global emphasis on the market economy with the United Nations pronouncement on promoting sustainable development and the survival of its human population at an adequate level of the quality of life, demand a whole range of skills from the graduates of humanities, social sciences, sciences and commerce, as well as from the various professional disciplines such as agriculture, law, management, medicine or engineering. We can no longer continue the model of general education as we have been persisting in for the large bulk of the student population. Rather, it will require a major investment to make this large human resource productive by coupling the older general disciplines of humanities, social sciences, sciences and commerce to their applications in the new economy and having adequate field based experience to enhance knowledge with skills and develop appropriate attitudes" (UGC, 1996, p. X).

It is needless to day the UGC which is an apex body to co-ordinate and maintain standards of higher education has number of schemes such as its Academic Staff Colleges for Orientation and refresher course for college and university teachers, Special Assistance Programmes for Departments to achieve excellence, funding for major and minor research projects, junior research fellowship etc. However, the problem of a quality remains because of poor attraction to teaching and research on account of salaries and other benefits and poor institutional physical infrastructure.

Another worry spot found in higher education is private sector expansion which has been happening already and will continue to grow but there need not to forget the fact in the post reform period but there need not forget the fact that when private entrepreneurs set up higher education facilities, there is the worrisome dimension of wide variation in quality because most of them pay scant attention to quality as they are only interested in maximizing net revenues. Only a few institutions provide top quality faculty and excellent infrastructure, targeting for high caliber output but such institutions are too costly to be admitted for low and middle-income groups. An increase in the cost of higher education in excess of price-indexed inflation, increasing privatization and reliance on contributions by corporations and the corporate wealthy and decreasing public and legislative support for higher education misfit in the Indian context because a large segment here belongs to low income strata and so for improving access to all and ensuring access to the weaker sections, building and sustaining quality and the regulation of the higher educational institutions including private sector, the state has to continue to play a dominant role in higher education in developing countries like India.

The most worry spot lies in this fact that in our country, the civil service is rated higher than academia with the best students opting for it, unlike in the US where the best go for research and this track needs to be changed in the national interest. Hereby it is worth noting the fact that most Indian universities and colleges function like government offices and VCs and principals donot understand academic considerations and they treat dissent as a malaise and not the essence of knowledge generation through high quality research. Real talent will not come to teaching to work honestly on the remuneration paid on the contract basis in the global era and in such scenario students get degrees but their position would not be better than an ass carrying its load of sandal wood knows only the weight and not the value of sandal wood. Indeed, education is imparted to students to enable them to think independently and to discriminate between right and wrong and between good and bad, and they are supposed to develop a scientific attitude and sympathetical outlook. But unfortunately, in India education that is imparted to Indian students is designed by Macaulay to produce clerks and not thinkers. There is no denying the fact that Macaulay was a farsighted man who was planning perpetuating the British Raj in India but British Raj ended and education designed for their interest continued till now. This is but ironical and needs to be revised in the interest of our nation. In 1800 Japan implemented the education policy of its country. In 1960-70 Taiwan, in 1970-80 Korea and in 1980-90 Ireland focused on education and Ireland which was the poorest country in Europe 26 or 27 years ago has the highest per capita income today and for this credit goes to education particularly higher education but in India the effort that we have made on education since Independence has been such that the outcomes donot come out focused (Arun Kumar, 2005). Unfortunately, India is spending only 0.6 per cent of its GDP on higher education and this is getting reflected in both the quantity and quality of infrastructure and faculty. While a small proportion of students are excelling globally, the general average does not reflect high caliber.

Concluding Remark

According to the May 2006, Report of the Technical Group on Population Projections Constituted by the National Commission on Population, the projected population numbers in the age range 15-24 is 222 million in 2006 and 2.40 million in 2011 and we need to impart higher education at least a fifth of the projected numbers. Roughly estimated about 40 million students will be then for getting higher education that is 4 times the present enrolment. India is confronting the challenge of providing access to quality higher education to a large proportion of population across the country with focus on weaker sections of society with a view to make higher education inclusive. Hereby it is heartening to take down that the Eleventh Plan approach paper aims at 15 per cent enrolment towards the end of this plan. We are in dire need to improve the standing of our university and college academics and the programmes they offer in order that the institutions eventually gain international reputation and prove instrumental in eradicating poverty through generating employment opportunities in the economy. There is need for adopting such a strategy in the field of higher education which makes higher growth rate as well as reduction of poverty possible, which can be, if we succeed in making labour more productive, which is the best way to reduce poverty.

REFERENCES

1. Gunnar Myrdal (1972), *Asian Drama: An Inquiry into the Poverty of Nations,* Vintage Book, New York.
2. Gunnar Myrdal (1971), *The Challenge of World Poverty,* Penguin Books.
3. C. Rangarajan (1999), *Indian Economy: Essay on Money and Finance,* UBSPD.
4. Jha, B.K. (2006), *89th IEA Annual Conference.*
5. Nighat Ahmed (2005), *88th IEA Annual Conference.*
6. Arun Kumar (2005), *In Social Sector: Development* (ed.), Dolly Arora.
7. A.B. Desai (1999), *Higher Education at the Cross Roads of the 20th and 21st Centuries.*
8. K.C. Reddy (2006), *On Reforming and Repositioning the Higher Education Sector.*
9. Professional Competency in Higher Education by CPDHE (1995).
10. *Indian Journal of Labour Economics Conf.*, Issue Vol. 48, No. 4.
11. *Indian Journal of Labour Economics Conf.*, Issue Vol. 47, No. 4.
12. Swami Vivekananda (1985), *On India and Her Problem,* compiled by Nijr Vedanda.
13. *A.P.J. Kalam's Address* (2003), in Vigyan Bhavan.
14. R. Ramchandram (2004), *Warning Bell Fronltine,* March 26.

23

Access and Equity in Indian Higher Education System: Problems and Prospects

DR. SHYAM SUNDER SINGH CHAUHAN AND
DR. (MRS.) SANGITA GUPTA

Higher education system is passing through a phase of transition. At the apex level, institutions like IITs, IIMs, IIS, TIFR, DSE etc. have proved their excellence and attained the world-class status. While at the lower level hundreds of affiliated degree colleges and in some cases even the State Universities are running without basic infrastructures. Nearly 70 thousand posts of teachers are lying vacant and contract teachers have filled equal number of posts. Colleges established under self-financing schemes are running on 'substitutes'. The policy makers are busy in preparing a road map for the smooth entry of foreign players in the field of higher education. The principles of access and equality in higher education have been overcome by profit making.

In these circumstances a plan for the development of higher education on market friendly basis is on card. Two strong forces of demand and supply, if applied to a sector like higher education, than the whole system of higher education will convert into a market and the noble profession having ethics in its core base and access, equity, relevance, quality, social values and educational technologies its five goals will turn into a commodity, which would be sold and purchase like anything. The educational institutes will run on commercial principles and profit maximisation will be their sole objectives.

In the light of the above scenario, the present article analyse the (*i*) present status of higher education, (*ii*) State in higher education, (*iii*) Higher education in relation to access and equity and finally, (*iv*) Some suggestions to improve the standard of higher education in India.

Higher Education in India

India has a strong tradition of higher education since ancient times. Western and secular education, with an emphasis on scientific inquiry came to India only with the British. The first college imparting Western education in India was set up in Serampore in Bengal in 1818. The three Central Universities of Calcutta, Bombay and Madras were established in 1857 with the sole aim of producing English knowing people to assist British officers of military and civil administration. Initially 27 colleges affiliated to them. Subsequently, more universities and colleges were set up. At the time of independence there were 19 universities in India.

Since independence, the higher education system has grown rapidly. By 1980, there were 132 universities and 4738 colleges in the country enrolling around five per cent of the eligible age group in higher education. Expansion of higher education got momentum during the era of liberalisation by with different pace. Central as well as State Governments, hitherto the sole crusaders of higher education allotted comparatively low budgetary resources to higher education as a part of the process of curtailing high fiscal deficit, which was one of the main factors of economic crises of 1990-91. Instead of creating new infrastructure, particularly establishing new teaching institutions or opening up of new sections in the colleges and universities government allowed private institutions, colleges and universities on self-finance basis to be established under the norms of UGC, AICTE and NCTE etc. This resulted into mushrooming growth of degree colleges, management schools, engineering colleges and other professional colleges.

Today, India is the third largest higher education system in the world (after China and the USA) in terms of enrolment. In terms of the number of institutions, India is the largest higher education system in the world with 17,973 institutions (357 universities and 17,625 colleges). However, the average number of students per educational institution in India is lower than that in the US and China.

Following types of institutions are imparting higher education in India:

- Universities under the Government
- Private Universities
- Deemed Universities (Aided)
- Deemed Universities (Unaided)
- Colleges under Government
- Private Colleges (Aided)
- Private Colleges (Unaided) established under self-financing scheme
- Distance Learning (Open Universities like IGNOU)
- Non-University Sector (Polytechnics and Industrial Training Institutes)
- Foreign Institutions

Student enrolment grew at an estimated rate of 7 per cent between 1987 and 1993 but has now declined to 5.5 per cent compound rate of growth. Today, there are 10.5 million students enrolled in all higher education institutions, with the teaching staff numbering 321,000. In spite of this phenomenal growth, the total enrolment forms only about 11 per cent of the relevant age-group (17-23) population. Tables 23.1, 23.2 and 23.3 illustrate the status of various educational institutions in India.

Table 23.1: Growth of Higher Education Institutions and Enrolment in India

Year	*Universities*	*Colleges*	*Total HEIs*	*Enrolment (in million)*
1947-48	20	496	516	0.2
1950-51	28	578	606	0.2
1960-61	45	1,819	1,864	0.6
1970-71	93	3,277	3,370	2.0
1980-81	123	4,738	4,861	2.8
1990-91	184	5,748	5,932	4.4
2000-01	266	11,146	11,412	8.8
2005-06	348	17,625	17,973	10.5

Source: UGC (Universities include central, state, private and deemed-to-be universities as also institutions of national importance established both by the central and the state legislatures).

Along with these statistical achievements of Indian higher education system has also the some bare facts as mentioned below:

- Just 200 million children enter primary school, 33 million secondary school and 10 million into colleges, finally churning out 3 million graduates every year (Ravi Krishnan, 2006). It means just one out of 66 students entering primary school go on to graduate.

Table 23.2: Stage-wise Enrolment

Courses	*Number in Thousand*	*As Percentage of Total Enrolment in Classes XI-XII*
Ph.D./D.Sc./D.Phil.	65.5	0.545
M.A.	427.2	3.56
M.Sc.	234.4	1.95
M.Com.	142.0	1.18
B.A./B.A.(Hons)	3824.8	31.87
B.Sc./B.Sc. (Hons)	1614.1	13.45
B.Com./B.Com. (Hons)	1613.4	13.44
B.E./B.Sc. (Engg.) B.Arch.	772.9	6.44
Medicine, Dentistry, Nursing, Pharmacy, Ayurvedic and Unani	223.2	1.86
B.Ed./B.T.	114.7	0.95
Others	973.9	8.11
Total	10009.1	

Table 23.3: State-wise Number of Institutions Imparting Higher Education

(as on 31st January, 2004)

S. No.	*States/UTs*	*U*	*DU*	*INI*	*RI*	*Coll.*	*En.C*	*MC*	*TTC*	*Oth.*	*Tot.*
1	2	3	4	5	6	7	8	9	10	11	12
1.	Andhra Pradesh	18	5	0	5	1330	238	53	87	93	1801
2.	Arunachal Pradesh	1	0	0	3	10	1	1	2	0	14
3.	Assam	5	1	1	0	317	3	7	40	21	388
4.	Bihar	11	1	0	11	743	7	23	15	63	851
5.	Chhattisgarh	9	0	0	0	213	2	2	1	43	250
6.	Goa	1	0	0	0	24	4	7	2	5	42
7.	Gujarat	10	2	0	16	422	32	41	51	111	657
8.	Haryana	4	3	0	0	163	41	8	24	35	271
9.	Himachal Pradesh	4	1	0	2	69	2	7	7	24	109

(Contd.)

1	2	3	4	5	6	7	8	9	10	11	12
10.	Jammu & Kashmir	5	0	0	0	73	4	6	8	34	125
11.	Jharkhand	4	2	0	1	146	5	8	9	14	182
12.	Karnataka	13	6	0	1	930	120	172	70	214	1506
13.	Kerala	7	1	1	1	186	66	40	21	82	395
14.	Madhya Pradesh	14	3	0	0	513	56	28	21	209	827
15.	Maharashtra	19	13	1	21	1208	177	116	251	128	1880
16.	Manipur	2	0	0	0	58	1	1	3	1	64
17.	Meghalaya	1	0	0	0	48	0	0	2	0	50
18.	Mizoram	1	0	0	0	26	0	0	2	2	30
19.	Nagaland	1	0	0	0	36	0	0	2	18	56
20.	Orissa	8	1	0	0	567	19	16	16	153	771
21.	Punjab	5	2	1	0	209	16	42	23	53	343
22.	Rajasthan	9	6	0	0	456	39	24	51	96	666
23.	Sikkim	1	0	0	1	2	1	1	1	1	6
24.	Tamil Nadu	16	9	2	1	441	96	97	22	184	840
25.	Tripura	1	0	0	0	14	1	1	1	5	22
26.	Uttar Pradesh	22	7	1	10	733	69	34	121	273	1230
27.	Uttaranchal	4	2	1	0	47	2	1	1	28	79
28.	West Bengal	14	1	2	11	354	43	19	26	46	488
29.	A&N Islands	0	0	0	0	2	0	0	1	1	4
30.	Chandigarh	1	0	1	0	12	2	4	3	3	24
31.	D&N Haveli	0	0	0	0	0	0	0	0	0	0
32.	Daman & Diu	0	0	0	0	1	0	0	1	0	2
33.	Delhi	5	8	2	1	63	16	18	19	56	163
34.	Lakshadweep	1	0	0	0	11	5	0	0	0	0
35.	Pondicherry	1	0	0	0	11	5	6	5	6	33
	INDIA	**217**	**74**	**13**	**85**	**9427**	**1068**	**783**	**900**	**1991**	**14169**

U: University; **DU**: Deemed University; **INI**: Institutions of National Importance; **RI**: Research Institutions; **Coll.**: Arts, Science and Commerce Colleges; **En.C**: Engg., Tech. and Arch. Colleges; **MC**: Colleges (Allo/Ayur/Homeo/Unani/Nurs./Pharm.); **TTC**: Teacher Training Colleges; **Oth.**: Others (includes Law, Management, CA/IT, Agriculture etc.); **Tot.**: Total Higher Education Institutions (col. 7 to 11)

Source: Association of Indian Universities (AIU).

- Nearly 10 million students pass their intermediate examination every year and out of these only 8 million are fortunate enough to get admission in a college or an university.
- Dropout rate is 62.7 per cent in 2003-04.
- India has one of the lowest public expenditure on higher eaucation per student at US $406 (GOI, 2005).
- The share of higher education in total planned resources has declined continuously since Fourth Five Year Plan.

Table 23.4: Functioning of Various Higher Education Institutions in India

Type	*Owner-ship and Financing*	*Number of Institutions*	*Number of Students*	*Growth Trends*
Universities under the Government	Public	240	1,000,000	Not growing
Private Universities	Private	7	10,000	Emerging on the scene
Deemed Universities (Aided)	Private or Public	38	40,000	Growing slowly
Deemed Universities (Unaided)	Private	63	60,000	Growing rapidly
Colleges under the Government	Public	4,225	2,750,000	Not growing
Private Colleges (Aided)	Private	5,750	3,450,000	Not growing
Private Colleges (self-financing)	Private	7,650	3,150,000	Mushrooming growth
Foreign Institutions	Private	150	8,000	Emerging on the scene
Total		**18,123**	**10,468,000**	

Source: Pawan Agarwal, *Higher Education in India: The Need for Change*, ICRIER Working Paper, June 2006.

- A recent evaluation of universities and research institutes all over the world, conducted by a Shanghai University, India has not a single university in the world's top 300 (Basu, 2006) despite the fact that Indian technocrats, scientists, managers and doctors have registered their presence and proved their worth in almost all the countries, developed as well as developing, of the world.
- As per latest statistics, gross enrolment ratio, in 18.25 age group, in India is about 13 per cent, which is far below than 40-50 per cent in developed countries.
- Central Universities, with more than 50 per cent share in total allocation for higher education providing quality education to only 10 per cent of the students entering into graduate courses remaining 90 per cent students go to the state universities or affiliated colleges.
- Pace of development, in terms of number of institutions has been significant during the era of LPG. However, it could result into an impressive increase in enrolment ratio. As a result of liberalised rules, in view of the government's policy to prune budgetary allocations to social sector so as to bring down the fiscal deficit, mushrooming growth of self-financing institutes/colleges has taken the space vacated by the public sector. The entry of private sector, has no doubt, created many additional seats in lucrative

professional courses, but with little care for quality. Many of these colleges/institutions are in short of qualified teaching faculty. Many colleges are running on 'substitutes' (unqualified teachers appointed in place of qualified teachers as included in the official records).

- There has been a rapid expansion of higher education, with student enrolment growing at about 5 per cent annually over the past two decades. This growth is about 2.5 times to population growth rate, and results from both a population bulge in lower age cohorts as well as increased demand for higher education. However, even today's gross enrolment ratio of Indians in institutions of higher education is approximately 7 per cent of the age cohort, which is considerably higher than developing country average, but lower than the average for Asia as a whole (11 %) and much lower than OECD countries. Enrolment ratios vary across Indian states, with the Southern and Western States faring well than their eastern counterparts (Table 23.5). Women now constitute about 40 per cent of all student enrolments, varying from 24 per cent in Bihar to a high 60 per cent in Kerala (Table 23.5). The bulk of students are enrolled in arts and science (nearly two thirds), with another 18 per cent in commerce/ management (Table 23.6) (Kapur and Mehta, 2004).

Table 23.5: Student Enrolment in Higher Education by Academic Discipline (2002-03)

S. No.	*Faculty*	*Total Enrolment*	*Percentage Share*
1.	Arts	4158606	45.07
2.	Science	1834493	19.88
3.	Commerce/Management	1660238	17.99
4.	Education	132572	1.43
5.	Engineering/Technology	692087	7.50
6.	Medicine*	300669	3.25
7.	Agriculture Science	55367	0.60
8.	Veterinary Science	14765	0.16
9.	Law	298291	3.23
10.	Others	80745	0.88
	Total	**9227833**	**100.00**

*Allopathy, Unani, Ayurvedic, Homeopathic, etc.
Source: University Grants Commission, New Delhi.

Table 23.6: State-wise Enrolment in Higher Education (2002-03)

S. No.	State/UTs	Boys Enrolment		Girls Enrolment		Total	
		Number	% share	Number	% share	Number	% share
1.	Andhra Pradesh	456146	60.70	295330	39.30	751476	100.00
2.	Arunachal Pradesh	3862	71.01	1577	28.99	5439	100.00
3.	Assam	119674	59.50	81458	40.50	201132	100.00
4.	Bihar	376407	76.19	117628	23.81	494035	100.00
5.	Chhattisgarh	96731	63.30	56082	36.70	152813	100.00
6.	Delhi	92998	54.00	79220	46.00	172218	100.00
7.	Goa	8966	41.50	11371	58.50	19437	100.00
8.	Gujarat	289538	55.79	229483	44.21	519021	100.00
9.	Haryana	146980	59.00	102138	41.00	249118	100.00
10.	Himachal Pradesh	51531	57.31	38383	42.69	89914	100.00
11.	Jammu & Kashmir	31528	52.90	28071	47.10	59599	100.00
12.	Jharkhand	137355	69.60	59994	30.40	197349	100.00
13.	Karnataka	329799	59.14	227846	40.86	557645	100.00
14.	Kerala	100475	40.00	150682	60.00	251157	100.00
15.	Madhya Pradesh	290183	62.80	176630	37.20	474813	100.00
16.	Maharashtra	742327	59.00	515868	41.00	1258195	100.00
17.	Manipur	20264	55.70	16115	44.30	36379	100.00
18.	Meghalaya	15195	52.10	13970	47.90	29165	100.00
19.	Mizoram	5991	53.30	5249	46.70	11240	100.00
20.	Nagaland	7551	61.20	4788	38.80	12339	100.00
21.	Orissa	221942	64.31	123171	35.69	345113	100.00
22.	Punjab	115332	47.32	128411	52.68	243743	100.00
23.	Rajasthan	245756	67.67	117416	32.33	363172	100.00
24.	Sikkim	2449	59.69	1654	40.31	4103	100.00
25.	Tamil Nadu	391462	54.90	321583	45.10	713045	100.00
26.	Tripura	11926	59.20	8219	40.80	20145	100.00
27.	Uttaranchal	69191	60.00	46127	40.00	115318	100.00
28.	Uttar Pradesh	725531	61.60	452279	38.40	1177810	100.00
29.	West Bengal	392786	60.60	255382	39.40	648178	100.00
30.	A&N Islands	518	42.23	1164	57.77	1164	100.00
31.	Chandigarh	15104	44.50	18838	55.50	33942	100.00
32.	Daman & Deu	312	53.15	275	46.85	587	100.00
33.	Pondicherry	8616	47.40	9562	52.60	18178	100.00
	All India	**5581869**	**59.95**	**3695964**	**40.05**	**9277833**	**100.00**

Source: University Grants Commission, New Delhi.

State in Higher Education: Post-Liberalisation Era

In broader terms, state played a key role in the development of higher education after the independence. But, the situation changed after the introduction of LPG—Liberalisation, Privatisation and Globalisation. As a matter of policy, central government and its key bodies (UGC, AICTE, NCT, MCI) allowed the entry of private entrepreneurs in this field, which was, hitherto treated as a 'philanthropists area'. Subsequently state governments and their universities liberalised the whole system of affiliation. Public spending on higher education, either by central government, or by state governments curtailed in the name of reduction of fiscal deficit. Central government's expenditure on higher education, as a per cent of GDP, as a per cent of total public expenditure and as a per cent of total public expenditure on education was 0.12, 0.42 and 2.89 during 1999-2000, which came down to 0.07, 0.25 and 1.90 respectively in 2006-07 (BE) (Table 23.7).

Table 23.7: Public Expenditure on Higher Education in India by Central Government

(Rs. crore)

Year	*Plan Expenditure*	*Non-Plan Expenditure*	*Total*	*Public Expenditure on Higher Education as % of*		
				GDP	*Total Public Expenditure*	*Total Pub-Exp. on Education*
1999-00	419.09 (19.36)	1745.56 (80.64)	2164.65 (100.00)	0.12	0.42	2.89
2000-01	499.72 (19.28)	2091.48 (80.72)	2591.20 (100.00)	0.13	0.45	3.14
2001-02	545.00 (33.02)	1105.49 (66.98)	1650.49 (100.00)	0.08	0.27	2.06
2002-03	569.41 (32.59)	1179.96 (67.43)	1748.37 (100.00)	0.07	0.26	2.04
2003-04	566.22 (37.37)	1183.18 (67.63)	1749.40 (100.00)	0.07	0.24	1.96
2004-05	710.95 (35.53)	1290.22 (64.47)	2001.17 (100.00)	0.07	0.24	1.91
2005-06 (RE)	788.80 (34.62)	1489.59 (65.38)	2278.39 (100.00)	0.07	0.25	1.91
2006-07 (BE)	1260.85 (45.44)	1513.56 (54.56)	2774.41 (100.00)	0.07	0.25	1.90

Source: GOI, Budget documents of various years.

If the expenditure on education and higher education by the

states and UTs is also added to the above than expenditure on higher education, as per cent of GDP was at its peak during 1998-99 (0.46 %), subsequently it came down to 0.36 per cent during 2005-06 (BE). As per cent of total expenditure on education, the expenditure of higher education came down from 15.6 per cent in 1989-90 to 9.71 per cent in 2005-06 (BE) (Table 23.8).

Table 23.8: Expenditure on Higher Education in India (Centre + State)

Year	*Expenditure on Education as per cent of GDP*	*Expenditure on Higher Education as per cent of Expenditure on Education*	*Expenditure on Higher Education as per cent of GDP*
1989-90	3.59	15.6	0.34
1990-91	3.52	12.8	0.33
1991-92	3.44	9.78	0.41
1992-93	3.78	10.79	0.40
1993-94	7.68	10.97	0.39
1994-95	3.61	10.81	0.37
1995-96	3.60	10.14	0.35
1996-97	3.57	9.77	0.35
1997-98	3.53	10.01	0.38
1998-99	3.85	9.93	0.46
1999-00	4.17	10.21	0.41
2000-01	4.27	10.72	0.43
2001-02	3.81	9.83	0.38
2002-03	3.79	9.75	0.39
2003-04	3.50	9.27	0.35
2004-05 (RE)	3.68	9.63	0.37
2005-06 (BE)	3.73	9.71	0.36

Source: *Analysis of Budgeted Expenditure on Education*, Ministry of HRD, GOI, New Delhi.

Escalating costs on the one hand, and shrinking budgetary resources on the other, characterise the higher education system in India. The share of higher education in total planned resources increased from 0.60 per cent in the First Five Year Plan to 1.19 per cent in Fourth Five Year Plan. But ever since, it has declined continuously to 0.55 per cent in Seventh Plan and further down to 0.46 per cent in ninth Five Year Plan. Though the actual expenditure on higher education has increased by more than 340 times from Rs. 11.72 crore in the First Five Year Plan to Rs. 3994.21 crore in the Ninth Five Year Plan at current price (Table 23.9). Thus, although higher education in India is characterised by massive public investment, this investment is still regarded as much below the required level.

Table 23.9: Plan Expenditure on Education (Centre + State)

S. No.	*Five Year Plan*	*Elementary Education*	*Secondary Education*	*Adult Education*	*Univ. & Higher Education*	*Technical Education*	*Other Programmes*
1.	First	87.03 (57.55)	8.30 (5.49)	NA	11.72 (7.75)	21.45 (14.19)	22.70 (15.01)
2.	Second	95.00 (34.80)	51.00 (18.68)	NA	48.00 (17.58)	49.00 (17.95)	30.00 (10.99)
3.	Third	201.00 (34.13)	103.00 (17.49)	NA	87.00 (14.77)	125.00 (21.22)	73.00 (12.39)
4.	Fourth	234.23 (31.34)	140.00 (18.73)	12.60 (1.68)	188.32 (25.20)	78.61 (10.52)	93.63 (12.25)
5.	Fifth	327.28 (28.62)	166.00 (14.52)	24.81 (2.17)	318.77 (27.88)	107.12 (9.37)	101.48 (8.87)
6.	Sixth	841.39 (32.12)	534.39 (20.41)	153.36 (5.86)	560.40 (21.40)	272.86 (10.42)	256.31 (9.79)
7.	Seventh	2849.41 (36.75)	1831.51 (23.62)	469.57 (6.06)	1201.13 (15.49)	1083.34 (13.97)	318.45 (4.11)
8.	Eighth	10393.97 (47.68)	5231.12 (24.00)	1142.05 (5.24)	2094.40 (9.61)	2198.73 (10.08)	739.78 (3.39)
9.	Ninth	26107.42 (57.06)	9757.83 (21.33)	785.58 (1.72)	3994.21 (8.73)	3721.96 (8.14)	1385.14 (3.03)

NA: Not available.

Figures in parenthesis showing percentage share.

Source: GOI, Drafts Plan for I to IX Five Year Plan, Planning Commission, New Delhi.

Another point that reminds about government's apathy towards higher education is continuously declining share of higher education in planned expenditure ever since Sixth Five Year Plan (Table 23.9). Share of university and higher education's plan expenditure in the total plan expenditure on education was at its peak during Fifth Five Year Plan (27.88 %). It came down to 8.73 per cent in the Ninth Five Year Plan. Now the higher education is low priority area for the central as well as state governments and elementary education acquired highest priority.

Thus, declining public budgets for education, especially for higher education, aggravates the problem. With respect to funding, while efforts to raise fees and other private sources initiation, hardly any serious attempt has been made to raise budget allocations to higher education; in fact, there have been severe cut. As a result, many universities and other institutions of higher education are in impoverished condition. Thousands of faculty positions remain vacant for more than a decade. Many universities and colleges are running with alarming numbers of under-qualified contract teachers and teaching assistants. A large number of study programmes are offered on a self-financing basis (Tilak, 2006). Policy makers and administrators are 'advising' or rather 'forcing' the universities to generate their own resources through self-financing root. This phenomenon of cut in budgetary allocations and allowing the opening of new colleges under self-financing schemes has provided green pastures to the private players. The country would not have been in such a sorry state of affairs had public education at all levels been strengthened and expanded with heavy investments, instead of reducing public expenditure on education, allowing the unbridled growth of private sector and legitimising self-financing courses.

Foreign University in India

Green pastures in Indian higher education system attracted many foreign universities and companies that operate in the higher education sector. They have shown keen interest to enter India. American major universities like Yale, Stanford and Georgia Institute of Technology have announced that they are keen to set up Greenfield campuses in India. India had opened its education sector in 2001, when 100 per cent FDI was allowed. However, tough entry regulations prevented top foreign education providers (FEPs) from opening campuses in India. By 2006, only 150 FEPs entered into joint ventures with Indian institutions and could attract just, 8000 students even as the number of Indians seeking education in the US, U.K., Australia and New Zealand crossed 1.10 lakh annually (Chauhan, 2006).

Advocates of privatisation and commercialisation of Indian higher education system argue that opening up the doors to the foreign universities would imply that foreign educational institutions would be allowed to establish wholly owned subsidiaries in India, leading to a foreign education and certification for students, while this would make foreign education/ certification more accessible to Indian students at a substantial cost. The experts are optimistic that it will improve quality, efficiency and accountability in the educational institutions. Mr. G.K. Pillai, Special Secretary, in the Ministry of Commerce, GOI, is of the opinion that every year the outgo from India on education to foreign countries is more that $4 bn. "If foreign universities are allowed to set up shop in our country, this huge money can be very well saved" (George, 2006). This argument must be taken with caution. As some players in the field argue that a lot of foreign universities in India, which have tie-ups with institutions here, are not recognised on their soil and award MCA and MBA degree of lower value than that awarded by an Indian Institute. Prof. Vinayshil Gautam, founder Director of IIM, Calcutta is of the view that FDI in education sector is a channel of international benchmarking and should be welcome. But, it should be monitored and regulated well, keeping in mind the national interest.

Even as Prime Minister Dr. Manmohan Singh is seeking more and more private investment in higher education, educationists wants privatisation and commercialisation of higher education to be restricted "to the minimum desirable level." Such is their anger against privatisation and commercialisation of higher education that majority view at a recent meeting on the issue-organised by National Institute of Education Planning and Administration (May 2, 2006) favoured a law banning such commercialisation. 64 eminent educationists, attending the meeting recommended unanimously that:

- All commercialisation of education, which should be unambiguously defined, should be banned by a suitable Act of Parliament.
- Private investment in education may be encouraged. However, it must be made clear that this cannot be for profit making purpose, in however disguised a form.

Union Commerce Ministry's proposal regarding FDI in education is being opposed not only by educationists, but by Minister of HRD Arjun Singh and left parties. The Ministry of HRD has recommended a 'cautious approach' to FDI in education, considering that other countries in the Third World and Muslim nations have told the W.T.O. that they will not open their education sector as doing so might affect the local political and cultural sensitivities. D. Raja, National Secretary of the CPI opposes the proposal on the ground that "you cannot treat education as an industry, opening up of the education sector for foreign players will be cultural attack on India. It will lead to rampant commercialistion of education which is already suffering from commercialisation."

Conclusions and Suggestions

Indian higher education system has reached to a point at this juncture that it is beyond the reach of common people. Admission to the prestigious courses such as MBBS, B.E./B.Tech/B.Arch., MBA, MCA, B.Ed. etc. has become so costly now-a-days that no students of ordinary financial background can think even to get admission in any institution in and outside India. The situation is comparable to pre-independent India when only the ward of rich people could go to Britain to attain higher education. Common people had to satisfy themselves with the domestic system of education, which was developed to create English knowledge official assistants who can help their British bosses.

The standard of education at primary, junior and secondary level, is so different in the urban and rural areas, that it makes rather impossible for students of rural background to fight for competitive examinations. Only the wards of rich rural elite opt for such competitions through huge investment in coaching and only a few of them are successful. Rest seeks their future in the colleges with bare minimum facilities.

Higher education in India is fragmented, scattered and takes place in nearly 16000 institutes called affiliated colleges, many of which are tiny and trace better than higher secondary schools. These colleges have libraries and reading rooms worth the name. Out of the sanctioned faculty more than 50 per cent is non-Ph.Ds. working on contractual basis. These institutes of higher learning provide only the classroom teaching. Unfortunately, the entire higher education in India takes place only in the ill-equipped, understaffed, affiliated colleges which absorb more than 90 per cent of undergraduate students and more than two thirds of post-graduate students, but of little use of research. Only 1 per cent of research scholars are in these affiliated colleges. That is the reason; none of the post-graduate students is able to carry on further research independently. Universities are overwhelmed by administration and cumbersome procedures and end up doing very little research. Vice-Chancellors to these universities are appointed on political considerations leaving little room for autonomy. These V.Cs. remain so busy with routine affairs of the universities that they seldomly have time for calling meetings of academic council, senate or executive council. How unfortunate the students of CCS University Meerut are that students of class 6th or so were evaluating their answer books and none other than the registrar of the university operated the racket. The VC of Dr. B.R. Ambedkar University, Agra cannot spare time to give approval for conducting meetings of RDCs, which are due for the last two years or more. Thousands of the students of such universities do not know when their results would be declared and they would get their mark-sheets.

In nutshell the privatisation and commercialisation of higher education system in India has the following weaknesses, which require urgent attentions:

- Private institutions never consider the demands of weaker sections of the society as they function on the principle of profit maximisation.
- State's apathy towards higher education resulted into the poor performance—qualitatively as well as quantitatively.
- The whole system of higher education in India is working under poor regulatory mechanism despite the multiple regulatory bodies.
- The universal pay structure for the faculty throughout the country has kept talented brain away from joining the institutions of higher education as teacher or researcher.
- When India had a few universities treating them all alike, with the same travel and research funding, same salary and the same autonomy (or lack thereof) was fine. But in today's India to tie all universities to the same level of support and rules is to commit them all to mediocrity.
- Higher education system in India continues to be constrained by strong entry barriers, poor regulatory framework, resource crunch and the inability to cater to the industry demands.

Following steps should be taken to overcome the difficulties faced by higher education system in the country:

- Provision of well subsidised, if not free, quality higher education for all.
- Government has to allow pockets of excellence to emerge and to allow them to bid for best researchers and teachers.
- Switch over to the 'star system' for the colleges and universities where for leading academics salaries and research funding are allowed to rise to match productivity.
- To attract some of the best minds to fundamental research, especially with top corporate salaries on the rise, we have to permit research funding to match a scholar's productivity.
- Instead of fully government funded or totally unaided private funded higher education institutions system of public-private participation should be introduced.
- Make disclosure norms more transparent and mandatory regarding affiliation, approval, infrastructural facilities, placements, fee structure and finances of the institutions.
- Instead of multiple regulatory mechanisms, develop single regulatory mechanism with more power to punish guilty.
- Tax on the industry to raise resources for higher education.
- All forms of commecialisation of higher education should be defined unambiguously and banned by a suitable Act of Parliament.
- Industrial houses should be encouraged to contribute towards establishment of departments/chairs of their choice with full say on the governance.
- Indian higher education system should be allowed to develop on the principles of (*i*) competition, (*ii*) flexibility, (*iii*) the authority of ideas, (*iv*) generous philanthropy, (*v*) combining research with undergraduate study.
- The government should do everything possible to ensure that more and more young men and women become capable of benefiting from higher education irrespective of what kind of family background they come from, and as and when they do, they should be helped financially to spend a few years at a university.
- Universalise the fee structure for the country as a whole.

- Make the higher education services a central cadre like Indian Administrative Services and create central recruiting body to select the teachers of various categories on regular basis.
- System of self-financing institutes should be abolished immediately.
- Develop postgraduate colleges in such a manner that they are capable enough to provide conducive environment for research.
- It should be mandatory for the universities to encourage research activities on priority basis.

REFERENCES

Agarwal, Pawan (2006), "Higher Education in India: A Need for Change", *ICRIER Working Paper*, June 2006.

Basu, Kaushik (2006), India's Faltering Education System; *BBC News*, http://newsvote.bbc.w.uk./mpapps/south-asia/4793311.stm.

Chauhan, Chetan (2006), Centre Plans New Ground Rules for Higher Education, *Hindustan Times*, September 13, New Delhi.

George Lype, *Foreign University in India*, http:/inhome.rediff.com/cms.

GOI (2005), *Higher Education in India and GATS: An Opportunity*, Ministry of Commerce, Discussion paper.

Kapur, Devish and Pratap Bhanu Mehta (2004), *Indian Higher Education Reform: From Half Backed Socialism to Half Backed Capitalism*. CID Working Paper No. 108, September 2004, Harvard University, p. 4.

Krishanan, Ravi (2006), Young Millions, Missing Classrooms, *The Financial Express*, September 16, New Delhi.

Raghuram, N., *Ugly Face of the Knowledge Economy Combat Law*, Vol. 5, Issue 1, 15 March, 2006.

Sunder, Pushpa (2000), *Beyond Business: From Merchant Charity to Corporate Citizenship*, Delhi, Tata McGraw Hill.

Tilak, B.G. (2006), "Quota in Higher Education: Must not be in Perpetuity", *The Hindu Business Line*, New Delhi.

Times Higher Education Supplement (2005); http://:llwww.epfl.ch/soc/etudes/pdt/world-rankingsos.pdf.

24

Commercialisation and Privatisation of Indian Higher Education System in Relation to Quality

DR. SANJEEV BHARADWAJ AND
MANISH DEV

Introduction

The modern higher education system of India is only 140 years old. When the first three universities—Calcutta, Madras and Bombay—were established in 1857 on the guidelines given by Macaulay and Wood's Dispatch (1854). To begin with, colleges, set up in India were affiliated to British Universities. The period 1857 to 1947 was the period of slow development of institutions of higher education in India. Colleges and universities were set up mostly in administrative headquarters and port towns. The rate of development was so slow that in a period of 90 years only 18 universities could set up in the country. Erstwhile rulers, zamindars, tallukedars and some rich persons of business community established colleges in their towns. British administration also established colleges in the cities of importance for them. The situation changed after independence, especially during the era of liberalisation, privatisation and globalisation. At present there are 357 universities (including central, state, private, deemed to be universities and institutes of national importance) 9427 colleges, 1068 engineering colleges, 782 medical colleges, 900 teacher's training colleges, 1991 other colleges, enrolling more than 10 million students. Quantitatively these figures seem quite impressive, but qualitatively India stands nowhere. It is not the irony of the situation that even after the significant presence of Indian technocrats and scientists in almost every country of the world, not a single university or institute of India is in the world's top 300 universities/institutes (Basu, 2006).

The Indian Institute of Science, Bangalore, come in somewhere in the top 400 and IIT, Kharagpur, makes an appearance after that. However, Times Higher Education Supplement (2005) rejects this claim. According to this survey, IITs get 50th rank among overall universities, 3rd rank (after MIT and Berkeley) in technology, 36th place in science, IIsc, which is not an university but a research institute is ranked higher than IITs in research).

Philanthropy in Higher Education in India

The pre-independence period, or that between 1892 and 1947, may be termed as the "Golden Age of Indian Philanthropy" (Sunder, 2000). Institutions of world repute, such as, BHU, AMU, Jamia Millia, IIS etc. were established largely through voluntary donations. Higher Education, especially institutes of research were widely considered to be 'pioneering' established by big industrial houses of the country. Of the sixteen largest, 'non- religious' trust established during this period, fourteen were major patrons of higher education. Leading industrial houses of India—Tatas, Bajajs, Birlas, Lalbhai, Sarabhai, Murugappa, Naidu, Ramco, Maftlal, Mahindra etc.—were behind these trusts. Some of erstwhile rulers of Indian states, such as Maharaja of Jaipur, Nawab of Rampur, Raja of Ram Nagar, Awagarh, Nijams of Hyderabad etc. also established colleges for the welfare of their subjects.

Constitution of India, paved the way for the private sector to enter in the field of education through following provisions. Article 19(g) conferred upon citizen the right to practice any profession or to carry on any occupation, trade or business subject to the provision of certain power of state to make any law or to carry on any business or trade. Likewise, Article 30 says that all minorities, whether based on religion or language, shall have the right to establish and administer educational institutions of their choice.

Christian public school established either by missionaries or church flourished taking advantage of this provision. Subsequently, Muslims and Sikhs entered into in this field and established educational institutions with minority character. It is another thing that they never considered the problems of their own communities so far as admission in these institutions are concerned and gave admissions purely on monetary basis.

Philanthropic commitment to public institutions of higher education has been steadily declining, except in case of minority institutions, since the middle of the nineteenth century. Philanthropic is being "Privatised" in two senses. **One**, donors for higher education are more likely to retain effective control over the resources they donate. **Second**, philanthropy is being conflated with creating not far profit, but financially sustainable institutions (Kapur, 2004). However, the practice of so-called philanthropy changed during the last two decades. Many educational trust/societies came into existence especially, in Tamilnadu, Karnataka, Andhra Pradesh and Maharashtra and established many institutions (engineering/medical/management college) purely on monetary considerations, Uttar Pradesh, Rajasthan, Madhya Pradesh, Chhattisgarh followed the suites. The number of educational trusts is increasing; most of them are generating revenue by charging for services rather than through donations or endowments.

As a result, there has been a rapid growth of private institutions of all kinds, more sub-standard and commercialised in nature, outnumbering by several times the number of public institutions in many states (Tilak, 2006). Motive of profit making in the garb of 'Charity' substituted philanthropy in higher education.

Privatisation and Quality Concern in Higher Education

Barring a few, most of the private colleges in India do not care for the quality of the education. Since they are rich in endowments so they have constructed beautiful and huge buildings. But so as the faculty is concerned, majority of them are running with under qualified teachers.

Scheme of self-financing colleges, failed completely, so far as, quality of higher education is concerned. Majority of the self-financing colleges have beautiful buildings and campuses but do not have qualified teachers. Even the engineering colleges, lack qualified teaching faculty. A system of 'substitutes' has been evolved in U.P. where the management of self-financing colleges appointed qualified teachers, merely on papers so as to obtain clearance from governing bodies like AICTE/NCTE/BCI/MCI and an affiliation from the universities concerned. These fake teachers never visit the colleges. For the purpose of teaching, the management acquires the services of locally available unqualified substitutes.

FICCI conducted a survey called "Developing an understanding of private higher education in India: A Stakeholder Perspective". This survey was carried out between December 2005 and January 2006 and covering 11 cities country-wide and 4000 respondents—including students, parents, faculty, recruiters and promoters were interviewed. Survey reveals some interesting points (Business Standard, March 23-24, 2006).

- 70 per cent students of private higher education institutes have sought government intervention in monitoring and accreditation of such institutes.
- 55 per cent students said they felt that such institutes charged exorbitant fees and 50 per cent said they selected courses based on employment potential leaving little scope for research.

Another area of concern regarding the sad state of affairs of higher education in India is the poor standard of teachers of which majority of them are either unqualified or less qualified. According to Damodar Acharya, AICTE Chief, out of the three lakh technically trained degree holders in India, only 30 per cent are worthy of getting a job and another 30 per cent fit to be trained. He further lamented that technical education was facing acute shortage of qualified faculty. "In engineering alone, the demand is for 1.20 lakh teachers, but the system today has hardly 7000 Ph.Ds, 20000 M.Techs. and rest fresh B.Tech. degree holders. This is mainly because graduates consider teaching the last career option." Probably that also explains why around 30000 seats remain vacant in technical institutes and 1.5 lakh students going abroad for higher education.

Higher education in India is fragmented, scattered and takes place in nearly 16000 institutes called affiliated colleges, many of which are tiny and trace better than higher secondary schools. These colleges have libraries and reading rooms worth the name. Out of the sanctioned faculty more than 50 per cent is non-Ph.Ds.

working on contractual basis. These institutes of higher learning provide only the classroom teaching. Unfortunately, the entire higher education in India takes place only in the ill-equipped, understaffed, affiliated colleges which absorb more than 90 per cent of undergraduate students and more than two thirds of post graduate students, but of little use of research. Only 1 per cent of research scholars are in these affiliated colleges. That is the reason, none of the post graduate students is able to carry on further research independently.

Government's Apathy Towards Higher Education

Apathy on the part of the government towards higher education is a major cause of increasing presence of private sector in this sector of low social return. Entry of politicians into the arena fueled the situation and finally the schemes like 'Member of Parliament Local Area Development' (MPLAD) scheme and MLALADS in case of states provided easy funds for the construction of buildings and development of campuses of the institutions of higher education under self-financing schemes. According to NSSO data, the government's share in overall education expenditure has been declining steadily, from 80 per cent in 1983 and 67 per cent in 1999. For states like Kerala, the decline is steep, from 75 to 48 per cent, while for Madhya Pradesh it is from 84 per cent to 68 per cent. On the contrary to this, private expenditure on education has increased 10.8 times during 1983 to 1999 in general, and 12.4 times for poor (NSSO, 2002).

The presence of private sector is more visible in medical, engineering, management and other professional courses such as BBA, BCA, MCA, B.Ed. In case of engineering, private colleges, which accounted for just 15 per cent of the seats in 1960, now accounts for 86.4 per cent of the seats and 84 per cent of the all the engineering colleges. In case of medical college the trend is not so fast. The proportion of seats in private medical colleges increased from 6.8 per cent in 1960 to 40.9 per cent in 2003. Data regarding number of medical and engineering colleges in selected 17 states shows that private medical colleges dominates the scene in the states like Karnataka where 22 out of 26 medical colleges are in the private sector (84.6 %), likewise in Maharashtra 53.3 per cent, in Andhra Pradesh 50 per cent medical colleges are in private sector. Northern states lag behind in this matter, but now all the states are pursuing the private sector to establish and run the medical colleges.

So far as, the engineering colleges are concerned, 84 per cent engineering colleges are in the private sector. Andhra Pradesh (95.5 %) is at the top and Tamilnadu (93.6 %) is at the second place, followed by Maharashtra (89.3 %), Madhya Prdesh (88.7 %), Orissa (86.4 %), and Karnataka (88.4 %). A large number of engineering colleges have been established in private sector during the last decade in the states of Uttar Pradesh, Madhya Pradesh, Rajasthan, Haryana and Punjab.

A recent decision of Government of Uttar Pradesh resulted into mushrooming growth of B.Ed. colleges not only in U.P. but also in her neighbouring states M.P., Rajasthan and Haryana. Government of Uttar Pradesh gave appointment to nearly 40,000 B.Ed. graduates in primary schools under '*Vishistha* B.T.C. scheme' in a single stroke. Suddenly it increased the demand for B.Ed. degree. The large number of applicants seeking admission to B.Ed. courses motivated private players to invest into this sector, which was not so lucrative a few years ago. Now the rate for the admission in B.Ed. is as high as Rs. 1.5 lakh.

How the private players make the loopholes of legal provisions, making of the system can be understand from the example of newly created Chhattisgarh state. Ajit Jogi led Congress Government saw a loophole and enacted the Private University Act, 2002. 108 such universities came up in Chhattisgarh, with 94 in the state capital Raipur alone. These universities were using the state's regulatory largesse, and even to the limited extent they were delivering educational services, they were doing so outside the states, under the nomenclature of these being off-campus centre, many of them running in a room having least infrastructure. Thus these so called private universities earned lakhs of rupees under the protection of the state government.

Thus, it is clear that proliferation of private institutions is largely in the area of professional education. It is not the result, as is being argued, of middle class or upper class's pressure or demand. The mushrooming growth capitation fees colleges is an outcome of entrepreneurial activities of politicians. Majority of these institutions are being run or managed or supported by the direct involvement of politicians. As has been said earlier, the schemes like APLADS/MLALADS have provided easy funds, on the reciprocal basis, for the construction of buildings. Some clever MPs/MLAs, established private colleges under the dummy management and allotted the funds freely to these institutions without being questioned its legality.

The second important phenomenon, that gave boost to the private institutions, is the entry of business class in this sector purely for the making money in the name of social service. Several trusts came up during the last decades. Theoretically their objective is not to earn profit from these institutions, but practically all the educational institutes, which are run by these trusts, charge hefty sums from the students and earn profit.

With privatisation reducing education to a commodity, teachers are reduced tutors and teaching is reduced to coaching (Raghuram, 2006). The consumerist boom and the growing salary differentials between teachers and non-teachers professionals and the value systems of the emerging free market economy have made teaching one of the least attractive professions that demands more work for less pay. Yet, the society expects teachers not only to be inspired but also to do an inspiring job.

Foreign University in India

Green pastures in Indian higher education system attracted many foreign universities and companies that operate in the higher education sector. They have shown keen interest to enter India. American major universities like Yale, Stanford and Georgia Institute of Technology have announced that they are keen to set up Greenfield campuses in India. India had opened its education sector in 2001, when 100 per cent FDI was allowed. However, tough entry regulations prevented top foreign education providers (FEPs) from opening campuses in India. By 2006, only 150 FEPs entered into joint ventures with Indian institutions and could attract just, 8000 students even as the number of Indians seeking education in the US, U.K., Australia and New Zealand crossed 1.10 lakh annually (Chauhan, 2006).

Advocates of privatisation and commercialisation of Indian higher education system argue that opening up the doors to the foreign universities would imply that foreign educational institutions would be allowed to establish wholly owned subsidiaries in India, leading to a foreign education and certification for students, while this would make foreign education/ certification more accessible to Indian students at a substantial cost. The experts are optimistic that it will improve quality, efficiency and accountability in the educational institutions. Mr. G.K. Pillai, Special Secretary, in the Ministry of Commerce, GOI, is of the opinion that every year the outgo from India on education to foreign countries is more that $4 bn. "If foreign universities are allowed to set up shop in our country, this huge money can be very well saved" (George, 2006). This argument must be taken with caution. As some players in the field argue that a lot of foreign universities in India, which have tie-ups with institutions here, are not recognised on their soil and award MCA and MBA degree of lower value than that awarded by an Indian Institute. Prof. Vinayshil Gautam, founder Director of IIM, Calcutta is of the view that FDI in education sector is a channel of international benchmarking and should be welcome. But, it should be monitored and regulated well, keeping in mind the national interest.

Even as Prime Minister Dr. Manmohan Singh is seeking more and more private investment in higher education, educationists wants privatisation and commercialisation of higher education to be restricted "to the minimum desirable level." Such is their anger against privatisation and commercialisation of higher education that majority view at a recent meeting on the issue-organised by National Institute of Education Planning and Administration (May 2, 2006) favoured a law banning such commercialisation. 64 eminent educationists, attending the meeting recommended unanimously that:

- All commercialisation of education, which should be unambiguously defined, should be banned by a suitable Act of Parliament.
- Private investment in education may be encouraged. However, it must be made clear that this cannot be for profit making purpose, in however disguised a form.

Union commerce ministry's proposal regarding FDI in education is being opposed not only by educationists, but also by Minister of HRD Mr. Arjun Singh and left parties. The Ministry of HRD has recommended a 'cautious approach' to FDI in education, considering that other countries in the Third World and Muslim Nations have told the W.T.O. that they will not open their education sector as doing so might affect the local political and cultural sensitivities. D. Raja, National Secretary of the CPI opposes the proposal on the ground that "you cannot treat education as an industry, opening up of the education sector for foreign players will be cultural attack on India. It will lead to rampant commercialisation of education which is already suffering from commercialisation."

Conclusions

Thus, declining public budgets for education, especially for higher education, aggravates the problem. With respect to funding, while efforts to raise fees and other private sources initiation, hardly any serious attempt has been made to raise budget allocations to higher education; in fact, there have been severe cut. As a result, many universities and other institutions of higher education are in impoverished condition. Thousands of faculty positions remain vacant for more than a decade. Many universities and colleges are running with alarming numbers of under-qualified contract teachers and teaching assistants. A large number of study programmes are offered on a self-financing basis. Policy makers and administrators are 'advising' or rather 'forcing' the universities to generate their own resources through self-financing root. This phenomenon of cut in budgetary allocations and allowing the opening of new colleges under self-financing schemes has provided green pastures to the private players. The country would not have been in such a sorry state of affairs had public education at all levels been strengthened and expanded with heavy investments, instead of reducing public expenditure on education, allowing the unbridled growth of private sector and legitimising self-financing courses.

REFERENCES

Basu, Kaushik (2006), India's Faltering Education System, *BBC News*, http://newsvote.bbc.w.uk./mpapps/south-asia/4793311.stm.

Business Standard, March 23-24, 2006, New Delhi.

Chauhan, Chetan (2006), Centre Plans New Ground Rules for Higher Education, *Hindustan Times*, September 13, New Delhi.

George, Lype, *Foreign University in India*, http:/inhome.rediff.com/cms.

Kapur, Devish and Pratap Bhanu Mehta (2004), *"Indian Higher Education Reform: From Half Baked Socialism to Half Backed Capitalism."* CID Working Paper No. 108, September 2004, Harvard University, p. 4.

Raghuram, N., Ugly Face of the Knowledge Economy Combat Law, 5(1), 15 March, 2006.

Sunder, Pushpa (2000), *"Beyond Business: From Merchant Charity to Corporate Citizenship"*, Delhi, Tata McGraw Hill.

Tilak, B.G. (2006), "Quota in Higher Education: Must not be in Perpetuity", *The Hindu Business Line*, New Delhi.

Times Higher Education Supplement (2005), http://:llwww.epfl.ch/soc/etudes/pdt/world-rankingsos.pdf.

25

Need of Examination Reforms in Higher Education

DR. A.K. TOMAR AND MS. NEERAJA SHARMA

During the last 50 years, higher education in India has taken long steps leading to the Indian higher education system decaning one of the largest systems in the world. Unfortunately this expansion in quantity has overshadowed the quality of Indian Higher Education. One of the important components of higher education is the manner in which student's academic performance is evaluated. A debate has been going on to determine the best system of assessment to be followed by universities. A great degree of diversity has been observed in terms of assessment and grading of the students in the university system at present. It is desirable that a certain optimum degree and standardization in the examination system and in the amusement of students is put in place before grades all awarded to them.

Our system of education is completely dependent on annual examination. It is the only criteria for the pupils growth, development assessment of their capacity, future performance teachers, efficiency and the success of the particular curriculum. These annual examination are mostly dominated by essay type question.

Such examination has reduced students to 'mere machines of memory' and made education synonymous with creaming large amount and knowledge.

This is the reason of making our examinations ill serving and it needs drastic and overall change in the present system of evaluation. This system of examination which dominated by essay type question is loaded with several defects.

(*i*) There exists subjectivity puncheon as the same answer can be marked different examiners having different viewpoints giving a wide range of marks. They are thus not accurate measure of achievements.

(*ii*) These examinations measure cramming than higher mental because original answers by brilliant students need 10 of time as compared to the crammed doorish answers given by average student in the stipulated time of two to three hours.

(*iii*) The marking is also affected by the handwriting vocabulary and the language ability of the students.

(*iv*) Limited time of exam (2-3 hours) requirement no of questions which do not cover the whole course.

(*v*) Students safety ignore the parts of syllabus without damaging their chances of securing high marks.

(*vi*) The use of mother tongue as medium helps students to secure high percentage with making too much efforts.

(*vii*) The instruction issued to the paper sellers and makers differ from subject to subject.

(*viii*) While marking, subjects in which there exists wide range of marks carry more weight as compared to those in which range is narrow.

(*ix*) The examinations are conducted only once a year which results in selective study of only one or two months before the exams and the students are indifferent towards studies throughout the year.

(*x*) Since the annual papers are external in nature the students do not pay project respect to their teachers.

(*xi*) Internal assessment by the teachers if present in the examination system is affected by 'hole effect' i.e. students having good and pleasant personality good nature get good marks.

Despite of all these weaknesses and limitation of traditional examination they are still widely used.

Recommendation of Different Committees

Before independence in 1854 first three universities were set up by Wood despatch, at Calcutta, Bombay and Madras. The main function of these universities were to conduct examination and award degree. The system of examination has been received from time to time to higher or weaken and suggest reforms. The first emphasis on improvement in examination was given by Indian Commission 1881-82. Then the first Indian University Commission of 1902 expressed dissatisfaction with the pre-relate examination system in the colleges, universities. It observed the greatest exile from which the system of university educate in India suggests is that teaching is subordinated to examination and not examinations to teaching.

Then the Calcutta University Grants Commission of 1917-19 pointed out several effects in the systems of university examination. But no step will be taken to improve it since it was serving the purpose of selecting clerks and junior officials to the Britisher in Indian officers.

In All Indian Education Conference 1944, Mr. D.N. Mukharjee chairman of examination section said, "The conclusion irresistible that education in India dominated by entered-control and tutelage in the form of fragmentary and unscientific examination has resulted in the perpetuation and mediocrity and realisation of genius, facts which are necessary concommitants, if not invitable consequences of the prevailing system.

The Hartog Committee (1929) remarked that examinations had become so predominant in our educational system that passing in them was the main objective of educational system. Rather than development of human being, Sargent Plan (1944) also observed the domination of examination system.

After achieving independence in 1947, the University Education Commission (1948-50) headed by Dr. Radha Krishan was set up to investigate into the condition of the system of university education. It remarked that the single reform required in university education is that of examination.

The Secondary Education Commission (1952-53) observed:

> "The examinations today dictate the curriculum instead of following it, preventing examination, hamper the proper treatment of subject and sound method of teaching, foster a dull uniformity rather than originality, encourage the average pupil to concentrate too rigidly upon too narrow a field and this help him to develop wrong value in education. In short internal examinations are exercising a restricting profluence

over the entire field of education to such an extent as almost to millify in real purpose."

The Commission made the following recommendations (Natayam, 1980):

1. The number of internal examinations must be reduced. The element of subjectivity in essay type examinations should be minimised by introducing objective type tests and also by changing the type of questions.
2. In the final assessment of students due credit should be given to the internal tests and the school records of the students.
3. A system of symbolic rather than numerical marking should be adopted for evaluating and grading the work of the students in external and internal examinations and in maintaining the records.
4. The certificates awarded should contain, besides the results of the public examinations in different subjects, results of the school tests in subjects not included in public examinations as well as the list of school records.

The Bhopal Seminar on Examination Reform (1950) also gave valuable suggestion for the improvement of examinations.

The S.R. Dongerkery Committee appointed by University Grants Commission in September 1957, recommended means to improve the academic and technical aspects of examination.

The UGC then invited Dr. Benjamis Bloom, head examiner of the University of Chicago to advise the Commission on measures to be adopted to reform the examination system in the Indian universities, it resulted in 10-year phased programme of examination reform which was approved by the Central Ministry of Education and the State Education Departments. The establishment of central evaluation unit in 1958 was the first major step towards the implementation of this programme.

In 1965, the UGC appointed a committee to review the standards of university education and to outline ways and means to make examinations more reliable and free from many errors.

The Education Commission headed by Dr. Kothari (1964-66) dealt with the importance of effecting examination reforms in the community in phased manner. It remarked:

"In the present system, when the future of the students is totally declared by one Eternal examination not the end of the year, the students pay minimum attention to the teachers, do little independents study through most of the academic year and cram accurately for final examinations on the quality of work in higher education is so great that examination reform has become to all progress."

In 1965, a Committee was appointed by the UGC to review the standards of university education in India and to formula the ways and means to increase the reliability of examination and reduce subjectivity and errors. This was followed by appointment of another Committee (1969) to workout some modalities of examinations reforms in central universities. It suggested concrete measure to improve the nature of evaluation and sessional work.

The National Policy on Education (1968) made several proposals on examination reforms and stated:

"A major goal of examination reforms should be to improve reliability and validity of examinations and to make evaluation a continuous process."

The inter-university board of India and Ceylon organised session examination reform at Madurai (1970) in which the board gave recommendations, in 1971.

1. Developing question bank in each subject.
2. Deciding relative emphasis on different type of questions such as objective type and short answer type.
3. Setting up of an examination research unit in each university to study continuously the nature of question, preparing question banks, and improving question in setting practices.
4. Introduction of grading system to replace the present marking system.

In 1972, the UGC published a document entitled 'Examination Reforms: A Plan of Action' (1972). The outlines of these reforms are:

1. Greater freedom should be given to college in conducting

examination under vigilant supervision of university authority.
2. The examination results should be analysed and then records be maintained.
3. The board of studies in the university department school frame syllabus and develop 'Bank of Questions' in each of the courses, the questions, in which, may be contributed by the teachers as well as students covering the entire course and should be changed every year.
4. The colleges should conduct their examinations by selecting questions from the question bank. The guidelines for such selections should be provided by the university.
5. The answer book should be evaluated by the teacher in the college and evaluated scripts may be returned to the students. In case of any problem student can appeal to the committee constituted for this purpose.
6. The university may finalised a minimum grade for the award of degree. The students, who do not achieve the minimum grade may be asked to respect the course of re-appeal in the examination after a semester or a year.
7. The colleges should maintain the cumulative record of students progress and the copy be sent to the university every year.
8. The record of examination internal assessment (sessional) and terminal examination both may be shown separately on the mark-sheet.

The Examination Reforms Implementation Committee appointment by University Grants Commission in 1978 recommended every university/deemed to be university to adopt the following minimum examination reforms:

1. The syllabus in each should be demarcated into well-defined units/areas of content alongwith a topic-wise breakdown.
2. Examiners should be free to repeat the questions set in previous examination so that the students do not leave out important portion of the syllabus.
3. Overall choice should not be given rather choice may be provided by alternate question in each unit of the syllabus.

4. The examination should not be held without fulfilling the requirement of a minimum number of lectures/tutorials/ laboratory sessions etc. which should be clearly laid down by the University.
5. Examination should be conducted in fair and impartial manner. Cheating is a cognizable offence effected security measures, proper supervision and invigilation, condoning off the examination centres from the ranges of loudspeakers and other interference, flying squads and stern action in all cases involving copying and use of uniform means.

The National Policy on Education (NPE, 1986) made certain proposals for evaluation process and examination reforms:

1. The elimination of excessive element of chance and subjectivity.
2. The de-emphasise of memorization.
3. Continuous and comprehensive evaluation that incorporates both scholastic and non-scholastic aspects of education spread over the total span of instructional time.
4. Effective of the evaluation process by teachers, students and parents.
5. Improvement in the conduct of examinations.
6. The introduction of concomitant changes in instructional materials and methodology.
7. Introduction of semester system from the secondary stage in a phased manner.
8. The use of grades in place of marks.

Suggestions for Improvement

The suggestion for improvement in the traditional method of examination in accordance to the different committees as tested below:

Continuous Internal Assessment

The evaluation procedure should be incorporated by continuous assessment by the teacher throughout the year (NPE, 1986) in the form of:

- Periodic Tests
- Library Work
- Practical Work
- Assignments
- Class Attendance
- Social Service
- Terminal Papers
- Regular Classroom Observation.

All of the above components of internal assessment use instruments of judging the seriousness of the students towards studies throughout the year. The weightage of each component applied would be decided before hand by the Committee set up by the university authority. This internal assessment should compliment the annual extend examination and the marks should be shown separately on the final marksheet.

Care should be taken by the teachers that their marking should not be affected by pleasant and extrovert nature and personality of an student or his/her religion, sex, region etc. In addition to this, the evaluation should be carried out stricty throughout the year.

Semester System

The academic year and the whole syllabus should be divided into two or three equal homogenous parts and exams should be taken at the end of each part. This reduces the chances of selective study and the stress. Through which students pass at the end of the year. This system result in regularity among students due to frequent examination and through study of the course since it is divided into small parts.

Since this system may increase the workload of the teachers, the teacher should be writing to accept the challenge as they would chance to undergo refresher courses for the new topics indeeded in the syllabus and carry on the examination two or three times an year with cooperative spirit.

The Grading System

The grading system with a linear 10-point and its equivalence in terms of percentage of marks should be followed uniformly across universities and disciplines. However, the evaluation methodology may bring across discipline/institutions.

The traditional question papers requiring essay type answers do not cencern the whole course, as long answers require a lot of time resulting in less number of questions. The examination papers should contain the short answer type and objective type questions also besides the essay type ones (NPE, 1986). This would cover the whole syllabus through the question paper and impures the reliability of testing as the number of question also increases.

Question Banking

A question bank is defined as a retailing large collection of easily test questions. These banks contain as many question as can be used for several tests together without repetition of items (UGC, 1972). Question banks should be made through experts for each discipline and should be revised every year, such banks enable the teacher to construct a wide vanity of tests in very little time in accordance to the sample and the purpose for which test is to be taken, the process of maintaining, recording, analysing and scrutinizing the question banks and examination reports can be easily done will the help of computers.

Pre and Past

Examination should be made transparent i.e. the pattern of paper, evaluation methodology, disciplinary rules etc. should be properly documented and communicated to the students well in advance.

Proper eventuation on accessment methods should be given to all the teachers particularly to the newly appointed teachers. The academic staff colleges set up by the University Grants Commission at different universities may be assigned this task.

A proper structure for examination reforms units for the universities should be evolved, supported by UGC to keep the nation-wide evaluation process at universities under continuous sinuosity.

Research on the desirability and relevance of existing examination patterns and improvements thereon in any given institution should be encouraged and facilitated. Innovative practices related to examination reforms should be empirically tested and institutionalised.

The UGC may encourage universities to organise regional level experts workshops to look into various qualitative aspects of examination reforms such as:

- Testing creativity.
- Testing application aspects.
- Testing both fundamental and in-depth knowledge, continuous evaluation strategies.
- In addition to above suggestions, proper care should be taken by the university authorities for the payment of teachers regarding the checking of answer books so that they are internally motivated to carry on the reforms as recommended.

REFERENCES

1. Chamber, C.P.S., *Emerging Trends in Educational Evaluation*, Commonwealth Publishers, New Delhi, 1993.
2. Chamber, C.P.S., *Essay Type Examination: Some Theoretical Issues*, Education Quarterly, Ministry of Education & Cullini GOI, New Delhi, 1984.
3. Government of India, *Report of the University Education Commission* (1948-49), Delhi, 1949.
4. Government. of India, *Report of the Secondary Education Commission*, Ministry of Education (1952-53).
5. Government of India, *National Policy on Education*, 1986.
6. Gupta, A.K., *Examination Reforms, Directions, Research and Implications*, Sterling Publisher Pvt. Ltd., New Delhi, 1975.
7. Harper, A.E. Jr., "Ninety Making Ten: A Study of Examination", *Indian Education Review*, Vol. 2, 1967.
8. Internet website of UGC: www.ugc.ac.in

26

Teaching and Research: Relationships and Implications for Learning in Higher Education

DR. BHAVNA AGRAWAL

A number of articles on the relationship between teaching and research, pointing to the failure to demonstrate statistically a connection between them, have indicated that efforts should be made to actively bring research and teaching together. Pinkler and Bates (1990), for example, suggest that research may serve as a model for teaching, while Barnett (1997) calls for teaching to become more research-like. Hattie and Marsh (1996) suggest that marrying teaching and research by enhancing the relationship between them is a desirable aim of institutions of higher learning.

The suggestion that teaching and research should be more firmly drawn together should not be seen as an argument for educating all students to become academics, nor is it merely an academic exercise to prop up arguments that all academics should engage in research. Rather, it is a response to a number of changes in higher education which have challenged the relationship. These include:

- The move to a mass higher education system;
- The amount of time available both for teaching and for research, as well as changes in the nature of research; and
- In the nature of teaching in higher education and changes in the nature of knowledge.

Also of relevance is a changed policy context, which Elton (1992) argues has given urgency to questions about the relationship between teaching and research. Not only do our institutions have diverse missions—commitments to serving a wide range of scholarly needs within region, states and action—but also there is the special commitment to the education of an increasingly diverse population, to the intellectual preparation of the educated citizenry necessary for making a genuinely democratic society possible. Scholarship in this context takes on broader meaning. A model is needed which explains the relationship between teaching and research in a changing higher education context and which takes account of these different understandings. Such a model can be used to understand and to guide how we can bring research and teaching closer together to enhance both.

Understanding Variation in Conceptions

Here, I draw on research to understand the variation in conceptions of research, conceptions of scholarship, conceptions of knowledge and approaches to teaching. This provides the groundwork for developing the two alternative models of the relationship between teaching and research to follow.

Conceptions of Research

In delineating variation in academics' conceptions of research, I have earlier made a distinction between, on the one hand, conceptions of research which are atomistic and synthetic with an orientation towards external products and where the intention is to produce an outcome, and on the other, conceptions which are holistic and analytical with an orientation towards internal processes and where the intention is to understand (Brew, 1999a; Brew, 2001b). The latter may more readily be subsumed under the notion of inquiry and result in curricula designs focusing on engaging students in various forms of investigation. However, the former opens up ideas of research as a social phenomenon and may suggest engagement in a wide range of social networks and outputs.

Research is oriented towards ↓	Research aims to ↓	The researcher is presentto, or the focus of,awareness	The researcher is absent from, or incidental to, awareness
External products	Produce an outcome	Trading view	Domino view
Internal processes	Understand	Journey view	Layer view

Fig. 26.1: Relationships Between Conceptions of Research

Conceptions of Scholarship

Many different frameworks to describe scholarship have been suggested in the literature and a wide range of teaching, research and community service activities have been presented as important elements of it. The scholarship of discovery, Boyer (1990) suggests, comes closest to the idea of "research". It contributes to the "stock of human knowledge" and also to the intellectual climate of the institution. The scholarship of integration is concerned with making inter-disciplinary connections. In calling for a scholarship of integration, what we mean is serious, disciplined work that seeks to interpret, draw together, and bring new insight to bear on original research.

The third type of scholarship is the scholarship of application. This draws attention to the application of knowledge in the wider community. There is a caution against seeing theory and practice separate, for what is envisaged is a dynamic interaction where the "one renews the other." Finally, there is the scholarship of teaching. This involves well informed teachers and teaching which is carefully planned, continuously evaluated and relates to the subject taught. It is teaching, which encourages active learning and encourages students to be critical creative thinkers with the capacity to go on learning after their university days are over; and recognition that teachers are also learners. There was firstly the view among some researchers that the distinction between research and scholarship is unclear, non-existent even. Scholarship was equated with research and interpreted as not making any sense on its own.

Alternatively, scholarship was interpreted as the preparation for research. Elton (1992) refers to this as the interpretation of what is already known, the primary work that feeds into everything else academics are supposed to do. Otherwise, scholarship was viewed as building on the idea of preparation and interpreted as the process of adding new knowledge to the existing literature. In a more complex idea of scholarship, the focus was on grounding new ideas and discoveries in the literature and then disseminating them through publication and teaching. Quite distinct from conceptions of scholarship which focus on particular activities, is the notion of scholarship (Neumann, 1993) as a quality of the ways in which academic work is done.

Scholarship in this conception is interpreted as the way academics demonstrate professionalism. It is demonstrated in an emphasis on attention to detail which includes logic, use of evidence, work properly referenced, spelling and grammar correct, etc. It was also about having the technical knowledge to engage in inquiry. A heightened knowledge about the ways in which academic researchers conceptualize research and scholarship throws new light on the relationship between teaching and research. However, before examining this, we need to look at the variation in conceptions of knowledge and conceptions of teaching.

Conceptions of Knowledge

The relationship between teaching and research has been changing and that different conceptions of teaching and different conceptions of knowledge have different consequences for bringing research and teaching together. While there have been a number of studies examining children's conceptions of knowledge and much discussion of changing ideas of knowledge in the theoretical literature, there has not been, as far as I have been able to ascertain, an empirical study of conceptions of knowledge among academics. There are two conceptions of knowledge. On the one hand there is the idea that research is the creation or discovery of a body of knowledge which is perceived as detached or separated off from the people who developed it. Knowledge tends to be crudely viewed here as a quantity of something which we are building up, frequently presented as having a correspondence relationship with the world and giving descriptions of a pre-existent reality. The other way of viewing knowledge can be seen in traditions such as hermeneutics, phenomenological psychology and critical theory. Here, knowledge is viewed as more subjective; as a product of interpretation and negotiation. It explicitly recognizes that learning always takes place in a particular context and influences and is influenced by that context; that it always takes place within a cultural tradition of knowledge much of which is derived from past research. If knowledge which is generated through research is viewed as objective and separate from knower, it would seem consistent to think that it requires transmission and absorption through a separately conceptualized teaching process. If on the other hand knowledge is viewed as a product of communication and negotiation, the links between research and teaching are, I believe, viewed quite differently since the relationship between research and learning becomes an intimate one. In other words, relationships between teaching and research are different in a tradition which views itself as heavily dependent on an empiricist or Enlightenment philosophy to those which become evident within a pluralistic context. When research and teaching are both viewed as being founded on a traditional empiricist framework, the relationship is always problematic. A move towards a more pluralistic view of knowledge which fully takes on board the interpretative nature of academic work means that research and teaching can be viewed as being in a symbiotic relationship.

Approaches to Teaching

Higher education teachers hold qualitatively different conceptions of teaching and learning and that the different ways in which they approach their teaching are related to the differences in these conceptions. For example, those teachers who conceptualize their teaching as being about transferring information from the syllabus to students are associated with an approach to teaching based on an idea of the teacher as the focal point. This is labelled an "information transmission/teacher focused" approach to teaching. On the other hand, an approach to teaching which is focused on endeavouring to change the students' conceptions of the phenomena of their study is associated with an emphasis on the student as central. This has been called a "conceptual change/ student focused" approach. These approaches have been found to be related to students' approaches to learning in that an "information transmission/teacher focused" approach to teaching is associated with a surface approach to learning and a conceptual change/student focused approach to teaching is associated with a deep approach to learning.

Models of the Relationship Between Teaching and Research

Looking at the relationship between teaching and research with these understandings of the ways in which academic researchers conceptualize research and scholarship, and different conceptions of knowledge and teaching, two different models of the relationship are clearly seen. One model is based on an idea of academic disciplines more or less aligned with academic departments, with a conception of knowledge as objective and separate from knowers, research being concerned with the building up of bodies of knowledge within a research culture consisting of other academics and researchers. The conception of teaching in this **model** of the relationship between teaching and research is focused on the teacher and concerned with the transmission of information to the students within a separate learning milieu which has little overt connection with the research culture. This is graphically represented in Figure 26.2. The two lines in the middle represent the way that in this model teaching and research constantly pull away from each other, vying for resources and academics' time. The model also allows the possibility of teaching and research to take place quite independently of each other in separate institutions. This as an old model, but of course it is still current. Indeed it currently defines the ways in which the relationship between teaching and research is conventionally viewed. Many suggestions for ways to enhance the relationship between teaching and research implicitly assume this model.

A New Model

However, as conceptions shift, we need a new model, one which focuses on a conception of teaching as student-focused, conceptual change and a conception of knowledge as constructed within a

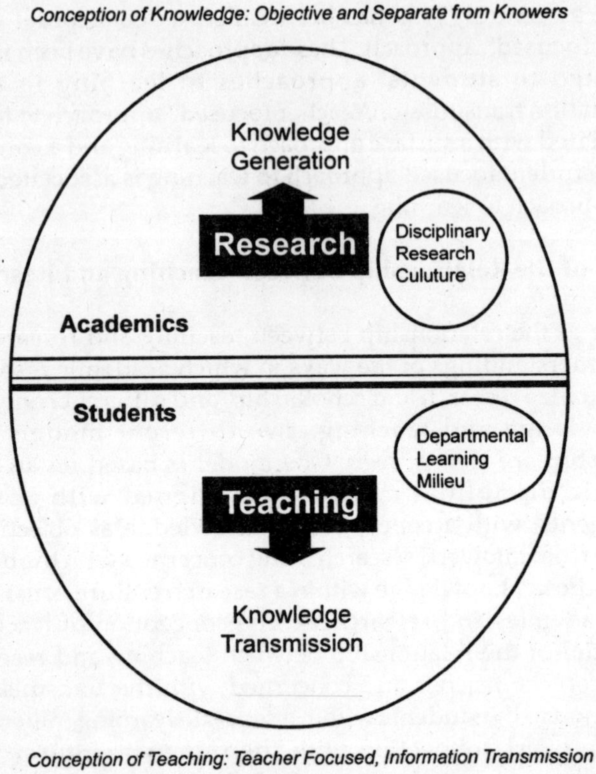

Fig. 26.2: Model of the Relationship Between Teaching and Research

socio-political context. The new model integrates ideas of situated learning. It presents a new, albeit somewhat idealistic, vision which challenges us to re-think the nature of higher education.

In the new model, research and teaching are both viewed as activities where individuals and groups negotiate meanings, building knowledge within a social context. What researchers understand research and scholarship to be are key influences in how we conceptualize the nature of student learning within this new context. For when academics talk about research and scholarship, different aspects are in the foreground of their awareness and other aspects recede to the background as we have seen. In the new model, teachers' and students' activities are not viewed as separate. In engaging in research, scholarship or learning, they engage as legitimate peripheral participants in academic communities of practice.

Implications for Teaching and Learning

So what are the implications of this new model of the relationship between teaching and research for teaching and learning in higher education? What does the model mean for the kinds of teaching and learning practice we engage in? The challenge which faces us is how to develop academic communities of practice where participants are, on the one hand, prepared to cope with uncertainty and super-complexity in a pluralistic world (Barnett, 2000) and, on the other, ready and able to change (world) views in the light of new information. We know that this is what research is essentially about.

Reconceptualising Higher Education

Meeting this challenge requires no less than radical reconceptualisation of higher education itself. The reconceptualisation to which I am referring implies that there is a critical challenge of ideas for both teachers and students. This means seeing problems as discrete but interconnected, developing the strategies, techniques, tools, knowledge and experience needed to solve unforeseen problems. Critical challenge means changing world views and being prepared to change them sometimes radically so that the ways we saw the world before are completely overturned, and being open to the unplanned and unexpected. It means learning which appreciates the importance of context, the significance of different interpretations and revision on the basis of looking again. It also points to teaching which encourages active learning, critical creative thinkers and lifelong learning.

Reconceptualising higher education in a community of practice where teaching and research are integrated also means that we should be open to the dissemination through teaching not just of academic teachers, but also of students. We should educate graduate students as apprentice teachers. The trading view of research and the integration conception of scholarship both point to the role of teaching in research and scholarship.

This might mean the use of peer teaching for both teachers and students, the production of published or publishable work recognition and reward coming from student peers. It might mean encouraging student publications, e.g., journals and it might also mean the encouragement of collaborative networks with opportunities to engage in student conferences and debates (perhaps electronically). Perhaps the most radical aspect of this reconceptualisation of higher education is the integration of the personal and professional. We saw with the journey conception of research that research fulfills the personal aims and existential needs of the researcher. It thus has an important role in teaching researchers about themselves. This point to the possibility of placing a greater emphasis on the personal relevance of the subject of study to the student, the development of self-knowledge or an exploration of existential life issues in curricula, personal growth and development becoming an integral part of university study. Clearly students do this to some extent anyway, particularly where they live away from home, but what I am suggesting here is more radical. Within such a culture of inquiry a negotiated conception of knowledge and a breaking down of the distinction between subjective and objective is implied in the integration of the personal and the professional.

Changed Relationships Between Teachers and Students

The development of academic communities of practice where both students and academics engage as legitimate peripheral participants cannot take place without the relationships between students and their teachers changing. What I have suggested means breaking down the distinction between teaching and learning as both teachers and students explore the issues which confront them. The development of what I have called academic professionalism among both students and their teachers is to reconceptualise that relationship. Both learning and research are about making meaning. Research and learning both involve the pursuit of intellectually challenging ideas. Both learning and research are concerned with discerning the critical features of phenomena. Both teaching and research involve exploring existing knowledge and trying to go beyond it. Both involve the human act of making sense of the world. This is essentially the layer conception of research since in this conception; research is interpreted as a process of discovering or generating underlying meanings. Using resources to aid the process, using evidence, setting goals and planning; for both learning and research involve thinking and critical reflection. If the task is to mentor students to become professional scholars, then the ways in which they are treated even in the early years of their study are crucial. There is a need to stress the importance of emphasizing uncertainty, encouraging a deep approach to learning and emphasizing the construction rather than the imparting of knowledge, involving students in "artistic and scientific productivity". Following an investigation of students' conceptions of their teachers' research, it is argued that opportunities for motivating students through involving them in discussions of their teachers' research are frequently lost. Students are often ignorant of the research their teachers are doing yet would like to know more. Students should not only have opportunities to benefit from their teachers' research, they should be more often involved in helping to carry it out. Attention should be given in curriculum design to how staff research can benefit student learning. A community of practice implies a much greater degree of sharing than perhaps is common in our institutions of higher education currently. All too often, students are alienated from the studies because they are treated as second class citizens. The implications of bringing research and teaching together within academic communities of practice mean that students would be treated as the adult people they are, with something valuable to contribute as well as to learn.

I am not merely referring here to those students who are likely to engage in further study or become academics themselves as a career. Neither am I merely referring to students in small, elite, research-based institutions. Rather, what I am suggesting is that for all students, no matter what their ability or study motivation, the pursuit of professionalism embodied in the quality conception of scholarship can be a useful foundation for whatever the student engages in when they graduate. The ability to carry out a rigorous systematic process of inquiry and the capacity to apply the skills so acquired in a range of different contexts needs to be developed. As such, the model I have proposed is a key to the future of a mass higher education system. Research needs to teach us how to live. This is where and how it can happen.

Conclusion

If higher education is to be reconceptualised, and if relationships between teachers and students are to change, as I am suggesting here, we need, to change reward systems for academics. There is a need to ensure public awards for teaching. They argue that creativity, commitment, inquisitiveness and critical analysis should be rewarded in both teaching and research. Bringing research and teaching together requires policy and management decisions. It requires policies requiring measures of teaching quality to include how individuals integrate their research into their teaching. What is needed are policies requiring departments to monitor and identify how research impacts upon and supports the undergraduate curriculum. Such policies might at the very least ensure the best researchers teach across all levels of students. They might, however, go beyond this to do and remove barriers to interdisciplinary education. In this Chapter, I have argued that if we are truly serious about developing the links between teaching and research, we must take account of how academics conceptualize research and scholarship. If we do this we are led to consider working with students in academic communities of practice. This means reconceptualising higher education. It means sharing power and it means being open to challenge. So the final question is this: Are we ready to really take up the challenges of bringing research and teaching together? Is this where the future of higher education lies?

REFERENCES

Barnett, R. (1997), *Higher Education: A Critical Business,* Buckingham: Society for Research in Higher Education and the Open University Press.

Barnett, R. (2000), *Realizing the University: In An Age of Super-complexity,* Buckingham: Society for Research in Higher Education and the Open University Press.

Boyer, E. (1990), *Scholarship Reconsidered: Priorities for the Professoriate,* Princeton, NJ: Carnegie Foundation for the Advancement of Teaching, University of Princeton.

Brew, A. (1993), Unlearning through Experience, in D. Boud, R. Cohen and D. Walker, *Using Experience for Learning,* pp. 87-98. Buckingham: Society for Research into Higher Education and The Open University Press.

Brew, A. (1998), Understanding Research: Exploring Different

Conceptions in J. Higgs and R. Cant, *Writing Qualitative Research*, pp. 9-20, Sydney: Hampden Press.

Brew, A. (1999a), Research and Teaching: Changing Relationships in a Changing Context, *Studies in Higher Education*, 24(3), pp. 291-301.

Brew, A. (1999b), The Value of Scholarship, Paper Presented at the Annual Conference of the Higher Education Research and Development Society of Australasia, Melbourne, Vic., July.

Brew, A. (2001a), *The Nature of Research: Inquiry in Academic Contexts*, London: Routledge Falmer, Brew, A. (2001b). Conceptions of Research: A Phenomenographic Study, *Studies in Higher Education*, 26(2), pp. 271-285.

Brew, A. and Boud, D. (1995), Teaching and Research: Establishing the Vital Link with Learning, *Higher Education*, 29, pp. 261-73.

Gibbons, M.; Limoges, C.; Nowotny, H.; Schwartzman, S.; Scott, P. and Trow, M. (1994), *The New Production of Knowledge: The Dynamics of Science and Research in Contemporary Societies*, London: Sage.

Hattie, J. & Marsh, H.W. (1996), The Relationship between Research and Teaching: A Metaanalysis, *Review of Educational Research*, 66(4), pp. 507-42.

Jenkins, A.; Blackman, T.; Lindsay, R. and Paton Saltzberg, R. (1998), Teaching and Research: Student Perspectives and Policy Implications, *Studies in Higher Education*, 23(2), pp. 127-41.

Lave, J. & Wenger, E. (1993), *Situated Learning: Legitimate Peripheral Participation*, Cambridge: Cambridge University Press.

Leatherman, C. (1990, December 5), Definition of Faculty Scholarship must be Expanded to Include Teaching, Carnegie Foundation says, *Chronicle of Higher Education*, 37(14), A15-A17.

Marton, F.; Hounsell, D. and Entwistle, N. (1997), *The Experience of Learning*, 2nd Edn., Edinburgh: Scottish Academic Press.

Mooney, C.J. (1990), Higher Education Conferences applaud Carnegie Plan to Broaden the Definition of Faculty Scholarship, *Chronicle of Higher Education*, 36, 30, A1, A16, April 11.

Podgorecki, A. (1997), *Higher Faculties: A Cross-national Study of University Culture*, Westport, CT: Praeger Publishers.

Ruscio, K.P. (1987), The Distinctive Scholarship of the Selective Liberal Arts College, *Journal of Higher Education*, 58, 2, pp. 205-22.

Scho¨n, D.A. (1995), The New Scholarship Requires a New Epistemology, *Change*, 27, 6, pp. 26-34.

Shore, B.; Pinkler, S. and Bates, M. (1990), Research as a Model for University Teaching, *Higher Education*, 19, pp. 21-35.

Sundre, D.L. (1992), The Specification of the Content Domain of Faculty Scholarship, *Research in Higher Education*, 33, 3, pp. 297-315.

Trigwell, T.; Prosser, M. and Waterhouse, F. (1999), Relations Between Teachers' Approaches to Teaching and Students' Approaches to Learning, *Higher Education*, 37, pp. 57-70.

27

Economic Reforms and Financing Higher Education in India

MS. BHAWANA

Knowledge is the driving force in the rapidly changing globalized economy and society. Quantity and quality of highly specialized human resources determine their competence in the global market. Emergence of knowledge as driving factor results in both challenges and opportunities. It is now well-recognized that the growth of the global economy has increased opportunities for those countries with good levels of education and vice versa. The benefits of globalization accrue to the countries with highly skilled human capital and it is a curse for the countries without such specialized human capital. Developing and transition countries are further challenged in a highly competitive world economy because their higher education systems are not adequately developed for the creation and use of knowledge. Converting the challenges into opportunities depend on the rapidity at which they adapt to the changing environment. Though the higher education system and the pattern of financing higher education vary a great deal across countries in terms of their size and strength and degree of diversification of higher education institutions, yet they all face a severe financial crisis in the public finances available for higher education.

India is no exception to this global phenomenon. As part of globalisation, the economic reform packages were introduced in India in the beginning of 1991. These reform packages imposed a heavy compression on the public budgets on education sector, more specifically so on higher education. Following the introduction of structural adjustment policies, that include macro economic stabilization and adjustment, a fiscal squeeze is experienced in all social sector investments in many developing countries, including in India. This has trickled down to public expenditure on education in general, and higher education in particular. With economic reforms, cuts in public budgets for higher education have been very steep, severely impairing the growth of higher education. Paradoxically, under the reforming economic conditions, integration of the Indian economy with world economy presupposes efficiency and competitiveness in the domestic front as well as in the international arena. As the process of globalization is technology-driven, and knowledge-driven, the very success of economic reform policies critically depends upon the competence of human capital. But, what is observed is the reverse. Even within the education sector, relative priority assigned to higher education has been on the decline. It is to be recognized that higher education institutions play an important role in setting the academic standard for primary and secondary education. They are also responsible for not only providing the specialized human capital in order to corner the gains from globalization, but also for training inside the country, provide policy advise, etc.

In federal polity like India, education being subject since 1976, the commitment of the centre equally at all level of education is important. Given the spill over benefits of higher education, it became mandatory for the center to finance an increasing share of expenditure on higher education. But, this has been declining in the recent years. Even in secondary education, center's share of expenditure is minimal ranging around 5 per cent. However, federal role in elementary education is on the rise since the middle of 1980s. Indeed, the momentum of interest in universalizing elementary education began in the country in 1987 with a centrally sponsored scheme namely, Operation Blackboard to improve the educational infrastructure in primary schools all over the country. Around the same time another two important nationwide schemes have been initiated—on teacher education and non-formal education as a result of all these efforts and initiatives by the federal government, the flow of plan transfers from central to states in elementary education have improved since the late 1980s

It is to be realized that while primary education is a fundamental to the nation, higher education determines its economic and technological progress in the globalised era, which are the necessary and sufficient conditions for growth and development respectively. Even for very low enrolment ratio in higher education in India, it is increasingly realized that public budgets cannot adequately fund higher education, particularly when sectors of mass education are starved of even bare needs. Hence, the resources from higher education are being diverted to the development of primary education. But it is stressed that while it is mandatory that the nation achieves universal elementary education and total literacy, it cannot at the same time afford to relegate to a neglected position to achieve global standards in higher education.

With this perspective, the present paper attempts to examine financing of higher education in India during the previous two decades by looking at different sources of funds for higher education, highlighting the changes therein terms of the hike in students fees, introduction of student loans operated by commercial banks and rapidly increasing role of private sector and self-financing courses within public higher educational institutions.

Sources of Income for Higher Education

The fund for higher education in India come mainly from three different sources, viz., government, fee income from students and other sources of income from philanthropy, industry, sale of publication, etc. reliance on government for resources has almost doubled that is from 49.4 per cent in 1950-51 to 75.9 per cent in 1986-87. On the other hand, fee income has drastically declined from 36.8 per cent to 12.6 per cent during the same period. Other sources contribute around 10 per cent throughout the period. Higher education has been largely a state funded activity with about three-quarters of the total expenditure being borne by government. The relative share of non-government sources such as fees and voluntary contributions have been declining. It is to be noted that the latest year for which such information available is 1986-87.

The demand for higher education has been growing rapidly with comparatively faster growth in enrolment in higher educational institutions than the growth in number of higher educational institutions. The growth rates are doubled among the students enrolled in postgraduate and research, while the number of institutions for postgraduation and research studies has grown at a slower rate in 1990s than 1990s.

Distinct signals from the government towards hike in fees and shift of resources from higher to primary education can be noticed from the approach paper to the Tenth Five-Year Plan, "since budget resources are limited, and such resources as are available, need to be allocated to expanding primary education, it is important to recognize that the universities must make greater efforts to supplement resources from the government. University fees are unrealistically low and in many universities have not been raised in decades. A substantial hike in university fees is essential. The Tenth Five-Year Plan document as well notes that it is important to recognize that the universities must make greater efforts to supplement resources apart from the government.

As far as the financial allocation to higher and technical education during the plan periods is concerned, the downward trend in resource allocation can be noticed from Chart 3 that the plan expenditures on higher and technical education has been on the decline since Fifth Five-Year Plan onwards in the case of general higher education and Fourth Plan onwards in technical education. Elementary education has got the highest priority in first plan, which again seemed to gain momentum in the 9th plan. In the first plan higher education got 9 per cent allocation, which is the case again in the Ninth Plan. The financing strategy even under economic reforms seems to be developing one level of education. It should be noted that higher education institutions play an important role in setting the academic standard for primary and secondary education. They are responsible for not only providing the specialized human capital in order to corner the again from globalization, but also for research and development, training inside the country, provide policy advise, etc., it is to be realized that higher education is no longer a luxury; it is essential to national, social and economic development.

Student Fees

In this section we examine the recommendation of various committees set up by UGC on resources generation through revision of fees and fee income as a source of financing higher education. Government of India had constituted a number of committees to examine the issue of mobilization of resources for central universities and for technical education. Further, committees were formed by UGC to specifically look into the recommendations of Punnayya Committee on unit cost of higher education; to review the norms of maintenance grant for Delhi colleges and to formulate the revision of fee structure. The important recommendations of these committees on student fees are recapitulated below. All these committees have a consensus that one of the major sources of income is the fee from students has not been revised upward revision for decades in most of the universities. Hence, there is an urgent need for upward revision of fees chargeable by universities and colleges from a reasonable to a substantial limit.

Tuition Fees

Tuition fee may be revised upwards with immediate effect and may be periodically adjusted keeping in view the inflation and rise in costs of higher education. The revision of fees must be related in a meaningful manner to the recurring cost of the course of study and employment opportunities offered by the course. Full cost recovery is suggested in government funded/aided colleges may be allowed to start new specialized programmes for specific target groups on self-financing/net revenue earning basis. Tuition fee will seek to recover the actual cost of imparting education. Tuition fee and all other fees, which are not to be charged on one time basis should be tenable for 12 months. Modified unit cost method i.e. 3 per cent of the unit cost worked out by Punnayya Committee should be the basis of fee structure, annual upward revisions may be made at 2 per cent of the suggested rate and after five years the commission may consider the entire issue again for upward revision in the fee structure. It is recommended that certain mandatory provisions be made to ensure that the revised fee structure being suggested by the committee is implemented.

Other Fees

With regard to fees for admission and examination fee, it is recommended to recover the recurring cost of operations. While in library, laboratory, sports and similar other facilities are concerned, it is suggested that these fees must be revised to recover a significant part of the recurring cost. It is recommended to revise the development fee to meet the actual recurring cost on no-loss-no-profit basis. Hostel and mess fees is recommended to meet the actual recurring cost and to cover part of the capital cost over time.

Fees as a Source of Income

Various committees recommended that institutions should raise the fee levels in such a way that at least 15 to 25 per cent of the annual recurring cost per student is recovered from the students in the form of fees and from other sources at the end of ten years. Government should in course of time shift the funding of universities to a system of students funding. The tuition fee for the government funded and government aided institutions to be revised to at least 20 per cent of the recurring expenditure per student per year. Fees so fixed may be reviewed and refixed once in every three years.

As against the general perception that fees are extremely low and not revised for decades, the reality is that most universities have not revised some components of fees, like tuition fees. But tuition fee is only one of the components of total fees chargeable. Many services especially student welfare services, viz., hostels, water, electricity, food charges and the development fees are revised to a substantial extent. This can be evidenced from the components of household expenditure on education that 40 per cent of the household expenditure on higher education goes to tuition and other fees.

Other Sources of Income

Income from other sources comprises income from endowments, university press, rent from university land, space, infrastructure, etc., income from consultancy services and research projects, etc. Income from sale university publications, self-financing courses, and interest income are some other sources of internal income of the universities. The search for additional resources and the introduction of income generating activities has been on the rise in many institutions. However, it should not sideline the primary goal of academic quality and relevance.

It is unambiguous that policy of the government of India now encouraging augmentation of resources by each institution for covering a larger portion of cost of education recent policy directions in India exacerbate full cost recovery from students even in public higher education institutions through hike in fees and introduction of self-financing courses and seat in tune with liberalization policies. Under the deep waves of globalization and competition, important economic rationale for government funding for higher education is neglected. With economic reforms and other pressures of the government, higher education has been shifted to the list of non-merit good from the list of merit good. It has ignored expenditure on education as social investment and the complementary nature of public and household expenditure on education. It is to be realized that the funding of higher education requires both public and private resources under economic austerity. However, the role of the state and public support to higher education remains essential to ensure its educational, social and institutional missions.

Student Loan

Student loan are currently in operation in more the 80 countries around the globe. Of late, educational loan is very popular among students because of its simple and appealing logic, despite its inherent weaknesses. It is argued that in order to safeguard poor students from the rising cost of higher education, a number of countries in the developing and developed world have established student loan programmes. However, cost recovery cannot be implemented equitably without scholarship programmes that should guarantee necessary financial support to academically qualified poor students. Further, imperfection in capital markets related to the lack of collateral security for education investments restricts the ability of poor students to borrow for education.

Following the wave of changes around the world, the present Educational Loan Scheme was introduced in India following the announcement in the budget 2000-01. The scheme is administered by the commercial banks. The scheme covers a wide range of courses in higher studies from post-metric to research studies, both in India and abroad. Eligibility criterion is that any student who secures admission in domestic/foreign educational institution is eligible for loan. The loan covers both instructional cost and living expenses. A maximum of Rs. 7.5 lakh for studies in India and Rs 1.5 lakh for studies in overseas institution/universities is envisaged under the scheme.

However, it is to be noted that there is no income ceiling on students/parents for the eligibility of this loan scheme. Neither the academic achievement is considered as an eligibility criterion, that is, there is no minimum qualifying marks required. There are no special provisions of any kind for the weaker sections in terms of security, government guarantee, lower rate of interest or repayment period, repayment in accordance with earnings, waivers, etc. It is to be noted that the scheme neither adheres to the efficiency nor the equity principles unlike in many other countries, where merit-cum-means determine the eligibility for student loan.

Given the world experience on student schemes, the new scheme in India is insensitive to the needs of the poor and does not concern equity aspects as there are no special provisions of any kind for the weaker sections. The present loan scheme neither takes into consideration the various details, such as eligibility, interest rates, repayment terms and conditions as recommended by various committees. Hence, an alternative scheme specifically for the weaker sections needs to be evolved as the present scheme is not flexible to the needs of the weaker sections.

The world experience on student loans suggests that recovery rate from student loan is very low. In addition, administrative cost of the student loan programme is quite high. Hence, total cost incurred on default and administration would be much higher and eventually the scheme may not be financially viable. Hence the idea of self-sustaining student loan schemes in the long run seem to be elusive. Further, student loan schemes require huge start-up amount. Apart from financial non-viability of student loan, its psychological impact and societal attitude is adverse on student's family and society.

Privatisation

In India, over the years, there have been private initiatives in education initially for philanthropic reasons and eventually in professional and even in general higher education not only to meet the growing demands but also to realize the huge and quick profits potential. Privatization of higher education has emerged in several forms and types in the recent decade in India. One, privatisation within government higher education institutions take place in the form of introducing self-financing courses within government institutions; two converting government-aided private institutions into private self-financing institutions; three, allowing to expand self-financing private institutions with recognition and also without recognition, which may be termed as commercial private higher education institutions.

Commercial private higher education emerges from market forces and tied to economic and global forces. They thrive on the principles of commercialism, primarily focus on vocational courses and highly pragmatic. Their commercial thrust is training jobs, indeed, part of the curriculum is industrial training. Not only training for jobs but also place their students in well-paid jobs. This indeed speaks about the strong industry institution linkages. They are narrowly focused, rather micro-specific in designing their course and training. This narrow focus is their strength as well weakness. It is a strength as long as there is demand for such specific nature of the courses and a weakness once such a demand is satiated. Moreover, the built-in set up/infrastructure do not allow them to diversify. They cater to the unmet demands or rather demand-absorbing from the non-university higher education sector.

Ownership of these private institutions ranges between a spectrum of substantially weaker and stronger commercial institutions. Indeed, there are chain of institutions from Kindergarten to higher levels of education by well-known business groups and corporate sector. Since 1993 with the Supreme Court judgment, growth of commercial higher education in the name of capitation fee of self-financing colleges is mushrooming. The private institutions include colleges, training centers, etc. Neither the Department of Education nor the University Grants Commission collect, compile and publish the information on the size and growth of institutions and enrolments on this rapidly growing private higher education.

There are also different types of these private institutions—many of self-financing engineering colleges and management institutions are affiliated to the conventional universities. In which, the course structure, design, curriculum, and the pattern of examination fall within the purview of the national or state pattern. On the other side, several of these self-financing private institutions are also non-affiliating to any universities and cater to the demands of the corporate sector nationally and internationally. Whether the private institutions follow multi-faculty or discipline is decided by the individual institutions. Since the programmes and courses are market-driven and each private institution decides on their own the course and subjects it offers. Hence, they also have a free hand to introduce new programmes and discard the old.

Pull Factors

All over world including India, there has been rapid expansion and demand for higher education known as massification of higher education. The conventional university sector is not able to cater to the demands of the new sections of the rapidly growing eligible age group population for higher education. As an alternative, private enterprises are sought to accommodate this evolving pressure on higher education in various forms, types and levels.

Conventional university courses are not able to cater to the immediate demands of the market as it takes considerable amount of time for a change within the formal higher education/university system. This academic inflexibility boosted the rapid development of private initiatives in higher education. Perhaps, many providers/stakeholders in many of these private institutions are the one who struggled to changed the formal system to suit to the needs of the students who, in turn, demand depending upon the marketability of a course, the emphasis being pragmatism.

The conventional institutions lack the responsiveness of higher education to labour market demands implying business participation in governing boards of institutions, the creation of financial incentives for joint industry-university research, corporate-sponsored internships for students, and part-time academic appointments for professionals from the productive sector. Alternatively, such a nexus between academics and industry is met by private institutions with multi-disciplinary and/or inter-disciplinary courses, which are short-term in nature with a very narrow focus. However, leaving a few reputed private higher learning institutions, majority of them are education shops catering to the majority of the students, who are willing to pay with a desperate hope to get into the job market.

In short, these private institutions marketed their service in technology course varying from hi-tech to fashion technology; management courses ranging from institutional management to hotel management; and promised to produce not only employable youth but also to place them in jobs.

Push Factors

Expenditure compression referred as resource constraint of the government on account of economic reforms led to financial privatization of higher education in various forms such as reduced allocation to higher education introduction of cost-recovery measures within public institutions and directed policy measures toward privatization of higher education. Government of India introduced the Private Universities Establishment and Regulation Bill—primarily on the clause on the provision of scholarship for the economically and socially backward sections of the population. Though, there have been deliberations on the private sector initiatives in higher education in different forums, there is no clear perspective on the issue. Yet another important factor is the deteriorating quality of the higher education over the years has indirectly made the students to look for alternatives.

External Factors

In the phase of internationalizing higher education, foreign universities and institutions have been allowed to come into India and establish franchise centers in the country, offering degrees or diplomas, which are not necessarily recognized by the parent universities in their own countries. India providers also set up institutions in other countries.

Based on the rates of returns analysis, World Bank focus on basic education, whereas its involvement in higher education is guided by calls for equitable and cost effective financing. It highly favours cost sharing and the promotion of private higher education to free up scarce public resources for improving basic education. It recommends forcefully that further enrolment expansion in higher education should take place in the private sector. Further,

World Bank indicates that the higher education systems in developing countries and institutions can only survive if they are flexible for change. The message is clear that the most flexible systems as well as institutions survive and those do not decay. More differentiated systems, including private and non-university institutions can help meet growing demand and make higher education more responsive to labour market needs. The examples are the successful higher education systems found in Australia and New Zealand other than US. It may also be noted that the European system, perhaps many of European countries are undergoing series of policy debates on financing higher education focusing on the extent and degree of cost recovery in higher education for enabling the transition from elite to mass oriented higher education.

To sum up, even though, private institutions offer course on any discipline, the viability and sustainability depends upon their demand. However, it is to be noted that private institutions in developing countries like India are not efficient, competitive and complement as found in developed countries. The absence of coherent long-term policy perspective on higher education reflected on the government's ambiguity to regulate private institutions. The unfettered growth of private higher education combined with the international economic and political events created a surplus in the labour market in the recent years.

The indicators in terms of allocation of resources to higher education in GDP and intra-sectoral allocation to university and higher education and technical education show a declining trend. It is also evident that enrolment growth has not been accompanied by the growth in public expenditure. This rapid erosion of public resources for the rise in enrolment will have a negative impact on the quality of educational services. It is unambiguous that policy of the Government of India and State Governments now encourages augmentation of resources for covering a larger portion of cost of higher education. Recent policy changes in India often favour to divert resources from higher education to primary level of education. While it is essential that the nation achieve universal elementary education, it cannot afford to neglect higher education in the period of globalization. Further, it needs to be realized that all levels of education are inter-dependent; the principle should not be the growth of one level of education at the cost of another.

Private investment alone in higher education would be socially sub-optimal. It is because the private and households do not come forth to invest on non-market oriented courses in higher education and research and development. Further, increased role of market jeopardizes the participation of meritorious students from economically disadvantageous groups, women and minorities. Further, markets can crowd out important educational duties and opportunities.

Increasing reliance on student fees, student loan and privatization without considering the low-income groups may produce regressive effects in the society. Hence, an alternative student loan scheme specifically for the weaker sections should be evolved. Such a programme must be flexible enough to suit their requirements, which may involve government guaranteed loans, subsidized interest rates, liberal terms of repayment, waivers for those students with less future incomes, etc. in addition to a strong student support system. Under the deep waves of globalization and competition, important economic rationale for government funding especially for higher education is neglected. Public support for higher education remains essential to ensure a balanced achievement of educational and social missions, apart from surviving in the knowledge-based society. Sequencing of policies, i.e., universal primary education first, secondary and higher education later would be very costly strategies in the era of globalization.

It is equally important to note the required fundamental transformation at both system level and at institutional levelling higher education. Effective financial management at institutional level is mandatory. It is essential that funding sources must be diversified but cost sharing with students has social and political limits, and excessive commercialization of higher education should be forbidden. Before concluding, the challenge to public policy on higher education in India remain to combine private providers with continuing responsibility of governments to guide, regulate, monitor and continuing the provision of subsidized higher education with a view to strike a balance between equity and efficiency principles.

28

Indian Higher Education in the New Millennium: Challenges and Opportunities

G.M. BHAT AND SHABIR AHMAD PADDER

Role of Higher Education in National Development

Higher education aims at contributing to national development by way of dissemination of knowledge, skills and attitudes, excellence of standards of achievement; providing opportunities to reflect upon the social, political, economical and moral issues facing the country; and its key role in generating leadership and manpower resources. Higher education is of great significance for the all round development of a country especially a country like India. The institutes of higher education can act as bridges between the community and government. These can serve as the brain of the Government in generating creative ideas and creative people. Higher education is vital for the society.

The *World Bank* document itself states: "Higher education is of paramount importance for economic and social development. Institutions for higher education have the main responsibility for equipping individuals with the advanced knowledge and skills required for positions of responsibility in government, business and the professions. Estimated social rates of return of 10 per cent or more in many developing countries also indicate that investments in higher education contribute to increases in labour productivity and to higher long-term economic growth which are essential for poverty alleviation" (World Bank, 1994). It goes on to add: "Higher education investments are important for economic growth. They increase individual's productivity and incomes, as indicated by rate-of-return analysis, and they also produce significant external benefits not captured by such analysis."

UNESCO in a policy paper "Documents of Policies for the change and development of higher education" (UNESCO, 1995) maintains that there is a well established correlation between investment in higher education and the level of social, economic and cultural development of a country. It expresses concern over the observed trend towards a reduction in state contribution for higher education and its reallocation to earlier educational levels. It maintains "state and society must perceive higher education not as a burden on federal budgets but as a long-term domestic investment, in order to increase economic competitiveness, cultural development and social cohesion. As a conclusion one could say that the public support to higher education is still essential in order to ensure its educational, social and institutional mission" (UNESCO, 1995).

Development of Higher Education After Independence

There is no doubt that expansion of higher education in India has received a great impetus after independence. However, it may be mentioned here that the expansion of higher education has not taken place in accordance with the new needs and interests of the country. There is admittedly a state of near anarchy even in administration of existing facilities leading to social tensions and mediocrity of output. Much of this confusion is traceable to ethical, moral and social well-being divorced from the educational process. Quality is being sacrificed at the cost of quantity. This has far reaching consequence on the quality of manpower, which holds the key to our country's progress.

At Independence in 1947, India inherited a system of higher education which was not only small but also characterized by the persistence of large intra/inter-regional imbalances. Determined efforts were made to build a network of universities, and their affiliated colleges which provided tremendous outreach to a country of vast diversities in language as also in the prevailing standards of education at the lower levels. The feeder schools differentially impacted on the higher education system leading to significant qualitative imbalances within it.

When India became independent, it had only 20 universities and 500 colleges located in different parts of the country. It enrolled around a hundred thousand students in higher education. Participation of women was limited and those who graduated annually were no more than a couple of dozens or so. The policies and aspirations of people influenced the development in the following decades. In the post-independence period, higher education has expanded fast, and it is mostly public in nature. Today, India ranks very high in terms of the size of the network of higher education institutions, with 6.75 million students enrolled. The teaching force numbers about 321,000. Student enrolment increased from 263,000 to 6,755,000 by 1996-97. It grew at an estimated rate of 7 per cent between 1987 and 1993 but has now declined to 5.5 per cent compound rate of growth, with 14 states having a lower rate. In spite of this phenomenal growth, the total enrolment, however, forms only about six per cent of the relevant age-group (17-23) population.

The number of students per 100,000 population has increased significantly since independence. It was only 48 per 100,000 in 1951 increasing to 613 per 100,000 in 1997.

India's higher education system compares favourably with the other countries of South Asia and Africa in its enrolment, while our South East Asian neighbours show much higher enrolment such as in the Philippines (27.8%), Thailand (19.0%), and Malaysia (10.1%). Hence, in spite of the rapid expansion of the system in 50 years, access to higher education still remains an issue as the pressure of India's very youthful population continues to bear on it.

With this scientific and technical manpower India has the potential to become the largest reservoir in the world. Compared to the situation that the country inherited from the colonial rulers about half a century ago, these numbers mark a phenomenal expansion of the system as is exhibited by Tables 28.1 and 28.2.

The number of women's colleges has recorded a substantial increase from 780 colleges in 1986-87 reaching a figure of 1195 in 1996-97. Of the total enrolment, women's enrolment accounts for 34 per cent.

Table 28.1: Growth in Higher Education in India

Institutions	*1950-51*	*1990-91*	*1996-97*
Universities	30	117	214
Colleges	750	7346	9703
Enrolment ('000s)	263	4925	6755
Teachers ('000s)	24.0	272.7	321

Note: Includes institutions deemed to be universities, but excludes other institutions.

Source: UGC Annual Report 1996-97 (New Delhi: University Grants Commission); and Selected Educational Statistics (New Delhi: Ministry of Human Resources Development) (relevant years).

Table 28.2: School and College Education

No. of Institutions	*2000-01*	*1999-00*	*1998-99*	*1990-91*
Primary ('000s)	514.8	641.7	626.7	560.9
Middle ('000s)	169.0	198.0	190.2	151.5
High/Higher secondary ('000)	106.2	116.8	112.4	79.8
General education colleges (No.)	4,966	7,782	7,494	4,862
Professional colleges (No.)*	1,702	2,124	2,129	886
Universities (No.)**	245	244	237	184

* Medicine, Engg. Technology and Architecture, teachers training colleges only.

** Including deemed universities and institutions of national importance.

Source: Statistical outline 2002-03, Tata Services Limited, Department of Economics and Statistics.

As a system expands, it absorbs a population of students who come from a wide spectrum of socio-economic groups. The "massification of education" has occurred in India at the lower levels of education which feed into higher education. The quality of that education impacts on higher education. Inevitably, therefore, the higher education system has had to cope with the problems of a very diversified student body from first generation learners to those from professional and higher income families whose children are exposed to many other opportunities besides education. The first generation learners have mostly attended the publicly funded schools with far poorer preparation than the latter who patronize the private institutions. Increasing access and decrease in quality have been major issues confronting higher education with a very large young population and increasing strain in government resources.

Education can have a great role to play in decreasing social disparities between groups and in promoting social mobility. For instance, the tremendous expansion of the middle class in India can be confidently attributed to the investment in education, especially in higher education. In this respect, the Indian ethos is echoed now in the Delors Report.

There is a need to place greater emphasis on enrolment of students from underprivileged backgrounds such as the rural areas, the scheduled castes and tribes and other backward groups, minorities, the disabled and others who have suffered from discrimination which has existed for centuries. Hence, special attention has to be given to all these groups through various strategies to be adopted in the university system, especially for access to the system, retention in the system and qualitative development of performance.

Most of the higher education institutions in India are public institutions. There are no private universities so far, though efforts have been initiated to allow opening of private universities. There are, however, a large number of private colleges. A majority of the private colleges are financially supported by the State. The rapid growth of self-financing private colleges is a recent phenomenon.

Financing of Higher Education

The expenditure on education is viewed as social investment in man which creates an orderly social life based on the values of socio-economic justice, freedom and equality of opportunity and raising the general economic condition. Education at the primary level is very important as it helps in removing the stranglehold of traditions, which characterize the society in under-developed countries and is inimical to growth and development.

Education at the secondary level provides the base for higher and technical education. Higher education is important as it provides manpower for higher cadre posts both in the private and public sectors. It hastens and facilitates the process of national development by encouraging scientific temper in students and inculcating in them the urge to develop, to progress, to be able to live a satisfying existence.

A global review clearly shows that in most countries of the world education is almost exclusively financed by the government. In countries of the OECD public source of funding was in 1991, as high as 99 per cent in Denmark, 98 per cent in the Netherland and 90 per cent in Canada. Even in the United States it was as high as 78 per cent. In India it was 89 per cent, in Indonesia 62.8 per cent and in Kenya 62.2 per cent *(World Bank, 1995)*. Cost sharing between government and beneficiaries is a relatively new suggestion, and has not really been put into practice. Tilak (1997) points out that in most societies government is the most important financer of higher education. According to the data given by him in the last decade state finances for the higher education sector in the OECD countries were high. It was 88 per cent in Australia (1988), 89.5 per cent in France (1984), 68.5 per cent in Germany (1986), and 90 per cent in Norway (1987). The contribution was relatively lower in the United States (59.3%) and United Kingdom (55%). Tilak believes that government financing "is held not only to be necessary for the development of education, but also as a desirable form of providing education, because, markets cannot provide the socially optimum quantities and qualities of education, as markets do not capture externalities."

In most countries there has been a rethinking on the role of government in financing higher education following the transition of education from elite systems to mass systems. *Ziderman* and *Albrecht* (1995) point out that as long as education was reserved for elite groups governments were able to meet the full costs without much budgetary strain. With the 'massification' of education governments of most countries find it difficult to spare proposal for cost recovery. However, it is significant that many Latin American countries increased their expenditure on higher education during the late eighties. Between 1985 and 1990 government financial of higher education, in terms of GDP, has increased from 1.5 per cent to 3.1 per cent in Argentina, from 2.1 per cent to 2.7 per cent in Bolivia, and from 3.8 per cent to 4.6 per cent in Brazil. In Mexico there has been an increase from 3.9 per cent to 5.2 between 1985 and 1992 *Mungaray and Lopez (1996)*.

Growth in Expenditure on Higher Education in India

Higher education in India is in financial stress. However, it should be noted that huge investments have been made in higher education in independent India. Total expenditure on higher education has increased remarkably during the post-independence period. At the inception of planning in the country (1950-51), India was spending Rs. 172 million on higher education. Government expenditure alone was of the order of Rs. 42,035 million in 1996-97, and it has risen further during the subsequent period. This impressive growth is, however, considerably offset by increase in prices, and increase in population, more particularly student numbers in higher education. Inflation has had an adverse effect on education. Nevertheless, on the whole, the trends suggest that higher education had a good start during the 1950s (with real growth of 7.5 per cent per annum), and had its golden days during the 1960s, with the real expenditure increasing at an annual rate of growth of 11 per cent; but it suffered significantly during the 1970s, with the rate of growth coming down to a meagre 3.4 per cent as educational planners aimed at consolidation of higher education instead of its rapid expansion; and showed some tendencies to recover during the 1980s. Though the growth in expenditure on higher education has been erratic during the 1980s, it had increased on the whole at a rate of growth of 7.3 per cent per annum. The 1990s heralded an era of austerity and higher education suffered greatly.

Share of Higher Education

The relative priority accorded to higher education can be measured in terms of the share of higher education in GNP. Starting from a very low figure of 0.19 per cent of GNP invested in higher education in 1950-51, the share of higher education increased five-fold by 1980-81; but it came down to nearly one per cent of GNP after three decades of development. But ever since, allocation of resources has been steadily coming down: it tended to decline to 0.4 per cent of GNP by mid-1990s.

India has adopted Five Year Plans as an important development strategy since 1950. The Five Year Plans set new directions for development—quantitative expansion, improvement in quality and relating to several other dimensions of educational development—and represent the serious intention of the planners to further develop the system.

The share of higher education doubled in the total education outlay from 9 per cent in the First Five Year Plan to 18 per cent in the Second Five Year Plan, and increased to an all time peak of 25 per cent in the Fourth Five Year Plan, and ever since it has been consistently declining, and was about 15 per cent in the Seventh Five Year Plan. The share of higher education in the total education outlay in the Eighth Five Year Plan was estimated to be 8 per cent. In Ninth Five Year Plan it has again increased to 12 per cent as is revealed by Table 28.3.

Reasons

- Facilities for higher education available at the time of independence were insignificant. Independence had created an abnormal increase in the social demand for higher education, and public expenditure has had to cope with the demand.
- Building up a new socio-economic system after the end of the colonial rule required large scale manpower with varied skills; so the government had to expand investment in higher education.
- The very development models emphasised high skilled labour force, and building up of huge social infrastructure for excellence in science and technology, and research and development.
- Government policies towards equality in education led to the growth in public investment in education, since it involves huge subsidies at all levels of education to a substantial number of students, belonging to weaker sections.
- The rapid growth of school education naturally pushed the demand for higher education.

Recently, efforts are being made to mobilize resources, and it has been recommended that while the government should make a firm commitment of funding higher education, colleges and universities should also make efforts to raise their own resources.

Table 28.3: Plan Expenditure on Different Sectors of Education.

Sectors of Education	*Ist Plan Expdt. 1951-56*	*2nd Plan Expdt. 1956-61*	*3rd Plan Expdt. 1961-66*	*Plan Holiday Expdt. 1966-69*	*4th Plan Expdt. 1969-74*	*5th Plan Expdt. 1974-79*	*6th Plan Exptd. 1980-85*	*7th Plan Expdt. 1985-90*	*1990-92 Expdt.*	*8th Plan Expdt. 1992-97*	*9th Plan Expdt. 1997-2002 (Central)*
Elementary	56 (850)	35 (950)	34 (2010)	24 (750)	30 (2390)	35 (3170)	33 (8360)	37 (28490)	37 (17290)	47 (92010)	58 (118428)
Secondary	13 (200)	19 (510)	18 (1030)	16 (530)	18 (1400)	17 (1560)	21 (5300)	24 (18320)	22 (10530)	18 (34980)	13 (26035)
Adults							9 (2240)	6 (4700)	9 (4160)	9 (18480)	3 (6304)
Higher	9 (140)	18 (480)	15 (870)	24 (770)	25 (1950)	22 (2050)	22 (5590)	16 (12010)	12 (5880)	8 (15160)	12 (25000)
Others	9 (140)	10 (300)	12 (730)	11 (370)	14 (1060)	14 (1060)	4 (1080)	3 (1980)	2 (1180)	4 (7510)	2 (4314)
Technical	13 (200)	18 (490)	21 (1250)	25 (810)	13 (1060)	12 (1070)	11 (2730)	14 (10830)	17 (8230)	14 (27860)	12 (23735)
Total	100 (1530)	100 (2730)	100 (5890)	100 (3230)	100 (78.70)	100 (9120)	100 (25300)	100 (76330)	100 (47280)	100 (196000)	100 (203816)

Source: Vide Table No. 5.1 of India 2002, Publication Division, Ministry of Information and Broadcasting, Government of India.

Current Policy Issues in Financing

Generally it is felt that the levels of fees in higher education in India are very low and that there exists much scope for increase in the fee and for rationalisation of the fee structure. This is more so in case of higher technical education. The UGC and AICTE Committees recommended that at least 20 per cent of the recurring expenditure per student has to be generated through student fees (and other sources).

Student loan programme has been one of the most prominent methods that is currently suggested as an effective solution to the problem of financing higher education. This is also advocated as an effective antidote to check the regressive effects of increase in fees. Many nationalised banks in India have begun to offer a variety of loans to students for higher education within the country and abroad.

An idea has been mooted to levy an educational cess on industries and other organisations that use technical manpower.

Efficiency and Economy in Expenditure

Several measures are being suggested for efficient utilisation of resources in educational institutions and to effect economy in expenditures, including the one related to the consolidation of uneconomic institutions. For effective utilisation of available resources, it is necessary that an optimum size of the institutions is worked out. Institutions with small size would be uneconomic and in the institutions with large student numbers, the resources might be over-optimally utilised. The AICTE felt that institutions of technical education should have enrolments in the range of 1,500-2,000, with a minimum annual intake of 180, and with an intake of 40-60 for every course/discipline. The Committee has also suggested staff-student ratios to vary between 1:15 and 1:20. Available data on some engineering institutions show that more than half the institutions were having enrolment below 1,500, and more than 80 per cent of the institutions have a staff-student ratio of less than 1:15. All this suggests the need for consolidation of technical education institutions, through proper institutional planning.

Privatisation of Higher Education

The new trends of thinking and overall constraint in resources call for private initiative and community support. In the Indian mixed economy, while the contribution of private sector has been significant in general, its contribution to higher education has not been encouraging.

While until now there is no formal private university in India, there are a large number of private colleges in the general and technical education spheres. Private colleges that form about three-fourths of the total number of colleges, are of two types: privately managed but publicly funded colleges familiarly known as (government) "aided" colleges, and privately managed and funded colleges, known as "unaided" colleges. A substantial number of private colleges belong to the former category, and they receive government aid to meet almost the whole recurrent expenditure. The private aided colleges have not contributed significantly to easing the financial burden of the government, as more than 95 per cent of the recurring expenditure, and sometimes even the capital expenditure, is met by public exchequer. Hence strictly from the point of view of finances, such private colleges do not have any significant role.

Pure or "unaided" private colleges do provide financial relief to the government in providing higher education, but at huge and long-term economic and non-economic cost to the society. Such institutions have been really a recent phenomenon. They are the result of private enterprise and initiative. In the very recent period, growth of private engineering and medical colleges has been remarkable. They charge donations and capitation fees. While other colleges are, by definition, non-profit institutions, many of these institutions not merely cover their costs, but also make profits, which are not necessarily re-invested in education. The government wants to encourage private initiatives in higher education but not commercialisation.

Measures for Financial Self-Reliance

Now-a-days with declining or stagnant budgets for education, specifically for higher education, institutions of higher education increasingly feel the need to become financially self-reliant by generating resources not only through increase in fees, but also through other measures, such as augmentation of resources from corporate sector in the form of donations and other similar contributions, by forging effective relationships with industry. The government has already promised incentives both to the institutions and to the individual donors. The institutions that generate such resources are promised matching grants by the government, besides stating that such resources would not be taken into account in giving bulk/maintenance grants. The donors are offered fiscal incentives in income tax savings (tax deduction at the rate of 125 per cent of the contributions to professional institutions and 100 per cent to other institutions of education).

It is, however, recognised that none of these measures for mobilisation of additional resources should aim at reducing the demand for higher education.

Quality Control in Higher Education

In this age of a techno-scientific revolution, when the sheer quantity of knowledge and information is expanding exponentially, when the needs of a constantly growing and increasingly varied student population are burgeoning, the quality of training for teachers and the quality of teaching in higher education institutions demand top priority.

The higher education system in India recognises its key responsibility in training teachers, in establishing links with teacher training institutions at other levels and in training teacher trainers. Efforts are being made to bring in teachers from the commercial and social sectors to facilitate interchange and build links with the education system. The higher education system in India is facilitating access to the common heritage of knowledge and research. It is fulfilling its moral obligation to society in exchange for the resources assigned to it by society. Recently, a Task Force on Fundamental Duties laid down in the Constitution has been constituted so that the same can be reflected in the curriculum. This would also lay down a code of accountability of all stakeholders in the educational system.

The University Grants Commission [UGC] was set up in 1956 as an agency for coordination and maintenance of the standards of teaching examination and research in universities. During the last 40 years, thee UGC has taken a number of measures to improve quality and to introduce innovations.

Quality Improvement through Infrastructural Development

Here the policy is to ensure a minimum level of facilities such as laboratories, libraries, classrooms and hostels, by the provision of development grants. Special grants have also been provided to improve in quality humanities, social science and science streams.

Financial support has also been provided for creating new inter-disciplinary oriented universities such as the Jawaharlal Nehru University.

Curriculum, Human Resources and Research Development

Another quality assurance measure is the provision of resources in the form of Research Fellowships for M.Phil. and Ph.D. programmes undertaken by university and college teachers, University Leadership Programmes (ULP) for college teachers, and seminars, workshops, summer schools in various subjects so as to help the teachers upgrade their knowledge.

Such programmes reach a large number of teachers in the system. In 1987, Academic Staff Colleges (ASC) were set up to provide opportunities for general orientation and subject refresher programmes for academic staff. Under the scheme, more than hundred thousand teachers have received orientation and subject refresher programmes of 3-4 weeks duration. Such measures are expected to have greater impact on the quality of teaching and learning in the system of higher education in the country.

Other measures within this broad category are restructuring of courses, improving the quality of research and curriculum development by constituting various subject panels and encouraging universities to undertake constant revision and improvement of curriculum. In order to implement relevant curricula, a scheme of restructuring of undergraduate programmes was initiated. The scheme envisaged flexible and socially relevant undergraduate curricula with a provision for foundation, core, application and skills-oriented course components.

A recent innovation has been the introduction of the vocational education scheme, at the undergraduate level. Under this scheme one of three subjects required for having a Bachelor's Degree could be a vocational education subject. The scheme has suggested 35 vocational subjects and recently some more vocational subjects related to agriculture and rural areas have been introduced. Nearly 1,500 colleges have been given facilities for vocational education and a large amount has been invested to support the implementation.

Centres of Excellence in Higher Education

Centres of excellence in different subject specialities have been established under the scheme of Centres of Advanced Studies (CAS), Department of Special Assistance (DSA) and Inter-University Research Centres at internationally comparable standards. The objectives of these centres are to provide quality input in higher education and in research areas.

Great strides in science and technology, on the one hand, and high cost of inputs for good research, on the other, have made it necessary to develop interactive institutional arrangements between teaching institutions, national research laboratories and the development sectors. The UGC has established Inter-University Centres to enable cooperation and joint use of facilities in nuclear science, crystal growth astronomy and astrophysics, social sciences and humanities. Information Centres to facilitate information flow have been set up at the Indian Institute of Science, Bangalore, M.S. University of Baroda and SNDT Women's University, Bombay.

Sudden expansion in the higher education system required the development of excellence. A major strategy has been devised by the UGC for establishing Advanced Centres and Departments of Special Assistance within the university system. At present, about 411 departments are participating in these schemes and 157 in the scheme for strengthening the infrastructure facilities for postgraduates and research in science. These schemes have had a major impact on raising standards and promoting excellence in higher education.

Research and Development

Research is promoted by encouraging students to do M.Phil. and Ph.D. research. The UGC provides financial assistance to those who are meritorious and propose to pursue research. Meritorious students are selected through National Level Test. Nearly 50,000 scholars are receiving Fellowships for conducting research. Those who are enrolled for research programme account for 74,000, i.e. 1.1 per cent of total enrolment in higher education. Nearly 10,000 students are awarded Ph.D. degree every year.

Teachers are encouraged to do research through award of minor and major research projects. Nearly 500 major research projects and 650 minor research projects were awarded during the last year. Besides, there are schemes of Research Associateship, Scientistship, Emeritus Fellowship, Teacher Fellowship and Career Awards through which research work is supported by providing financial assistance to teachers. These Fellowships are available for Science, Social Sciences, Humanities and Engineering and Technology. Besides UGC, support for major and minor research projects is provided to teachers in higher education by Department of Science and Technology and various Councils related to Social Sciences, History and Philosophy.

Training of teachers is an important component of any policy, which aims at maintaining high standards of teaching in the universities and colleges. The review of Educational Policy (1992) stressed upon a comprehensive programme of professional development of teachers through Academic Staff Colleges. The scheme of Academic Staff Colleges was started in 1986-87, under which 45 such colleges have been set up so far. These colleges conduct four-week orientation programmes for training new teachers with innovative techniques and also three to four weeks refresher courses in various disciplines for in-service teachers to enable them to update their knowledge. Since these Academic Staff Colleges cannot cater to the needs of all the teachers, 72 departments of universities and specialized institutions have been selected to conduct refresher courses, in addition to the Academic Staff Colleges. These centres have prepared reading material for the use of teachers. The Academic Staff Colleges also conduct seminars of two to three days' duration for the principals located under the catchment area. The Academic Staff Colleges sensitize the teachers about students' expectations and perceptions and provide them an understanding of the academic context of higher education.

To enrich the quality of higher education, a country-wide classroom scheme was launched. Under this scheme, special fil on various subjects were prepared and broadcast for the benefit of students and teachers. To carry this out, institutional audio-visual research centres and educational media research centres were set up throughout the country. Such centres already number 21 and are likely to increase. These centres are producing a large number of video tapes that are transmitted on the national TV network.

Structural Reforms

The regulatory system was introduced as early as in 1857 along with the establishment of the modern university in India. The main purpose was to ensure the standardization of curriculum in undergraduate programme, as well as objective and impersonal evaluation of students. The system of affiliated colleges involved determination of curriculum by the university. Implementation of this curriculum was carried out by the affiliated colleges and university departments and evaluation of students through comprehensive examinations. So long as the system remained small in size, it worked reasonably well.

But, with the expansion in the number of institutions and students, this system has become counter-productive and has caused serious damage to the process of teaching and learning; diversification of higher education, social relevance of the curriculum and evaluation of students. In order to remedy this situation, the following steps have been taken:

Scheme of Autonomous Colleges

These are intended to ensure quality relevance and appropriate assessment of students. Under this arrangement, teachers in the colleges decide the curriculum and conduct the evaluation of their students through systems of continuous evaluation. At present, there are 119 autonomous colleges.

Critical Inputs and Recognition

Other regulatory measures, such as creation of minimum level of infrastructure, the specified number of qualified staff and well-defined administrative procedures, are insisted upon before any institution is affiliated to a university, or before a university can be recognised by the UGC for financial assistance. These measures discourage the opening of substandard institutions.

Evaluation and Monitoring

UGC review committees and visiting committees oversee and assess the quality of university programmes. These committees are constituted for different areas and disciplines and for all the universities which receive financial assistance from the UGC.

Another UGC measure is the National Educational Testing (NET) programme. The UGC and the Council of Scientific and Industrial Research (CSIR) conduct tests in science subjects twice a year for Junior Research Fellowships (JRF) and an eligibility test for the teaching profession.

Universities and colleges are required to consider the candidature of only such persons who have qualified for teaching jobs. Those who qualify for JRF tests are awarded Junior Research Fellowships of Rs. 5,000/- per month. These tests have proved to be important indicators of quality of students engaged in the teaching and research profession.

As a part of coordination and maintenance of standards of higher education, the UGC has set up an Inter-University Institution of quality assessment and accreditation. This is named as National Assessment and Accreditation Council (NAAC) and it was set up in 1994 under Section 12 CCC of the UGC Act.

NAAC's responsibility is to assess and accredit institutions of higher education that volunteer for the process, based on certain criteria which can be applied to the functioning of the institution in totality. NAAC's process of assessment and accreditation involves the preparation of a self-study report by the institution, its validation by the peers and final decision by the Council.

Though assessment and accreditation is voluntary on the part of the institutions, UGC has already indicated that its plan-based development support to educational institutions will be related to the outcome of assessment and accreditation. It has already extended financial support to the extent of Rs. 5 lakh to each university to meet the expenses involved in undergoing the accreditation process. Likewise, the autonomous colleges are provided with financial support for this purpose as a part of their annual grant from the UGC.

New Challenges

India recognises that the new global scenario poses unprecedented challenges for the higher education system. The University Grants Commission has appropriately stated that a whole range of skills will be demanded from the graduates of humanities, social sciences, natural sciences and commerce, as well as from the various professional disciplines such as agriculture, law, management, medicine or engineering.

India can no longer continue the model of general education as it has been persisting in for the large bulk of the student population. Rather, it requires a major investment to make human resource productive by coupling the older general disciplines of humanities, social sciences, natural sciences and commerce to their applications in the new economy and having adequate field based experience to enhance knowledge with skills and develop appropriate attitudes.

Responding to these emerging needs, the UGC stated: "The university has a crucial role to play in promoting social change. It must make an impact on the community if it is to retain its legitimacy and gain public support." It seeks to do so by a new emphasis on community based programmes and work on social issues.

Emphasis has to be laid on curriculum change; interdisciplinary courses gradually replacing discipline-oriented learning, especially at the master's degree level; greater emphasis on field based learning experiences for students both in undergraduate and postgraduate programmes; more career oriented courses and response to local needs for human resource in specific work-related opportunities. The university is required to be seen not only as a seat of learning and new knowledge through its research and extension functions but also as a focal point for the dissemination of information to the community through continuing education, extension education and through field outreach activities. It will have a major role to play in directly impacting on the community for social development and change. It should be facilitated in this task which is described by the UGC as the third dimension of education.

As a very small proportion of the relevant age group (around 6 %) is enrolled in higher education in India, compared to the developed countries (about 40%) with which the country is going to engage itself in the international market, efforts will need to be directed towards raising the enrolment in higher education sector and meeting the increasing costs of such enrolment.

Access means costs but access cannot be overlooked when the base is narrow, not in absolute numbers but in the percentage of the educated in the country's structure. We have to acknowledge the need to prepare a human resource capable of accepting the challenges of the new millennium.

We have also to realise that social changes and transformation can only be brought about by people and not through technology alone which itself is a product of human endeavour. Hence, human resource development, at all levels, needs to be given priority and made a part of the nation's overall strategy.

Educational system of India is confronted with a serious crisis due to the huge population explosion. India has to do the twin task of keeping optimum pace with the enormous advancements of modern technology on one hand, and on the other, they have to develop educational programmes which are work-related, employment-oriented and need-based to meet the requirements of their modern industrial sectors, and unidentified economic sectors.

A large number of the Educational Centres in India and in several other developing countries are badly affected by the political and ethnic conflicts. These centres are dominated by unacademic activities of the semitized trade unions of students, teachers and others who derive their strength from their respective political and caste-based mafias. Education is treated as a process of stuffing the minds of the students with contents of books, forcing them to vomit the same out in the examination halls, and return empty-headed. Increasing number of persons are seeking education not for learning but acquiring the means to gratify their desires and glorify their social status. This has badly affected the quality and standards of education at all levels. The university and colleges have turned into centres of unhealthy environment and corruption.

As long as the degrees can be bought and sold, marks have

their heyday, happiness gets equated with material success, till then, life-giving human values will remain unhonoured.

There is no uniformity in higher education in respect of programmes and their course-structures. Irrelevant courses and syllabuses, overcrowded classrooms, denominated teaching-learning methods, and sub-standard evaluation systems have all combined to make educational institutions as centres of commercial transactions. The mushroom growth of institutions have turned centres of educational excellence into those of mediocre mass production units. The educational institutions of India do not offer the much desired work-based education or application-oriented educational programmes and continue with the traditional system of instruction-based education. As a result, there is a big gap between what is being produced, and what is needed by the society. Some of the educational institutions live in their own world without being accountable to the society. They have no interaction with the trade, industry and technology to provide employment opportunities for their students.

The educational system will have to overcome its credibility crisis by ensuring students' keenness to acquire knowledge and competence, teachers' commitment to contribute to the educational growth of their institutions, and the administrators sincerity for smooth functioning of the educational institutions.

REFERENCES

1. Roa, D.B. (2003), *"Higher Education in 21st Century"*, Discovery Publishing House, New Delhi.
2. World Bank (1994), *"Higher Education: The Lesson of Experience"*, The World Bank, Washington DC.
3. World Bank (1994), *ibid.*
4. UNESCO (1995), *"UNESCO Policy Paper for Change and Development in Higher Education"*, Reproduced in Frontiers in Education.
5. World Bank (1995), "Priorities and Strategies for Education", *World Bank Review*, The World Bank, Washington D.C.
6. Tilak, J.B.G. (1997), *The Dilemna of Reforms in Financing Higher Education in India,* Higher Education Policy.
7. Zidermann, A. and Aibrecht (1995), *Financing Universities in Developing Countries,* the Falmer Press, London.

8. Munjaray, A. and Lopez, R. (1996), *Introduction to Latin American Challenges and Perspectives in the Nineties,* Higher Education Policy.
9. Hanumanthappa, K. (1993), *Challenges, Responses and Higher Education in India: Relevance of Sri Sathya Sai System of Education, University News,* November 8.
10. Sen, Rajkumar (2005), *"Social Sector Development in India"*, Deep and Deep Publication, New Delhi.
11. Madan, V. D. (2002), *"Higher Education in Beyond 2000—An Omni-Tech Approach"*, Kanishka Publishers, New Delhi.
12. Narkhede, S.P. (2001), *"Challenges of Higher Education in India"*, Sarup and Sons, New Delhi.
13. UNESCO (1998), *UNESCO Policy Paper on Higher Education,* World Conference on higher education in the 21st century, Paris.

29

Higher Education: Opportunities and Challenges for Women and Weaker Section in India

PROF. RAM NARESH THAKUR

Centuries ago, women in India were highly placed in society. During the Mahabharata era, the children were named after their mothers as Kaunteya, Radheya etc. Women were considered highly placed in the society. People believed in the idiom "where women are celebrated, there resides the God." But with the change of time males got edge over the females. Manu wrote, "In childhood a woman must be subject to her father, in youth to her husband, and when her lord is dead, to her sons. A woman must never be independent." She began to be viewed solely as the mother and the wife, and these roles became idealised. The ideal wife should be faithful and uncomplaining and her virtues should be in the services she renders to her husband. Since then exploitation to women started.

Foreign invaders shook the foundation of our cultural heritage also. They plundered the fortune, and robbed the chastity of women. Consequently people sent the women behind the curtain to save them from the atrocities of invaders. Gradually the 'purda system' developed and women began to be treated as the weaker section of the society and as the assets or wealth of men. Thus the deformity in social structure began. The fundamental rights were denied to the female from their childhood. Beginning of discrimination between male and female children started in this way. The concept took place that the female is designed to deliver child and for performing domestic duties. It was also conceived that the girls would go to other families after their marriage, and so they would not be useful for the parents. Dowry system added fuel to fire. It is why the girls began to be neglected from the very beginning. Such type of treatment created inferiority complex in them and their mental development began to be retarded. In this way their role in the society either in education or higher education or in the economic development of the nation began to play a negligible part.

But time changed. Importance of women began to be realised day-by-day. The role of women became vital and the Indian women became the key to the process of economic development. Though the actual and inevitable progress of the women could not happen. Yet the development of women as well as the development by the women became the inter-related issues for the academic height as well as the economic development of India. Women's participation in education, social life, industrialisation, science and technology, employment as well as in politics began to increase here day-by-day. The women in the last decade of the 20th century occupied the key role in different sectors of the society. They are sharing with the men not in the academic life and economic growth process, but in the field of administration and political system also on the virtue of their achievement in higher education. Education is the root of the development process. It is actually the key to the door of economic development. After independence, Indian women has succeeded in the field of education and in higher education too.

Higher Education

The growth in the number of women students in higher education since independence has been phenomenal. While women constituted only 9.3 per cent of all students in institution of higher education on the eve of independence, the percentage of women students enrolled in all colleges and universities was 33.2 in 1993-94 according to the report of the University Grants Commission.

Women Students per Hundred Men Student

Year	*Total Women Enrolment*	*Enrolment Per Hundred Male Student*
1950-51	40,000	14
1993-94	16,64,000	50

Growth in Enrolment of Women in Higher Education

The pace of growth has been particularly faster in the last two decades or so. The number of women enrolled per hundred men registered a four-fold increase during the period 1950-51 to 1993-94.

State-wise Distribution of Women Enrolment

While the enrolment of women as a percentage of total enrolment has gone up in all the states, the extent of this increase has varied across the states. As in earlier year Kerala, having 53.4 per cent enrolment, continued to lead other states in terms of women enrolment as percentage of total enrolment in 1993-94, followed by Punjab—48.6 per cent enrolment of women, Delhi—46.7 per cent, Haryana—42.6 per cent, Meghalaya and Nagaland—39.5 per cent and Tamil Nadu, West Bengal, Tripura, Sikkim—38.9 per cent, while Bihar remained at the bottom with 16.9 per cent enrolment in women in 1993-94.

State/U.T.	*Total Enrolment*	*Women Enrolment*	*Percentage of Women*
Andhra Pradesh	341057	95257	27.9
Assam	98749	31028	31.4
Bihar	350328	59057	16.9
Gujarat	294093	105315	35.8
Haryana	106537	45377	42.6
Himachal Pradesh	10793	8355	27.1
J. & K.	39191	14856	37.9
Karnataka	322152	95761	29.7
Kerala	186139	99335	53.4
M.P.	343649	118948	34.6
Maharashtra	691776	257384	37.2
Manipur	16124	5549	34.4
Meghalaya/Mizoram/Nagaland	14589	5763	39.5
Orissa	102040	26057	25.5
Punjab	179201	87053	48.6
Rajasthan	111450	54808	24.6
Tamil Nadu	491072	191039	38.9
U.P.	656713	150666	22.9
West Bengal/Tripura/Sikkim	388165	151005	38.9
Delhi	131757	61508	46.7
Total	**5006575**	**1664121**	**33.2**
1993-94	—	—	**33.2**
1998-99	—	—	**35**

Stage-wise Distribution of Women Enrolment

Women's enrolment as percentage of total enrolment has consistently increased during the period 1984-85 to 1993-94 at all levels of higher education—graduate, postgraduate, research and diploma etc.

Percentage of Women Enrolment of Total Enrolment (Stage-wise)

Years	*Graduate*	*Postgraduate*	*Research Certificate*	*Diploma*
1	2	3	4	5
1982-83	29.1	30.5	29.7	24.7
1993-94	33.1	35.1	37.6	26.2

Faculty-wise Distribution of Women Enrolment

While there are women students in all the faculties, the pattern of their distribution across faculties differs from the pattern that obtain for all the students in the system except for the faculty of science where the percentages are almost the same both for all students and women students. There are four notable differences in the enrolment patterns of the two categories of students:

(*a*) The percentage of women students became almost double in percentage share of all students enrolled in the faculty of Education.

(*b*) The percentage of women students were, however, markedly lower as compared to the percentage of all students in the faculties of Law, Engineering and Technology.

(*c*) This was more or less true for Commerce. As against nearly 22 per cent of all students, only a little over 14 per cent of women students were enrolled for Commerce courses.

(*d*) The highest concentration of women students was in the faculty of Arts, which also includes Humanities. As against 40 per cent of all students, 54.4 per cent women students were enrolled in various courses in Arts and Humanities.

Faculty-wise Women Enrolment (1993-94)

Faculty	*Women Enrolment*	*Percentage of Women*	*Percentage of All Students*
1	2	3	4
1. Arts	9,05,125	54.39	40.4
2. Commerce	2,35,309	14.14	21.9
3. Science	3,34,439	20.01	19.6
4. Law	30,039	1.08	6.3
5. Engineering/Technology	20,026	1.02	4.9
6. Education	65,086	3.97	2.3
7. Others	74,097	4.04	5.6
Total	**16,64,121**		

Women's Colleges

The number of Women's Colleges had recorded a substantial increase during the period 1984-85 to 1993-94 as follows:

Year	*No. of Women's Colleges*	*No of Total Colleges*
1	2	3
1984-85	712	—
1986-87	780	—
1988-89	821	—
1990-91	874	7346
1991-92	950	7761
1993-94	1070	8210
1994-95	—	11,000
2003-04	—	18,000

Promotion of Women's Studies in Universities

The Central Government, under the sponsorship of the University Grants Commission has established various centers for promoting women's studies. As on 31st March, 1994, U.G.C. had provided assistance to 22 Universities and Colleges/University departments for setting up Women's Studies Centres/Cells. In addition, UGC also provided assistance for the research projects concerning women's studies.

In all developing countries, till 1970 the women's enrolment in higher education was 50 per cent of men's enrolment, which had become more than 70 per cent in 1990. In 32 countries this enrolment rate of women is higher than men.

Education has been regarded both as an end in itself and as a means of realising other desirable ends. It develops the personality and rationality of individuals, qualifies them to fulfill certain economic, political and cultural functions and thereby imposes their socio-economic status. It has been recognised as a major instrument which societies can use to direct goals. It provides for vertical mobility and can thereby help to equalise status between individuals coming from different social strata. 'The Universal Declaration of Human Right' regards it as one of the basic rights of every human being. In 1945, the U.N.O. has declared to grant equal political and social rights to both men and women. Since then the movement for improving women's status all over the world has always emphasised education as the most significant instrument for changing women's subjugated position in society.

The Indian social reformers of nineteenth century also accepted this view. Their aim, however, was to use education to make women more capable of fulfilling their traditional roles as wives and mothers and not to make them more efficient and active units in the process of socio-economic as well as political development. The colonial authorities generally supported this limited view of women's education. The expansion of education in the twentieth century, however, precipitated a need for women teachers and doctors.

The attainment of independence and constitutional guarantee of equality introduced new dimensions with the call of women to play multiple roles in the policy, economy and the society in the years after the Second World War. International agencies also emphasised the role of education as an instrument that can equip women to build the new social order. In spite of the new emphasis, however, attitudes to women's education in India have displayed an ambivalence between the traditional view on the one hand and this broad new concept on the other and has influenced academic planning, allocation of resources and development of values in society.

In spite of all the expansion that has taken place in the formal education system, the vast majority of Indian women have remained outside the reach of all educational progress and are illiterate. In fact, the female literacy rate has increased from 0.69

per cent in 1901, 8.86 per cent in 1951, 39.29 per cent in 1991 to 54.2 per cent in 2001 census.

Social attitudes to girls' education varies from acceptance to absolute indifference even now. We found the acceptance of girls' education most in urban areas, being the highest among the middle classes. A small group of affluent/elite families still oppose it for traditional reasons, but others regard it as an accomplishment and a symbol of modernisation. Among the lower middle class, an increasingly large section is now ready to make substantial sacrifices for girls' higher education because of economic need, but a very large section still find itself unable to do so for economic and social difficulties. For the majority of the people below subsistence level, poverty is the predominant factor that governs their attitude to girls' higher education.

The employment holds the key to improvement in status; yet education and particularly higher education is equally important. Education determines aspirations, productivity mobility. Education also changes perception of costs and values of human beings and their contribution to the economy of the household as well as of the nation too.

The educational system is the only institution, which can counteract the deep foundations of the inequality of the sexes they are built in the minds of men and women through the socialisation process. It must make a deliberate, planned and sustained effort to replace the traditional value system, based on inequality by the new value system which accepts equality of the sexes.

Unfortunately, the educational system, instead of accepting this responsibility has helped to perpetuate traditional prejudices through its classification of subjects on the basis of sex and the unwritten code of conduct enforced on the pupils. This is one area where a major change is needed in the content and organisation of education.

In the Fourth World Women's Conference (Beijing, 1995) it was realised that "women literacy is essential for making women able for taking decisions in society for health and education of the families." It further appealed for eliminating discrimination between men and women in the field of education as well as for making 'basic education' available for all women essentially till the end of this century. This reflects the path to higher education.

There is no doubt that the constitution contemplates a social revolution brought about through the use of law as an instrument of directed social change. The attainment of equality of status of women was one of the specific objectives which is implicit in the preamble, fundamental rights and the directive principles of state policy. We have to achieve the goals and to go miles before we can sleep. Indian women have to march on the path of gaining literacy, education and particularly higher education too, health, employment, social and political recognition and status in due course. The struggle is not over. Certainly they will prove as a key to the process of economic development.

We will have to make a continuous effort to guarantee equal participation of both men and women in public health, education, (Specially higher education), employment, housing, sanitation or environment. All have their roles relating to women. It is essential to make the women full of rights for solving the problems relating to these roles. The main obstacle in making women full of rights is to change the existing social attitude. The women has become the prey of exploitation in almost all the political and economic systems. It is essential to bring change in this mentality. In our country considerable economic development took place, but vast inequality exists even now due to increase of population and lack of just and equitable distribution. In this situation it is necessary that the community development system in place of human-oriented development system should be adopted.

Indian Record in Academic Achievements

"From very beginning upto now during the different five year plans the importance, role and relevance of higher education in economic development was enforced. India has developed much in the spheres of higher education, technical education, management education as well as in the areas like innovations and development. It is observed generally that India is facing the problem of 'brain drain' due to the plight of brilliant and trained scientists, engineers, doctors, computer specialists and management scholars into the other developed countries. It is very attracting feature that India is producing such brilliant persons from very beginning. So, today in India the number of such meritorious academic persons is six times more than China. India has developed very fast in establishing the academic and educational based infrastructure in the face of academic institutions, enrolments, and able teachers. According to the 'Economic Survey Report 2000-01' there has become increase in the number of universities from 27 to 185 (which remained 740% increase) during the period of 1951 to 1995. The number of colleges became 11,000 in this period. In addition to it there were 42 deemed universities and 5 other institutes established by central and states' statutes. There has become enormous increase in the enrolment of students, particularly girls students in the plan periods (1951-2006) gradually." (Provision of Education in India-Economic Development of India after Independence/IGNOU-2004).

There has become effective increase in the sphere of university and higher education. The number of enrolment in higher education became 9.2 million in 2002-03 increasing from 7.26 million became 1997-98. The enrolment or women students became 3.69 million by being tremendous increase in the said period. In 2002-03 the number of 40 per cent of the total enrolment was only of women. So it is observed that there has become overall heavy increase in the enrolment of women in the plan-periods. Open university system is the step forwarded in the direction of diversification of curriculum in which the academic needs of women and the persons of rural sector has been considered seriously. There has become tremendous increase in the enrolment of students under the distance education system in the sphere of higher education.

"The technical and commercial education had attained higher qualitative number of manpower which has provided important role in the economic and technical development. At the degree level there are 1,265 recognised engineering colleges. In addition to it, there are 1,034 computer centers teaching at 'Master of Computer Application' level, 958 registered Management Institutes are teaching M.B.A. Courses." (Source-Selected Academic Statistics, 2001-02, Ministry of Human Resource Development).

Care for Scheduled Castes/Scheduled Tribes Students

According to the '172nd Report of Universities and Higher Education' placed in the Parliament on 22nd May, 2006, between the period of 1990-91 to 2002-03 the percentage of the students of scheduled castes is recorded between 8.6 to 11.3 per cent, whereas their reservation requires upto 15 per cent according to the constitution. The students coming from scheduled tribes record 2.1 to 3.6 per cent their enrolment, when it should be 7.5 per cent. Today it seems that to achieve higher education for scheduled castes/scheduled tribes students is still like "Obstacle Race" in India. The drop-out rate of these classes viz. SC/ST is also enormous due to many socio-economic constraints.

The condition for the higher education to scheduled castes/ scheduled tribes students is being worsened by leaps and bounds and is likely to be worsened more in future.

(*i*) The very first cause of it is the adaptation of the liberalisation, privatisation and globalisation policies and the division of state from welfare works, i.e., path of economic development adopted by the administrators and planners of nation and to pursue 'pay more for higher education policy.'

After independence the Indian Government had adopted such 'model of economic development' under the mixed economic policy was consisted of public works-oriented. But during the nineties, in the way to implement economic reform, under the decision of open discretion to the market power, the process of privatisation and commercialisation of higher education became so fast, has effected the common education system adversely. The procedure of grabbing education world by the market power has made the educational progress of the dalit and down-trodden people full of obstacles and miseries.

(*ii*) The technical transformation also had created the digital divide in a new way. The mostly effected adversely are the dalit and tribes (adivasi) only. Gail Omved (2005) has rightly observed in his article 'Untouchable in the World of Information Technology', how we talk of revolution in the age of the explosion of information technology but the dalits and the backward class people are out in the whole race of this game. Now also the real right and entitlement of dalits and tribes are not given to them easily.

The real successors are being deprived off from their right. The different universities of India record the rising number of cases of violence against dalit-adivasi students in the universities/ colleges' campuses or in their hostels. Just recently it has been focused of 'the caste-wise divide issue' against dalit students in the All-India Institute of Medical Sciences (AIIMS). The 'caste-based violence report' of the central university, Hyderabad by the institute named 'Anveshi' of Hyderabad reveals the fact that how divide is enormous and widespread. In the data of the results of entrance test examinations of IITs and AIIMS of 2005 and 2006 reveals the fact that there is no difference between the 'reserved' and 'unreserved' students. In different IITs and its allied institutes 3.5 lakh students appeared against their 5,000 seats. But the students of scheduled castes and scheduled tribes fetched more marks than the 'general or common students'.

This analysis shows that students of scheduled castes and scheduled tribes are not less brilliant. But the government itself is cold minded and ignorant towards their academic interest.

Article 14 of Indian Constitution confers on men and women equal right and opportunities. Article 15 prohibits the State as well as private persons from discriminating against any citizen on grounds of religion, race, caste, sex, place of birth or any of them. Ironically these words are more on paper than in practice particularly when it comes to sex or in other words 'Gender Equality is ensured but not pursued'. The Constitution of India enjoins upon every citizen of India the duty to promote common brotherhood of all the people of India and renounce any practice derogatory to the dignity of woman. Contrary to this, women are prone to multiple discrimination. In the remote past too, we have examples that depict the pathetic and deplorable condition of women—Sita was exiled, Draupadi was humiliated in the court, Ahilya was converted into a statue, in-laws of Meerabai attempted to put her to death. In the present scenario also women's position is still subordinate to that of men—since her birth to her last breath.

REFERENCES

1. *Report* (1995), UGC.
2. *Report* (2004), UGC.
3. *Report* (2006), UGC, 172nd of Universities and Higher Education.
4. IGNOU (2004), Provision of Education in India—Economic Development of India After Independence.

5. Selected Academic Statistics (2001-02), Ministry of Human Resource Development.
6. Gail Omved (2005), Untouchable in the World of Information Technology.
7. Thakur, R.N. (2000), "Education and Political Status of Indian Women; Key to Economic Development", *Women and Economic Development*, EDS A. Banerjee and R.K. Sen, Deep and Deep Publisher, New Delhi.
8. Thakur, R.N. (2006), *Minor Research Project of UGC*, Gender Gap of Education—Its Economic Factors: A Case Study of Samastipur Dist. (Bihar).
9. Thakur, R.N. (2006), *Gender Justice in Education in Bihar*, Paper for IEA 89th Conference, Kurukshetra (Haryana).
10. Thakur, R.N. (2006), *Empowerment of Women in Bihar*, IXth Annual Conference of E.A.B., A.N. College, Patna.
11. Thakur, R.N. (2004), *Empowerment of Poor People Under Panchayati Raj in Bihar*, VIIIth Annual Conference of E.A.B., P.K. Roy Memorial College, Dhanbad.
12. Thakur, R.N. (2006), *Empowerment of Weaker Section Under Panchayati Raj in Bihar*, National Conference, R.N.A.R. College, Samastipur.

30

Knowledge Economy: A Development Perspective

RANJU NARANG

Education plays a pivotal role to in the process of socio-economic development of every nation and it has a very close link with the nations growth. Knowledge forms human capital and investment in human capital assists in progress of individuals and nation. The returns on investment in education are higher than in investment in physical capital because education enhances the production and productivity of factors of production.

Economists right from Adam Smith have realised that education plays an important role among the factors that contribute to economic development. Marshall regarded education as a national investment and most valuable of capital and the most valuable of all capital is one that is invested in human beings. Studies in this regard are in great number and recent studies made by Schultz, Kuznets, Denison and Bowmen started a new era of economics—'Economics of Education'. Schultz analysed the contribution of education to growth in national income in the United States from 1900-56 and came to the conclusion that investment in education contributed 3.5 times more to the increase in gross national income than investment in physical capital.

Following this revolutionary economic thought of human investment, India too, like many other developing economies made heavy investment in education. The government accorded special importance to education not only in the country's constitution but also in the Five Year Plans. Education Commission (Kothari, 1966) stressed the relationship between education and productivity and considered education as an instrument of Social 'Change on Grand Scale' in India.

National policies on education 1968, 1986 and 1992 (modified) emphasised the role of education. Considering acculturating role, they all led emphasis on universalisation of elementary education, equalization of educational opportunities for children from all strata and retention of children in the school. For secondary education vocationalization of education was emphasized. They also laid special emphasis on improvement in quality in higher education and above all eradication of illiteracy was given top priority. Also, a number of schemes and programmes were launched over the past 55 years especially after the constitutional amendment in 1976 vide which education was included in the concurrent list, making it a joint responsibility of both Union and States.

Consequent upon these efforts India made enormous progress in terms of increase in number of schools, teachers and students. The education system in India is the second largest in the world. The percentage of literacy which was hardly ten at the time of independence has risen to 52 in 2002. The expansion of education since the independence period has made sufficient contribution to economic growth.

More than 40 years ago, when D.S. Kothari submitted the report of the Education Commission to the then Education Minister, M.C. Chagla on June 29, 1966, he noted, "It is characteristic of a world permeated by science that in some essential ways the future shape of things is unpredictable. This emphasises all the more the need for an educational policy which contains a built in flexibility so that it can adjust to changing circumstances. It underscores the importance of experimentation and innovation." He added, "...the single most important thing needed now is to get out of the rigidity of the present system. In a rapidly changing world of today, one thing is certain: yesterday's educational system will not meet today's, and even less so, the need of tomorrow."

This prophetic statement is equally and perhaps more relevant today in the context of enormous change taking place in the society and economy.

Education is a basic condition for a knowledge economy. The effective use of knowledge is becoming most important factor for international competitiveness and for creating wealth and social welfare. **The knowledge economy of today needs a set of new competencies, which includes not only ICT skills, but also such soft skills as problem solving, analytical skills, group learning**

working in a team based environment and effective communication.

A good education system is essential to enhance further the productivity and efficiency of the economy. Skills matter more than ever in present day's more competitive global market. Firms and farmers alike must be able to learn and develop new skills.

In the present scenario, in the area of scientific and technical education, even though India produces almost 200,000 scientists, engineers and technicians a year, it has not been obtaining the full benefit from this skill base, because of mismatch between education and labour market. When technology is changing, India needs to develop various job training programmes to be globally competitive. These programmes must be flexible, cost effective and able to adapt quickly to new skill demands generated by changing markets and technologies.

Developing ICTs in India in the recent years has affected economic and social activities. It has affected the use of knowledge. In the area of economic development ICT can provide access to markets and jobs and promote competition and efficiency. In the area of personal development ICT can help to improve the quality of life for the individual by providing access to education, entertainment and health care. In the area of social development ICT can help to facilitate free flow of information and lead to increased transparency of Government operations through eGovernment initiatives India's ICT industry has become popular since 1990s. India has a lot to gain from the new technologies and is putting efforts to do so. The increasing number of skilled manpower in this sector has contributed to both domestic industry and industry abroad India has large number of English speaking engineers. The quality of their service is high. As India is doing well in this sector it is pertinent to look at the size of software and services industry in India in the recent times.

Recent developments in technology, which have made possible to digitise information and pass it on at negligible cost to any part of the world with the help of internet, have made trade in services a global phenomenon. These developments in ICT are advantageous to Indian Economy in form of faster economic growth, employment growth and support to balance of payments. The interesting part of outsourcing is that it has brought remarkable economic growth without much exploiting natural resources and creating pollution in India. ICT is the driving force of globalization. The Indian ITES BPO industry is a high potential and high growth segment within the country. ICT industry accounts for around 60 per cent of ICT revenues in 2004-05. **This segment has been amongst the largest employment generator segments within the country (as is evident from Table 30.1).**

Table 30.1: Employment in ITES-BPO Segment in India

Year	*Employment (No. of people)*
2002-03	171,000
2003-04	245,000
2004-05	348,000
2005-06	470,000

Sources: www.nasscom.org

According to NASSCOM-McKinsey estimates, this country would create jobs for over one million professionals by 2008-09. Within the country they are penetrating Tier-II cities such as Mysore Nasik, Indore, Chandigarh, Kochi, Shimla and Trivandrum. This will contribute to employment generation on one hand and help removing regional disparities on the other. A new work-culture would be spread to these cities. It is also hoped that this primary employment generation will also have a trickle down effect in that the newly employed skilled workers will create lots of secondary employment for semi-skilled and unskilled workers. This would be an extent to help in the solution of the equity and employment problems of the country.

Table 30.2 provides a broad view of employment in Indian software industry.

Table 30.2: Employment in Indian Software Industry, 2000-04

No. of Employees in thousands

	1990-00	*2000-01*	*2001-02*	*2002-03*	*2003-04*	*CAGR**
Software Export Sector	110	162	170	205	260	24
Software Domestic Sector	17	20	22	25	28	13
Software Captive User Org.	115	178	224	260	280	25
Business services (ITES-BPO)	42	70	106	171	245	55
Total	**284**	**430**	**522**	**661**	**813**	**30**

Note: CAGR represents cumulative average growth rate in employment in per cent during 1999-00 to 2003-04 in category.

Source: NASSCOM, Indian Industry Factsheet.

With increased trend in offshoring of services employment in this sector has also shown substantial growth in India with about 30 per cent CAGR in industry total employment.

Indian IT and ITES-BPO services sector is also showing a **remarkable increase in exports**. In absolution terms, Indian and ITES-BPO services exports during 1995-96 and 2003-04 have increased from $754 million to $8600 million (See Table 30.3).

Table 30.3: Trends in Indian IT and ITES-BPO Services Exports

Year	*IT Services-Exports*		*ITES-BPO Exports*	
	Amount in Million Dollars	*% of Total*	*Amount in Million Dollars*	*% of Total*
1995-96	754	100	–	0
1996-97	1,100	100	–	0
1997-98	1,759	100	–	0
1998-99	2,600	100	–	0
1999-2000	3,397	86	565	14
2000-01	5,287	85	930	15
2001-02	6,152	80	1,495	20
2002-03	7,045	74	2,500	26
2003-04 (Estimates)	8,600	70	3,600	30

Source: NASSCOM as quoted in RBI Annual Report.

While composition of Indian services exports, have greatly changed due to outsourcing of software service at the same time it appears that services exports in Computer and Information Services (CIS) sector is also showing shift in composition and mode of global delivery. Share of BPO services, which was zero per cent till 1998-99 has increased to 30 per cent in 2003-04. So this segment is the largest employment generator as well as high revenue generator segment.

India is facing some challenges in this field in the form of issues related to data protection, legal and infrastructural environment and emerging competition from other developing countries like China, Malaysia, Philippines, Thailand and Vietnam which have raised their challenge due to low cost English speaking labour force.

India has a long way to go to fully tap the advantages of knowledge. There is a great potential to increase new knowledge based activities. India should concentrate its strength to become a leader in knowledge creation and use. This may require promoting new institutions and strengthening the existing ones. Policy shift may also be necessary especially in case of education sector. This policy regime has to focus on strengthening the economic and institutional regime, developing educated and skilled workforce, creating an efficient innovation system and building a dynamic information infrastructure. Educationists are working in this direction. On behalf of National Knowledge Commission (NKC) Sam Pitroda has submitted a report on January 12, 2007. This report suggests certain reforms to face current and future challenges. A few of them are allowing foreign education institutions in India, granting autonomy for academic self-governance to individual colleges with proven record of academic excellence, inviting private initiatives in higher education without diluting academic standards. This report is being criticized too.

The acceptance or rejection of these suggestions depends on government. India is in a position to reap significant economic gains by developing policies and strategies that focus on effective use of knowledge to increase the overall productivity of the economy. In this process India will be able to perk up its international competitiveness. Information technology is an important part of knowledge. Economy and traditional knowledge and wisdom flourished in our country for centuries is an integal part of knowledge economy as well. So the knowledge traditional as well technical must not only be generated but must also become available and accessible to all. Wealth generation through the application of technology is primarily a product of knowledge generation and utilisation for which we have to flourish lots of technopreneurs instead of entrepreneurs. Recently established National Knowledge Commission is expected to work in this direction.

REFERENCES

Economic and Political Weekly (17-23 February, 2007), Vol. XLII, No. 7.

NASSCOM (2005), *"Indian IT Industry Fact Sheet"*, Available online http://www.nasscom.org.

NASSCOM (2005a), *"Indian ITes-BPO Industry: Nasscom Analysis"*, Available online http://www.nasscom.org.

RBI Annual Report (2004), August, htp://www.rbi.org.in/Upload/Annual/ReportDocs/56240.doc.

Surjeet Singh, "India and the Knowledge Economy" published in Vol. 48, No. 4, 2005, *Indian Journal of Labour Economics.*

The Economic Survey of India (2004-05), Government of India.

The Economic Times (2004), "Karan Bahree, Part-II, Shot in Australia", August 16.

The Economic Times (2004), "Sun's sting operation maligns Indian BPO Industry", June 24.

World Economic and Social Survey (2005), UN Publishers.

31

Economics of Education in Reference to New Policy on Education

DR. A.K. TOMAR AND DR. JYOTSNA CHAUHAN

During the 19th century, nothing occupied a more prominent place among the requirement for Economic and Social change than public education and population enlightenment. Today also, among the areas of the prime concern are the runway growth of population in the developing world, the threat to our natural environment and the role of the educational process in dealing with our present situation. India's 350 million people who need literacy and many more who have to acquire employable skills to suit the emerging modern India and the globe. It is essential that we enlighten and create widespread awareness of Education among all sections of society particularly in rural areas and among urban poor. We should use our technology for this important social purpose, mobilize resources and allocate them properly for full literacy and quality education and for this, not only the government (central and state) but the corporate sector, NGOs and other social institutions etc. have to come forward for creation of awareness, mobilization of resources and overall development of educational facilities having formal and informal, technical and non-technical, professional and quantitative and qualitative aspects. In creating awareness among the masses, media has also an important role to play.

They have good results. Expenditure on education has increased multiple times, number of schools, colleges and universities and other institutions—the literacy ratio has risen 18.3 per cent in 1951 to 64.8 per cent in 2001 (Economic survey 2005-06. Nevertheless, India continues to lag behind several other developing countries in the region such as China (86 %) and Sri Lanka (92 %) there are inter-regional and intra-regional disparities in the country itself. Likewise the enrolment ratio has gone up progressively from 32.1 in 1950-51 to 84.91 in 2003-04 but the dropout ratio, even after a declining trend, still continues to be higher being 31.4 per cent at the primary level (Class 1 for). Several Schemes/programmes for universal and quality education are in operation and we have high hopes from them in near future but still there are some problems which must be diagnosed properly and cured so that we can have the better result.

Education Policy and Programmes in India

Government is firmly committed to providing education for all, the priority areas being free and compulsory elementary education, covering children with special needs, eradication of illiteracy, eradication of woman's inequality and special focus on education of SC/ST and minorities. In relation to elementary education, the (NPE) National Policy on Education, 1986 as modified in 1992 emphasizes three aspects:

1. Universal access and enrolment.
2. Universal retention of children upto 14 years of age.
3. A substantial improvement in the quality of education to enable all children to achieve essential levels of learning.

The NPE had set a goal of expenditure on education of 6 per cent of GDP and the National Literacy Mission launched in 1988 has set the objective to attain a sustainable threshold literacy rate of 75 per cent by 2007.

There are various programme of elementary and primary education sponsored by the central government include Sarva Shiksha Abhiyan (SSA) main goal is all children in school, education guarantee center, alternative school relation by 2010.

National Programme for Education of girls at elementary level (NPE, GEL) Rs. 1064.50 crore has been earmarked for special programme of NPE GEL. Education Guarantee Scheme and Alternative Innovative Education (EGS/AIE). EGS/IJE is designed for specially provide access to elementary education to children out of school children.

Mid-day Meal Scheme. This scheme is provisional Rs. 3345.26 crore for current year 2005-06.

Prarambhik Shiksha Kosh (PSK). PSK is a separate dedicated, non-lapsable fund to be maintained by the ministry of Human Resource Department.

Kasturba Gandhi Balika Vidyalaya (KGBV). This programme launched for specially backward area girls.

National Literacy Mission (NLM) with its Total Literacy Campaign (TLC) is involved in raising the level of literacy through adult education and at the level of secondary and higher education which is highly subsidised by the centre and state governments, several schemes are going on having emphasis on vocational/ professional/technical and equality education. A Constitution Amendment Bill has also been passed by the Parliament in December 2005 enabling the state to make special provisions, by law for admission of students belonging to SC, ST and socially and economically backward classes to educational institutions including aided and unaided private educational institution except minority institution referred to in Article 30(i) of the Constitution.

Sarva Shiksha Abhiyan (SSA) implemented in partnership with the states, addresses the needs of 209 million children in the age group of 6-14 years. It covers 9.72 lakh existing primary and upper primary school and 36.95 lakh teachers. By 2011, the government hopes that its efforts with the Sarva Shiksha Abhiyan (SSA) with ensure that all children between the age of 6 to 14 years will be in the school.

National Programme for Education of Girls and Elementary Level (NPEGEL) and Education Guarantee Scheme and Alternative and Innovative Education (EGS/AIE) are the important component of SSA. NPEGEL provides additional support by way of girl child friendly schools, stationary, uniforms etc. for girls education in Educationally Backward Blocks (EBB) and other area for elementary education of under privileged and disadvantage sections, whereas EGS and AIE is specially designed to provide access to elementary education of children.

The centrally sponsored Mid-Day Meal Scheme which was revised and universalised in September 2004 makes a provision for providing cooked meals to child studying in Government. Government aided and Local Body schools and EGS and APE centres. Besides providing foodgrains free of cost to the State/UTs and foodgrains transportation subsidy, the Central Government provides assistance for converting foodgrains into cooked meal at a rate of Re. 1 per child per day. The KGBV programmes was launched in August 2004 to set up 750 residential schools at elementary level for girls belonging predominantly to the SC, ST, OBC and minorities in EBBS. The National Literacy Mission (NLM) was launched on May 5, 1998 as a technology mission to impart functional literacy to non-literates in the country in the age group of 15-35 years in a time bound manner. This age group has been the focus of attention because they are in the productive and reproductive period of life. The NPE, 1986 are modified in 1992, recognises the NLM as one of the three instruments to eradicate illiteracy from the country.

The Total Literacy Campaign (TLC) has been the principal strategy of NLM and at present, 137 districts are implementing TLC. 165 districts post literacy programmes and 295 districts continuing education programme. At the higher education level, our policy and programmes are putting emphasis on qualitative education with a favour towards technical vocational and competitive education. Professional courses are gaining prominence. In the current economic scenario, students have to be exposed and taught skills, which leads to vocationalising of education. If higher education is to remain competent, meet emerging challenges and serve the needs of the nation, it has necessarily to undergo a major revolution.

Expenditure and Achievement on Education

The total expenditure on education by Central and State Governments was 3.9 per cent of GDP in 2004-05 Central Plan Allocation for education was increased from Rs. 8,225 crore in 2004-05 to Rs. 15,244 crore in 2005-06 with Rs. 12,242 crore for elementary education, Rs. 290 crore for adult education and Rs. 2712 crore for secondary and higher education (Economic Survey, 2005-06).

Allocation for elementary education in the Tenth Five Year Plan period (2002-07) at Rs. 28750 crore is 75 per cent higher than the allocation in the Ninth Plan. Resources for elementary education have been augmented through imposition of the education at the rate of 2 per cent on direct or indirect central taxes imposed through finance (hoz) Act, 2004 with the imposition of education, budget outlay for elementary and adult education more than doubled from Rs. 6000 crore in 2004-05 to Rs. 12,532 crore in 2005-06.

As a result of efforts and schemes, during the plan period, the literacy ratio has increased 18.33 per cent in 1951 to 64.84 per cent in 2001 (Table 31.1) with the states like Kerala having 90.86 per cent literacy. Mizoram 88.80 per cent and Goa 82.01 per cent and the state like Bihar it is only 47 per cent. Literacy which is much lower than the national average.

The Gross Enrolment Ratio (GER) at Classes I to VIII has increased significantly from 32 per cent in 1950-51 to 80.91 per cent in 2003-04 primary education, from standard I to V age-group has gone up to 98.31 per cent in 2003-04 (Table 31.2) and the states like Goa, Gujarat, Arunachal Pradesh, Chhattisgarh, Himachal Pradesh, Karnataka, M.P., Maharashtra, Manipur and Mizoram have crossed the 100 per cent figure, though the states like Bihar, Punjab and Haryana are still hangging with 72.57 per cent, 73.45 per cent and 75.25 per cent respectively.

Table 31.1: State-wise Literacy Rates (1951-2001)

S.No.	*State/Union*	*1951*	*1961*	*1971*	*1981*	*1991*	*2001*
1.	Jammu & Kashmir	–	12.95	21.71	30.64	NA	55.52
2.	Himachal Pradesh	–	–	–	–	63.86	76.48
3.	Punjab	–	NA	34.12	43.37	58.51	69.65
4.	Chandigarh	–	NA	70.43	74.80	77.81	81.94
5.	Uttaranchal	18.93	18.05	33.26	46.6	57.75	71.62
6.	Haryana	–	–	25.71	37.13	55.85	67.91
7.	Delhi	NA	61.95	65.08	71.91	75.29	81.67
8.	Rajasthan	8.5	18.12	22.57	30.11	38.5	60.41
9.	Uttar Pradesh	12.02	20.87	23.09	32.65	40.71	56.27
10.	Bihar	13.49	21.95	23.17	32.32	37.49	47.00
11.	Sikkim	–	–	17.74	34.05	56.94	68.81
12.	Arunachal Pradesh	NA	7.13	11.29	25.55	41.59	54.34
13.	Nagaland	10.52	21.95	33.78	50.28	61.65	66.59
14.	Manipur	12.57	36.04	38.47	49.66	59.89	70.53
15.	Mizoram	31.14	44.01	53.80	59.88	82.26	88.80
16.	Tripura	NA	20.24	30.98	50.1	66.44	73.19
17.	Meghalaya	NA	26.92	29.49	42.5	49.1	62.56
18.	Assam	18.53	32.95	33.94	–	52.89	63.25
19.	West Bengal	24.61	34.46	38.86	48.65	57.70	68.64
20.	Jharkhand	12.93	21.14	23.87	35.03	41.39	53.56
21.	Orissa	15.80	21.66	26.18	33.62	39.09	63.08

(Contd.)

S.No.	State/Union	1951	1961	1971	1981	1991	2001
22.	Chhattisgarh	9.41	18.14	24.08	32.63	42.91	64.66
23.	Madhya Pradesh	13.16	21.41	27.27	38.63	44.67	63.74
24.	Gujarat	21.82	31.47	36.95	44.92	61.29	69.14
25.	Daman & Diu	–	–	–	–	71.20	78.18
26.	Dadra & Nagar Haveli	–	–	18.13	32.90	40.71	57.63
27.	Maharashtra	27.91	35.08	45.77	57.24	64.87	76.88
28.	Andhra Pradesh	–	21.19	24.57	35.66	44.08	60.47
29.	Karnataka	–	29.80	36.83	46.21	56.04	66.04
30.	Goa	23.48	35.41	51.96	65.71	75.51	82.01
31.	Lakshadweep	15.23	27.15	51.76	68.42	81.78	86.66
32.	Kerala	47.18	55.08	69.75	78.85	79.81	90.86
33.	Tamil Nadu	–	36.39	45.40	54.39	62.66	73.45
34.	Pondicherry	9	43.65	53.38	65.14	74.74	81.24
35.	Andaman & Nicobar Islands	30.30	40.07	51.15	63.19	73.02	81.30
	All India	18.33	28.30	34.45	43.57	52.41	64.84

Source: Quoted in *Economic Survey*, Government of India, 2005-06, S. 114.

Table 31.2: Gross Enrolment Ratio in Classes I-V, VI-VIII and I-VIII (2003-04)

S. No.	States/UTs	Classes I-V (6-11 Years)			Classes VI-VIII (11-14 Years)			Classes I-VIII (6-14 Years)		
		Boys	Girls	Total	Boys	Girls	Total	Boys	Girls	Total
1.	Andhra Pradesh	87.42	88.03	87.72	67.10	62.49	64.86	79.80	78.58	79.20
2.	Arunachal Pradesh	115.35	103.47	109.56	67.99	59.06	63.60	98.68	87.64	93.29
3.	Assam	88.22	88.09	88.16	66.02	61.15	63.65	80.10	78.32	79.23
4.	Bihar	80.20	64.20	72.57	30.64	19.21	25.33	62.37	48.5	55.82
5.	Chhattisgarh	123.69	122.86	123.29	78.51	62.21	70.52	106.99	99.97	103.58
6.	Goa	100.30	95.50	97.96	104.77	97.55	101.23	102.07	96.31	99.26
7.	Gujarat	117.67	108.62	113.41	81.88	57.40	70.40	104.19	89.38	97.23
8.	Haryana	73.53	77.31	75.25	68.24	62.40	65.51	71.53	71.49	71.51
9.	Himachal Pradesh	106.10	106.88	106.47	99.91	96.49	98.24	103.62	101.61	103.13
10.	J & K	87.47	76.42	82.10	65.20	52.95	59.28	78.77	67.31	73.21
11.	Jharkhand	46.10	71.10	79.09	42.47	32.19	37.54	70.51	57.15	64.04
12.	Karnataka	110.53	107.23	108.91	78.95	73.32	76.2	97.95	93.76	95.89
13.	Kerala	97.25	96.59	96.92	95.69	91.49	93.64	96.61	94.51	95.58
14.	Madhya Pradesh	112.11	110.68	106.59	71.78	53.88	63.30	96.89	83.43	90.44
15.	Maharashtra	108.32	16.84	107.60	89.41	85.52	87.55	100.71	98.31	99.56
16.	Manipur	139.30	135.64	137.51	86.95	81.57	84.33	118.85	114.60	116.77
17.	Meghalaya	104.19	106.88	105.51	60.27	62.02	61.14	88.01	90.34	89.16
18.	Mizoram	122.54	117.71	120.17	77.25	76.70	76.98	105.10	101.86	103.51
19.	Nagaland	80.95	79.97	80.48	43.56	45.85	44.66	66.11	66.50	66.30
20.	Orissa	114.23	107.44	110.91	58.13	49.69	54.01	93.28	85.86	89.65
21.	Punjab	71.04	76.38	73.45	59.31	60.93	60.06	66.52	70.25	68.22
22	Rajasthan	120.18	109.41	115.07	74.30	47.22	61.54	103.65	87.19	95.87
23.	Sikkim	116.54	116.48	116.51	52.02	61.63	56.75	90.63	94.77	92.68
24.	Tamil Nadu	117.47	115.49	116.51	102.28	98.44	100.41	111.57	108.88	110.26
25.	Tripura	125.73	119.68	112.76	75.34	70.23	72.84	105.01	99.41	102.27
26.	Uttar Pradesh	96.69	92.58	94.74	53.61	42.97	48.68	81.09	74.86	78.16

(Contd.)

S. No.	States/UTs	Classes I-V (6-11 Years)			Classes VI-VIII (11-14 Years)			Classes I-VIII (6-14 years)		
		Boys	Girls	Total	Boys	Girls	Total	Boys	Girls	Total
27.	Uttaranchal	106.10	107.66	106.85	81.08	79.59	80.36	96.57	96.88	96.72
28.	West Bengal	1107.45	107.21	107.33	65.90	62.57	64.28	91.57	900.20	90.90
29.	A&N Islands	118.78	113.23	116.05	100.13	91.41	95.85	111.27	104.47	107.92
30.	Chandigarh	72.00	70.77	71.44	69.19	69.85	69.510	70.95	70.42	70.71
31.	D&N Haveli	133.92	117.88	126.06	95.75	66.08	81.64	120.14	99.86	110.30
32.	Daman & Diu	111.66	111.01	111.35	100.85	94.11	97.62	107.76	104.81	106.36
33.	Delhi	90.34	89.87	90.10	84.83	85.91	85.34	88.26	88.33	88.30
34.	Lakshadweep	111.65	100.93	106.37	104.04	89.77	97.09	108.51	96.38	102.56
35.	Pondicherry	121.94	118.72	120.37	121.89	117.37	119.68	121.92	118.18	120.09
	India	100.75	95.67	98.31	66.87	57.69	62.49	88.02	81.51	84.91

Source: *Selected Educational Statistics*, 2003-04, Ministry of Human Resource Development, Government of India.

The Table 31.3 show that the number of educational institutions have also gone up several times. In the year 2003-04, the number of primary/junior basic school at 710,471 and that of middle/senior basic schools at 2,62,649. High school/Higher secondary/ Intermediates and Junior college 46,796 for general education 9427 and professional education 1068 but even after this numerous growth, we find the number very limited in a vast country like ours.

The primary level education is generally being provided by the government schools having about 95 per cent share in the number of primary level educational institutions but most of these government primary schools lack basic infrastructural facilities and not only the quality teachers but also the required number of teachers. Despite the rising rate of literacy, the quality of primary education is so poor that the children, even after going through four to five years of schooling of the primary classes eventually join the rank of illiterate.

Secondary and higher education is concerned, there has been an impressive growth in the area of higher education with an increase in annual student enrolment from 7.26 million in 1997-98 to 9.95 million in 2003-04. Enrolment of woman students rose from 2.45 million in 1997-98 to 4.03 million in 2004-05, constituting 40.22 per cent of the total enrolment. But as per NSSO survey (55th round, 1999-00) there are inequalities in enrolment in higher education a cross various social groups in rural and urban areas

Table 31.3: Total Number of Recognized Educational Institutions in India 2003-04 (Provisional)

S. No.	State/UTs	Primary/ Junior Basic School	Middle/ Senior Basic School	High Sch/Hr. Sec./ Intermediate Education Research	Universities/College for Professional Deemed Univ.		
					General Education	Education Research Instt.	Instt. of National Importance
1.	Andhra Pradesh	63897	15215	3267	1330	238	28
2.	Arunachal Pradesh	1364	449	74	10	1	4
3.	Assam	30068	8143	731	317	3	7
4.	Bihar	40337	9922	685	743	7	23
5.	Chhattisgarh	32556	9350	1439	213	2	9
6.	Goa	1009	79	80	24	4	1
7.	Gujarat	7233	30646	2427	422	32	28
8.	Haryana	11500	2171	1776	163	41	7
9.	Himachal Pradesh	11013	2076	820	69	2	7
10.	Jammu & Kashmir	10488	3976	380	73	4	5
11.	Jharkhand	16417	4324	122	146	5	7
12.	Karnataka	26163	25612	2237	930	120	20
13.	Kerala	6717	2975	1286	186	66	10
14.	Madhya Pradesh	66592	30592	4211	513	56	17
15.	Maharashtra	41258	26033	4212	1208	177	54
16.	Manipur	2552	832	112	58	1	2
17.	Meghalaya	5851	1559	80	48	0	1
18.	Mizoram	1504	908	71	6	0	1
19.	Nagaland	1495	480	52	36	0	1
20.	Orissa	42104	11510	744	567	19	9
21.	Punjab	13265	2493	1695	29	16	8
22.	Rajasthan	55757	23942	3159	456	39	15
23.	Sikkim	497	126	41	2	1	2
24.	Tamil Nadu	32242	6825	4136	441	96	28
25.	Tripura	2075	453	242	14	1	1
26.	Uttar Pradesh	119404	35427	7369	433	69	40
27.	Uttaranchal	14304	3557	1071	47	2	7
28.	West Bengal	49865	1984	2868	354	43	28
29.	A & N Islands	209	56	49	2	0	0
30.	Chandigarh	24	9	52	12	2	2
31.	D & N Haveli	127	91	9	0	0	0
32.	Daman & Diu	53	24	6	1	0	0
33.	Delhi	2126	681	1212	63	16	16
34.	Lakshadweep	20	4	4	0	0	0
35.	Pondicherry	329	125	77	11	5	1
	India	710471	262649	49796	9427	1068	389

Note: Professional Education, includes Engineering, Technology and Architecture, Medical and Teacher Training Colleges.

Source: *Selected Educational Statistics 2003-04*, Ministry of Human Resource Development.

and also in terms of gender. Women belonging to SC and ST and those living in rural areas are the most disadvantaged. However, a Constitution Amendment Bill has been passed by the Parliament in December 2005, which enables the state to make special provisions, by law for admission of student belonging to SC, ST and socially and educationally backward classes to educational institution except minority insitution referred to in Article 30(1) of the Constitution. But only enactment may not solve the problem. It require general awareness, Government, support people's cooperation further all over the world higher education is in university institution having big campus with a critical mass of students and staff strength and can large libraries, modern laboratories and advance centers with adequate infrastructure, whereas in India a vast proportion of the entire higher education takes place only in the ill-equipped, understaffed, affiliated college as can be seen from the fact that 89 per cent of undergraduate students, 66 per cent of postgraduate students and 82 per cent of faculty are in the affiliated college.

The total numbers of universities/deemed universities institutes of national importance, research institutes, etc. stood at 389 in the year 2003-04 (Table 31.3). This number is very small for the size of India comparison with other countries like Japan, U.S. etc.

Conclusion

It appears from the above discussion that education the engine of growth is in a poor condition in the country both quantitatively and qualitatively. Whether it is at the elementary level or at the secondary or higher level. 35 per cent of our adult population are yet to achieve literacy. The expenditure on education is still much below the accepted international standards near about 4 per cent GDP as against the accepted and declared goal of 6 to 7 per cent of GDP which is required for 100 per cent literacy. The quality of education is so poor especially in government school and rural areas that even at distant places with higher fee structure. The delivery of quality education is possible only through quality teachers. The teacher has to be committed teacher who have teaching and children. And also the teacher has to be equipped with all the knowledge required for effective teaching. Some element of competition rewarding is to be done based on performance. This competency has to be built up through out the country through a massive teachers education programme delivered through a tale-education system and continuously updated. This can be funded and implemented by a consortium of government, educational institutions with the corporate sectors providing value added services there is also un urgent need that every school should have basic amenities, such a good building equipped with ventilated, light, air and spacious classroom beside library, laboratories, including the latest tools and infrastructure, safe drinking water, clear toilets and playground. This is possible by making additional investment in education and increasing expenditure upto 6-7 per cent of GDP in this field.

The funds allocated for education and channelized through different schemes and agencies must be utilized properly, leakage of funds must be restricted strictly and last but not the least we can suggest that not only the government, but the corporate sector, NGOs the philanthropists and others capable to do so should come forward on a massive scale for the development of education. So far as the management of schools in the rural area is concerned, a system of local community control and monitoring of school education may be explored through constitution of a village education council, wherever the village community is cohesive and enlightened leadership exists. Such Village Education Council (VEC) should be a non-political, NGO like body, possibly free from politics. Eventually the VES may be interested with the upkeep and development of the school infrastructures.

It may also be suggested that on experimental basis, wherever possible, the management of school and colleges may be handed over to reputed NGO's established educational agencies, industries and such other bodies. These schools, however, would be aided schools but managed privately. The tuition fees if any shall be compensated through scholarship. It may also be suggested that providing teachers with learning materials and encouraging parents to get more involved in the schooling of their children are more effective than a school feeding programme in reducing drop-out rates and increasing learning.

REFERENCES

1. Government of India (Planning Commission), *Economic Survey*, 2005-06.

2. Govinda, R. (2005), Elementary Education, Progress and Challenges, *Yojna*.
3. Kulandaiswamy V.C. (2005) Reconstruction of Higher Education, *Yojna*.
4. A.O. Hirschman (1969), *"The Strategy of Economic Development"*.
5. T.W. Schultz, *"The Role of Government in Promoting Economic Development."*
6. Shastree, Nalin K. (2004), *"Privatizing Higher Education Global Challenges and National Responses"*, University New.
7. Jandhayala, B.G. Tilak (2004), "Public Subsidies to Education in India", *Economic and Political Weekly*, January 24.
8. Guhan, S. (1995), "Social Expenditure in the Union Budget", *Economic and Political Weekly*.
9. Mehta, P.L. & R. Poonga (1999), *"Free and Compulsory Education"*, Deep and Deep Publication, New Delhi.
10. Natarajan, S. (1999), *"Introduction to Economic of Education"*, Sterling Publishers Pvt. Ltd., New Delhi.

32

A Case for Great Books in Management Education

ANUJ AGRAWAL

Introduction

In our "electronic age" it is hard to image life or the academic enterprise without books. In a few colleges a select group of "great books" are so highly regarded that the entire curriculum is built around reading and understanding the ideas contained within them. Some people devoted to this great books tradition equate education with mastery of these works because, according to them, they require us to deal with humanity's greatest questions—the existence of God, the nature of love, the possibility of immortality, the achievement of freedom. Advocate of great books believed it is better to read selectively and wisely than extensively and widely. Business schools, as a general rule, do not attach such importance to great books or to what might be "great books in the making."

Best sellers in management are rarely written by management professors. That distinction goes to consultants, journalists, business executives and coaches. The paradox is that much, if not most, of the conventional wisdom of a discipline is chronicled in the books written by its academic masters. And research has shown that mastery of a discipline is an essential foundation for expanding the frontiers of knowledge. A study of 70 European composers, for example, found that "no composer created a great work without having dedicated at least 10 years to mastering the craft". Similarly, Edmund Learned (1993) related a story of how Dean Donham of the Harvard Business School told him, immediately upon completion of his doctorate, that he should "do research in his field for 15 to 25 years and then write one of the field's great books." Is it likely that present and future intellectual pioneers of management will push back the knowledge frontiers without first mastering the wisdom of the discipline?

The Case for Great Books

The study of great books in the field of management education is an integral part of study. Undergraduate and master's students would also learn much from studying classic management works, but the case is less compelling. In making this argument, I will avoid the elitist position that management scholars are not truly "educated" unless they master the great books of the field. Such a contention would not serve the argument well since many of today's outstanding management scholars have probably read relatively few of the generally agreed on "great books" of management.

What Makes a Management Book Great?

My review of the writings on great books revealed many reasons why books have been labelled as "great". These include the potential of a few books to preserve and transmit the traditions of a discipline, the ability of great books to focus our thinking but not dominate it, the capacity of a few great books to teach us something new regardless of how many times we read them, and so on. The long list of what makes a book great, however, can be summarized under four general headings:

- Great books are central to the development of a discipline;
- Great books continue to be relevant to today's issues;
- Great books allow us to locate our own time in the discipline's evolution; and
- Great books allow broad access to some of the great minds of the field.

In the discussion that follows, I examine these reasons using illustrations from a few generally agreed on great books and assessments by recognized contributors to the field of management.

Great Books are Central to the Development of the Discipline

Science is not so much the accumulation of knowledge as it is conversation. If science is conversation, books are major voices that tell the story of a discipline.

If Science is Conversation, Books are Major Voices that Tell the Story of a Discipline

To be central to a discipline books must represent integral parts of that discipline's story and convey the spirit and substance of the field. Thus, a book may be central to the development of a discipline by documenting the importance of the field in improving the human condition, by establishing a methodological orientation for knowledge development or for a variety of other reasons. Thompson's work (1967) represents an important counterpoint in the evolution of modern management and organization theory. By illustrating the importance of contingencies, incorporating uncertainty, acknowledging complexity, and recognizing the interdependence of organizations and their environments, he rejects the radical absolutism of scientific management and the one best way. At the same time he puts forth his view of *patterned variations* and illustrates that no useful theory can rest on the assumption that every decision and management challenge is unique—radical situationalism. This emphasis on patterned variations was instrumental in elevating management to a more mature discipline not bound by the necessity of absolutism or unrestrained by relativism.

Thompson stated that he wrote *Organizations in Action* to call attention to developments that tend to go unnoticed when we stay within the boundaries of a single discipline. His goal was to "link at important points several now independent approaches to understanding of complex organizations". This came at an extremely opportune time when increasing numbers of behavioral scientists were migrating to business schools and applying their research methods to problems of industry. Larry L. Cummings (1992) indicated, for example, how Thompson influenced his intellectual development.

Great Books Continue to be Relevant to Today's Management Issues

Management fads, fashions, and facades waste executive time and organizational resources. It has been shown, for example, that although management fads and fashions are nothing new, more recent ones have shorter life cycles than earlier ones, require substantially more effort to implement, and are more quickly abandoned. These "relatively transitory collective beliefs, disseminated by the discourse of management-knowledge entrepreneurs" usually result from the need for a quick fix to a managerial problem. The fact that fads and fashions are "relatively transitory" highlights the need to understand the origins of management ideas rather than fall prey to Urwick's (1944: 40) *practical man fallacy* in which he contended that by the time executives become successful they attribute their success to personal characteristics rather than adherence to principles and theory. Thus, they come to believe that the only way to learn to be successful is through experience. Each new generation of managers reinvents for itself the principles of success when, in fact, a vast store of conventional wisdom is available and can be effectively applied to contemporary issues. Urwick believed that "most people share a weakness for quick answers and easy remedies that do not require the painful discipline of thought." Great books help us avoid this reliance on such *potted knowledge* gleaned from experience and devoid of theory.

Great Books Help us Avoid this Reliance on Such Potted Knowledge Gleaned from Experience and Devoid of Theory

It is probably accurate to say that few topics have been discussed more and systematically researched less than informal communication networks in organizations. Virtually every business trade magazine has something to say about the grapevine. Although the subject is of interest to office managers and factory supervisors, prescriptions are rarely based on rigorous research or sound theory. Yet, there is a long tradition of management research on the grapevine that can be traced directly to classic management books. Keith Davis (1992) indicates that his interest in the grapevine was stimulated by experiences at the Hughes Tool

Company before he entered academics. While he was a manager, he tried to learn as much about it as possible. However, when he accepted his first faculty position he was "introduced" to Roethlisberger and Dickson's *Management and the Worker* (1939) and Mayo's *Social Problems of an Industrial Society* (1945) and discovered that social scientists also were interested in informal communication in organizations. The "ideas in these books seemed so impressive that even today. Davis' *Harvard Business Review* (1953) article on the grapevine, for example, was reprinted in books of readings more than 3 decades after its publication. Many topics in management have "come and gone" during this period but a number of organizational challenges reported in classic books remain as relevant as ever.

Great Books Assist in Locating Our Time in the Evolution of the Discipline

Managers often do absolutely stupid things that they do not have to do and would not have done if they only understood more about the whole historical sequence. Managers make decisions and researchers conduct research within a context provided by history even if the historical context is not consciously recognized. Managers and researchers think in *time streams* that assist in determining whether or not current events are part of a continuous trend or represent discontinuities. If books are the voices that tell the story of management, no one tells the story better than Chandler (1977). Although best known in management for *Strategy and Structure* (1962), Chandler's *Visible Hand* is an important part of the saga of management field because it traces the emergence of management as a modern institution. Chandler contends that the first modern business administrators were managers of railroads because the administrative tasks of the railroad were too varied and complex to be handled by a single family member or entrepreneur. Managers of railroads argued for the development of policies, procedures and principles and they were among the first to appreciate the importance of delegation of authority, supervisor—subordinate relations, and control systems. Chandler skillfully traced the demise of Adam Smith's invisible hand and the emergence of the visible hand of modern management. Just as Chandler provided a context within which we can observe the emergence of modern management, a similar point of departure for contemporary behavioral research in organizations is provided by classic books by Douglas McGregor (1960) and Victor Vroom (1964). The intellectual debt owed to McGregor is acknowledged by Golembiewski (1992), Schein (1993), and Strauss (1993). Porter (1993) noted that his thinking was "mightily influenced" by Vroom's (1964) "explication of an expectancy theory approach that had great applicability to our own data and ideas" (Porter, 1993: 13).

Great Books Allow Us Access to the Great Minds of Management Field

Perhaps the primary reason why history teaches us so well and prepares us for future challenges is not so much the lessons we learn but the people we meet. Reading great books of management allows us access to the great minds of our field. Herbert A. Simon, in addition to winning the Nobel Prize for economics, wrote or co-authored two classic books on management (March & Simon, 1958; Sherwood, 1990; Simon, 1946). His focus on decision making provided us a new way to view human beings as problem solvers. Simon's analysis of human problem solving and decision making has been instrumental in the modern concept of the executive as an individual forced to satisfy the demands of multiple stakeholders, deal with uncertainty and ambiguity, and make choices with less-than-complete information. Moreover, the intellectual climate created by the entire "Carnegie School" greatly influenced the evolution of management thought. Victor Vroom (1993: 266-267) indicated that the promise of this intellectual climate at Carnegie Mellon is what attracted him to the faculty. Everyone interested in management can be exposed to these great minds through their books. In a similar manner all the great books of management are available to us and provide unique access to the great thinkers in our field. It has been my contention that prospective scholars of management can benefit from reading and mastering the great books of the field because they are central to the development of our discipline, continue to be relevant to today's management issues, assist us in locating ourselves in the evolution of the discipline, and allow us the only access we have to many of the great minds of our field. However, there are challenges that must be addressed—if not overcome—if we are to effectively utilize the great books of management for purposes of instruction. One of the most important questions is how to organize the content of great books of management and present them to students in a way that will obtain maximum synergy. In concluding here, I discuss an approach I have found useful around the great books of management.

A Model for Integrating the Great Books into Management Education

To imagine that management students would read at least a large sample of the great books of management during their collegiate experience would be encouraging. In reality, this is at best a pipe dream, because time is limited in management programmes and many competencies must be developed to prepare young scholars to be successful in their chosen careers. Admittedly, mastering the great books of management is not a critical determinant of academic success in management. However his mastery, in association with other competencies could greatly influence the quality and direction of management research. Perhaps more important, it could add to the quality of management instruction because management concepts would be presented accurately in their historical context. Recognizing the reality of constraints in management education, I offer below a pedagogical approach have used for more than a decade management education. The purpose is to analyze, familiarize, and summarize the essential lessons taught in the great books of management and expose management students—to the extent possible—to the content of the classic works in the field. The administrative theory was added to management curriculum because of a recurring problem that faculty noted during the comprehensive examinations: Students seemed to respond reasonably well to questions asked on the examinations, but when reference was made to historical topics, they were often baffled and unfamiliar with concepts that seemed essential to an understanding of the context of management. Frequently their understanding of historical issues was simply inaccurate. As a faculty, we decided to alter the content of the programme to include an overview of management history. I was assigned responsibility for the course and used several moderately successful approaches until we decided to focus on the great books of management.

Conclusions

In the above I have attempted to make a case for the inclusion of great books in management education. An understanding of these works provides prospective scholars with an appreciation of the ideas that are central to the development of the discipline, allows today's students to understand the origins of management's concern with the important contemporary issues, assists us in locating our present time in the ongoing evolution of our field, and helps us obtain access to some of the greatest minds of management theory and research. On a pragmatic level, we as management educators must grapple with one of the most important questions facing management education: how to provide prospective scholars with the intellectual history of the field while ensuring they obtain all the competencies necessary for a successful research and teaching career. Although unfortunate, in my opinion it is unlikely that most management students will read the great books of management. A pedagogy such as the one proposed here can be effective in filling that gap by requiring students to read a few classic books and providing a model for summarizing the content of the larger collection.

REFERENCES

Abrahamson, E. (1996), Management Fashion, *Academy of Management Review*, 21: 250-60.

Abrahamson, E. and Fairchild, G. (1999), Management Fashion: Lifecycles, Triggers, and Collective Learning Processes, *Administrative Science Quarterly*, 44: 708-740.

Bedeian, A.G. and Wren, D.A. (2001), Most Influential Management Books of the 20th Century, *Organizational Dynamics*, 29(3): 221-25.

Berube, M. (1997), Great Books and Good Intentions, *Dissent*, 44:107-12.

Carson, P.P.; Lanier, P.A.; Carson, K.D. and Guidry, B.N. (2000), Clearing a Path Through the Management Fashion Jungle: Some Preliminary Trailblazing, *Academy of Management Journal*, 43: 1143-58.

Casement, W. (1995), Some Myths about the Great Books, *Midwest Quarterly*, 36: 203-09.

Chandler, A.D., Jr. (1962), *Strategy and Structure*, Cambridge, MA: MIT Press.

Chandler, A.D., Jr. (1977), *The Visible Hand: The Managerial Revolution in*

American Business, Cambridge, MA: Belnap Press of Harvard University Press.

Cummings, L.L. (1992), Calling, Disciplines, and Attempts at Listening. In A.G. Bedeian (Ed.), *Management Laureates: A Collection of Autobiographical Essays* 1: 239-266.

Greenwich, CN: JAI Press, Cyert, R.M. and March, J.G. (1963), *A Behavioral Theory of the Firm*, Englewood Cliffs, NJ: Prentice-Hall.

Czarniawska, B. (1997), *Narrating the Organization: Dramas of Institutional Identity*, Chicago: University of Chicago Press.

Davis, K. (1953), Management Communication and the Grapevine, *Harvard Business Review*, 31(5): 43-49.

Davis, K. (1992), A Journey Through Management in Transition. In A.G. Bedeian (Ed.), *Management Laureates: A Collection of Autobiographical Essays*, (Vol. 1): 269-300, Greenwich, CN:JAI Press.

Denby, D. (1997), *Great Books: My Adventures with Homer, Rousseau, Wolf and Other Indestructible Writers of the Western World*, New York: Simon & Schuster.

Ford, E.W.; Duncan, W.J.; Bedeian, A.G.; Ginter, P.M.; Rousculp, M.D. and Adams, A.M. 2003, Mitigating Risks, Visible Hands, Inevitable Disasters and Soft Variables: Management Research that Matters to Managers, *Academy of Management Executive*, 17(1): 46-60.

Furchgott, R. (1997), Read Any Great Books Lately? *Business Week* (October 13) :30-31.

Golembiewski, R.T. (1992), Mid-career Perspectives, In A.G. 2004, *Duncan* 427.

Bedeian (Ed.), *Management Laureates: A Collection of Autobiographical Essays* 1: 373-416, Greenwich, CN: JAI Press.

Hafner, A.W. (1992), In defense of the great books, *Education Digest*, 57: 70-71.

Hartley, J.E. (2001), The Great Books and Economics, *Journal of Economic Education*, 12: 147-59.

Howe, M. (1988), Perspiration Bests Inspiration, *New Scientist*, 31 (December 24): 32-36.

Kantrow, A.M. (1986), Why History Matters, *Harvard Business Review*, 64(1): 81-88.

Learned, E.P. (1993), Reflections on Leadership, Teaching and Problem Solving Groups. In A.G. Bedeian (Ed.), *Management Laureates: A Collection of Autobiographical Essays* (Vol. 2): 151-175. Greenwich, CN: JAI Press, March, J.G. & Simon, H.A. 1958, *Organizations*, New York: Wiley.

Matteson, M.T. (1974), Some Reported Thoughts on Significant Management Literature, *Academy of Management Journal*, 17: 386-89.

Mayo, G.E. (1945), *The Social Problems of an Industrial Society*, Boston, MA. Graduate School of Business Administration, Harvard University.

McGregor, D.M. (1960), *The Human Side of Enterprise*, New York: McGraw-Hill.

Micklethwait, J. and Wooldridge, A. (1996), *The Witch Doctors: Making Sense of the Management Gurus*, New York: Times Business.

Miller, T.R. and Vaughn, B.J. (2001), Messages from the Management Past: Classic Writers and Contemporary Problems. *SAM Advanced Management Journal*, 66(1): 4-11.

Neustadt, R.E. and May, E.R. (1986), *Thinking in Time: The Uses of History for Decision Makers*, New York: Free Press.

Nord, W.R. (2003), Augmenting the Role Books Play in Organization Management Studies, *Academy of Management Review*, 28: 154-55.

Patzig, W.D. and Wisdom, B.L. (1988), Some Words of Caution About Having Students Read the Classics. In Dennis F. Ray, (Ed.), *Proceedings of the Southern Management Association*, 25th Anniversary Ed.

Pfeffer, J. and Fong, C.T. (2002), The End of Business Schools? Less Success than Meets the Eye, *Academy of Management Learning and Education*, 1: 78-95.

Porter, L.W. (1993), An Unmanaged Pursuit of Management. In A.G. Bedeian (Ed.), *Management Laureates: A Collection of Autobiographical Essays* (Vol. 3): 1-30, Greenwich, CN: JAI Press.

Roethlisberger, F.J. and Dickson, W.J. (1939), *Management and the Worker*, Cambridge, MA: Harvard University Press.

Schein, E.H., The Academic as Artist: Personal and Professional Roots. In A.G. Bedeian (Ed.), *Management Laureates: A Collection of Autobiographical Essays* 3: 31-62, Greenwich, CN: JAI Press.

Sherwood, F.P. (1990), The Half-Century's Great Books in Public Administration, *Public Administration Review*, 50(3): 249-62.

Simon, H.A. (1946), *Administrative Behaviour*, New York: Free Press.

Spell, C.S. (2001), Management Fashions: Where do They Come from and are They Old Wine in New Bottles? *Journal of Management Inquiry*, 10(4): 358-73.

Staw, B.M. and Epstein, L.D. (2000), What Bandwagons Bring? Effects of Popular Management Techniques on Corporate Performance, Reputation, and CEO pay, *Administrative Science Quarterly*, 45: 523-56.

Strâuss, G. (1993), Present at the Beginning: Some Personal Notes on OBs Early Days and Later. In A.G. Bedeian (Ed.), *Management Laureates: A Collection of Autobiographical Essays* 3: 145-90, Greenwich, CN: JAI Press.

Thompson, J.D. (1967), *Organizations in Action*, New York:McGraw-Hill.

33

Reengineering Management Education: Role of Faculty Response

VIPIN AGRAWAL

Introduction

Recent years have witnessed a variety of efforts to reengineer higher education into closer alignment with market principles and management approaches drawn from business. Such reengineering efforts often entail an intermingling of three distinctively different organizational paradigms within higher education:

- A professorial paradigm characteristic of traditional higher education organization;
- A bureaucratic machine paradigm representative of traditional business organization; and
- Innovative or "adhocratic" paradigm defended by proponents as a timely alternative to traditional bureaucratic organization.

This intermingling is often carried out in a fashion oblivious to the nuances of organizational design and with little or no attention to the conflicts likely to result. The increasing stakeholder pressure exerted on the institutions of higher education has elevated the relative importance of teaching as a central school activity in the eyes of institutions' constituents as well as the society as a whole. Because they service the largest percentage of university students, business schools are expected to develop competence that yields learning outcomes that can be documented in terms of how and what they add to students' cognitive, practical, and creative bases of knowledge during or after their educational experience.

Many business schools have embraced a number of innovative practices, such as distance education, action learning (i.e., classes built around social problems where the students act as consultants), and team teaching, which are designed to enhance student-learning experiences. This expansion of educational innovations in modern business schools has in turn imposed new pressures on the traditional faculty role and has produced new challenges to business school administrators. The purpose in this article is to examine the administrative challenges of change management in business schools, which are facing a changing and more competitive environment. The author has used the traditional faculty role content as the unit of analysis to address change management issues from a school administrator's perspective. On the basis of the administrator's commitment to the mission-based status quo versus the vision-based change, the author developed a framework to analyze possible faculty responses to the change management initiatives and offer practical recommendations for the advancement of administration in business schools.

The Changing Role of Business Schools

A business school is both the custodian and the communicator of knowledge about the business practices used in the society. Beyond storing and communicating knowledge, the business school also fosters the research process that enhances general understanding and the cognitive capacity of society. The overarching mission of the business school is to be responsible both for the continuous dissemination of new and evolving bodies of knowledge available to practitioners and for the institutionalized development of new faculty to continue the process discovering and developing knowledge (see Figure 33.1). This multifaceted role of the business school as an institution engenders contradictory administrative demands for stability and change. On the one hand, for smooth functioning of the business school as the repository and disseminator of knowledge, stability of the business school as an institution is encouraged—perhaps demanded—in the public domain. On the other hand, the business school is expected to be a

Social Creation of Knowledge	Knowledge for Understanding	Knowledge for Use
Institutionalization of Knowledge	Scientific Research	Scientific Development
Dissemination of Knowledge	General Education	Professional Education

Social Organization of Knowledge

Fig. 33.1: The Business School's Multiple Roles in the 21st Century: A Matrix Model.

creative and bold wellspring of new practices because the snare of the population serviced by the business school has grown and the complexity of the required administration has significantly increased. The juggling of stability and change in business schools is administratively challenging in the public arena where new competitive pressures and budgetary constraints are placed on the schools as institutions. This juggling is further made more palpable as faculty positions continue to go unfilled. The resulting interplay among competitive, budgetary, and understaffing factors has only exacerbated business schools' need to use their faculty resources more efficiently.

The Changing Role of Faculty in Business Schools

Institutions of higher education have historically provided their faculty with the privilege of a quiet life. An important element of a faculty member's quiet life is slack or X-inefficiency within an organization, inefficiency being captured in low levels of effort by its faculty members to reduce costs, improve quality, and introduce innovative new ways of doing things, and correspondingly high levels of leisure. The labelling of faculty as the *leisure class* had been originally articulated in 1776 by Adam Smith (1981), a century before Verblen (1899) elaborated this concept. In particular, Adam Smith (1981) depicted the leisure of faculty in the 18th century at Oxford, where "the greater part of the public professors have, in these many years, given up altogether even the pretence of teaching". In other words, like many tenured professors today, faculty of those times had monopolistic discretion in how much of their leisure time would be allocated to their various academic priorities because their status was not affected by their choice. With the onset of the 21st century, the faculty role in business schools is changing as the demand for knowledge development and use has rapidly increased and, moreover, as knowledge is created and disseminated by many sources other than business schools (i.e., corporate, private, and government research and development centers). In addition, the traditional modes of teaching are being challenged by new methods enabled by technological development and by changes in the student demographics (i.e., many of them employed, older, and with higher expectations), and the availability of resources (i.e., mostly money) for business schools has been under serious taxpayer scrutiny and resistance to additional funding (i.e., their refusals to commit to higher taxes makes future resource increases doubtful). In response, business schools have been pursuing change initiatives to match the alignment with these external developments. Over time, change initiatives may contribute to the institution's operational efficiency, but only if accompanied by the support of insiders (i.e., faculty), whose "buy-in" may ensure that the changes are lasting. Therefore, the crucial task of administrators is how to manage the changing faculty role effectively in the new competitive and resource-constrained educational environment to elicit faculty cooperation in a goal-congruent manner.

Administrative Motives for the Redefinition of Faculty Roles

One of the main incentives for administrators to use faculty role redefinition as a means to increase institutional effectiveness arises from the growing acceptance of educational performance comparisons based on the plethora of business school or college rankings. The rank-driven competition motivates administrators of business schools to channel their change initiatives toward the rating criteria that are valued by the school's primary constituents (i.e., students, employers and regulatory officials). However, the rating related measures of academic "quality" are seldom true indicators of the actual quality of education received by the average postgraduate student. In fact, because ratings of postgraduate education are crucial for the reputation and prestige of the institution, the students and their families do not know that the postgraduate learning environment is likely to be drained of limited resources to enhance the post graduate rankings. In spite of their limited validity, rankings have the most powerful impact on the actual choices that business schools' constituents make (e.g., in terms of funding, enrolment and recruiting). As administrators face the increasing constituent pressures to improve the ranking of their individual institutions, cost-effectiveness of the faculty role is becoming one of the primary targets of their initiatives because colleges and business schools are human capital intensive institutions where as much as 70 per cent of the cost is related to personnel, and, if the faculty role is differentiated (i.e., if faculty functional tasks can be discretely represented), then faculty time and effort can be more efficiently managed. From an administrative perspective, shifting the focus from an individual faculty role to the efficiency of the faculty as a whole is necessary to lower the costs of inevitable role-related dissatisfaction with increasing demands on the faculty. To implement such a shift, it is necessary for administrators to initiate the process of identifying or specifying the associated tasks or activities within each functional component that are integral components of the faculty role. A common rhetoric of administrators is that the specification of these tasks or activities is also required by accreditation agencies, whose imprimatur is eagerly sought in order to validate what the faculty is doing. Such validation in a professional programme (e.g., business administration) is often seen (either rightly or wrongly), as impressive to prospective employers and business schools. In the murky world of institutional politics and budgetary maneuvering, the validation provided by accreditation is also thought to yield a positive "edge" to the accredited programme. Therefore, the transparency of a faculty role is a part of both the internal and external business school agendas. In general, a faculty role incorporates three main functional components: (*a*) teaching, (*b*) research, and (*c*) service.

For efficient management of these components, educational administrators should consider the risks and benefits of either outsourcing or internally contracting any and each of these functions to clinical or part-time teachers, researchers, professional advisors, and administrators. The analysis of these two structural alternatives requires discrete representation (i.e., identification and specification) of function-specific tasks and activities. The tasks comprising the teaching-related activities of the faculty members' job are: (*a*) designing course and curriculum; (*b*) developing course, curriculum, methods, and materials; (*c*) mediating the learning process; (*d*) delivering the subject matter; (*e*) assessing student learning though methods, assignments, or grading; and (*f*) advising students academically. Management of these tasks or activities should be primarily analyzed from an efficiency perspective. The technology-enabled, resource intensive and competency-driven new rivals of traditional institutions are increasingly contracting discrete tasks of instructional activities. Design is contracted into committees or out to national authorities; development is contracted out to providers of educational solutions; mediation is contracted in and out to instructional or teaching professionals; delivery is contracted in and out to institutional or teaching professionals, Webmasters, and instructional technologists; and assessment is contracted in or out to competency testing or assessment centers. Also, the rivals are subcontracting research to specialized institutions and advising to advising specialists. It appears that virtually no core activities, other than contract coordination, require the crucial agency of a full-time professor in these "mean and- lean," and often virtual, entrants to the educational arena. Administrators in traditional institutions face difficulties when trying to replicate efficient solutions of new rivals because business schools are governed like governments (i.e., faculty exercise democratic control over a range of significant decisions), whereas they compete like firms (i.e., offering service for a price and competing against each other both in input and output markets). In other words, administrative discretion in decision-making is constrained by faculty participation in business school governance, which safeguards academic freedom while making the decision-making processes slow to change, cumbersome to implement, and protective of entrenched interests. Because of this inert nature of governance, any change initiative planned by administrators should be assessed in terms of the desired extent of change (i.e., commitment to the vision versus commitment to the mission of the institution). This assessment should be particularly focused on possible responses by the faculty body as a whole.

Faculty Responses to Change Initiatives

The challenge of business school administrators is how to craft, through consultations, a statement of purpose and direction of change that is inspiring to both the internal and external constituents of the institution. The crafting of the statement requires administrators to seek a balance between anchoring the change initiative either in the stable mission of the school or in the dynamic vision of its change. The dilemma of the appropriate trade-off in administrator's commitment choice should be addressed in terms of possible responses to the change initiative by the faculty as a whole (see Figure 33.2). The faculty response that is ideal for the administrator would be a support for the vision of change, which is unconstrained by the inertia or strings of the institution's mission. For support to occur, the administrator needs to exhibit transformational leadership in influencing change in faculty preferences for acceptance of the change initiative in terms of the proposed innovations, cost reductions, and the associated degree of faculty role unbundling. When the strings of the mission are pulled along with the vision (as shown in the lower right corner of Figure 33.2), the administrator has to be charismatic in influencing faculty to sacrifice their self-interest while complying with the change initiative that is to align the mission with the vision.

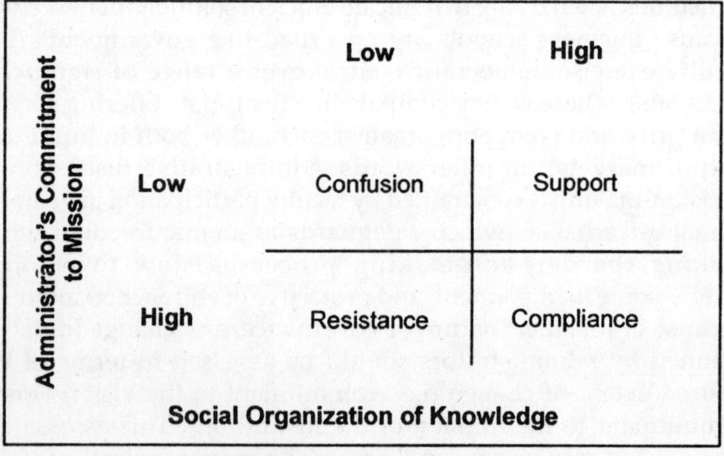

Fig. 33.2: Faculty Response to Change Initiative.

The drawback of this response is that the faculty is less likely to exhibit organizational citizenship behaviour. When the administrator is neither firmly committed to the vision of change nor to the stable reliance on the institution's mission, the administrator will commonly try to imitate the "best practice" initiative pursued by some flagship business school. The likely faculty response, confusion (see Figure 33.2), as the anarchic implementation of change initiative, will evolve in a suspended animation because of the lack of anchoring in the institution's direction and purpose. When the administrator is primarily committed to the institution's mission, a bias toward status quo will occur, as the change initiative will be likely pursued involuntarily under external pressure. The faculty will exhibit resistance (Figure 33.2) because they will have no understanding of how the change initiative contributes to the institution's goals.

Linking Faculty Development and the School Mission

A business school's goals and student learning outcomes only have meaning when they are intimately linked to the core values of the school. Accordingly, core values are used to link faculty development with the school mission. The process of linking faculty development and school mission can be broken into four phases: focus, alignment, integration and review (FAIR).

In the **focus phase**, the mission statement is converted into actionable steps. The process begins by breaking the core values inherent in the mission statement into an explicit list. This is used to generate single-focus actionable goal statements. These are the goals of the school. The goals are ranked and rated according to the current strategic intent. The ordered list of goals with associated ratings is called the "ranked and rated goals of the school." The ranked and rated goals of the school reflect the current strategic positioning of the school.

In the **alignment phase**, all resources are directed toward the attainment of the mission statement. The presumption is that the resources available can effectively implement the mission statement. The school initiates a request for proposals and provides a rubric for evaluating the proposals. This faculty proposal rubric is the key link in the chain connecting faculty development and the school's mission. Rubrics are typically used for assessing student work. Extending rubrics to faculty development provides a common lens for all business schools. The faculty proposal rubric must be based on the ranked and rated goals of the school. Therefore, each proposal is evaluated in light of the current strategic positioning of the school.

In the **integration phase**, a desired future is designed. This is the crucial link between faculty development and the business school's mission. The values embedded in the goals as rated and ranked by the present strategic intent will be meaningful to the faculty only if they are widely shared. This should provide direction and motivate faculty toward the kinds of activities most valued by the school. Here the role of the departmental mentor is crucial in helping individual faculty members determine their individual needs and in matching these to the call for proposals. It falls on the mentor to ensure that not only are the school's current needs integrated with those of individual faculty, but also that every faculty member's needs are being met from iteration to iteration. However, the individual faculty member has responsibility to generate a proposal and to link it to the school's mission through the use of the rubric. The faculty member is intimately aware of how his or her development needs are being played out against the mission of the school. The school then makes the assessment of the proposals in an open forum and allocates the resources accordingly. The open forum enables individual faculty members to witness the alignment of resources to proposals of the ranked and rated goals of the school, enabling a common vision of direction.

In the **review phase**, the process is mastered through improved iterations and disseminated best practices. First, the school evaluates the allocation plan in light of the ranked and rated goals of the school in an open forum. The transparency of the process allows all to see exemplary proposals in light of the current strategic positioning of the school as well as pitfalls in the process. To integrate this feedback into the learning cycle, the school surveys the faculty to elicit feedback from the process and from the evaluation of the allocation plan. The ultimate goal of this approach is to generate faculty support of the development and implementation of the school mission. Hence, as a final step in the review process, the school takes inventory of faculty contributions so as to assess the tool's effectiveness in eliciting faculty buy in.

Although the process is iterative, the iterations do not need to be done annually. The iterations can be carried out on any predetermined time period (e.g., annually or once every 3 years) that suits the strategic needs of the school.

Conclusion

The static, hierarchical, tradition bound business schools have been reluctant to improve their operating productivity, to adapt to the needs of their students, or to predict what employers expect their students to know. Most of all, business schools have not found a formal way to motivate faculty members to accept initiatives for change. Because the focal point of any needs analysis or change initiative is faculty role redefinition, the administrators must seek an appropriate way to recognize faculty responses to change initiatives. The need to overcome faculty resistance to change is becoming critical for administrators because the inertia of historic institutional governance and inefficiency facing the rapid globalization, deregulation, and technological advances in education are of growing concern to the business school's critical constituents (i.e., legislators, administrators, students and their families and recruiters). The concern grows as a new set of technology enabled institutions, coming from various geographies, has entered the educational market to challenge the seemingly monopolistic position of business schools. Unfortunately, a typical response of many administrators in institutions of higher learning has been hesitation until the new practices become widespread. The basic premise of article is that the strategy of hesitation should be terminated by the use of the anticipatory frameworks proposed.

Each individual faculty member must prepare an FDP. The FDP would address the need to accommodate individual differences among faculty members that may be in different stages of their career. At Step 1, A mentor should assist the faculty member in reviewing and updating the FDP and help find points of commonality with the strategic direction of the school as set out in the call for proposals. The mentor will estimate how much support the faculty member is likely to receive at the college level and assist the faculty member when the FDP is not in line with the call for proposals. Because there will be points of commonality between the strategic intent of the college and the FDP of individual faculty members, the individual faculty members would be responsible for generating proposals and for making initial assessments of the proposals on the basis of the rubric developed in Step 2. The final evaluation would be carried out at the college level. Step 3 is an open forum that makes the resource allocation decision transparent. Review the resource allocation plan maps the resource allocation decision across all proposals. As such it can be mapped against the "ranked and rated goals of the school" (Step 4). The school faculty as a whole would then be surveyed to assess satisfaction with the resource allocation decision (Step 5). It could be that some faculty members might not have participated in the request for proposals while others might not have been awarded their requested resources. Assessing faculty participation will review the actual link between faculty development and the school's mission.

REFERENCES

Armstrong, J.S. (1995), The Devil's Advocate Responds to an MBA Student's Claim that Research Harms Learning, *Journal of Marketing*, 59, 101-06.

Association to Advance Collegiate Schools of Business (AACSB) (2003), Sustaining Scholarship in Business Schools, *AACSB eNewsline*, 7(3): 1-2, Retrieved August 15, 2005, from www.aacsb.edu/publications/dfc/default.asp

Atkinson, M. (2001), The Scholarship of Teaching and Learning: Reconceptualizing Scholarship and Transforming the Academy, *Social Forces*, 79(4), 1217-30.

Bartem, R. & Manning, S. (2001), Outsourcing in Higher Education, *Change*, 33(1), 43-47.

Bedeian, A. (2002), The Dean's Disease: How the Darker Side of Power Manifests itself in the Office of Dean, *Academy of Management Learning and Education*, 1(2), 164-73.

Burke, J. & Modarresi, S. (2000). To keep or not to keep performance funding: Signals from stakeholders, *Journal of Higher Education*, 71(4), 454-73, Commission on the Academic Presidency (1996).

But Can You Teach It? Are Business Schools Teaching the Right Things? (2004), *The Economist*, 371(8376), 61-63.

Carpenter, R. (1997), What's an MBA Worth? Canadian Business, 70(14), 41-48.

Crainer, S. & Dearlove, D. (1999), Gravy Training: Inside the Business of Business Schools, San Francisco: Jossey-Bass.

de Russy, C. (1996, October 11), Public Business Schools Need Rigorous Oversight by Activist Trustees, *Chronicle of Higher Education*, B3-B4.

Delbecco, A. (1999), Review of Rethinking Management Education, *Administrative Science Quarterly*, 44, 439-43.

Dreher, G.F. & Ryan, K.C. (2002), Evaluating MBA-programme Admissions Criteria: The Relationship between Pre-MBA Work Experience and Post-MBA Career Outcomes, Research in Higher Education, 43, 727-44.

Dreher, G.F.; Dougherty, T.W. & Whitely, B. (1985), Generalizability of MBA Degree and Socio-economic Effects on Business School Graduates' Salaries, *Journal of Applied Psychology*, 70, 769-73.

Ferris, W. (2002), Students as Junior Partners, Professors as Senior Partners, the B-school as the Firm: A New Model for Collegiate Business Education, *Academy of Management Learning and Education*, 1(2), 185-93.

Fisher, A. (2004, June), Why an MBA may not be Worth it, *Fortune*, 149(12), 56.

Gallos, J. (2002), The Dean's Squeeze: The Myths and Realities of Academic Leadership in the Middle, *Academy of Management Learning and Education*, 1(2), 174-84.

Gillaspy, J. (2004, July), Letters to Fortune: A Matter of Degree, *Fortune*, 150(1), 18.

Glaser, R. (1990), The Reemergence of Learning Theory within Instructional Research, *American Psychologist*, 45, 29-39.

Goldhor, H. (1974), The Use of late Respondents to Estimate the Nature of non-respondents, Washington, DC: U.S. Office of Education (ERIC Document Reproduction Service No. ED083309).

Green, R. (2003, January), Market, Management and "reengineering" Higher Education, *The Annals of American Association of Political and Social Sciences*, 585, 196-213.

Harvey, M.; Buckley, M.; Novicevic, M. & Elfessi, A. (2002), Developing a Times Cape-based Framework for an Online Education Strategy, *International Journal of Educational Management*, 16(1), 46-54.

Hazelwood, K. (2003a, May 6), Striking Out on their Own, *Business Week*, 98-99.

Hazelwood, K. (2003b, May 6), The Worst of Times for New MBAs, *Business Week Online*, Retrieved March 23, 2006, from http://www.businessweek.com/bschools/content/may2003/bs2003055_0596_bs001.htm

Hindo, B. (2004, April 26), Don't Hire Him—He's a Harvard MBA, *Business Week*, 16.

Laber. G. (2004, July), Letters to Fortune: A Matter of Degree, *Fortune*, 150(1), 18.

Leslie, D. (1996), Strategic Governance: The Wrong Questions? *The Review of Higher Education*, 20(1), 101-12.

Levin, H. (1991), Raising Productivity in Higher Education, *Journal of Higher Education*, 62, 241-62.

Massy, W. & Zemsky, R. (1994), Faculty Discretionary Time: Departments and Academic Ratchet, *Journal of Higher Education*, 65(1), 1-22.

Masten, S. (in press), Authority and Commitment: Why Universities, Like Legislatures, are not Organized as Firms, *Journal of Economic and Management Strategy*.

McCowen, M.; Ewell, B. & McConnell, P. (1995), Creative Conversations: An Experiment in Interdisciplinary Team Teaching, *College Teaching*, 43, 127-31.

Miller, L.E. & Smith, K.L. (1983), Handling Non-response Issues, *Journal of Extension*, 21, 45-50.

Mintzberg, H. & Gosling, J. (2002), Educating Managers Beyond Borders, *Academy of Management Learning and Education*, 9(1), 64-76.

Mintzberg, H. (2004), Managers not MBAs: A Hard Look at the Soft Practice of Managing and Management Development, San Francisco: Berrett-Koehler.

Moallem, M. (1997), Review of Instructional Planning: A Guide for Teachers, *Educational Technology Research and Development*, 45(4), 88-95.

Newman, S.W. (1962), Differences between Early and Late Respondents to a Survey, *Journal of Advertising Research*, 11, 37-39.

Pfeffer, J. (1977), Effects of an MBA and Socioeconomic Origins on Business School Graduates' Salaries, *Journal of Applied Psychology*, 62, 609-705.

Renewing the Academic Presidency: Stronger Leadership for Tougher Times. Washington, DC: Association of Governing Boards of Business Schools and Colleges.

34

Teaching and Research: Need for Proper Linkage in a Developing Country Like India

DR. SANDEEP SHANDILYA

Indian Higher Education System has rapidly grown in magnitude after independence. However, this growth has been more quantitative and less qualitative. Quality seems lost in the chaos of quantity and mushrooming educational organisations with an unprofessional and orthodox attitude. "In India, over the last several years there has been a phenomenal increase in enrolment, the number of universities increased from 28 (1950-51) to 224 (1996) and colleges from 695 to 8,613 during the same period. The students population increased from 2.5 lakhs to over 60 lakhs while the number of teachers increased from 12,000 to 3,00,000. We have now 238 universities, over 11,000 colleges and 3,42,000 teachers with a total student enrolment of nearly 7.5 million. It may however be pointed out that while India has the second largest system of higher education, next to the U.S., the total number of students hardly represent 6 per cent of the relevant age group between 18 and 23 years, which is much below the average of developed countries (47 %) and less than that of developing countries which is 7 per cent."[1] Above information is more than sufficient to give an idea about the vastness of Indian Education System. A total student enrolment of nearly 7.5 million makes us the second largest education system in the world. However, on qualitative front, Indian higher education system legs behind. There is an urgent need to upgrade its quality.

Education was a state responsibility until 1976, when it was brought into a concurrent list of the Constitution of India that gave more powers and responsibilities to the Union Government. Though education is a concurrent subject, state governments enjoy considerable freedom with respect to several aspects, in general. At higher education level, the University Grant Commission (UGC) plays significant role. Universities are established by the union or state government and are funded by the UGC and state governments.

Higher Education in India is coordinated by several agencies. While most of general higher education falls within the jurisdiction of the UGC, professional institutions are coordinated by different bodies. The All India Council for Technical Education (AICTE) is responsible for coordination of technical and management education.

Table 34.1: Role of University in Higher Education

Total number of universities in India	259
Central universities	16
Total number of colleges	11,089
Deemed to be universities (Declared under UGC Act, 1956)	49 institutions
Total enrolment of students	74.18 lakh
Total number of teachers	3.42 lakh

Source: India 2002, Ministry of Information and Broadcasting, Government of India, p. 93.

Table 34.2: State-wise Distribution of University Level Institutions

	1993	*1994*	*1995*	*1996*	*1997*	*1998*	*1999*	*2000*
Universities								
(*i*) Central	12	14	15	15	15	7	17	17
(*ii*) State	156	159	160	163	164	172	182	182
Deemed to be Universities	33	34	36	39	39	40	43	45
Institutions of National Importance	8	10	10	11	11	11	12	13
TOTAL	**209**	**217**	**221**	**228**	**229**	**240**	**254**	**256**

Source: Association of Indian Universities, University Institutions in India (1993-99, 2000) AIU, New Delhi.

Table 34.3: State-wise Distribution of University Level Institutions

	1993	*1994*	*1995*	*1996*	*1997*	*1998*	*1999*	*2000*
Andhra Pradesh	18	18	18	18	18	20	21	21
Arunachal Pradesh	1	1	1	1	1	1	1	1
Assam	4	6	6	6	6	6	6	6
Bihar	17	17	17	17	17	17	17	17
Chandigarh	2	2	2	2	2	2	2	2
Delhi	11	11	11	11	11	11	13	13
Goa	1	1	1	1	1	1	1	1
Gujarat	10	11	11	11	11	11	11	12
Haryana	4	4	5	5	5	5	5	5
Himachal Pradesh	3	3	3	3	3	3	3	3
Jammu & Kashmir	3	3	3	3	3	3	3	3
Karnataka	12	13	13	15	15	16	16	16
Kerala	5	6	8	8	8	8	8	8
Madhya Pradesh	14	15	16	17	17	17	19	19
Maharashtra	21	22	22	24	24	27	28	28
Manipur	2	2	2	2	2	2	2	2
Meghalaya	1	1	1	1	1	1	1	1
Nagaland	–	1	1	1	1	1	1	1
Orissa	5	5	5	5	5	5	8	8
Pondicherry	1	1	1	1	1	1	1	1
Punjab	4	4	4	4	5	6	7	7
Rajasthan	10	10	10	10	10	10	11	11
Sikkim	–	–	–	1	1	1	1	1
Tamil Nadu	19	19	19	19	19	22	22	22
Tripura	1	1	1	1	1	1	1	1
Uttar Pradesh	28	28	28	28	28	28	30	31
West Bengal	12	12	13	13	13	14	15	15
TOTAL	**209**	**217**	**221**	**228**	**229**	**240**	**254**	**256**

Source: Association of Indian Universities, University Institutions in India (1993-99, 2000) AIU, New Delhi.

University Grants Commission

It was established in 1956 under an Act of Parliament to take measures for promotion and coordination of university education for determination and maintenance of standards in teaching, examination and research in the universities. To fulfill its objectives, the commission can enquire, among other things, into financial needs of the universities, allocate and disburse grants to them; establish and maintain common services and facilities, recommend measures for improvement of university education and give its advice relating to the allocation of grants and establishment of new universities.

Indian Higher Education system is passing through fast sweeping changes. Unplanned mushrooming of organisation imparting higher and professional education is a serious threat to sustainable development of higher education in India. Teaching, research and extension work are considered as three inseparable tasks of higher education. Teaching and research are in fact two faces of the same coin. Proper linkage between these two is one of the most vital ingredient for steady growth of Indian higher education. India legs in properly synchronising her teaching and research activities. The situation becomes even more ridiculous when heads of the educational organisation themselves create unnecessary problems in the way of budding researchers. Writer of this article has faced such problem. Only lip service cannot serve the purpose of making research a viable tool for the development of higher education. Growing application of modern technology in education. "Both globalisation and computer communication technology have caused and resulted in the growth of each other, they have emerged as two sides of the same coin and have impact on one another in complex and multiple way. New trends in education has also came about, and new challenges have been thrown up to reckon: At the same time there is an indisputable need to maintain continuity, change and growth, all at once."[5] In such a scenario importance of research and its meaningful linkage with teaching becomes even more significant. Proper inclusion of modern technology to serve higher education definitely needs a planned research. Distance education has emerged as a way of teaching and learning where modern technology is being extensively used for instructional purposes.

Teaching, research and extension are considered inseparable in any efficient higher education system. Unfortunately in Indian higher education this linkage is not so intense and effective. In some cases the situation becomes extremely pitty when even the heads of the educational organisations fail to appraise this vital linkage. In some cases the heads of the higher education organisations are not even Ph.D. themselves. There is discrimination among teachers on the issue of liberty and facility to pursue research work. Writer has also faced such apathy. On same dates two teachers present two different papers in two different national seminars, one is granted seminar leave and other is shown absent from duties. It is ridiculous that, recently twelth convention of U.P. Government Colleges Academic Society was held at Rampur during 13-14 January, 2007. The theme of this convention was "Access and equity v/s Quality and relevance in higher education." Only lip service will not serve the cause. The organisers must understand the meaning of equity in practial terms. Equity is not equality which is more concerned with physical distribution of some items whereas equity is social justice. Equity is far bigger a domain. Glamorous and catchy themes of seminars and conferences cannot do justice. We must learn to be practical and sincere in our approach and application.

There is one more area of concern, which needs a mention here, and it is the area of inter-disciplinary research. Inter-disciplinary research is considered an excellent and meaningful way of overall development of higher education all over the globe but unfortunately several bright careers have been ruined due to it in India. They paid the price of pursuing inter-disciplinary research. They are constantly falling victim to conservative and traditional approach being followed when the question of recruiting these poor researchers as teacher comes. Writer of this article is a unique victim of this apathy in India.

REFERENCES

1. K. Venkatasubramanian, "Financing of Higher Education", *The Hindu*, New Delhi, 19 February, 2002.
2. India 2002, *Ministry of Information and Broadcasting*, Government of India, p. 93.
3. Association of Indian Universities, University Institutions in India (1993-99, 2000), AIU, New Delhi.
4. *Ibid.*
5. Vasanth Vasudev, "Challenges of e-learning", *The Hindu*, New Delhi, September 18, 2001.

35

Restructuring of Indian Educational System

DR. POOJA GUPTA

Introduction

Education is the most important national activity, the backbone of a country's progress. It helps to strengthen the fabric of a nation "to produce men of education enlightenment and character". However, the rising has of unrest and growing population of the educated unemployed in India strongly suggest that there is something fundamentally wrong with the System of Education. One thing is admitted by all that the education given at present is narrow, bookish and far removed from the practical needs of society. The real aim of education is to develop the physical, intellectual and moral qualities of a student so as to make him into an integrated personality, capable of living a purposeful life. At present, this aim is hardly fulfilled by universities.

The essence of education, said Mahatma Gandhi, "lies in drawing out the very best that is in you." In today's scientific and competitive world of the twenty-first century, education is a basic requirement for survival if we wish to understand things in a rational manner in order to face the vicissitudes of life. Education is a training that we imbibe from our parents, teachers, elders and friends. We get the benefit of their experience and the clouds of ignorance gradually fade away. Even though we complete our formal education in school or college, there is no end to self-improvement and learning. There is abiding truth is the saying, "The more a person learns, the less it is." Education is thus the soul of society.

Review of Literature

Most of the economists have suggested their views in this respect. Some of them are given below:

Brahm Prakash and Y.P. Aggarwal have concluded that over the period of the past five decades, there has been a very significant expansion of the educational sector as a whole in India. The sector has following positive achievements to its credit.

It has thrown open the doors of education at the point of admission at every level—primary secondary and higher levels—to all the people of India.

There has been a veritable explosion in education. Indian educational system is now colossal, teeming with almost 100 million students and three million teachers, and costing billions of rupees each year. This colossus is the result of conscious public policy in independent India. Two basic features of this policy have been (1) Access-based strategy, and (2) Incentive-based strategy. The principal focus of educational policy has been to increase access to education at all levels. Now, almost everyone in rural areas (over 93 per cent) lives within 1 km of a primary school. Similarly, over 92 per cent of the people in rural areas have a middle school within about 5 km. and 82 per cent of the rural population now lives within 8 km. of a high school. A district headquarter town without at least an arts college is now an anomaly in most cases. Colleges have proliferated at even faster rate than have schools.

- India has the second largest (next only to China) pool of education and skilled men and women in the world.
- There has been the development of institutions of excellence at every level.

All this contributed to self-dependency for manpower in every area, including policy planning, administration and governance of the huge economy.

Marline Lockheed has depicted that it has a very narrow coverage of the entire population of the country. Only 2.5 per cent of the Indian population in the relevant age group attends colleges and universities, compared with 66 per cent in the US and Canada, 7 per cent in the OECD countries, 37.7 per cent in Korea and over

20 per cent in countries such as Cuba, Costa Rica and Venezuela. Moreover, it has a very low retention rate. Of 100 children entering class-I, only 47 make it to the end of primary school (class V). In contrast, 68 per cent of world's children complete primary education. Further, less than 3 children complete class XII. The extremely poor retention rate at the primary level has been traced to the general neglect of the sector.

D. Nguyan and K.C. Roy have suggested that the quality of the education is fairly low and the content less relevant to the 'needs' of the individual and the society. The educational system suffers from what has been called 'diploma disease', i.e., it does not aim at conveying knowledge and skills at all, but is more concerned with certification and credentialling. As such, its contribution to the growth of human capital is minimal.

Cf. Resonance, has given that India have one of the most rigid educational systems in the world. At every stage in one's educational career, doors are being shut, rather than opened. The prospectus of the Cambridge University tells potential applicants for admission: 'You can arrive in Cambridge expecting to become a physicist or zoologist, and emerge after three years as a metallurgist or a psychologist. Unfortunately, this cannot happen even in the best universities or institutes in India today.

Drawbacks of the Educational System

The greatest defect of the present day educational system is its excessively passive and mechanical character. The student does not play an active part in the attainment of knowledge, but knowledge remains floating on his mental surface. He mugs up the facts given to him for cramming and vomits them out on paper in the examination hall. That is why a student who does well in his college examinations, often fails miserably in the examination of life. Thus, the present system of examinations has ceased to be a reliable test of a student's ability.

The present educational system is purely academic and theoretical. The best product of this system is an owlish looking boy, a mere bookworm, who knows nothing of the world beyond the world of books. He has no proper grasp, no views and no vision of his own. There is no co-relation between the system of education and the needs of life. The students are taught lessons from books, but not lessons from life. They are provided with knowledge, but not wisdom. They are committed to memories the characters of fiction, but they are unable to read the characters of their own friends.

The system lays too much stress on the head but neglects the heart. This lop-sided development of personality produces scholars who are morally destitute and physically bankrupt. The education that he receives, fails to activate the virtue and righteousness in the students. This is why the students of today have no passion for the worship of the true, the good and the beautiful. The sacred bond between the teachers and the students is broken. Again, one can see crowds of youth at the portals of colleges because there is no adequate provision for systematic physical training, games and sports.

Another drawback of the system of education is that it slack of vocational guidance. Colleges and universities have become the factories and mills that manufacture graduates and postgraduates by the thousands, who only swell the ranks of the educated unemployed in the country.

Examinations are another evil in the prevailing system of education. The present method of examination encourage the dependence of the students on ready-made answers and renders them incapable of thinking for themselves. This system of examinations is unnatural, unscientific and uncertain.

Strikes and agitations have become a common feature of educational institutions. Every day every one read and hear about these things. Students boycott classes, raise slogans and take out processions in order to protest against some action or order of the authority concerned, or to get some of their reasonable or whimsical demands accepted. If the authority refuses to yield, they run riot. In the authority refuses to yield, they run riot. In their frenzy, they indulge in lawlessness and violence and damage public and private property. However, the students alone are not responsible for this state of affairs. Educational system and the teachers are equally responsible for these strikes and agitations. Our educational system is breeding a race of discontented and frustrated young men and women. They drink, smoke and gamble even in the presence of their elders. The sacred bonds of kinship between the elders and the youngsters in a family stand shattered. The self-seeking politicians use the students as cat's pay. They instigate them to resort to strikes and demonstrations in a bid to grind their own axe.

Further, this system is very expensive. The parents with modest means find it hard to give higher education to their children. For the students, education has become a pass-time and luxury. Over-crowded classrooms wear the looks of a cinema hall. The students pay heavy fees to purchase entry tickets to these intellectual theatre houses. Since the situation is deteriorating rapidly, it is imperative that some concrete steps are taken to completely restructure our educational methods and ideals.

At this critical juncture, Mother India needs dynamic sons and daughters who possess muscles of iron and nerves of steel inside which may dwell a mind cast of the same metal of which the thunderbolt is made. To produce such heroes and heroines, country require a dynamic education policy which may strike a judicious balance between physical mental and moral perfection.

Measure Undertaken

Over the last five decades, a number of measures have been taken to reform the educational system. The various measures can be grouped in three parts, viz. (*i*) equality reforms, (*ii*) quality reforms, and (*iii*) reforms for administrative ease. A recent study on the effectiveness of these reforms further classifies each of these into two categories, viz., class-oriented reforms and mass-oriented reforms, and reaches the following conclusions:

1. Equality reforms meant for the masses have turned out to be, by and large, less successful than equity reforms meant for the classes. Thus equality reforms at higher less successful than equity reforms higher levels of education have been found to be more successful than at lower levels of education.
2. In the case of quality reforms also the mass-oriented reforms are less successful as compared to the class-oriented.
3. In an educationally advanced environment the educational reforms seem to have achieved a success but in a less-developed socio-economic and educational environment, educational reforms seem to have been less successful.

4. It appears that reforms meant for the classes seem to have taken relatively shorter period to succeed.
5. In the case of majority of the educational reforms the primary initiative was taken by the government and the mass involvement was very much limited. The people, both target group as well another, simply followed this initiative on the part of the government or the leadership.
6. The global approach to educational change seems to have received great attention by the policy-makers than the specific measures for educational change meant for specific target groups. The global measures have an implicit bias towards the socio-economically better-off sections of society, as major benefits from such measures could be cornered by them.
7. In short, educational reforms have not been successful in overcoming the weakness of smaller coverage, lower quality and higher inequality. In some cases, the problems seem to have been aggravated with widening inter-regional disparities, inter-community disparities and still larger inequalities as between the male and female learners.

Resource Allocation in Plans

Education has been a low priority area in terms of the resource allocation in our plans. A glance at percentage share of funds for education in the total plan would reveal that it has been decreasing from the third plan onwards, as shown in the table.

Financial Outlay on Education

Plan	*Amount (Rs. Crores)*	*% of the Total Outlay*
I	149	7.9
II	273	5.8
III	589	6.9
Annual	307	4.6
IV	774	5.0
V	1285	3.2
VI	2521	2.6
VII	8568	3.6
Annual 1990-92	5290	3.9
VIII	17892	4.1
IX	31594	3.61

In simple words education has been a low priority area in the Indian economy. After the higher priority areas like industry and agriculture had their required shares, whatever used to be left in the resource-pot would be distributed among the low priority areas, among which education also figured. There is need for planning education expenditure on some priority basis. This calls for a proper manpower planning in the country.

Conclusion and Suggestions

Although reforms have been introduced from time to time to make our educational system relevant to needs of the day, it still remains archaic and obsolete. We are still producing an army of clerks and white-collar workers through the system, which was introduced by Macaulay more than a hundred and fifty years ago. The present system needs far-reaching reforms and radical changes in the form and content of our educational system. The people of India, must accept the inescapable truth that the quality of education in most of our educational institutions is abysmally low. Our educational system is full of flaws and loopholes which must be plugged immediately to stop further degradation and make the system relevant to the fast-changing times.

The best education is that which gives to the body and to the soul all the beauty, all the perfection of which they are capable. New education policy should be an instrument of social change; it must destroy the narrow partition walls that divide people on the ground of caste, class and colour. It should help in eradicating the social evils of casteism, dowry menace, female infanticide, atrocities on women and the like by inculcating enlightened thinking in the minds of the students. Emphasis should be laid on self-employment, job oriented courses vocational education, etc., so that they can peddle their canoes early in life. Aptitude and ability tests should be conducted regularly in schools so that we may have lesser number of square pegs in round holes. Re-orientation of the syllabus that has become outdated is necessary. The western concept of "earn while you learn" must be introduced in India so that students learn to appreciate the dignity of labour. Moral education should form an integral part of the syllabus with greater emphasis on practice than on theory Study of the lives of great men and women should be made compulsory to in spite and encourage them to hitch their wagon to a shining star. In tune with Tagore's Shanti Niketan and Vishwabharati meditation, yoga, field work occasional outings and recreation should be undertaken to develop independent thinking decision-making ability and creativity among the students. Sports, NSS, NCC and other extra curricular activities should be brought within the reach of every student so that they don't remain mere bookworms but blossom into strong pillars of the nation. Thus, if the lessons of cosmic love, brotherhood and peace are imbedded in the minds of the tiny tots, they will grow up into mighty oaks, taught enough to withstand the stresses and strains of life.

"Purpose of education is to dispel error and discover truth", said Socrates. The new education policy must inculcate the scientific spirit plus authentic sense as also teach children to respect age and wisdom, admire beauty and appreciate merit; even of the enemies. It must bring about a silent social revolution and ring out the old and ring in the new and nobler modes of life. Mahatma Gandhi too felt that "education is an all-around drawing out of the best in the child and man...body, mind and spirit", Literacy is not the end of education, not even the beginning. It is only one of the means whereby men and women can be educated.

One must develop such a system of education as encourages the students to develop their latent talents which, in most cases, lie antappec, irrespective of the fact that our system of education is Indianised or indigenized. The case for Idealization and indigenization of education should not be totally rejected. It should be pursued by the Government as well as the policy-makers subject to certain qualifications and reservation.

In the 21st century, education stands on the threshold or restructuring. As an important instrument of change and development, it must be depoliticized and modernized.

REFERENCES

Abusaleh Shariff and P.K. Ghosh, "Indian Education Scene and Public Gap", *EPW*, Vol. XXXV, No. 16, 21 April, 2000.

Amrik Singh, "Educational Imbalance in India", *EPH*, Vol. XXXIV No. 26, July 2, 1999.

Brahm Prakash and Y.P. Aggarwal, *Development of Human Resource*, Study Prepared for ESCAP, Bangkok, Mimco, 1987.

C. Upendranadh, "Structural Adjustment and Education, Issues Related to Equity, *EPN*, Vol. XXXVIII, No. 44, 30 October, 1993.

Cf. Resonance, *Journal of Science Education*, Vol. 1, No. 2, February, 1996.

D. Nguygen and K.C. Roy (Eds.), *Economic Reform, Liberalisation and Trade in the Asia Pacific Region*, Wiley, New Delhi, 1994.

Higher Education in India: Vision and Action, Paper presented at the UNESCO world conference on higher education, New Delhi, on 5 October, 1998.

Jandhyala, B.G. Tilak, "Five Decades of Under-investment in Education", *EPW*, Vol. XXXII, No. 36, 12 September, 1997.

K.L. Chopra, "Technical Education—Vision 2010", *Current Science*, Vol. 72, No. 8, April 25, 1997.

Marlaine Lockheed, *Primary Education in India*, World Bank, 1997.

S. Shukla and R. Kaul (eds.), *Education, Development and Underdevelopment*, Sage, New Delhi, 1998 and *Probe: Public Report on Basis Education in India*, OUP, New Delhi, 1999.

Index